Louisiana

Louisiana

Cynthia V. Campbell

FIRST EDITION

The Countryman Press ✳ Woodstock, Vermont

Interior photographs by the author unless otherwise specified.

Maps by Paul Woodward, © The Countryman Press
Text and cover design by Bodenweber Design
Composition by PerfecType, Nashville, TN

Explorer's Guide Louisiana
978-0-88150-980-9

Published by The Countryman Press, P.O. Box 748, Woodstock, VT 05091

Distributed by W. W. Norton & Company, Inc., 500 Fifth Avenue, New York, NY 10110

Printed in the United States of America

10 9 8 7 6 5 4 3 2 1

Travel
917.63
EXP 2013

Dedicated to my dear family and traveling friends,
who have never stopped looking beyond the horizon.

EXPLORE WITH US!

The entries in this first edition of *Explorer's Guide Louisiana* are the personal recommendations of the author, an experienced travel writer and editor and a longtime resident of Louisiana. This book also includes tips from locals on the best ways to enjoy festivals, plan outdoor adventures, visit mansions and historic sites, shop for Louisiana-made arts and products, and simply have a good time. No guide can be all things to all travelers, but this book intends to help readers enjoy Louisiana and learn to love it as those of us who live here do.

This guide does all it can to include phone numbers, addresses, and basic information. Still, it is probable that by the time you read it, some of this information will have slipped out of date. For that reason, we suggest you always confirm dates and hours of operation and costs.

Here are a few notes about the organization of the book.

WHAT'S WHERE

At the beginning of this book is an A-to-Z listing of the basics, some highlights, and some tips that will be helpful when traveling through Louisiana. For a quick reference, you'll find brief information on everything from area codes and alligators to zoos and zydeco.

Each chapter covers an area that can be easily explored from its listed inns. The chapters start with an overview, followed by general descriptions of the regional scenery.

TOWNS AND VILLAGES

This section gives details on Louisiana's major cities as well as smaller communities that a visitor might enjoy exploring.

TO SEE

Worthwhile destinations may be small or large, but they must be interesting. They must be authentic and not exploitive. Your hosts may be wearing Cajun garb from past centuries, but there will be nothing put on about the dance halls and music.

GREEN SPACES

These entries describe in broad terms large city parks and giant sections of publicly accessible lands, and identify the best of the parks, recreation areas, trails, and camping spots.

TO DO

Louisiana is an outdoor playground that can be enjoyed all seasons. These entries list outside activities and include some sports that are quiet and noninvasive. The Audubon Golf Trail and the Birding Trail are among the major attractions.

LODGING

This book lists independent and historic establishments with high standards of comfort, cleanliness, and hospitality. Not every worthy establishment can be listed, but we try to provide a good selection of unique places. We make an effort to list places that are accessible to the disabled and are family friendly or pet-friendly.

WHERE TO EAT

These listings are divided into informal places, Eating Out, and formal restaurants, Dining Out. In Louisiana the distinction blurs. The listings include unique, casual cafes with gourmet menus, and historically famous restaurants that for generations have served meals fit for a king.

ENTERTAINMENT

These are places with regular entertainment. Listings include places that present authentic jazz and zydeco performed by local musicians as well as well-known and respected international artists. Also listed will be highly regarded regional theaters and regularly scheduled classical music series.

SELECTIVE SHOPPING

This section includes shops with Louisiana flair and/or unusual offerings, as well as worthwhile shopping districts.

SPECIAL EVENTS

Louisiana has more than 400 festivals every year, many celebrating the state's agricultural, historical, and musical heritage. These listings include some of the most colorful and worthwhile. Also listed are major sports events that attract thousands.

KEY TO SYMBOLS

The book uses icons to denote entries with special characteristics:

🎗 This symbol represents spots that perform above and beyond the call of duty in terms of quality, service, or unique offerings. In many cases, the symbol is used to indicate free admission.

✎ The crayon denotes a family friendly place that welcomes young children. Most bed & breakfasts have some restrictions or prohibit children younger than 12.

♿ The wheelchair is intended to note locales that either meet the standards of the Americans with Disabilities Act or at least have ramps or paved paths.

🐾 The dog paw indicates a place that allows pets—very unusual among boutique inns and bed & breakfasts. Most recreational vehicle (RV) sites require that pets be kept on a leash. An establishment with a dog paw might charge an extra fee or restrict pets to certain units or areas.

⚭ This symbol represents places that arrange special weddings, such as parks, gardens, and plantation homes.

⊸ Many sites in Louisiana are eco-friendly. The symbol denotes those that are easily accessible for children and families.

((ᵠ)) WiFi accessible. The WiFi symbol appears beside lodgings and other establishments that provide wireless Internet access.

☂ Rainy day. The umbrella icon points out places where you can entertain yourself but still stay dry in bad weather.

🍸 The "martini glass" icon appears next to restaurants and entertainment venues with good bars.

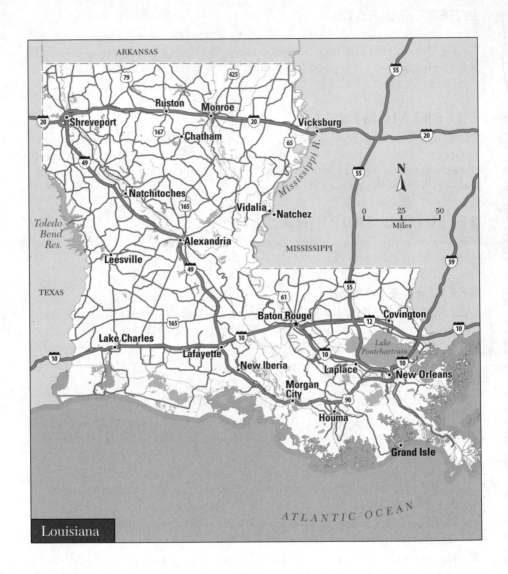

Louisiana

CONTENTS

MAPS

ACKNOWLEDGMENTS

Louisiana challenges visitors and residents to look beyond the obvious. Big cities and small villages alike contain off-the-path sites, cafes, or events that reveal the depth of the state's heart and soul.

Lieutenant Governor Jay Dardenne, who oversees the Louisiana Department of Culture, Recreation and Tourism, often remarks about the variety of things to do and see in the state. "There's literally no place in America like Louisiana," he said. "We are a human gumbo that dates back centuries." With his suggestion, we seek to give travelers a hunger to discover that gumbo for themselves.

To write this guide, I sought help from road warriors who advised, "Never stop looking." I thank the many travel experts from the Louisiana Office of Tourism and from convention and visitors' bureaus throughout the state. From Shreveport to Cocodrie, New Orleans to Natchitoches, many people generously assisted with gathering information for this guide.

Special thanks go to Allison Blake, fellow journalist and travel writer, who conceived of a Louisiana guide and encouraged me to take up the project. She contributed greatly to the Lafayette portion of the chapter on Cajun Country. I also thank my husband, Larry B. Campbell, for his patience while I buried my head in a laptop. Also, credit goes to Kermit Hummel, the editorial director of Countryman Press, whose encouragement kept me on the right track, and to Lisa Sacks and Lucia Huntington, incomparable editors.

INTRODUCTION

Louisiana, one of the United States' oldest settled areas, enchants and mystifies visitors. This is a land of dramatic contrasts—rolling hills covered with towering pines, and shimmering swamps filled with exotic wildlife. Ask a resident to describe Louisiana and you'll get a different answer every time. Often, the state is explained in terms of a favorite dish, a well-seasoned gumbo. Louisiana is a mix of cultures, politics, music, and food, tempered by time and climate into a rich, satisfying blend.

Many people visit the state for a few days or weeks to experience Louisiana's unique culture. They step away from their daily routines to throw aside their cares, listen to jazz and zydeco, mingle with crowds enjoying the good life, eat spicy gumbo and etouffee, visit riverboat casinos, and party until sunrise. Some seek the quiet, still waters of ancient bayous where fish, herons, and alligators roam freely. Birders walk wetlands and piney woods trails looking for rare species. Some search for family roots or seek solace in welcoming religious centers. Many find themselves seduced by Louisiana, and decide to stay.

For those whose ancestors settled here decades or centuries ago, this is home. It's where people have enjoyed great wealth and dealt with devastating economic downturns. They have survived yellow fever, floods, fires, military bombardments, and hurricanes. Talk with locals and you'll understand why, after the hard times, celebrations such as Mardi Gras and myriad other festivals are so important.

This guide will lead you to the time-honored sights and unexpected haunts of Louisiana. To help you truly understand the state, I encourage you to take time to delve into the culture of the cities, each different in character. Explore Louisiana's scenic byways, incredible waterways, and rural communities. Discover Louisiana's differences and its greatest treasure, its people.

Before you explore the state, learn a little of its history, which stretches back thousands of years. Keeping in mind that historians continually discover or rediscover facts, this is only a brief overview of Louisiana's colorful past. As you travel through the state, you'll learn more intriguing details that shaped Louisiana as an exciting destination.

HISTORY The first inhabitants of the region left fascinating traces of their existence. Archaeologists have discovered prehistoric mounds at Watson Brake in the floodplains of the Ouachita River near West Monroe. The earliest known mound complex in North America, Watson Brake has 11 mounds that range between 3 and 25 feet tall, and it has been dated to about 3400 B.C. According to the archaeologist Joe W. Saunders, retired professor, University of Louisiana at Monroe, the mounds may have been built by mobile hunter-gatherers. Watson Brake is on private property and not available to the public.

Poverty Point National Monument, a Louisiana State historic site near Epps in the northeast section of the state, is open year-round. It is considered one of the most important archaeological sites in America. Here, between 1700 and 1100 B.C., prehistoric people built a huge complex of mounds and ridges. Artifacts discovered on the site reveal that the inhabitants traded with others along the Mississippi River corridor. Numerous Native American tribes had created settlements and well-established trails in the region before Europeans arrived in the area.

Soon after Columbus reached the Americas, Europeans began exploring the New World. The Spanish explorer and cartographer Alonso Alvarez de Pineda led an expedition in 1519 along the northern shore of the Gulf of Mexico and discovered the mouth of a great river that may have been the Mississippi. While exploring the Mississippi River in 1682, the French explorer Rene-Robert Cavelier, Sieur de La Salle, took possession "of the country known as Louisiana," naming it for the reigning king of France, Louis XIV. France thus claimed all the land along the Mississippi from the Gulf of Mexico to Canada.

In 1699, a French Canadian military officer, Pierre Le Moyne d'Iberville, founded Fort Marapas on the site of Ocean Springs, Mississippi. That same year

THOUSANDS OF EGRETS ROOST AT THE JUNGLE GARDENS ROOKERY ON AVERY ISLAND.
Cynthia V. Campbell

he explored the Mississippi River with his brother, Jean-Baptiste Le Moyne, Sieur de Bienville, and 48 men. During the trip up river, the party discovered a site with a red pole or tree apparently marking a division between Indian tribal territories. In his ship's log, d'Iberville named the site Baton Rouge, today Louisiana's capital city.

Fort St. Jean Baptiste was established on the Red River at Natchitoches in 1714 by Louis Juchereau de St. Denis. Natchitoches is considered the oldest permanent settlement in the Louisiana territory. The fort had two purposes: to establish trade with the Spanish in Texas, and to deter Spanish advances into Louisiana.

The territory experienced a surge of growth in the early 1700s as a colony of the Company of the West and after 1719, of its successor, the Company of the Indies. In 1718, Sieur de Bienville founded the town of New Orleans. By 1721 New Orleans had a population of more than 370 people, including adult colonists, children, servants, slaves, and Indians.

The French continued to explore and found outposts throughout its territory, although they were not the only colonists. The French introduced slavery in Louisiana in the early 1700s. They enslaved Native Americans, including members of the Atakapa, Bayougoula, Choctaw, Chickasaw, and Alabama tribes. Slave ships from Africa and the Caribbean continued to bring in large numbers to bolster the economy. The Spanish period gave slaves and free people of color more security and rights than other regimes. Slavery was officially abolished on December 18, 1865, with the 13th amendment to the U.S. Constitution.

In the 1720s, Germans settled along the Mississippi upriver from New Orleans in an area called the German coast. Successful in farming, the Germans were soon providing food for themselves and for New Orleans residents. The German immigrants began speaking French from the time of their arrival, and they intermarried with early French settlers. Over subsequent decades they also intermarried with Acadians—people of Canada's Maritime Provinces who had been deported by the British between 1764 and 1788. With the aid of Spain, many resettled in south

COTTON FIELDS ABOUND IN THE RURAL PARISHES OF LOUISIANA'S CROSSROADS REGION.

Larry B. Campbell

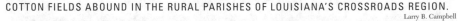

Louisiana's wetlands and prairies. Their dialect, which adapted expressions to suit their new climate and living conditions, are now termed Cajun French. While few people today speak Cajun French, the accent and numerous expressions have lingered. It doesn't take new residents long to start picking up a phrase or two. While they may not be Cajun, they soon learn how to "pass a good time."

Along with their language, the Catholic French brought their celebration of Mardi Gras, a day of celebration prior to Ash Wednesday, which marks the start of Lent, a solemn period. The colonists also brought their music, both folk tunes and dances and court music, to Louisiana. Blended with African traditions, these are the roots of the grand celebrations and American music we now enjoy.

In the 1700s, various sections of the Louisiana territory were ruled by France, Spain, and Britain. In 1762, France ceded Louisiana lands west of the Mississippi River and the Isle of Orleans to Spain. In 1763, the Treaty of Paris gave Britain the French territory east of the Mississippi and north of the Isle of Orleans. Colonists had to deal with new tax structures, laws, and often religious affiliations during each of the territorial changes. As a result, the colonists developed a strong sense of independence and wily methods of dealing with political change.

When Thomas Jefferson purchased Louisiana from Napoleon in 1803, Americans began moving into the territory. With their foreign customs and languages, Louisiana's people seemed different. The newcomers brought vitality and traditions that added to the distinctive culture found in the region today.

GEOGRAPHY Geographically, Louisiana is defined by its rivers: the Mississippi, Ouachita, Sabine, Red, and Atchafalaya. There are numerous lagoons, oxbow lakes and manmade lakes. The state offers exceptional opportunities for fishing and hunting. There are three land areas: the East Gulf Coastal Plain, east of the Mississippi River, with low lands and marshes; the Mississippi Alluvial Plain, along the Mississippi from Arkansas to the Gulf of Mexico, with ridges and hallows; and the West Coastal Plain, west of the Mississippi Alluvial Plain, which has barrier beaches and inland prairies gently rising to Arkansas. The highest point in the state is Driskill Mountain, at 535 feet, and the lowest point is 8 feet below sea level in New Orleans. The ridges along the Mississippi River are the most fertile. The barrier beaches, islands, and lowland marshes are home to an incredible array of wildlife. Yet the wetlands are highly susceptible to erosion.

The landscape captivated early explorers as they vied for control of the New World. Whoever controlled the great Mississippi River and its tributaries held the key to vast commercial wealth. Establishing colonies on sites with protected bays was the top priority for these seafarers. Until the advent of the steamboat, rivers were Louisiana's thoroughfares. The earliest "roads" were established along Indian trails, and today some highways still follow the same routes.

The state's main highways are I-20, in the north, and Interstate 10, crossing the southern section of the state. I-12 runs from Baton Rouge to Slidell, on the northern side of Lake Pontchartrain bypassing New Orleans, and connects with Interstate 10 East and Interstate 59 North.

Interstate 49 runs from I-20 near Shreveport to Lafayette where it connects with I-10. Long-term plans are for I-49 to run from New Orleans through Shreveport to Kansas City, Missouri. Interstate 55 runs from near LaPlace north into Mississippi. These are excellent roads with Louisiana visitor centers situated at all major entrances into the state.

The Louisiana Office of Tourism divides the state into five areas: Sportsman's Paradise in the north, Crossroads in the central part of the state, Cajun County in the south, Plantation Country around Baton Rouge, and Greater New Orleans in the southeast. To make it easier for travelers, this guide covers the state in a similar pattern. The culture and topography in each of these areas overlap somewhat.

When necessary, the guide shows how some towns and cities that border other states have strong ties with their neighbors. For example, Shreveport residents may tell you they live in the Ark-La-Tex area. Residents in Vidalia on the Mississippi River share a lifestyle similar to folks in Natchez, Mississippi, and Lake Charles exports its Cajun heritage to east Texas.

The guide also explains how to visit parks and heritage areas operate under the auspices of the National Park Service. Jean Lafitte National Historical Park and Preserve, which covers the lower Mississippi Delta region, has six units: Acadian Cultural Center in Lafayette; Prairie Acadian Cultural Center in Eunice; Wetlands Cultural Center in Thibodaux; Barataria Preserve in Marrero; Chalmette Battlefield and National Cemetery in Chalmette; and French Quarter Visitor Center in New Orleans. The New Orleans Jazz National Park, in and near the French Quarter, interprets the development and preservation of jazz in America.

Cane River Creole National Historical Park, near Natchitoches, interprets the distinct Creole region with a focus on Oakland Plantation and Magnolia Plantation, both of which still contain many original pre–Civil War buildings. This park falls within the Cane River National Heritage Area on a corridor on either side of Cane River Lake, once a section of the Red River. Poverty Point National Monument, near Epps, interprets the pre-historic mounds discussed above. History lovers can also visit sections of El Camino Real de los Tejas National Historical Trail, which runs from Laredo, Texas, into northwest Louisiana, ending at Natchitoches.

MAGNOLIA MOUND PLANTATION WAS OWNED BY A FRIEND OF THE MARQUIS DE LAFAYETTE.

Cynthia V. Campbell

Larry B. Campbell

LOUISIANA STATE MUSEUM-BATON ROUGE
FEATURES EXHIBITS ON STATE HISTORY,
INDUSTRY, CULTURE

The Atchafalaya National Heritage Area, established in 2006, stretches across 14 parishes in south-central Louisiana. The most ecologically varied region in the United States, the area is home to 200 bird species, some 85 animal species, alligators, and black bears. Just one boat ride in the Atchafalaya Basin makes clear its importance to America's ecology. During serous flood periods, such as occurred in 2011, the Morganza Spillway and Bonnet Carre Spillway floodgates are opened, and waters diverted from the Mississippi flow through the basin to the Gulf of Mexico. Carefully monitored, the process saves the lower Mississippi from flooding and at the same time renews the soil and waters of the Basin.

POLITICS Visitors often ask about Louisiana's colorful politics. The state's history has indeed included some rascally politicians as well as some rather remarkable leaders. Most residents take a philosophical attitude toward politicians. They find it entertaining to regale newcomers with tales of the misdeeds of past governors, senators, and sheriffs. But they take current politics seriously, and will engage in a vigorous debate with those ready for it.

RELIGION The average Louisiana resident is seriously proud of his or her church. You will find churches of every known denomination, and some you didn't know existed. You'll see simple wood-framed churches and grand brick and stone edifices. In the northern part of the state, Protestant churches are dominant, while the Catholic Church, established by the French and Spanish during the Colonial period, is predominant in the south. Religion is a private thing, but if you ask you will be directed to a church of your choice. Don't be surprised if you are invited to an evening supper or gospel service.

RECREATION Some states invite travelers to enjoy placid, peaceful settings for gentle pleasures, guiding visitors to simple meals and quiet corners. Others offer high-energy entertainment and recreational sites with plenty of outdoor opportunities. Louisiana does both. This book helps you journey through the state with a sense of exploration. It is a guide for finding your way to a tranquil bayou, shimmering lake, tree-shaded river, or relaxing cottage where mouth-watering biscuits are offered for breakfast. It's a guide for taking in a dynamic music festival where people dance the night away to local as well as internationally famed jazz and zydeco bands, to restaurants serving exquisitely seasoned seafood dishes, and to arenas known for their deafening sports competitions.

This guide doesn't list just the traditional tourist places and popular hangouts. For the most part it helps you discover places enjoyed by Louisianans themselves. There's always great live music in Louisiana, from opera spectaculars to country fiddle contests. You'll find large halls and intimate venues where legendary entertainers such as Louis Armstrong, Elvis Presley, Jerry Lee Lewis, and others have wowed audiences. You can attend concerts featuring contemporary stars such as Wynton Marsalis, Harry Connick Jr., and Tim McGraw. While two-stepping at a festival, stop and watch Louisiana's talented young musicians take to the stage with their parents. This guide will lead you to five-star restaurants, such as Emeril Lagasse's eponymous bistro in New Orleans, but it also shows you how to find a pie lover's haven in Lecompte, and succulent barbecue in Ruston.

Cynthia V. Campbell

A COMMON LOUISIANA SIGHT: A DRAGONFLY ALIGHTS ON A FENCE POST.

CULTURE Louisiana's culture is celebrated throughout the world. People unfamiliar with the state often consider it to be made up of French-speaking Cajuns, Catholics, and swamps. However, the state is divided geographically and philosophically into two regions. The north section of the state is predominantly Protestant and part of America's Upland South. Its culture was shaped mainly by Indians, Anglo, and African Americans in pioneer, sharecropping, and farm settlements. Studies at the Louisiana Folklife Center at Northwestern State University in Natchitoches reveal that the region's culture is the most traditional in the state. In contrast, Nicholas R. Spitzer, folklorist and creator of the public radio program *American Routes,* has written that predominately Catholic South Louisiana is more akin to societies in the Spanish and French West Indies.

Traveling through the state you'll find pockets of distinct groups. South of Natchitoches in the Cane River area, Creoles—highly respected African Americans, former slaves of mixed racial heritage—established communities and owned large plantations. Spanish-speaking Canary Islanders settled in St. Bernard Parish. Throughout the 19th and 20th centuries, immigrants from Italy, Hungary, Croatia, Yugoslavia, Greece, India, and Vietnam added their own foods and music to the state's rich blend.

As a result of this ongoing multicultural mix, Louisiana is one of the most diverse areas in America. While you undoubtedly will find spectacular jazz and delicious seafood in New Orleans, you'll also find spicy gumbo and heart-thumping zydeco in Opelousas, Lake Charles, Natchitoches, and Shreveport. You'll hear the Delta blues in Baton Rouge, swamp pop in Eunice and Lake Charles, and country and gospel music in Monroe and Ruston. In fact, most everyone cooks in Louisiana, and most can hum or dance to a good tune.

CELEBRATING 200 YEARS OF STATEHOOD

Louisiana loves a celebration. So, 2012 became "the year" to celebrate 200 years of statehood. The retired U.S. Army Lieutenant General Russel Honore was named to lead the commission planning a yearlong observance through education and celebration in every corner of the state.

On April 30, 1812, the United States admitted Louisiana as the 18th state in the Union. According to the commission's website, as a predominantly Catholic state, Louisiana was the first to have a majority French- and Spanish-speaking population. The road to statehood took some skillful political maneuvering. Lobbying efforts by the French-born congressman Julien Poydras and the American attorney Edward Livingston moved the territory closer to statehood. They convinced William C. C. Claiborne, the territorial governor, that the Orleans Territory qualified for statehood. Finally in 1811, President James Madison signed the bill allowing the people of Louisiana to form a state consti- tution. Following a constitutional convention, Madison signed the bill approving statehood. The bill designated April 30, 1812, as the day of formal admission.

Louisiana's French-Catholic Creole culture eventually blended with the American English Protestant tradition to create a distinct Creole American society. Two hundred years after statehood, Louisiana's rich Creole culture is evident in the use of the Civil Code, the use of parishes as units of politi- cal organization, and the celebration of Catholic traditions such as observ- ing Lent with Mardi Gras. To mark its bicentennial, Louisiana celebrates its Creole American heritage, a gumbo of New World ideas and folkways found only in the United States.

In 2012 and the years that follow, visitors will find hundreds of free activities that played a part in the Louisiana Bicentennial Bonanza and make the state a great travel bargain.

Here's a sampling of what can be discovered:

Learn about the Louisiana Maneuvers, the military exercises in Alexan- dria and Rapides Parish that trained about half a million soldiers at the onset of World War II.

Travel to the top of the tallest state capitol in the United States. The observation deck on the 27th floor offers a bird's-eye view of Baton Rouge and the Mississippi River.

See the LSU Indian mounds near Tiger Stadium that date back about 5,000 years and are among the oldest Native American sites.

Walk the Chalmette Battlefield near New Orleans, where General Andrew Jackson led his troops to victory against the British in one of the most significant land battles of the War of 1812.

Attend the International Rice Festival in Crowley that calls attention to the state's rice industry and its place in the world economy.

Learn about saving Louisiana's coasts from erosion while dancing to local music at blues musician Tab Benoit's Voice of the Wetlands Festival at Southdown Plantation in October.

See Louisiana's dramatic topographic changes through scenic overlooks in Kisatchie National Forest. The Forest's seven ranger districts cover more than 600,000 aces in central and north Louisiana Parishes.

Celebrate the state's French heritage at the Festival International de Louisiane as performers from around the globe gather in Lafayette the last full week of April.

Drive into Louisiana's Outback along the Creole Nature Trail, a 180-mile "All-American Road" that features prairies and lush marshes abundant with wildlife, including alligators and more than 400 bird species. Pick up a GPS Ranger at the Lake Charles/Southwest Louisiana Convention and Visitors Bureau to experience a self-guided tour.

Spend time at St. Augustine Catholic Church, part of the Cane River National Heritage Area, near Natchitoches. It is said to be the oldest Catholic church formed by free people of color in America.

Tour the Tabasco factory at Avery Island. The pepper sauce has been made in this town near New Iberia since 1868.

Stroll along Bourbon or Frenchman streets in New Orleans, where jazz, zydeco, rock, and new music pour out from the clubs, or duck into nightspots where musicians and fans share remarkable music experiences.

Learn to cook Cajun food at the Prairie Acadian Cultural Center in Eunice, which offers free cooking demonstrations led by locals every weekend.

Enjoy Cajun and zydeco music at Music and Market, Friday evenings in the fall and spring at the Opelousas Farmers Market.

Ride a bike or jog along the Tammany Trace, a 31-mile paved trail connecting the towns of Covington, Abita Springs, Mandeville, Lacombe, and Slidell.

VISITORS STROLL THROUGH TROPICAL GARDENS AT AVERY ISLAND, WHERE TABASCO SAUCE IS MADE.

Cynthia V. Campbell

In north Louisiana, you may hear an Arkansas expression pepper a conversation. Along the border with Mississippi, visitors are greeted with gracious comments softened by the lovely drawl of the Deep South. Spend some time along the Sabine River border with Texas and you may hear a Spanish word or two. In Cajun Country in the south, older folks still speak the French dialect of the Acadian settlers. In New Orleans, you'll hear many accents. The most pronounced is called the "Yat" accent of the Irish Channel and the Ninth Ward, as in "Where y'at?" French expressions are often a sign of welcome into the community. Both men and women are *cher*. Everyone is invited to "Laissez les bon temps rouler"—Let the good times roll.

Cynthia V. Campbell

STEAMING BOILED SHRIMP AND CRAWFISH ARE PILED HIGH ON A TABLE AT SUSIE'S SEAFOOD IN MORGAN CITY.

WHAT'S WHERE IN LOUISIANA

AREA CODE Whether you're contacting individuals, restaurants, or hotels, it helps to keep in mind the area codes in Louisiana. Baton Rouge is **225**, Lafayette **337**, and New Orleans and its surrounding areas have a single code, **504**. Shreveport in the northern section of the state shares the **318** code with Monroe-West Monroe. The Northshore of Lake Pontchartrain is north of New Orleans and shares the **985** code with the Houma area south of the Big Easy.

AIRPORTS AND AIRLINES
Louisiana is relatively easy to reach by plane. **Louis Armstrong New Orleans International Airport** (504-303-7500, www.flymsy.com) is served by American, JetBlue, Continental, Delta, United, U.S. Airways, Southwest, Air Canada, Aeromexico, and WestJet. It is open 24 hours a day and its facilities include a food court, restaurants, gift shops, Wi-Fi access, and the Louisiana Tax-Free Shopping kiosk for international visitors. **Baton Rouge Metropolitan Airport** (225-355-0333, www.flybtr.com), which was known as Ryan Field during World War II, serves the Plantation Country area including the Natchez, Mississippi, region. It is served by American and American Eagle, Delta and Delta

Connections, U.S. Airways, and Vision Airlines, with connections to major hubs. Facilities include a food court, restaurants, gift shop, Wi-Fi, airport shuttle, and parking shuttle. **Shreveport Regional Airport** (318-673-5370) www.shreveportla.gov/airport) serves northwest Louisiana and sections of east Texas and southwest Arkansas. It is served by American, Continental, Delta, Allegant, and Vision Airlines. Facilities include food concessions and gift shops. The **Monroe Regional Airport** (318-329-2200, www.flymonroe.org), original home of Delta Air Lines, serves a 13-parish area. It is served by Atlantic Southeast (Delta) and Continental. **Lafayette Regional Airport** (337-266-4400, www.lftairport.com) is served by American, Delta, Continental Express, and Vision with nonstop flights to Houston and Dallas. Facilities include Le Petite Cajun Cafe and Bar and the terminal building restaurant. American and Continental serve southwest Louisiana out of the **Lake Charles Regional Airport** (337-477-6051, www.flylake charles.com). **Alexandria International Airport** (318-449-3504, www .aexairport.org) is located within the England Industrial Airpark. It is served by American, Delta, and Continental Airlines.

Southwest LA/Lake Charles Convention and Visitor Bureau

ALLIGATORS The Louisiana legislature has designated the American alligator the official state reptile. The word gator comes from the Spanish el legato, meaning "the lizard." Alligators construct burrows for shelter and hibernation during winter months. They are known to seek shelter in swimming pools during dry periods. Gators can be found in ponds, lakes, rivers, canals, and swamps throughout the state. With 4.5 million acres of habitat, Louisiana's coastal marshes account for more than 3 million gators. You're not likely to see an alligator walking across the street in places such as New Orleans or Shreveport. If your time is limited, the quickest way to see gators is to visit a zoo or alligator farm. Many people enjoy taking a swamp tour in the coastal wetlands with an experienced guide. Depending on which city you're visiting, a drive to the nearest swamp tour can take anywhere from 30 minutes to several hours. It is wise to call ahead to secure a reservation. Tours usually run about two hours. Because alligators are plentiful here, the Louisiana Department of Wildlife and Fisheries has established an alligator-hunting season, which begins on the first Wednesday in September and lasts 30 days. For informa-

tion, go to the Wildlife and Fisheries Website at www.wlf.louisiana.gov and click on the wildlife icon or visit the Alligator Advisory Council website, www.alligatorfur.com/sport.htm.

AMTRAK (800-872-7245, www.amtrak .com) Amtrak has three passenger trains with service to the New Orleans Union Passenger Terminal, at 1001 Loyola Ave. The City of New Orleans runs from Chicago to New Orleans with a stop at the station in Hammond, Louisiana, from which the old Crimson Flower used to make the run to Chicago. The train offers superior sleeper service and excellent food in the Cross Country Cafe car. The Crescent runs daily from New York City through Philadelphia, Washington, D.C., and Atlanta to New Orleans. The train has sleeper service, a lounge car, and a dining car. It crosses a 6.2-mile trestle bridge over Lake Pontchartrain before it enters New Orleans. The Sunset Limited runs from New Orleans to Los Angeles, California. Three trains depart three days a week in each direction. There's sleeper service, a dining car, and a sightseer lounge. As part of its Trails and Rails program, National Park Service guides from the Amistad National Recreational Area are onboard the Sunset Limited from New Orleans to Houston. The New Orleans station is open daily from 5 a.m. to 10 p.m. Tickets are sold daily from 5:45 a.m. to 10 p.m.

ANTIQUES Antiques fanciers will find many Louisiana residents have a love affair with polished silver, 19th-century four-poster beds, and cherished family heirlooms. Antiques shopping in Louisiana is an art in itself. It can mean looking for an old garden gate to enhance a sunroom or a Philadelphia federal desk to set off a home office. Antiques shops can be found throughout the state. However, antiquing can also include consulting with a world-renowned dealer or browsing in a flea market for a tea kettle. Look for fine antiques in New Orleans along Royal and Magazine streets. The city includes a number of reputable auction houses. Ponchatoula bills itself as America's Antique City, but it's more a browser's spot for collectibles. Meander through the old high school turned into an antiques mall in Washington or the old theater antiques mall in Denham Springs. Shopping turns into an elegant jaunt along Line Avenue in Shreveport and a treasure hunt along Monroe's Antique Alley. If you're an avid collector, you'll find expert dealers in Louisiana who speak your language. When you find that special piece, ask for its provenance, the proof of authenticity. Otherwise, beware of false claims. When antiquing you will find some roadside shops loaded with flowery demitasse cups, rusty kitchen tools, dusty women's hats, bent musical instruments, and overpriced reproductions. Check them out carefully, and pass them up unless you spy that one thing you can't live without.

Cynthia V. Campbell

ARTISTS AND GALLERIES Art is definitely in the eye of the beholder, and what you find in Louisiana is a thriving interest in visual arts. Artists have always been attracted to the state's incredible beauty. The interplay of continually changing light, the climate that supports leafy forests and shadowy bayous, and the architecture influenced by 18th-century colonists are tempting subjects. People with colorful personalities and faces lined by smiles and tears draw artists' attention. John James Audubon completed many of his paintings for The Birds of America in the summer of 1821 while teaching the 15-year-old daughter of the Pirrie family at Oakley Plantation in St. Francisville. The French impressionist Edgar Degas captured the lifestyle of his Creole cousins while visiting New Orleans from October 1872 to March 1873. Conrad Albrizio, a muralist and painter, and Caroline Wogan Durieux, a painter, lithographer and social satirist, left indelible works recording the Great Depression of the 1930s. Fonville Winans documented the people, landscapes, and culture of the mid-20th century with his dramatic black-and-white photographs. Interest in visual arts extends into households, where people love to display inherited

Monroe-West Monroe CVB

or newly collected works. In the late 1800s and early 1900s, art schools in New Orleans, Baton Rouge, and Shreveport established traditions that survive today. Vernacular art by individuals without formal training appears throughout the state, often at festivals and church fairs. You can expect an abundance of swamp scenes, old cabins, birds, rural landscapes, and city courtyards. You'll also find contemporary works in metal, wood, and mixed media worthy of any modern museum. Drive through the state and you will find memorable art in museums and galleries in every region. They will be described in relevant chapters.

BIRDING On any given morning in Louisiana, you can wake up to a chorus of cardinals, mockingbirds, wrens, woodpeckers, and warblers. In just about any forest or wetland, you will find bird habitats. The Mississippi Flyway migration path crosses through the state, and Louisiana has the largest expanse of coastal wetlands in the country. Follow any loop of America's Wetland Birding Trail in south Louisiana for what is considered some of the best birding in the country. The trail includes 115 sites in 12 loops. They will introduce you to a variety of Louisiana's coastal habitats including fresh, brackish, intermediate, and saltwater marshes, *cheniers* (ridges), cypress-tupelo swamps, bottomland hardwood forests, upland hardwoods, longleaf pines, farmlands, barrier islands, headland beaches, and urban habitats. As a bonus, these trails offer views of other wildlife. Visit www .louisianatravel.com/birding for more information.

CASINOS Louisiana offers riverboat casinos, one land-based casino in New Orleans, racetrack slots, and video poker. There are also three land-based

Indian casinos in the state. Casino resorts have a wide variety of gaming, entertainment and restaurants. Harrah's Casino in downtown New Orleans has first-class restaurants and a convenient hotel with luxurious suites. Casinos in Shreveport-Bossier City in the northwest include Horseshoe Hotel & Casino, Sam's Town Hotel & Casino, DiamondJacks Casino Resort & Hotel, Eldorado Casino Resort & Hotel, Boomtown Casino & Hotel, and Harrah's Louisiana Downs, a horse track and casino. Lake Charles in the southeast offers the Isle of Capri Casino Hotel and L'Auberge du Lac Casino Resort. In Baton Rouge, visitors can enjoy the Belle of Baton Rouge Casino and Hollywood Casino, both on the Mississippi River. A third casino and resort, L'Auberge, is due to open in Baton Rouge the summer of 2012. Indian casinos in the state include the Paragon Casino Resort and Hotel in Marksville, Coushatta Casino Resort at Kinder, and Cypress Bayou Casino on Chitimacha Nation lands at Charenton. Horse racing fans can try their luck at tracks in Bossier City, Vinton, Opelousas, and New Orleans.

CAMPING Campgrounds are found throughout the state. Louisiana State Parks, operated by the Department of Culture Recreation and Tourism, offers excellent RV camping in a number of parks with hookups and electricity as well as primitive camping in certain areas. Well-maintained, many of these parks feature swimming areas, boating, fishing, and hiking trails. The parks are popular and it's wise to make camping reservations well in advance. The Louisiana Reservation Center is open Monday through Friday, 7:30 a.m.–6 p.m. (CST), but closed on all state holidays. Mondays are the busiest days for the center, so your best bet is to call midweek (Tuesday–Thursday) when telephone traffic has slowed. Reservations must be made 48 hours in advance and can be made up to 11 months ahead of time online at www .reserveamerica.com or by calling the reservation center at 877-CAMP-N-LA (877-226-7652). A $6 nonrefundable fee will be assessed on each reservation made, online, via phone or as a walk-in. If you want to share camping in Louisiana State Parks with family and friends, reloadable gift cards are available, and can be purchased at any state park. The gift cards can be purchased for any value with a $5 minimum, and are a great way to share Louisiana's parks with your family and friends. The Kisatchie National Forest, with five districts, offers outdoor stays from primitive camping to full hookup camping in motor homes. Contact www.fs.fed.us for more information.

Cynthia V. Campbell

CHILDREN, ESPECIALLY FOR

Louisiana is loaded with child-appropriate, family oriented things to do. The guide makes a major effort to mention anything that will be fun, exciting, and challenging, yet safe, for your kids. From Shreveport's Sci-Port to New Orleans's Aquarium of the Americas, you'll find imaginative children's museums and science centers, zoos, planetariums, and water parks. Outdoor adventures are never far away. With adult supervision, boat rides on rivers and bayous thrill children. Intriguing child-oriented programs in state parks range from eagle walks to spider identification. Hotels and campgrounds have inviting swimming pools, but it's best to call ahead for specific amenities. Some bed & breakfasts don't accept children under 12. The text will note family friendly lodgings and attractions.

CIVIL WAR Many places in Louisiana mark the events and sacrifices of the

Civil War. Louisiana, a slave state, seceded from the Union on January 26, 1861. It was considered a strategic location due to the Mississippi River running through the state and providing access to the Gulf of Mexico. Historic sites of note include battlefields, museums, and cemeteries. Brave Confederate and Union soldiers created legacies that are not forgotten. History buffs will want to visit the Port Hudson State Historic Site, near St. Francisville, which withstood the longest siege in U.S. history, and the Mansfield State Historic Site at Mansfield, where a series of engagements during the Union's Red River campaign concluded with a Confederate victory. The most significant sites are listed in each chapter. See www.louisianatravel.com /louisiana-civil-war-sites for more information.

CULINARY Food is a major topic in Louisiana. Residents love to catch, cook, and share their meals. The product of diverse influences, Louisiana's food is flavorful, prepared with the bounty from prairie farms and coastal fisheries. Celebrity chefs have made Louisiana cuisine famous, and every visitor owes it to himself to experience the explosion of flavors of southern fried chicken and cornbread in Monroe, candied yams and smothered pork chops in Opelousas, or oysters Rockefeller in New Orleans. To find famous and off-the-path restaurants, just follow Louisiana's Culinary Trail. The seven loop drives through the state include fine restaurants, farms, country stores, and truck stops. The loops are: Bayou Bounty in Acadian country; Capital Cuisine, with Baton Rouge sophistication and River Road gems; Creole Fusion, featuring New Orleans food like nowhere else; Delta Delights, which includes cafes in Monroe and Ruston serving smoked barbecue and great fruit cobblers; Prairie Home Cooking, which leads you to delightful small eateries in St. Landry and Avoyelles parishes; Red River Riches, where southern food like hot-water corn bread and country vegetables vie for attention with meat pies and jambalaya; and Seafood Sensation in Lake Charles, Vermillion, and Jeff Davis parishes, where spectacular seafood from Southeast Louisiana's coast can be found. A tip: Don't limit your gustatory adventures to the famous or recommended eateries. Often some of the best meals are found in one-light villages, unassuming strip malls, or service stations. If it grows in the sea or on the land, can be harvested or hunted, Louisianans know how to cook it and serve it with a smile. You can find a list of culinary driving tours and a map at www.louisianaculinarytours.com.

EMERGENCIES When traveling it's particularly frightening to have a medical emergency and not know where to go, so each chapter introduction in this guide includes the locations of convenient emergency rooms. To report roadway emergencies to the Louisiana State Police, dial *LSP (star 577) on your cell phone. The official state website for roadway closures is emergency.louisiana.gov.

FISHING Louisiana is truly a fisherman's paradise. The state's lakes, reservoirs, rivers, bayous and estuaries team with fish. For outdoor fun in the north, plan a trip to the Red and Ouachita rivers, which run through piney hills near Shreveport and Monroe and are known for their catfish and bass. In central Louisiana, visit Toledo Bend Reservoir on the Texas border. The North and South Toledo Bend state parks offer outstanding fishing and camping, as do private campgrounds. For deep-water action, don't pass up an opportunity for a charter adventure in the Gulf of Mexico. If you dream of landing a tarpon, amberjack, marlin, or other trophy fish, charter a boat from Venice, one of the top saltwater fishing spots in the world, or launch a boat from Grand Isle or Port Fourchon. To reserve a day of offshore fishing, contact the Louisiana Charter Boat Association at www.fishlcba.com. Louisiana requires recreational fishing licenses, which can be purchased from the Louisiana Department of Wildlife and

Cynthia V. Campbell

Fisheries online or by telephone using Visa or MasterCard; the toll-free number is 888-765-2602. An authorization number will be provided for immediate use and licenses will be mailed to the licensee.

FESTIVALS There are more than 400 festivals annually in Louisiana, so there's somewhere to go and join in the fun at any time. A really great festival brings together everything Louisianans love about their state and love to share with visitors. There's something for everyone. Most fairs and festivals are great family entertainment with delicious food, lively music, and outdoor experiences. We celebrate just about every crop harvested, every type of cuisine, every type of regional and national holiday. Themed festivals range from the Strawberry Festival in Ponchatoula in April to the Crawfish Festival in Breaux Bridge in May. Take in the Beauregard Watermelon Festival in June and Morgan City's Shrimp and Petroleum Festival on Labor Day weekend. Relish the good times at Shreveport's Mudbug Madness and Rayne's Frog Festival. Dance for hours at the Festival International in Lafayette, the Zydeco Festival in Opelousas, or the DeltaFest in Monroe. Certainly you want to take in the New Orleans Jazz and Heritage Festival and the family friendly French Quarter Festival. And the biggest party of them all—Mardi Gras—is celebrated big time in New Orleans and across the entire state. Each chapter of this guide includes major festivals, and there is a sidebar on how best to enjoy Mardi Gras. You can also visit www .laffnet.org and www.louisianafairs andfestivals.com.

GOLF Golfers will find world-class courses, both public and private, in every region of the state. While testing

Louisiana Office of Tourism

your skills, you can enjoy the beauty of ancient Spanish oaks, sunbeams reflecting off deep blue lakes, and birds taking wing overhead. The state's Audubon Golf Trail started in 2001 and was named for the famed ornithologist. It features 12 courses, all members of the Audubon Cooperative Sanctuary Program, which promotes ecologically sound land management and conservation of natural resources. The trail includes courses designed by Hal Sutton, David Toms and Pete Dye. Dye's TPC Louisiana at Fairfield opened in 2004 and hosts the Zurich Classic of New Orleans. Visit www .audubongolf.com or call 866-248-4652 for more information.

HIGHWAYS AND ROADS
Louisiana's highways and bridges are constructed and maintained by the Louisiana Department of Transportation and Development. In 2008, the DOTD began replacing the green-and-white shield with new signs that have a white silhouette design against a black background, and black letters and numbers. Drivers see road names such as Interstate (I-20); U.S. routes (US 65); and Louisiana highways (LA 1). Where highways have secondary routes, they are marked as such: US 190 [Spur; Business (Baton Rouge); Business (Covington); Business

(Slidell)]. Louisiana state law requires that drivers keep to the right lane on double or multi-lane roads, and use the left lane only for passing. Passengers are required to buckle up in the back seat as well as the front seat. Poor road conditions in some areas can be attributed to the moist, hot climate, which causes roads to deteriorate rapidly. Particularly in rural areas, you may encounter defects in drainage and shoulders, and missing or insufficient road markings. For more information, visit www.dotd.Louisiana.gov.

INFORMATION As much as we would like to provide complete coverage, we admit there is nothing like fresh, timely information. Each chapter of this guide lists relevant Convention and Visitors' Bureaus and Chambers of Commerce, along with their telephone numbers and websites. We also list the local tourist information centers so you can talk with someone in the know. For statewide information, visit the state's official website, www.louisianatravel.com. Request a copy of the official Louisiana Tour Guide, which is packed with information on areas, hotels, restaurants, and attractions, including phone numbers and websites. The guide has special "phone tags" where you can zoom in on Louisiana via your smart phone. Look for the MS tags that work much like a bar code. When you snap one using your phone, you will be immediately linked to additional information about the place, event, or attraction that interests you. The website also has links to hotel reservations, a Virtual Travel Center, Facebook, Twitter, and a Travel Advisory on weather-related conditions, such as flooding. You also can call 800-99-GUMBO for a copy of the travel guide.

MUSEUMS Louisiana's museums are magical places that tempt inquisitive visitors to learn about the state's fascinating history and people. The museums cover numerous topics, from Native Americans and African Americans to art, music, politics, cotton, oil and gas, architecture, and religion. The guide will lead you to both major museums and little-known gems that are worth going out of your way to see. One help is the Heroes and Heritage Trail program established by Lieutenant Governor Jay Dardenne, a former secretary of state. Travelers can obtain a Passport to Louisiana Adventure, a booklet that describes 17 museums under the Louisiana Department of State and allows for stamps after each visit. Once you gather your quota of stamps, you can spend a night on a cot in the Old State Capitol in Baton Rouge. Among the 17 museums are the Eddie G. Robinson Museum in Grambling; the Cotton Museum in Lake Providence; and the Louisiana Military Museum in Ruston. To obtain a passport booklet, visit www.louisiana travel.com/museums. Major properties are operated by the Louisiana State Museum, including the Cabildo and the Presbytere in New Orleans as well as the Louisiana State Museum—Baton Rouge. For an excellent listing visit the Louisiana Museum Association website, www.louisianamuseums.org.

Louisiana Office of Tourism

MUSIC The music never stops in Louisiana. Wherever you go in the state, you'll find music that is loved the world over. It gets into your system. Even if you don't play an instrument or dance, you'll find yourself shrugging and moving to jazz, zydeco, rock, rockabilly, country, hip-hop, bluegrass, salsa, and gospel. If your preference is more classical, choose an informal setting to hear the sweet melodies of a string quartet or a concert hall to enjoy a majestic symphony orchestra. The music comes from a long tradition that began with stately court dances from Europe and simple waltzes enjoyed by French Acadians. Blended with the sounds of Africa and the Caribbean, we soon had the new sounds of cornetist Buddy Bolton, clarinetist Sidney Bechet, and trumpeter Louis Armstrong. New Orleans nurtures world-class talent, and its stars have included Pete Fountain, Fats Domino, Trombone Shorty, and Wynton Marsalis. Cajun and zydeco music developed in southwest Louisiana, where pioneers like Amede Ardoin, Dennis McGee, and Clifton Chenier used accordions and *frottoirs* (rubboards) to create lively new tunes. Visit Shreveport's Municipal Theater, where Elvis Presley, Johnny Cash, and Hank Williams launched their careers, then head to Eunice on a Saturday for the weekly Rendezvous des Cajuns live radio show. In each chapter you'll find famed music venues and secluded spots where the state's musicians showcase their talent, and the youngest players of all take the stage with their parents and grandparents.

NATIONAL PARKS The National Park System has a strong presence in Louisiana, with highlights including Jean Lafitte National Park, the Cane River Creole National Historical Park, Poverty Point National Monument and National Landmark, and the Atchafalaya National Heritage Area. Distinctively different, each site has played a unique role in the history, geography, and culture of North America. The parks are described in detail in appropriate regional chapters.

PLANTATION HOMES Louisiana leads the nation in the number of sites listed on the National Register of Historic Places, including antebellum mansions and Colonial cottages. The state's dramatic history is reflected in its wide range of architectural styles, from Federal to Greek Revival to Caribbean-Creole, and numerous property owners are involved in historic preservation. Fantastic homes in romantic settings still stand along the Mississippi River from New Orleans through Baton Rouge and the Felicianas. You'll find more treasures traveling northward to the Red River area and Ferriday, just a short drive from Natchez, Mississippi. Some are still working plantations. Others are privately owned, and you may be welcomed by a member of the family. You'll hear stories of bygone eras, romances, hardship, and good times. When asking questions, keep in mind you are not just a tourist, but a guest

Cynthia V. Campbell

in someone's home. Many homes are open to the public daily. A few are opened on a limited basis or only for special events. Most charge admission. This guide singles out homes in every region that are especially worth visiting. Visit www.nps.gov/nr/travel /louisiana/riverroad.htm for more information.

SCENIC BYWAYS Louisiana has two road networks designated as among America's great scenic byways. The National Scenic Byways Program is part of the U.S. Department of Transportation's Federal Highway Administration. It is a grassroots collaborative effort established to help recognize, preserve, and enhance selected roads throughout the United States. The U.S. Secretary of Transportation recognizes certain roads as All-American Roads or National Scenic Byways based on one or more archeological, cultural, historic, natural, recreational and scenic qualities. The roads run through wonderful towns and amazing scenic areas. Louisiana's Creole Nature Trail, an All-American Road, is a 180-mile loop through Calcasieu and Cameron parishes and takes you through incredible wetlands. The Great River Road, a National Scenic

Louisiana Office of Tourism

Byway, is actually a series of roads from Lake Itasca in Wisconsin to Venice, Louisiana, linking 10 states along the Mississippi River. The guide gives more information on these byways in the appropriate chapters.

WEATHER Louisiana residents like to joke about the weather. You'll hear people repeat the old saw, "If you don't like the weather, stick around. It will change soon." In reality, Louisiana has a steady amount of rainfall and mild to hot temperatures most of the year. The state has a semitropical climate. North Louisiana has more variable changes in temperature and precipitation, while ocean currents keep conditions in the south constant. In north Louisiana, the average temperature in January is about 49 degrees Fahrenheit. The warmest month, July, has an average temperature of 82 degrees Fahrenheit. However, the northern part of the state holds the records for the highest and lowest temperatures in Louisiana: minus 16 degrees Fahrenheit in Minden, and 114 degrees Fahrenheit in Plain Dealing. The average annual temperature for southern Louisiana is 69 degrees, with the average January temperature 54 degrees Fahrenheit and the average in July, the hottest month, at 82 degrees. With ocean currents affecting the southern region's climate, rainfall averages 64 inches. There is a difference of almost 20 inches of rainfall between the southern and northern regions. Spring and fall are the most comfortable seasons. For the most part, summers are hot and humid and winters are mild.

Because Louisiana sits on the Gulf of Mexico and is North America's great watershed, the state is susceptible to tornadoes, hurricanes, and flooding. North Louisiana rests on the edge of Tornado Alley, and is at the greatest tornado risk in the spring months.

HURRICANES

People who live in south Louisiana know that tropical storms and hurricanes are as much a part of the Gulf as balmy, sunny days and abundant wildlife. A hurricane is a type of tropical cyclone, which is a generic term for a low-pressure system that generally forms in the tropics. A cyclone is accompanied by thunderstorms and, in the Northern Hemisphere, a counterclockwise circulation of winds near the earth's surface.

While great storms occur on an irregular basis, when they do touch down they are a fearsome force of nature. Thankfully, modern technology and weather casting allows us to be forewarned—unlike the first Europeans who explored the Gulf of Mexico.

One of the earliest references to hurricanes dates to October 13, 1527, as the Spanish explorer Panfilo de Narvaez, with five boats and less than 250 men, sailed westward from Florida. As they passed the mouth of the Mississippi River, a storm caught the vessels and tossed them like driftwood. The first well-documented hurricane to hit Louisiana occurred September 22–24, 1722. Having reached the mouth of the Mississippi on the 23rd, it passed through central Louisiana. Winds lasted 15 hours. Thirty-six huts were destroyed. The buildings had been hastily constructed in between 1717 and 1718, when New Orleans was selected as the capital of the Louisiana Company after a hurricane devastated Dauphin Island, near Mobile.

In subsequent centuries, communities in states along all of the Gulf south have recorded incredible damage from hurricanes. The further you go back in time, the more people died from hurricanes. The number of storm-related fatalities began to decline in the 20th century because of timely warnings by the National Weather Service and the spread of information from the public and private sectors about the dangers of storms. In Louisiana, public officials begin weather warnings on television and radio several days before expected landfall. People are given instructions on how to secure their homes; obtain water, food, and gasoline; and prepare for evacuation. When a hurricane is imminent, the state issues a counterflow order, which makes all traffic in all lanes head in one direction—away from the area where the hurricane is likely to make landfall. This helps vehicles flow more quickly along designated evacuation routes.

Hurricane season along the Atlantic and Gulf of Mexico usually lasts from June through November. Hurricanes have brought huge damage to southern Louisiana. On August 29, 2005, Hurricane Katrina caused catastrophic damage and loss of life in the New Orleans area, and Hurricane Rita, on September 24, damaged towns in the central coast. In 2008, hurricanes Gustav and

Hurricane Katrina, the most destructive hurricane ever to strike the United States, made landfall August 29, 2005, at 7:10 A.M. in southern Plaquemines Parish. As the center of the storm passed southeast of New Orleans, winds downtown were in the Category 3 range. In the city the

storm surge caused more than 50 breaches in drainage, canal levees, and navigational canal levees, causing the worst engineering disasters in the history of the United States. About 80 percent of the city was flooded. The French Quarter, located on a ridge, escaped inundation.

About 90 percent of the residents of southeast Louisiana were evacuated in the most successful evacuation of a major urban area in the nation's history. However, many remained, including the elderly and the poor. The estimated number of deaths was 1,577. National and international television coverage provided daily coverage of the disaster, yet never fully explained that central and northern Louisiana suffered little damage and no flooding.

Katrina stimulated local, regional and national discussion and research in urban disaster planning and economic issues. In Louisiana, the state addressed a number of its emergency response issues, including parish Community Emergency Response Team programs. By law, an annual sales tax holiday is now held on hurricane-preparedness items the last Saturday and Sunday of May. Tax-free purchases are authorized on the first $1,500 of the sales price on such items as portable self-powered radios, two-way or weather-band radios, tarpaulins, gas or diesel fuel tanks, and storm shutter devices.

The state also urges people to visit the Governor's Office of Homeland Security and Emergency Preparedness website, www.getagameplan.org. The site contains detailed information on evacuations, emergency shelters and Louisiana contraflow maps. You can also obtain a "Get a Game Plan" app for iPhones and iPads in Louisiana Apple iTunes stores.

Ike caused massive damage in Baton Rouge and southwestern Louisiana.

Flooding can strike Louisiana as a result of heavy storms or when heavy rain and melting snow in the northern United States floods the Mississippi. Fortunately, the Mississippi River levee system is one of the largest such systems in the world. It extends more than 600 miles from Cape Girardeau,

Missouri, to the Mississippi Delta. Under the direction of the U.S. Army Corps of Engineers, the system in Louisiana includes the Morganza Spillway and the Bonnet Carre Spillway above New Orleans. In the spring of 2011, the spillways were opened to divert water through the Atchafalaya Basin and Lake Pontchartrain. Carefully monitored, the systems kept the Baton Rouge and New Orleans regions from flooding.

Louisiana residents take weather warnings seriously. Wise citizens and visitors pay close attention to local and national media. When necessary, the governor announces a reverse flow of traffic—called contraflow—from all towns and villages in the danger zone. Evacuation routes on major roads and highways are publicized and people are expected to leave immediately. In addition, each year when hurricane season nears, people are reminded to start preparing for emergency situations. Complete information is on the website www.getagameplan.org.

WILDLIFE Louisiana's abundance of wildlife is not exaggerated. Outdoor enthusiasts can spend days hiking, biking, boating, fishing, and hunting, or

Louisiana Office of Tourism

just sitting quietly with a camera waiting for a beautiful heron to land a few yards away. Among the animals that make this home are American alligators, deer, squirrels, rabbits, raccoons, possums, coyotes, hogs, skunks, armadillos, rats, nutria, crawfish, turtles, frogs, snakes, herons, bald eagles, hawks, woodpeckers, ducks, warblers, brown pelicans, and black bears. Wildlife refuges and preservation areas throughout the state are managed by the U.S. Fish and Wildlife Service. The Bayou Sauvage National Wildlife Refuge, adjacent to the Pontchartrain and Borgne lakes, is a 20-minute drive from the French Quarter in New Orleans. More information is available at www.packyourgear.com, 504-646-7555, or refuges.fws.gov, 800-344-WILD. The Louisiana Department of Wildlife and Fisheries, www.wlf .louisiana.gov, issues regulations and licenses for fishing, hunting, and trapping. To report violations, call 800-442-2511. Animals prefer their own habitats, but invariably they will come in contact with humans. People who encounter animals in the wild are reminded to keep a safe distance and contact the proper authorities.

ZOOS Certainly you can see plenty of birds and animals in Louisiana's natural settings. However, to see a magnificent white tiger, a playful spider monkey, or an elephant show, head to one of the state's zoos. Children, parents, grandparents, and friends can meander for hours looking at animals and sharing a day's outing. The state's outstanding zoos, known for animal conservation and accredited by the Association of Zoos and Aquariums, include Alexandria Zoological Park, Audubon Aquarium of the Americas and Audubon Zoo in New Orleans, and BREC'S Baton Rouge Zoo. Also worth a family trip

Cynthia V. Campbell

the larger zoos include train rides, boat rides, and gift shops with quality items. Depending on the season, you'll get to see nature programs and special events such as Halloween fun nights or Christmas light displays. The state boasts several animal habitats that technically are not zoos, but are nonetheless especially fascinating. Global Wildlife Center at Folsom, near Hammond, focuses on hoof stock, including giraffes and antelope, and offers a delightful wagon safari through rugged pastures. Chimp Haven at Shreveport, www.chimphaven .org, is a National Chimpanzee Sanctuary, a secure haven for chimpanzees that have been retired from medical research or rescued from inappropriate caretaking. Visitors are welcomed on Discovery Days, which take place just seven times a year. Individual zoos are described in more detail in the appropriate chapters.

are Louisiana Purchase Gardens and Zoo in Monroe and the small, fun Zoo of Acadiana in Lafayette. Amenities in

Sportsman's Paradise

1

SHREVEPORT–BOSSIER CITY AREA

MONROE-RUSTON AREA

Larry B. Campbell

INTRODUCTION

M any first-time visitors expect to find all of Louisiana to be made up of French-speaking Cajuns, Catholics, and swamp dwellers, but the northern region is nothing like that. The fact is the state is divided geographically and philosophically into two regions, and the northern area is more akin to the Upland South and neighboring states of Arkansas and Mississippi. Yet north and south Louisiana meld into a fascinating mix. They're kissin' cousins, with an intriguing blend of traditions and culture. People in north Louisiana are more reserved, but they know a good party when they see it.

Stop at a local restaurant and you'll find simple, down-home classics of country cooking, such as stewed chicken, fried catfish, or barbecued pork. Meals are filled out with big biscuits or cornbread and fresh vegetables like snap beans, corn, or okra and tomatoes. The music that originated here has its roots in Appalachian folk tunes and, before that, songs and dances from the British Isles. Church music, gospel, bluegrass, and country are popular throughout the region. Voting leans conservative, and conversations are sprinkled with Southern expressions. While all faiths are observed, Protestant sects and values dominate. When you meet a local, one of the first questions you are likely to be asked is "What church do you attend?"

In the northeast corner of Louisiana, the inhabitants of Poverty Point built an array of mounds and ridges overlooking the Mississippi River flood plain between 1700 and 1100 B.C. Visit the archaeological site near Epps to learn about this civilized group. Later, the Tunica Tribe, formally known today as the Tunica-Biloxi, appeared in this area. The historical record of the Tunica begins with Hernando de Soto's expedition in the 16th century. The tribe, known for its agricultural and trading abilities, has continued to adapt to social and economic upheavals and thrives in Marksville today. Further west, tribes of the Caddo Nation occupied much of north Louisiana. They were woodland people and skilled farmers. Today, the Caddo Nation headquarters is in Binger, Oklahoma.

While the French and Spanish were establishing a stronghold along the Mississippi River in the northeast, trappers and traders were moving westward. In 1785, the French military officer Don Juan Filhiol established a fort on the banks of the Ouachita River and laid out a plan for the town that is now Monroe. In the early 1800s, families from Arkansas, Tennessee, and the Ohio Valley started settling in the area. The region opened to trade in 1836 after Captain Henry Miller Shreve and the U.S. Army Corps of Engineers cleared the Red River Raft, a 150-mile log

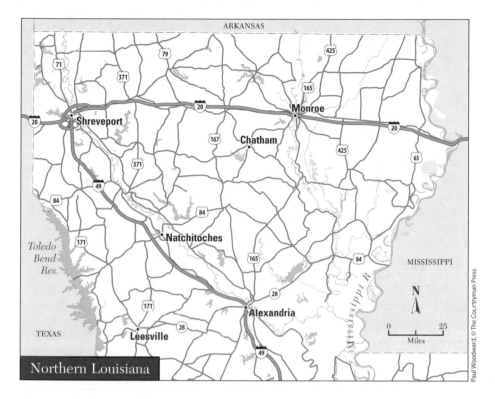

ARKANSAS

Monroe

Shreveport

Chatham

Natchitoches

Toledo
Bend
Res.

MISSISSIPPI

TEXAS

Leesville

Alexandria

N

0   25
Miles

Northern Louisiana

Paul Woodward, © The Countryman Press

jam, and Shreveport was established by the Shreve Town Company in 1836. It was part of a scheme that required establishment of a township at the junction of the Red River and the Texas Trail.

Through the years, the Sportsman's Paradise region has survived economic good times and bad. Along with homespun tales and country ways you will find people with plenty of savvy and sophistication. The communities have energy and excitement to spare. The sister cities of Shreveport and Bossier City offer great dining, fine shopping, and lovely art galleries. Young sports and old sports can seek 24-hour fun at five riverboat casinos and one horseracing track and casino.

Monroe and West Monroe, sister cities on the Ouachita River, form a vibrant and growing regional center with quality restaurants and lodgings along the I-20 corridor, extremely convenient to travelers. Antiques shopping, an eclectic Coca-Cola and Bible museum, an appealing zoo, and an excellent military museum will hold

A SODA JERK AT THE COKE MUSEUM AT THE BIEDENHARN MUSEUM & GARDENS IN MONROE TELLS VISITORS THE STORY OF HOW COCA-COLA WAS FIRST BOTTLED.
Monroe-West Monroe CVB

your attention for days. The University of Louisiana at Monroe (ULM) offers undergraduate and graduate degrees in five colleges ranging from agribusiness and art to gerontology and pharmacy. The university injects a youthful spirit into the region with its enthusiastic sports teams. Ruston welcomes visitors to sporting events at Louisiana Tech University and nearby Grambling University. And you can explore the community's art studios and sample true down-home cooking.

There's a good reason north Louisiana is called a paradise. Start your visit by studying the land. Meandering bayous and magnificent lakes create landscapes a master artist would envy. Throughout the region stands of tall longleaf pines and rolling hills meet blue skies and fluffy white clouds most days. Seven state parks offer plenty of outdoor entertainment. Listen as raindrops, falling gently on a canopy of trees, lull you to sleep at night. Listen as songbirds chirp along shadowy hiking trails. Beautiful Lake Claiborne State Park, near Homer, has a sandy beach for swimming. Cyclists will enjoy the challenge of hills and steep inclines at Lake D'Arbonne State Park. At Chemin-a-Haut State Park, near Bastrop and the Arkansas border, two playgrounds in the day-use area keep younger travelers occupied and a hard-surfaced trail goes along the high, scenic banks of Bayou Bartholomew. Lake Bistineau attracts freshwater fishermen with schools of black crappie, largemouth bass, yellow bass, catfish, bluegill, and redear sunfish. The park's trail system features nearly 10 miles of woodland trails and an 11-mile canoe trail. Serious hunters and fishers can also spend days in the Caney Ranger District and Winn Ranger District of the Kisatchie National Forest. Locally operated parks provide easy access to camping, boating, fishing, hiking, cycling, and birding. You don't even have to come in from the woods, unless you're so inclined.

I-20, which cuts across the region from Vicksburg, Mississippi, to the Sabine River on the Texas border, takes you to Shreveport, Bossier City, Ruston, Monroe, and West Monroe. Get off the big highway and follow the region's scenic byways to get a true feel of the area that captured the imagination of the first Europeans to arrive here. In some cases, the roads here began as trails used by the earliest inhabitants. Follow scenic back roads to places like the Germantown Museum in Minden, Bernice Depot Museum in Bernice, or the Caddo-Pine Island Oil and Historical Museum in Oil City. The roads will take you to postcard-perfect villages like Homer, Columbia, Mer Rouge, Lake Providence, and Transylvania. Asking directions from locals can result (depending on their outlook on life) in a mumble or a 20-minute discussion about weather conditions, their great-grandparents, and local ghosts. Smile and listen or graciously move on.

A MULE GUARDS DERELICT EQUIPMENT IN AN OIL CITY FIELD.

Louiisiana Office of Tourism

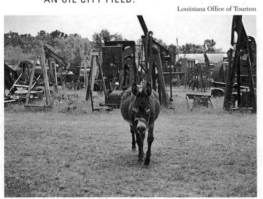

South of Shreveport, on US 84, is Mansfield, where you'll find the Mansfield State Historic Site, the location of the last major Confederate victory during the Civil War. Another museum is the Mansfield Female College Museum, site of the first college for women west of the Mississippi. The

1843 log courthouse is said to be one of the last two remaining in the state. Yogie and Friends, a big cat sanctuary, is in Frierson. Logansport on the Texas border has the last known international boundary marker between the United States and the Republic of Texas. The gravesite of Louis "Moses" Rose, the only survivor of the Alamo, is nearby. The town, on the banks of the Sabine River, has a delightful city park with picnic tables.

Local tourist information offices are usually open 8 A.M. to 4 or 4:30 P.M. In some villages, the offices are closed during lunch hours. Be prepared: Carry a good map and call ahead.

AREA CODE 318.

GUIDANCE Louisiana North Coalition (318-393-32274, www.explorelouisiana north.org). The tourist organization represents 29 northern parishes in both Sportsman's Paradise and the Crossroads region. The group promotes historic and cultural attractions, events, and recreation activities. Its annual full-page guide, which is very helpful, includes websites and phone numbers for towns and parishes in the entire region.

Greenwood Welcome Center (318-938-5613, www.crt.state.la.us), I-20 Eastbound, 9945 Interstate 20, West Greenwood. This is the official Louisiana Welcome Center for drivers entering the state from north Texas. It contains maps and brochures about every area of the state, as well as pamphlets listing accommodations, restaurants, etc. The staff here is welcoming and extremely helpful. They can give you updated details on north Louisiana area attractions and events; they're the ones who will know if a popular local festival has changed dates or a new cafe has opened nearby. You will often find an exhibit here related to Louisiana culture and history.

Mound Welcome Center (318-574-5674, www.crt.state.la.us), I-20 Westbound, 836 Interstate 20, Tallulah. This center welcomes drivers entering the state from the Vicksburg, Mississippi, area. Like other state Welcome Centers, it is well run, with trained travel counselors. Certainly, they can give directions to Poverty Point State Historic Site and nearby campgrounds. Ask, and they will tell you how the center got its name from a nearby Indian mound, which is no longer available to see. Also, you can pick up maps and brochures from well-stocked kiosks. You're welcome to help yourself to hot coffee and relax a while.

Shreveport-Bossier Convention and Visitors Bureau (888-458-4748, www .shreveport-bossier.org), 629 Spring St., Shreveport. This is the most comprehensive source for all things in Shreveport, Bossier City, and Caddo Parish. The website is easy to follow and filled with detailed information. Contact this visitors' bureau and ask for a city guide and map. The office and official visitor information center is housed at the corner of Spring Street and Crockett. **The Bossier City Visitor Center** (318-226-8884 or 888-458-4748), 100 John Wesley Blvd., is situated in a historic Victorian gazebo where you can sit and relax. Another visitor center is located at the Shreveport Regional Airport (318-222-9391, www.shreveportla .gov/airport), 5103 Hollywood Ave., Shreveport. The travel counselors are well versed in the region and friendly. You will receive the same assistance if you call one of centers.

HAY BALES AWAIT PICK-UP ALONG CADDO PARISH ROAD.

GETTING THERE Getting to northern Louisiana is relatively easy. While it's not a major hub, there are excellent airports at Shreveport and Monroe-West Monroe. I-20 links major towns and cities in the region. As in the rest of Louisiana, all roads, including some U.S. and state highways, seem to meander at times. This is because rivers, bayous, and lakes create a network of waterways and flat terrain that sometimes flood. Many roads follow paths that have proven to be the best routes over and around flooded terrain. Road conditions range from excellent in some parishes to dismal in others. Road repairs are ongoing projects in Louisiana, where rain and humidity create a constant need for upkeep.

By car: I-20 runs across the entire width of northern Louisiana from Vicksburg, Mississippi, on the east to the Texas border on the west. It travels through the cities of Monroe-West Monroe, Ruston, and Shreveport-Bossier. This is an extremely busy stretch of the interstate, heavy with commercial vehicles. If you're planning to drive north or south of I-20 in the northeastern section of the state, watch for the exit sign for US 65, a well-maintained, two-lane highway that connects with Arkansas in the north and US 425 and Natchez, Mississippi, to the south. Pick up US 165 at Monroe and US 167 at Ruston to reach byways in the heart of Sportsman's Paradise.

Shreveport's highway system has a cross-hair and loop freeway structure similar to those in Texas cities like Houston and Dallas. I-20 runs through the center of the metropolitan area. The loops consist of the Outer Loop Freeway, I-220, on the north, and the Inner Loop Freeway, LA 3132, on the south, which form a semi-loop around downtown. A second outer loop is formed by the Bert Kouns Industrial Loop (LA 526), which circles further south and bisects I-49.

The complexity of highway interchanges can be confusing. Watch carefully for signs directing you to I-49, which runs north to south from Arkansas through

and LA 1 north and south connecting with scenic roads in the western section of
the state.

For explorers who enjoy following back roads, we suggest following LA 2. The
highway runs the width of the state north of I-20 and connects rural areas, picturesque small towns, and Lake D'Arbonne and Lake Claiborne State Parks.

By air: **Shreveport Regional Airport** (318-673-5370, www.shreveportla.gov
/airport), 5103 Hollywood Ave., Shreveport. The airport, operated by the Shreveport Airport Authority, is served by American, Continental, Delta, and Allegiant
Air with connecting flights to Dallas–Fort Worth, Houston, Atlanta, and Memphis.
You should be at the airport two hours before departure and the checkpoint opens
at 4 A.M. You can't park a car curbside for more than a few moments to drop off or
pick up a passenger. Parking rates are $8.50 per day, standard; $7.50 per day, long-
term; and $9.50 per day, premium. Car rental companies include Avis, Budget,
Enterprise, Hertz, National, and Thrifty. The airport is southwest of downtown
Shreveport via I-20. The Airport Visitor Center, operated by the Shreveport Convention and Visitors' Bureau, is open weekdays. **Shreveport Downtown Airport**
(318-673-5398. www.shreveportla.gov/airport/dtnairport.htm), 1550 Airport Dr.,
Shreveport is a general aviation airport and is the city's original commercial airport
dating from 1931. Numerous owners of small planes house their aircrafts there,
and services include a maintenance shop and the Stone's Throw Café. **Monroe
Regional Airport** (318-329-2461, www.flymonroe.com), 5400 Operations Rd.,
Monroe, the original home of Delta Air Lines, serves a 13-parish area. It is served
by Delta and Atlantic Southeast Airlines, American, Continental Express, and
Masada. The airport provides free high-speed wireless connections. Parking is
50 cents an hour. The minimum rate for 24 hours is $5, and for a week, $20.
The Monroe Transit System operates bus service to the airport every 45 minutes
Monday–Saturday, 6:20 A.M.–6:30 P.M. Car rentals include Avis, Budget, Hertz,
and National. Taxi and limousine services are also available.

MEDICAL EMERGENCIES Christus Schumpert Health System (318-681-
4222, www.christusschumpert.org), 1 St. Mary Place, Shreveport. This hospital is a
Catholic, nonprofit system. The emergency departments of **Christus Schumpert**
and **Christus Schumpert-Highland** (318-681-5443, 1453 East Bert Kouns
Industrial Loop) are staffed 24 hours a day by highly trained physicians and nurses.
If an injury or illness is serious or life-threatening, call 911, if it is available in your
area. EMS technicians can provide emergency response during transport. When
time is critical to survival, EMS technicians will take you to the nearest hospital
that can handle the problem.

Willis-Knighton Health System of Shreveport (318-212-4500, www.wkhs.com),
2600 Greenwood Rd., Shreveport, and **Willis-Knighton Bossier Health Center**
(318-212-7500), 2510 Bert Kouns Industrial Loop, Bossier City. These hospitals
offer full-service, 24-hour emergency treatment. Each department is staffed by
experienced emergency personnel. The emergency departments are supported by
the hospital's Heart and Vascular Institute and are ideal locations for the treatment
of symptoms of heart attack. They also are supported by Life Air Rescue helicopter. Willis-Knighton offers two Quick Care/Urgent Care Centers for minor illnesses and accidents such as cuts, sprains, flu symptoms, sports medicine. They

are: Quick Care Shreveport (318-212-3520), 1666 East Bert Kouns Industrial Loop, and Quick Care Bossier (318-212-7520), 2300 Hospital Dr., Bossier City.

Glenwood Regional Medical Center (877-726-9355, www.grmc.com), 503 McMillan Rd., West Monroe. Glenwood offers comprehensive healthcare services, including emergency care and heart care 24 hours a day. Facilities include a private patient triage area, fast-track for minor illnesses and injuries, and helipad for emergency airlift services.

St. Francis Medical Center (318-966-4172, www.stfran.com), 309 Jackson St. and St. Francis North, 3421 Medical Park Dr., Monroe. The hospitals operated by the Franciscan Missionaries of Our Lady offer 24-hour emergency service daily.

Northern Louisiana Medical Center (318-254-2100, www.northernlouisiana medicalcenter.com), 401 East Vaughn Ave., Ruston. The emergency services staff is on duty 24 hours daily. Physicians, nurses and technicians work as a team to evaluate patients, prescribe treatment and follow through to see that emotional and physical needs are met.

Pafford EMS (318-255-9114, www.paffordems.com), 1109 Farmerville Highway, Ruston. This EMS ambulance service maintains crews on duty 24 hours a day. Each crew consists of an EMT-paramedic and an EMT basic. Pafford Air One provides air ambulance service across North Louisiana and South Arkansas.

SHREVEPORT–BOSSIER CITY AREA

T he northwest corner of the state, in and around Shreveport, enjoys the reputation of being a little bit different than the rest of Louisiana. The towns are a blend of wide-open Texas spirit, lively Cajun attitude, and homespun Arkansas practicality. There's a little of Vegas's free-wheeling pizzazz thrown in for good measure. Business is mixed with pleasure, so the serious side of seeking new enterprise is always a part of the scene.

Shreveport was founded in 1836 by the Shreve Town Company, after Captain Henry Miller Shreve and the U.S. Army Corps of Engineers cleared the long, natural log jam on the Red River. The site of the original town covered 64 blocks, which today comprise the city's historic district. The town quickly became the center of steamboat commerce, mostly cotton and agricultural crops. By the early 1900s, railroads replaced riverboats as the principal means of transportation and the town continued to grow. From 1863 to 1865, as the Civil War raged, Shreveport was the capital of Louisiana. The city was the headquarters of the Trans-Mississippi Department of the Confederacy, and local women were instrumental in raising funds and providing socks, blankets, and other goods for soldiers. Eventually the Red River again became unnavigable. In 1994 it was restored by the Corps of Engineers with a series of lock-and-dam structures and a navigation channel that is still in use today.

Along with growth came fun. By the 1920s, the blues singer and guitarist Huddie William Ledbetter, later known as Lead Belly, was entertaining in St. Paul's Bottoms, a notorious red-light district. He developed his own style picking up musical influences from Fannin Street, a section of saloons, dance halls, and brothels. From 1948–1960, *Louisiana Hayride*, a radio and television country music show broadcast from the Municipal Auditorium, helped to launch the

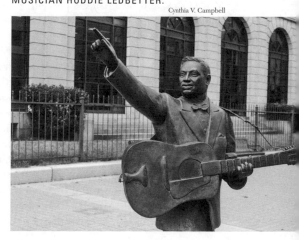

A STATUE IN DOWNTOWN SHREVEPORT HONORS THE LEGENDERY BLUES AND FOLK MUSICIAN HUDDIE LEDBETTER.

Cynthia V. Campbell

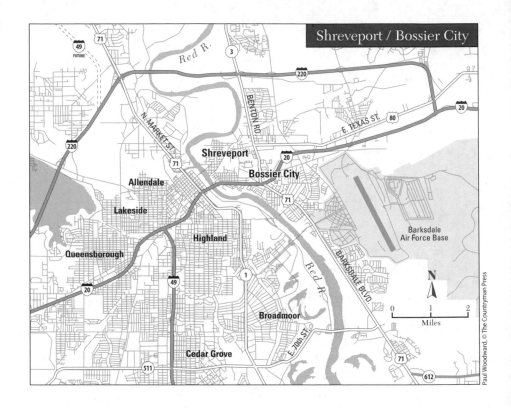

Shreveport / Bossier City

Paul Woodward, © The Countryman Press

careers of some of the greatest stars in American music. Elvis Presley performed on the radio show in 1954 and made his first TV appearance on the TV version on March 3, 1955. Among others who appeared in the show were Hank Williams, Tex Ritter, Webb Pierce, Kitty Wells, Jimmie Davis, Aretha Franklin, Smokey Robinson, B. B. King, Slim Whitman, and Johnny Cash.

Bossier City, originally known as Bennett's Bluff, was named after William Bennett, who owned Elysian Groves Plantation on the Red River along with his wife, Mary Ciley, and his business partner, James Cane. After Bennett's death, his widow married his business partner and the property became known as Cane's Landing, and later Cane City. In 1843, a section of the land was divided out of the Great Natchitoches district and Claiborne Parish areas, and was named Bossier Parish after Pierre Evariste Jean-Baptiste Bossier, a former Creole general who became a cotton planter. By 1850, hundreds of settlers on their way west passed through Bossier City. Some stayed and settled in the fertile river valley. In the late 1800s, the town became a railroad hub, and the east–west Dixie Overland Highway was built in 1918. In 1908, crude oil was discovered south of town and Bossier City boomed. In the 1930s construction began on Barksdale Air Force Base, which became a training school for the Army Air Corps. The airfield was used by both fighter and attack pilots. Among the units trained at Barksdale Field was the 17th Bomb Group, which was led by General Jimmy Doolittle during his daring raid on Tokyo during World War II. Today, Barksdale is a key U.S. military installation. The base is home to the Air Force's newest command, Air Force Global Strike

Command. The "Mighty Eighth" Air Force is headquartered at Barksdale. Visitors are welcomed to the Eighth Air Force Museum to view historical aircraft and artifacts.

Shreveport and Bossier City thrive because they are entrepreneurial and welcome new ventures. Equally welcomed are visitors. With five riverboat casinos and one horse-racing track and casino, the towns offer bright lights and fast-paced gaming. There's a fascinating range of things to do and see. Pick up a movie ticket at the Robinson Film Center in downtown Shreveport, which showcases international and foreign films, or tour the Municipal Auditorium to focus on the *Louisiana Hayride* country-rockabilly era. Specialty boutiques abound. The Louisiana Boardwalk and the Villaggio shopping village in Bossier City have endless options, from perfume boutiques to a tattoo parlor. Don't worry about finding great food. Go for scrumptious Southern cuisine at Ernest's Orleans. Try Cajun specialties at Herby K's or Bear's Restaurant and Sports Bar. You'll find Italian and Asian or cowboy and contemporary cafes throughout the two towns. Head outdoors to find natural habitats or head to Gator and Friends Alligator Park or Jubilee Zoo. Take in a horse race, baseball game or a round of golf. Go for the fun at Sci-Port and Splash Kingdom Water Town.

You'll find plenty to do on either side of the Red River, and don't miss the Texas Street Bridge lit up like a Christmas tree at night.

GETTING AROUND The listing at the beginning of the chapter explains the complex highway system in the Shreveport–Bossier City area. Traffic in the metropolitan areas can be extremely busy during rush hours. Watch carefully for signs directing you to major highways. Some exit signs come up rapidly, so stay alert and be prepared to move quickly to the proper lane.

STATE-OF-THE-ART BLADE STUDIOS IN SHREVEPORT HAS RECORDED WORK BY WORLD-FAMOUS MUSICIANS, INCLUDING THE ROLLING STONES.

Cynthia V. Campbell

Cynthia V. Campbell

MUSICIANS PLAY HUDDIE LEDBETTER'S SONGS FOR A PARTY AT HERBY K'S IN SHREVEPORT.

✳ To See

Antioch Baptist Church (318-222-7090), 1057 Texas Ave., Shreveport. Founded in 1866, this is the oldest Black Baptist church in Shreveport. The Romanesque Revival–style edifice is listed on the National Register of Historic Places. It was designed by the noted African American architect Nathaniel Skyes Allen, and features wonderful stained-glass windows. Open to public for group appointments only.

Barnwell Garden & Art Center (318-673-7703, www.barnwellcenter.com), 601 Clyde Fant Parkway, Shreveport. One of the South's few combined art and garden centers, the Barnwell has a spectacular view of the Red River, the Texas Street Bridge, and Louisiana Boardwalk. Under the dome of the botanical garden conservatory you'll see a collection of plants from the tropics. Palms, bromeliads, and unusual trees flourish here. The garden is especially colorful during Easter and Christmas. The center's galleries present visiting art exhibitions and flower shows. Experience the Fragrance Garden for the visually impaired or visit the gift shop filled with contemporary handmade works of glass, pottery, and jewelry. Open 10 A.M.–4 P.M. Tues.–Fri., 10 A.M.–5 P.M. Sat., and 1–5 P.M. Sun.

Caddo Lake Drawbridge (318-929-2806, www.caddolakedrawbridge.com), Mooringsport. In 1914, as modes of transportation developed, this historic drawbridge was built to replace the ferry. During World War II, generals Dwight D. Eisenhower and George S. Patton came to Mooringsport and led the Red and Blue Armies in the "capture" of the bridge. They also bombed the bridge with sacks of flour. In 1989, the Department of Transportation and Development received funds from the Federal Highway Administration to build a new two-lane bridge and destroy the original structure. A citizens' campaign saved the bridge and converted it to a pedestrian walkway, landmark and tourist attraction. It is now maintained by the Caddo Parish Department of Parks and Recreation. Open daily 7 A.M.–7 P.M.

Cemeteries, Oakland and Star (www.shreveportla.gov). These two historic cemeteries are especially helpful to visitors who are trying to learn more about their roots. Oakland Cemetery, 1000 Milam St., officially opened in 1847 and was originally called City Cemetery. At least 16 mayors are buried here, along with some 1,000 Confederate soldiers. Star Cemetery (at Levy and Texas Avenue, with entrance through St. Joseph's Cemetery) was established in 1883. It is the first cemetery organized by and for Shreveport's African American citizens. Some gravestones are assumed to be of people born into slavery as early as 1815. The site also contains the graves of blacks who served in the military, including one man who fought in the Civil War.

Elvis Presley and James Burton Statues (318-220-9434, www.stageofstars .com), 705 Elvis Presley Blvd., Shreveport. Standing in front of the Municipal Auditorium, the handsome, bigger-than-life bronze statues of Elvis Presley and James Burton, a Rock and Roll Hall of Fame guitarist, spotlight the place where they played together on the *Louisiana Hayride* radio show.

✂ ❧ **Eighth Air Force Museum** (318-456-3067, www.8afmseum.com), 88 Shreveport Rd., Barksdale AFB, Shreveport. The collections here take you on a journey from World War I to present. Uniforms, dioramas, and a barracks exhibit dating from World War II help visitors experience the history of aerial bombardment. Twenty-five aircraft and ground vehicles are displayed outside the museum. There is a gift shop. Access is through the North Gate of Barksdale AFB. Picture identification is required, and all vehicles are subject to search. No backpacks, briefcases, or large bags will be allowed in any buildings. Visitors are asked to sign in upon entering the museum. Open 9:30 A.M.– 4 P.M. seven days a week. Closed Thanksgiving, Christmas, and New Year's Day.

A BRONZE STATUE OF ELVIS PRESLEY MARKS THE ARTIST'S BEGINNINGS AT SHREVEPORT MUNICIPAL AUDITORIUM.
Cynthia V. Campbell

First United Methodist Church (318-424-7771, www.fumcshreveport .org), 500 Common St., Shreveport. Located at the head of Texas Street, the church appears to loom over downtown as travelers cross the Texas State Bridge from Bossier City. The way ends abruptly at Common Street directly in front of the church's entrance. Traditional Sunday worship services are held at 8:30 A.M. and 11 A.M., and there is a contemporary service at 11 A.M. The church complex recently added the new Emmett Hook Center for Performing Arts, which is available for concerts, theatrical productions, lectures, and contemporary worship (see Entertainment list).

Holy Trinity Catholic Church (318-221-5990, www.holytrinity-shreveport.com), 315 Marshall St., Shreveport. Records for the parish begin in 1849, before the first church was built. The second church was erected on Fannin Street in 1859. The current Romanesque Revival edifice, built in 1896, was listed on the national Register of Historic Places in 1984. One of the most dramatic events in the church's history occurred during a Yellow Fever epidemic in 1873, when between 2,600 and 3,000 residents came down with the disease. Five priests and two nuns died while caring for those who were ill.

✍ 🐾 **J. Bennett Johnston Waterway Regional Visitor Center** (318-677-2673, www.redriverwaterway.com), 700 Clyde Fant Parkway, Shreveport. Engineers and curious youngsters will love this center. This is the regional visitor center for the U.S. Army Corps of Engineers. Fashioned like a boat, it uses interactive exhibits and displays to educate people about Red River history, navigation, and exploration. Open 9 A.M.–5 P.M., Mon.–Sat., in winter and 9 A.M.–6 P.M. summer, and 1–5 P.M. Sunday.

Lead Belly Statue at Texas Ave. and Marshall St., Shreveport, stands the bronze statue of Huddie William "Lead Belly" Ledbetter (1888–1949), a legendary blues 12-string guitar player and singer. He could also play the piano, mandolin, harmonica, violin, concertina, and accordion. Ledbetter performed in an area called Bluegoose, on the southwest edge of Shreveport's Central Business District, which took its name from a speakeasy that operated during Prohibition. Ledbetter, who was raised in nearby Mooringsport, composed a wide variety of blues, gospel, and folk songs, and was inducted into the Louisiana Music Hall of Fame in 2008.

✍ 🐾 **Louisiana Oil and Gas Museum** (318-995-6845, www.sos.louisiana.gov), 200 South Land Ave., Oil City. About a 20-minute ride north of Shreveport, this museum interprets the drama of the region's early oil industry history. This area was the site of the 1911 Ferry No. 1 well, one of the world's first over-water discovery wells (basically drills loaded onto barges in order to access oil underneath lakebeds). Artifacts include a wooden flow line pipe, an electric motor patented in 1899, and other equipment. There's also a large collection of early boomtown and gusher photos. The museum's Caddo Indian Room features tribal relics and arrowheads dating back 10,000 years. Open 9 A.M.–4 P.M. Mon.–Fri. Free admission.

✍ ♿ 🍴 🐾 **Louisiana State Exhibit Museum** (318-632-2020, www.sos.louisiana.gov), 3015 Greenwood Rd., Shreveport. One of Louisiana's very special small museums, this is an architectural gem. The front portico features a two-story fresco by the famed muralist Conrad Albrizio and a beautiful diorama that is staggering. Inside, exhibits on Louisiana history include Native American and Civil War collections. Rotating art displays make it worthwhile to return time and again. Open 9 A.M.–4 P.M. Mon.–Fri.

✍ 🐾 **Mansfield Female College Museum** (318-871-9978, www.sos.la.gov), 101 Monroe St., Mansfield. The first women's institute of higher learning west of the Mississippi River, the college was established by the Methodist Church in the 1850s. Its buildings served as hospitals for wounded soldiers during the Battle of Mansfield. Supposedly, a ghost from that era even became something of a mascot

Cynthia V. Campbell

INCREDIBLE ART DECO MURALS ADORN THE ENTRANCE TO THE LOUISIANA STATE EXHIBIT MUSEUM.

for later classes of schoolgirls. The museum features much of the art, pottery and crafts produced by the students. You'll also see class rings, commencement dresses, yearbooks, and other items. The college operated for 80 years before merging with Centenary College in Shreveport in 1930. Open 9 A.M.–5 P.M. Mon.–Fri. Free.

♂ & ✿ **Mansfield State Historic Site** (318-872-1474 or 888-677-6267, www.crt .state.la.us), 15149 LA 175, Mansfield. This site played a crucial role in the Civil War. With the fall of Vicksburg and Port Hudson in July 1863, the Mississippi River was firmly in the hands of the Union Army. The Union next decided that a successful campaign would involve the seizure of cotton and prevent French-Mexican forces from providing supplies to the Confederacy. Like many battles, the Mansfield-Pleasant Hill engagement was actually a series of encounters taking place over several days. The Confederate General Richard Taylor (son of President Zachary Taylor) decided to defend a site about four miles from Mansfield. General Nathaniel P. Banks, commanding Union troops, did not expect the Confederates to fight until he reached Shreveport. After several days of battle, the Union forces turned back—a Confederate victory that prevented the Union from taking control of Louisiana. Visitors can walk a section of the battlefield. The museum contains exhibits about the battles, the soldiers who fought on both sides, and the importance of the conflict. Interpretive rangers host programs throughout the year. Watch for musket demonstrations and candlelight tours of the battlefield. Open daily 9 A.M.–5 P.M. Admission is $4 per person; free for seniors and children age 12 and under.

Meadows Museum of Art (318-869-5169, www.centenary.edu), 2911 Centenary Boulevard, Shreveport. The museum, located on the campus of the Centenary

College of Louisiana, was established in 1975 to house the collection of Jean Despujols paintings and drawings of Indochina, a large portion of which is normally on display. The museum was made possible by a gift from Algur H. Meadows, an oilman, art collector, and an alumnus of Centenary College. Visitors also will see works by Georg Grosz, Emilio Amero, Mary Cassatt, and Alfred Maurer. Open 10 A.M.–5 P.M. Tues.–Fri.; 10 A.M.–5 P.M. Sat.; 1–5 P.M. Sun.; late hours Thurs. until 9 P.M. Admission $8, adults; $6, seniors 65 and over; $4, students.

Multicultural Center of the South (318-424-1380, www.mccsouth.org), 520 Spring St., Shreveport. This center is dedicated to the appreciation of the diverse cultures of northwest Louisiana, as well as other regions of the state. Exhibits focus on more than 26 cultures, including African American, Asian, Greek, Hispanic, Japanese, and Vietnamese. Expect lively colors and a friendly staff. Exhibiting hours are 10 A.M.–4 P.M. Tues.–Fri. Guided tours on Saturday by appointment only.

𝄞 **Municipal Auditorium/Stage of the Stars Music Museum** (318-220-9434, www.municipalauditorium.homestead.com and www.stageofstars.com), 705 Elvis Presley Ave., Shreveport. The Shreveport Municipal Auditorium, built in the 1920s, is noted for its art deco architecture and superior acoustics. The building seats more than 3,000 and has a 54-foot proscenium arch. As home of the *Louisiana Hayride* radio show, it has played host to numerous stars, including the king of rock 'n' roll, Elvis Presley. Located inside the auditorium, the Stage of Stars Museum is a local treasure. Although small, it is packed with artifacts and memorabilia from performers who have played the auditorium. View sheet music, albums, theatrical costumes, and personal items donated by performers and their fans. Tour hours vary.

Once in a Millennium Moon Mega Mural (318-673-6500), corner of Cotton and Marshall, Shreveport. This is one of America's most amazing urban murals. Covering two sides of the 12-story AT&T building in downtown Shreveport, it's the nation's largest public mural, covering 25,000 square feet. It was designed by Meg Saligman and the staff of the Shreveport Regional Arts Council. The painting, designed on a paint-by-number grid, involved more than 2,600 people. Once painted, the cloth was "floated in acrylic" on the wall. The mural is a visual time capsule that portrays the people of Shreveport, their treasures, tragedies, and triumphs.

𝄞 ↬ **RiverView Park** (318-673-7703), 601 Clyde Fant Parkway, Shreveport. Not many cities have a downtown park as lovely and entertaining as Shreveport's RiverView. Terraced lawns, splashing fountains, and gardens invite people of all ages to relax outdoors in the middle of an urban setting. Children and adults can cool off in the spray of the fountains on hot summer days or watch movies in the evenings. Bring a lawn chair or blanket and just chill out.

𝄞 ⅋ ↑ 🌼 **The R.W. Norton Art Gallery** (318-865-4201, www.rwnaf.org), 705 Elvis Presley Blvd., Shreveport. A wonderful museum, the Norton is a true Louisiana surprise. It houses incomparable collections of American and European paintings, sculptures, and decorative arts spanning more than four centuries. Several galleries are devoted to an amazing collection of American Western art, with works by Charles Marion Russell, Frederic Remington, and Albert Bierstadt. The museum contains a number of Remington's famous bronzes like *The Bronco Buster* and *Coming Through the Rye*. The Norton's European collection includes works by Jacob van Ruisdael, Joshua Reynolds, Mary Cassatt, Jean-Baptiste-

Cynthia V. Campbell

WHIMSICAL SCULPTURES IN THE CHILDREN'S GALLERY DELIGHT YOUNG VISITORS TO THE NORTON GALLERY IN SHREVEPORT.

Camille Corot, and Charles Jacque. The rare book collection contains a broad selection of the printed word, including a Book of the Hours from the 14th century, the John James Audubon double elephant folio of *The Birds of America,* and a complete set of John Gould's masterpieces of ornithology. A more recent work is a limited edition *Alice in Wonderland* with original lithographs by Salvador Dali. One Saturday a month the Norton hosts an expert who presents a formal or informal talk. There's also a First Saturday Tour program. The museum has an artful gift shop. If nothing else, you can spend an hour or so strolling through the museum's dreamy garden. It's especially beautiful when the azaleas bloom in spring. Open 10 A.M.–5 P.M. Tues.–Fri., 1–5 P.M. weekends.

Texas Street Bridge (US 80 over the Red River). Built in 1934 and rehabilitated in 1984, the four-lane truss bridge connects Shreveport and Bossier City. It's nicknamed the Neon Bridge for a light sculpture by Rockne Krebs that illuminates it at night. While it doesn't always work as designed, city fathers deserve a tip of the hat for embracing the idea that a bridge structure can be a contemporary work of art. It certainly makes crossing the Red River at night an unusual experience.

✳ Green Spaces

American Rose Gardens (318-938-5402, www.ars.org), 8877 Jefferson Paige Rd., Shreveport. America's largest private park dedicated exclusively to roses draws rose fanciers from around the world. More than 60 specially designed rose gardens cover 118 acres of beauty. Many were donated by rose societies from across the United States. It's especially spectacular and fragrant in spring and fall, when it's cool enough to enjoy the stunning blooms. You can see antique and heritage plants, roses named for celebrities, climbing roses, and roses being tested by the American Rose Society. In addition, the gardens feature magnolias, camellias, and azaleas, a Japanese teahouse and an enchanting gift shop. Each Christmas season, the garden is adorned with thousands of lights and displays for Christmas in Rose-land. Open year-round, 9 A.M.–5 P.M. daily. Admission $5.

✐ ❧ **Arthur Ray Teague Park** (318-949-1804), Bossier City. This city park on Arthur Ray Teague parkway runs along the east side of the Red River. It offers scenic biking and jogging trails, picnic pagodas, and a boat launch.

✐ ❧ **Betty Virginia Park** (318-673-7727, www.myspar.org), 3901 Fairfield Ave. between Fairfield and Line avenues, Shreveport. The beauty and central location of Betty Virginia Park makes it one of the most visited in Shreveport. Open dawn to dusk, the 23-acre plot has a half-mile trail, picnic area, multi-purpose building, playground, and ball field.

❧ **Bodcau Dam and Reservoir** (318-322-6391, www.recreation.gov), 171 Ben Durden Rd., Haughton. A wonderful waterfowl management and upland game and management area, Bodcau is an outdoor paradise for anyone who wants the feeling of getting away from it all. There's plenty of room for biking, boating, camping, fishing, hiking, and horseback riding. Go for an afternoon of picnicking and wildlife viewing. The lake has good fishing for largemouth bass, various types of catfish, crappie, and sunfish.

❧ **Caddo Lake** (www.explorecaddolake.com). Caddo Lake spreads across the Texas-Louisiana border just north of Shreveport. Mysterious and beautiful, the lake covers 25,810 acres of Cypress swamp. There are many bayous, channels, waterways, and sloughs that delight fishermen and canoeists. Bird watchers have observed about 240 species at the lake. Other wildlife includes white-tailed deer, raccoons, beavers, minks, squirrels, armadillos, frogs, turtles, snakes, and alligators.

✐ ❧ **Cypress Black Bayou Recreation Area** (316-965-0007, www.cypressblack bayou.com), Bossier City. Exit 120 off Airline Drive north, turn right on Linton Road and follow signs to the park entrance. The family oriented park offers boating, fishing, swimming, nature trails, and a petting zoo. The camping area has 73 RV sites with full hookups and bathhouses. Simple cabins are available. Park is open 7 A.M.–9 P.M., Sun.–Thurs., and 7 A.M.–10 P.M., Fri.–Sat., March through September. After Labor Day, hours are 7 A.M.–7 P.M., Sun.–Thurs. and 7 A.M.–9 P.M., Fri.–Sat. Beginning Oct. 1, hours are 7 A.M.–5 P.M. Sun.–Thurs. and 7 A.M.–5 P.M. Fri.–Sat.

✐ ❧ **Clyde Fant Parkway**, downtown Shreveport. Named for Clyde Fant, Shreveport's visionary mayor, the parkway is one of the best-designed urban park areas in Louisiana Stretching eight miles parallel to the Red River, it slices through downtown Shreveport and is dotted with spots for disc golf, the Red River Bicycle and Jogging Trail, Hamel's Park, Veterans & Freedom Park, the Sci-Port Discovery Center, Riverview Park, the Barnwell Garden and Art Center, and the Eldorado and Sam's Town casinos. On any spot you will get spectacular views of the Red. Simply drive the parkway or stop anywhere along the way to enjoy the special sites here. Check for handicapped accessibility areas.

♿ ❧ ✿ **Lake Bistineau State Park** (318-745-3503 or 888-677-2478, www.crt .state.la.us), Doyline. Dating back more than 200 years, this lake was created in 1800 when several thousand acres were flooded by a log jam in the Red River. As the area was dredged, the lake gradually drained, and in 1935 a permanent dam was built across Loggy Bayou, creating the present body of water. Fishermen can get freshwater catches from January through spring, summer, and early fall. Black crappie, largemouth bass, yellow bass, catfish, bluegill, and redear sunfish are plentiful. Bistineau has a 10-mile hiking/biking trail, a half-mile nature trail, and a 6-mile equestrian trail. There's an 11-mile canoe route for people who want to see the park's beauty from the water. Area 1, the park's main section, has cabins, a group camp, and a beach open in the summer. Picnicking along the lake is very popular and there are tables, grills, and nearby restrooms. Area 2 is connected to the main part of the park by the lake. To reach the area by car, you have to return to the highway by going east off LA 163 and along Webster Parish Road 177 to the entrance. The park offers disc golf near the boat launch.

✺ ✿ **Robert A. Nance Park** (318-929-2806, www.caddoparks.com), 147 Odom Rd., Hosston. Take the kids and let them romp in this 20-acre park along Black Bayou Lake in a Shreveport suburb. There's a playground, restrooms, boat ramp, and picnic tables with grills. Open 6 A.M.–9 P.M. daily. Open to fishermen 24 hours a day.

✺ ♿ **Walter B. Jacobs Memorial Nature Park** (318-929-2806, www.caddoparks .com), 8012 Blanchard Furrh Rd., Shreveport. About three miles west of Blanchard, the 160-acre nature park is pine, oak, and hickory forest with five miles of nature trails. There's an interpretive building, a pavilion with restrooms, and a handicapped-accessible trail. Nature-oriented programs are available by appointment. Open 8 A.M.–5 P.M. Wed.–Sat. and 1–5 P.M. Sun.

✳ To Do

ANIMAL FARMS & ZOOS ✺ ↬ **Gators and Friends Alligator Park and Zoo** (318-938-1199, www.gatorsandfriends.com), 11441 US 80, Greenwood. Watch alligators wrestle and swim in a park with a petting zoo where you and the kids can

WILDFLOWERS FIND A HOME IN THE CENTER OF A WHEAT FIELD IN NORTHWEST LOUISIANA.

Louisiana Office of Tourism

walk among tame and cuddly miniature horses, ring-tailed lemurs, deer, kangaroos, goats, llamas, a camel, and more. You can even help out at feeding time. The park will remind you to wash and clean your hands after holding the alligator or feeding animals, especially before you eat. Wear comfortable clothes and bring a camera. Open 10 A.M.–6 P.M. daily May–August, and 10 A.M.–6 P.M. Wed.–Sun. September–April.

✍ ⤳ **Duck Pond** (318-673-7727, www.shreveportla.gov), 1200 East King's Highway, Shreveport. Officially East King's Highway, the park is nicknamed the Duck Pond by locals. It's a perfect outdoor spot for families, with picnic tables, a gazebo, and park benches. There's a large children's playground with swings and slides and a two-mile trail for walking or jogging. Not to mention the huge number of ducks that live and play on the pond. Photo op time.

✍ ⤳ **Hidden Oak Farm** (318-455-8102, www.hiddenoakfarms), 111 Hidden Oak Dr., Haughton. This petting zoo with kangaroos, zebras, and more started with a couple of goats. The snack shop offers burgers, hot dogs, fries, chicken strips, Natchitoches meat pies, pizza, nachos, funnel cakes, and other sweets. Open the first and third weekends of each month, 10 A.M.–4 P.M. Sat. and noon–4 P.M. Sun. Admission is $7. Children age 2 and younger admitted free.

✍ **Jubilee Zoo** (318-929-7387, www.jubileezoo.com), 6402 LA 1, Shreveport. The zoo offers pony rides and a safari hay ride. Spend the day and let your children pet and feed the animals, bounce in the moonwalk, or ride the carousel ponies. Get up close and personal with Zoe Zebra and her friends the llamas, ponies, and miniature cows. Soda and snacks are on sale in the picnic area. Open noon–6 P.M. Wed.–Fri., 10 A.M.–7 P.M. Sat., and 2–5 P.M. Sun. Admission: 2- and 3-year-olds, $5; age 4 and over (including adults), $7. Seniors age 55 plus, clergy, and military get $1 off admission.

ANIMAL SANCTUARIES ✍ ⤳ **Chimp Haven** (318-925-9575, www.chimp haven.org), 13600 Chimpanzee Place, Keithville. This is not a zoo. It is open to the public only for limited, prearranged programs like Discovery Days, held seven times a year. Chimp Haven is a National Chimpanzee Sanctuary 22 miles southwest of Shreveport in the Eddie D. Jones Nature Park. Its mission is to provide lifetime care for chimpanzees that have been retired from medical research or the entertainment industry, or are no longer wanted as pets. The haven gives the animals a permanent home in large, naturalistic enclosures in complex social groups. The voices of the haven's chimps were used in the 2011 movie *Rise of the Planet of the Apes*. On Discovery Days, guests can visit educational booths and walk in areas where they can view the animals in forested habitats. Visitors can bring specific items that the chimpanzees can safely use, such as used or new Little Tikes toys or board books. Food and treats you can bring for them include canned vegetables and fruit, dried fruit, and trail mixes.

✍ ⤳ **Yogie and Friends Exotic Cat Sanctuary** (318-795-0455, www.yogieand friends.org), 128 Fob Lane, Frierson. Yogie and Friends is the only big cat sanctuary in Louisiana. It gives a permanent home to tigers, lions, leopards, cougars, servals, and other exotic cats that have been abused, neglected, or unwanted. Yogie and Friends is open to the public on only a limited basis; the majority of the cats have been subjected to cruelty and the idea is to not add any more stress to their lives. Visitors are required to follow strict rules, including never leaving children unescorted and never running. Pets and weapons are banned, as are camera tripods and umbrellas, because they scare the cats. Several benches and large shade umbrellas are provided throughout the sanctuary. There are no paved walkways, but a covered picnic area accommodates about 30 people. Cold drinks are available for purchase. Since it's likely to be hot and humid during a summer visit, wear comfortable clothes, sunglasses, and perhaps a hat for shade. Open to visitors between April and October, noon–5 P.M. Sat., weather permitting. Admission is $5, adults ages 13 and up; $4, children ages 4–12; and free to children age 3 and under.

BASEBALL The Shreveport Bossier Captains (318-636-5555, www.sbcaptains .com), Fair Grounds Field, 2901 Pershing Blvd., Shreveport. The Captains are members of the American Association of Independent Professional Baseball. The team's mascot, Captain Jack, is a pirate with a big black mustache and a playful sense of humor. The Captains play teams from Amarillo and Grand Prairie, Texas; St Paul, Minnesota; and Lincoln, Nebraska, among others.

BASKETBALL Centenary College of Louisiana basketball (318-869-5067, www.centenarycollege.edu). The Centenary Gents and Ladies teams play in Division 3. Home games are played in the Gold Dome Arena on Kings Highway directly across from the campus at 2911 Centenary Blvd., Shreveport.

Louisiana State University-Shreveport basketball (318-797-5194, www.lsus .edu). The LSU-Shreveport men's team, the Shreveport Pilots, and women's team, the Lady Pilots, compete in Division 1. Home games are played in the Health and Physical Education Building on campus, 1 University Place, Shreveport.

Southern University-Shreveport basketball (318-670-9337, www.susla.edu /athletics). The Port City Jags and Port City Lady Jags play in Division 1 and the Miss-Lou conference. Basketball season runs November to March, and at-home games are played in the Physical Education Building on the SUS campus, 3050 Martin Luther King Dr., Shreveport, or at The Dock on campus.

BOWLING Holiday Lanes (318-746-7331, www.bowlholidaylanes.com), 3316 Old Minden Rd., Bossier City. Holiday Lanes is an exciting, 44-lane center that has been family-owned and -operated since 1960. You'll find state-of-the-art technology and a professional staff. Drop by to bowl on open lanes, but if you're in town for a while, you can always ask about joining a league. Striker's Cafe, known for its thick, juicy burgers, is open for breakfast, lunch, and dinner. For a refreshing beer or something more serious to drink after a game, head to the Ten Pin Lounge, open 4–11 P.M. through Mon.–Sat. Every Friday and Saturday night, Holiday Lanes offers Intergalactic-Glow-in-the-dark bowling. Bright lights go down and black lights come on, and strobes flash light everywhere. The more white or safety green you wear, the more you glow. Hours are Mon, 11 A.M.–11 P.M.; Tues.–Thurs., 9 A.M.–11 P.M.; Fri.–Sat., 9 A.M.–2 A.M.; and Sun., 11 A.M.–11 P.M. Check out hourly rates (according to day and time) on the website.

CASINOS Shreveport-Bossier City's five riverboat casinos and the horse-racing track at Harrah's Louisiana Downs draw visitors from all over the huge Ark-La-Tex area. There's 24-hour excitement. The casinos recall the post–Civil War era when gambling was a popular activity for cowboys and roughnecks. If you love a lively slot machine or enjoy a good table game like blackjack or roulette, you'll find plenty of action.

Boomtown Bossier Casino and Hotel (318-746-0711, www.boomtownbossier .com), 300 Riverside Dr., Bossier City. *Casino Player Magazine* readers voted that Boomtown has the Best Reel Slots and Best Video Poker. In addition, the casino has more than 29 table games. Hotel accommodations include garden suites and four themed suites. The 1800 Prime Steakhouse is named for the extremely hot broiling method that produces exceptional steaks cooked to your specifications, and also features a lobster and barbeque buffet. Open daily.

DiamondJacks Casino Resort (www.diamondjacks.com), 711 Diamondjacks Blvd., Bossier City. The resort contains a special high-limit area for high rollers. The sprawling resort complex has 570 guest rooms and mini-suites with a separate sitting area and separate bathtub and shower. There's a beautiful outdoor swimming pool, a full-service spa, a fitness center, and the Legends Buffet with all-you-can-eat breakfasts. Open daily.

Eldorado Casino (877-602-0711 www.eldoradoshreveport.com), 451 Clyde Fant Parkway, Shreveport. Table games include blackjack, roulette, and mini-baccarat. The Poker Room features Texas Hold 'Em and Omaha Hi. The three-story entertainment pavilion includes a 6,000-square foot spa, and the Vintage gourmet restaurant offers an extensive wine list, prime steaks, and seafood. Open daily.

Harrah's Louisiana Downs (318-742-5555, 800-847-5505, www.harrahslouisiana downs.com), 800 East Texas St., Bossier City. The John Fanks Turf Course is considered one of the best in the nation, featuring thoroughbred races at its 350-acre facility from May through October. Quarter horse racing takes place mid-November through mid-December and televisions in the entertainment complex air year-round horse racing simulcasts. The casino features more than 1,300 slots. Springhill Suites by Marriott is located within the grounds, and offers complimentary breakfasts. Mini-kitchens in the suites are handy.

Horseshoe Casino and Hotel (800-985-0711, www.horseshoebossiercity.com), 711 Horseshoe Blvd., Bossier City. Experience Vegas-style gaming traditions in a large gambling area with more than 1,500 slots and 60 table games. Spacious hotel rooms are comfy and decorated in soft, tranquil shades. There is a spa and health club, shops, and restaurants including the Village Square Buffet and the Oak Creek Cafe and Grille, with classic American fare. Open 24 hours.

Sam's Town Hotel and Casino (877-429-0711, www.boomtownbossier.com), 315 Clyde Fant Parkway, Shreveport. The casino offers blackjack, craps, roulette, various poker games, and more than 1,000 slots. Featured entertainment in the Grand Ball Room includes popular acts such as the Oak Ridge Boys and Charlie Daniels. Restaurants include William B's Steakhouse, Smokey Joe's Cafe, and the International Buffet. Java's Deli features gourmet coffees, deli sandwiches, and more. Open daily.

FOOTBALL AdvoCare V-100 Independence Bowl (318-221-0712, www .independencebowl.org), 401 Market St., Suite 120, Shreveport. This college football game featuring games from the Atlantic Coast Conference and Mountain West Conference is played at year's end in the Independence Stadium.

FUN CENTERS Party Central Family Fun Center (318-742-7529, www.party centralinfo.com), 94401 Viking Dr., Bossier City. North Louisiana's largest family fun center, this is just the place for the kids to use up a lot of energy. Activities include go-karts, bumper boats, rock climbing, batting cages, mini golf, kiddy rides, bungee trampoline, and a 10,000-square-foot arcade building. No admission. Pay as you go.

Sci-port: Louisiana's Science Center (318-424-3466, www.sciport.org), 820 Clyde Fant Parkway, Shreveport. This amazing, well-planned facility has more than 290 science, math, and space exhibits that engage people of all ages. Roam from floor to floor and explore the galleries, raise a 500-pound motor with a giant lever, hoist yourself with the mechanical advantage of a set of pulleys, estimate the number of gumballs in a huge graduated cylinder, or try your hand at 3D tic-tac-toe. The Red River Gallery focuses on the river's natural and cultural history. In the International Paper Nature Lab, you can dissect an owl pellet and identify skulls and skins of local animals. In the Space Dome Planetarium, you can see how the stars looked on the night you were born, and enjoy the astronomy show. Sci-Port has Imax Dome Theatre films as well as a cafe and a delightful gift shop. Open 10 A.M.–5 P.M. weekdays; 10 A.M.–6 P.M. Sat.; noon–6 P.M. Sun. Tickets for the Sci-Port only are $13, adult; $10, children 3–12. Imax tickets are $9.50 for adults, $8.50 for children 3–12. Combination tickets are available. Discounts for seniors and military.

Splash Kingdom (318-938-5475, www.splashkingdomwaterpark.com), 7670 West 70th St., Shreveport. Cool off during long, hot summer days at this play park with 13 water slides, wave pools, and kiddy pools. There is a lazy river with cooling sprays for those who just want to relax, as well as dry-land activities. When you're tired of splashing around, enjoy burgers, sandwiches and wraps, salads, and smoothies at the Courtyard Grill. Open summer 11 A.M.–6 P.M. Sun.–Thurs.; May–September, 11 A.M.–7 P.M. Fri.–Sat. Open Labor Day weekend. Call for admission.

GOLF Huntington Park Golf Course (318-742-0333, www.shreveportla.gov), 8300 Pines Rd., Shreveport. This 18-hole course in west Shreveport is two miles south of I-20 on Pines Road. *Golf Digest Magazine* called it one of the top courses in Louisiana, with a course rating of 74.8. Huntington Park is made-to-order for a big hitter, but it may bring a power hitter to his knees. It may help the shorter but more accurate golfer with out of bounds to the left on all but one hole, and six water hazards. The Huntington Restaurant serves a hearty golf breakfast and omelets as well as breakfast sandwiches. The lunch and dinner menu includes burgers, sandwiches, hotdogs, po-boys, and simple salads. Green fees are $18.61. Mon.–Fri.; $22.10

THE CALVERT CROSSING GOLF CLUB BETWEEN MONROE AND RUSTON FEATURES UNDULATING GREENS AND TREE-LINED WATERWAYS.

Monroe-West Monroe CVB

Sat.–Sun. and holidays. Fees for children and seniors are $14.10 Mon.–Fri.; $16.59 Sat.–Sun. and holidays. Golf cart fee is $11.41 for nine holes, $22.82 for 18. Open daily 7 A.M.–8 P.M. No weekday tee times.

Olde Oaks Golf Club (318-742-0333, www.oldeoaksgolf.com), 60 Golf Club Dr., Haughton. Olde Oaks is northwest Louisiana's premier daily fee golf course. Designed in collaboration with Hal Sutton, the PGA Ryder Cup captain, Olde Oakes is on the state's Audubon Golf Trail. With 27 holes winding through 340 acres of hilly terrain, the course presents a challenge to golfers of every level. The clubhouse features a pro shop, full-service bar and restaurant grill. Green fees are $45 and $35 for twilight play on weekends; $35, regular and twilight, Mon.–Thurs.; and $30 for juniors, seniors and military members. Tee times can be reserved by phone up to seven days in advance.

Querbes Park (318-673-7773, www.shreveportla.gov), 3500 Beverly Place, Shreveport. This 18-hole regulation course is exciting to play. From the longest tees it presents 6,207 yards of golf for a par of 71. The course rating is 71.0 with a slope rating of 118. Three sets of tee boxes make for a fun, but challenging, experience. Querbes Park, built in 1921, is a municipal golf course with an open-to-the-public guest policy. The course features a practice bunker, driving range, chipping area, pull carts, rental clubs, food, and beverages. Weekend green fees are $33.

Shreveport Country Club (318-631-4511, www.shreveportcountryclub.org), 3101 Esplanade Ave., Shreveport. The 18-hole course has a remarkable history going back to 1919. Among the golf greats who have played here are Walter Hagen, Ben Hogan, and Tommy Bold, as well as the Shreveport stars Perry Moss, Meredith Duncan, John Daly, David Toms, and Hal Sutton. The greens are fast and very challenging. The course rating is 71.9 and it has a slope rating of 130. Call for tee times and green fees. The club accepts limited nonmember play.

StoneBridge (318-747-2004, www.gcstonebridge.com), 301 StoneBridge Blvd., Bossier City. Designed by the PGS Tour professional Fred Couples and the architect Gene Bates, the golf club at StoneBridge winds through mature oaks, small lakes, and wetlands. The course has five sets of tees to provide fun for golfers of all ages. It is open for public play and tee times are available up to four days in advance for nonmembers, or six days in advance for Player's Card holders. Facilities include well-appointed men's and women's lockers, a clubhouse with a restaurant, a bar, and a full-service pro shop. Rates are $55 Mon.–Thu., $65, Fri.–Sun., and $20 daily after 2 P.M.

Westwood Executive Golf Course (318-636-3162), 5006 Jefferson Paige Rd., Shreveport. The 18-hole course features 3,485 yards of golf from the longest tees for a par 59. The course rating is 60, and it has a slope rating of 120. The pro shop opens at 8 A.M., and a snack bar is available. There is no driving range, chipping green, or practice bunker. The course is open to all guests. Open 7 A.M.–11 A.M. Mon.–Sat. and 7 A.M.–dark, Sun. from mid-March through mid-October; and 7 A.M.–dark, Mon.–Sun., mid-October through mid-March. Green fee is $16 weekends and $14 weekdays.

HORSE RACING Harrah's Louisiana Downs (318-742-5555, www.ladowns .com), 8000 East Texas St., Bossier City. It's not exactly Ascot and the royal family may not be there, but plenty of people go the races in Shreveport. Louisiana Downs has both thoroughbred and quarter horse races. An exciting blend of horses from Arkansas, Texas, and Louisiana, as well as other horse-breeding areas, can be found on Harrah's tracks. The John Fanks Turf Course is one of the best in the nation. Spring-Hill Suites by Marriott (see the Lodgings listings) is on site, as are restaurants including The Buffet and Fuddruckers.

✴ Lodging

Best Western Chateau Suite Hotel (318-222-7620, www.best western.com), 201 Lake St., Shreveport. Recently remodeled, the 101-room hotel is near many casinos and downtown Shreveport if you're here to participate in events such as Mudbug Madness and the Independence Bowl. Enjoy the complimentary Southern-style breakfast buffet, in-hotel restaurant, business center, free high-speed wireless Internet, outdoor pool, and free shuttle, or relax in Le Club cocktail lounge. Moderate.

Clarion Hotel (318-797-9900, www.choicehotels.com), 1410 East 70th St., Shreveport. The hotel has 261 deluxe rooms, five suites, and a penthouse, along with a restaurant and lounge, pool, fitness center, iron and ironing boards, coffee makers, refrigerators, free Wi-Fi, and more. Moderate.

Courtyard by Marriott (318-742-8300, www.courtyard.com), 100 Boardwalk Blvd., Bossier City. This attractive hotel is conveniently located at the Louisiana Boardwalk. The restaurant serves breakfast and dinner. The hotel also features an exercise room, outdoor pool and spa, business center, and market. Rooms have really comfortable king beds or two queens. The staff is friendly and attentive. If you need a good night's sleep, ask for a room on the top floor. Walk out of the lobby and you're within feet of a delightful carousel; a bit further and you come to an attractive overlook of the Red River, especially beautiful and romantic when walkway lamps are lit in the evening. Moderate.

Hilton Garden Inn (318-686-0148, www.hiltongardeninn.hilton.com), 5917 Financial Plaza, Shreveport. This

A FANCIFUL CAROUSEL WELCOMES VISITORS TO THE LOUISIANA BOARDWALK SHOPPING AND ENTERTAINMENT CENTER IN BOSSIER CITY.

Cynthia V. Campbell

midprice hotel near the airport features an indoor pool and a spa tub and business center. Guests can make use of the concierge desk and express check-out. On-site parking is complimentary. Features include comfortable, adjustable comfort mattresses and in-room microwave and mini-refrigerator. Saturday breakfasts are cooked to order. Moderate.

&. (((•))) **Hilton Hotel Shreveport** (318-698-0900, www.shreveporthilton.com), 104 Market St., Shreveport. The Hilton Shreveport Hotel boasts a top location in the heart of downtown Shreveport's Riverfront District. It's especially convenient for business travelers and convention attendees, since it is attached to the Shreveport Convention Center. There are 313 guest rooms with soft beds and all the amenities. There's a small rooftop swimming pool, a 24-hour business center, and complimentary Wi-Fi. Take a break in the lobby bar or the Coffee Talk Cafe. Louisiana cuisine is featured in the River Rock Grill. Moderate–expensive.

✎ ❀ (((•))) **Holiday Inn Express and Suites** (877-859-5095, www.hiexpress .com), 8751 Park Plaza, Shreveport. Situated off I-49 and Bert Kouns Industrial Loop, this hotel is convenient for people driving the interstate between I-20 and I-10. Connecting loops to downtown Shreveport and Bossier City (including casinos and the Louisiana Boardwalk) take 10–15 minutes. Complimentary breakfast includes a few hot items. There's free Wi-Fi access, a 24-hour fitness center, and a big outdoor pool popular for families. A number of restaurants are nearby. Moderate.

(((•))) **The Remington Suite Hotel** (318-425-5000, www.remingtonsuite .com), 220 Travis St., Shreveport. This is an excellent boutique hotel conveniently located in the center of town.

Spacious suites have king-size beds, television, comfy couches, and a tub with Jacuzzi jets. Furnishings have different themes in each suite. Indulge with facials and body treatments in the spa. The hotel has a saltwater pool and an indoor hot tub area. The staff is friendly and accommodating. The large reception area is a good place to relax with a coffee. Expensive.

BED & BREAKFASTS 2439 Fairfield (318-424-2424), 2439 Fairfield Ave., Shreveport. Featured in *Southern Living, Better Homes and Gardens,* and *Country Inn,* this elegant, two-story mansion is beautifully decorated. There's a balcony for each bedroom so guests can sit outside and relax, and the luxurious beds are piled with lots of pillows. Breakfast entrees are varied and delicious. Moderate–expensive.

Les Memories Cottage Home (214-321-8346, www.lesmemoires.com), 208 Jacquelyn St., Bossier City. The address is given only to guests with advance reservations. This six-room cottage features two guest rooms; one contains Elvis memorabilia, the other is furnished with white French furniture. Entertainment in the gathering room includes 1950s and '60s music on the jukebox, and there are cookouts on the patio. The cottage is a mile from Barksdale Air Force Base.

Medjoy Bed & Breakfast (318-861-4424), 601 Oakley Dr., Shreveport. Not far from Line Avenue and the First Baptist Church, Medjoy is an antiques-filled historic home on the National Register.

CAMPGROUNDS ✎ **Campers' RV Center** (318-687-9797, www.campers rvcenter.com), 7700 West 70th St., Shreveport. The campground is situated next to an RV dealership. Big rigs and clubs are welcomed. There's a pool and recreation hall. Amenities include ice, laundry, public phone, and RV supplies. Inexpensive.

𝄞 ((ᵖ)) **Tall Pines RV Park** (318-687-1010, www.tallpinesrvpark.com), 6510 West 70th St., Shreveport. The well-groomed site in Good Sam Park is large enough to accommodate the largest rigs on the road. There's plenty of room for slide outs and awnings. Facilities include clean restrooms and a bath house, free Wi-Fi and cable TV, and 24-hour laundry services. Inexpensive.

✳ Where to Eat

EATING OUT 𝄞 ⅁ **Big O's** (318-658-9649), 1129 Villagio Blvd., Bossier City. Most folks come here for the spaghetti made with fresh seasonings and the crispy fried catfish. One fan argues that the reason people like it so much is the tartar sauce, the recipe for which owner Odis Johnson said came to him in a dream. The red beans and rice at Big O's may be the best in town. Open 11 A.M.–2 P.M. and 5–8 P.M. Mon.–Sat. Moderate.

Blind Tiger Restaurant (318-226-8747, www.blindtiger.com), 120 Texas St., Shreveport. Situated in one of Shreveport's oldest documented buildings, Blind Tiger has built a reputation on laid-back atmosphere. The name was taken from a nickname given illegal bars and saloons during the Prohibition era. The menu features a mix of Southern and Cajun favorites. There's a wide selection of burgers and fried seafood for lunch. For dinner you might want to try the jumbo "voodoo" shrimp dinner or the Atchafalaya chicken—grilled chicken topped with sautéed mushrooms, hickory-smoked bacon, and melted Swiss cheese. Blind Tiger has happy hour 3–7 P.M. week-days and karaoke at 10 P.M. Sundays and Wednesdays. Moderate.

𝄞 **Geauxsicles** (318-865-8110, www.geauxsicles.com), 3970 Youree Dr., Shreveport. On a really, really hot day, there's nothing better than the sweet treats you'll find here. The artisanal popsicles are a spectacular sweet. After trying just one of the gourmet flavors, you'll want to try all of them. Catchy names give you a hint of the flavors: Banana Bliss, creamy banana pudding; Blackberry Blues, blackberry and blueberry; Java the Pop, sweet and strong, creamy coffee and chocolate; and Sublime, creamy key lime with a dark chocolate crust. The fleur de lis on the front of each pop makes it that much better. Also available are Geaux Low pops sweetened with Truvia instead of sugar. The shop also makes dairy-free and gluten-free ice pops. Folks buy bagfuls to take home, but if you don't like getting out of your car, just head for the drive-by window. Open noon–9 P.M. Mon.–Thurs.; 11 A.M.–10 P.M. Fri.–Sat. Moderate.

𝄞 **Herby-K's Restaurant** (318-424-2724, www.herbyks.net), 1833 Pierre Ave., Shreveport. This casual, hole-in-the-wall seafood restaurant offers an array of fried platters. If you're really, really hungry, try the Saturday Night Special, featuring sautéed catfish topped with etouffee, Creole rice, and salad. A children's lunch menu is available. Open 11 A.M.–9 P.M. Mon.–Thurs. and 11 A.M.–10 P.M. Fri.–Sat. Inexpensive–moderate.

𝄞 **Mariscos La Jaibita** (318-742-5595), 2242 Barksdale Blvd., Suite B, Bossier City. Get ready for a really great treat. This small restaurant specializes in seafood dishes popular on Mexico's Atlantic and Pacific coasts. It is flavorful and as authentic as any you will find north of the border. Large glass goblets filled with chilled shrimp or oysters in a spicy tomato sauce are a meal in themselves. Or choose a shrimp cocktail combined with oysters or octopus. Seafood entrees include huachinango a la Veracruzana (whole red snapper deep-fried and smothered in stewed tomatoes and onions) or oysters empanizados (breaded oysters) served with salad and French fries. Drop in on Thursday night to hear live Tejano music from a band dressed in vaquero gear. Inexpensive–moderate.

Noble Savage Tavern (318-221-1781, www.myspace.com/noblesavagetavern), 417 Texas St., Shreveport. Open Tuesday through Saturday for late lunch, dinner, and late-night dining, this is a good spot for hanging out and meeting locals. It can get a bit smoky, but regulars keep coming for the ambiance, good food, and beer on tap. The tavern serves an eclectic menu ranging from wild game and fresh seafood to pizzas and specialty sandwiches. It also serves more than 30 single-malt scotches and fine wines. Numerous live music events are held here, and the laid-back atmosphere attracts a savvy local crowd. Moderate.

Cynthia V. Campbell

THE NOBLE SAVAGE IN SHREVEPORT OFFERS EVERYTHING FROM SHRIMP REMOULADE TO EXOTIC MEATS.

✐ ♿ **Papa Fertitta's Delicatessen** (318-869-0931, www.papafertitta.com), 1124 Fairfield Ave., Shreveport. Fertitta's is famous as the home of the original "Muffy" sandwich in a variety of styles, including Sicilian, gondolier, centurion, and gladiator. The cafe also offers imported oils and foods. Open Monday through Saturday for lunch only. Inexpensive–moderate.

A BAND ENTERTAINS DINERS AT THE NOBLE SAVAGE IN DOWNTOWN SHREVEPORT.

Cynthia V. Campbell

⏎

✔ ⧖ **Cantina Laredo** (318-798-6363, www.cantinalaredo.com), 6505 Youree Dr., Shreveport. The restaurant serves homey, authentic Mexican dishes and gourmet Mexican food in a sophisticated setting. Look for daily fish specials, grilled chicken, and steaks accented with signature sauces. For lunch we suggest the avocado and artichoke enchilada topped with tomatillo sauce, or tacos al pastor with roasted marinated pork. For dinner, try the chile relleno featuring a picadillo filled with beef, almonds, raisins, Oaxaca cheese, and ranchero sauce. Try the mango tres leches cake with mango sauce for dessert. The cantina features a tequila flight with three different tequilas, special margaritas, wines, and mixed drinks. Moderate.

DINING OUT Bella Fresca (318-856-6307), 6307 Line Ave. Shreveport. The restaurant offers eclectic American fare with a Continental flare. Dinner entrées run more to the Continental style. Try the Gulf shrimp over curried rice with smoked habanero cream and garlic spinach, or the chile-rubbed 12-ounce Angus strip steak with blue-cheese butter, parmigiana truffle fries, and haricots verts. For lunch, try the smoked salmon sandwich with dill and caper dressing or the turkey burger with baby Swiss and basil mayonnaise. Expensive.

Ernest's Orleans Restaurant (318-226-1325, www.ernestsorleans.com), 1601 Spring St., Shreveport. Famous for its marinated crab claws and prime steaks, this restaurant is a Shreveport institution. Ernest's has been operated by the Palmisano family for more than 60 years. One look at the photos of national and local celebrities adorning the walls and you know this is a place to see and be seen. Relax in the cocktail lounge, then choose an intimate table in the main dining room. If

you're not in the mood for steak, try one of the restaurant's signature Italian entrees. Open 4:30–10:30 P.M. Mon.–Sat. Expensive.

Village Grille (318-424-2874), 1313 Louisiana Ave., Shreveport. Dimly lit, Vintage Grill has a romantic atmosphere with a touch of sophistication. The restaurant has no menu; your server verbally presents the night's offerings, which may be anything from shrimp Lafayette to Chicago prime rib or country lamb. Expensive–very expensive.

✴ Entertainment

Casinos It wouldn't be Shreveport-Bossier City without the gaming action provided by five riverboat casinos and one "racino" with live horse racing: Hollywood, Horseshoe, El Dorado, DiamondJack's, Sam's Town, and Harrah's Louisiana Downs. The casinos (see the To Do listings) attract travelers not only for gaming, but for the great entertainment they provide year-round. You'll find outstanding live music being programmed by the Horseshoe Riverdome, where recent performers have included Melissa Etheridge, G. Love and the Special Sauce, Bill Cosby, and Al Green.

Chicky's Boom Boom Room and Oyster Bar (318-828-2846), 205 Texas St., Shreveport. Popular with locals, this downtown spot has a handsome long bar and plenty of dancing space. Local and regional bands perform rock 'n' roll on a regular basis. Chicky's also serves fresh oysters on the half-shell as well as one of the best frozen daiquiris in town, the Dreamsicle, which really is amazing.

Emmett Hook Center (318-429-6885, www.emmetthookcenter.org), corner of Common St. and Milam, Shreveport. Built by the congregation of the First United Methodist Church for the enrichment of the community, the new theater is state of the art, with an open, airy atmosphere and comfortable seating. It was designed for concerts and theatrical productions as well as contemporary worship and seminars. Recent productions have included *It's a Wonderful Life: The Musical* and *I Remember Mama,* a classic American drama. See the website for production schedule and tickets.

Fatty Arbuckle's Pub (318-459-1448, www.fattyarbucklespub.com), 450 Clyde Fant Memorial Parkway, Shreveport. If you're looking for New Orleans–style live music, including some of the city's notorious groups such as Soul Rebels Brass Band and the Rebirth Brass Band, Fatty Arbuckle's is the place to find it. Shows start late here (often 11 P.M. or later), but the revelry is worth waiting for. The pub also frequently takes over the entire Red River District to host live musical performances by larger touring acts like the country star Robert Earl Keen, Citizen Cope, and more. Shreveport's best food trucks, like I Fry (late-night fried catfish) and the Burrito Man (self-explanatory!), also hang out in the Red River District area. The Shreveport police have a kiosk nearby to maintain order and safety.

✍ ♿ **Louisiana Boardwalk** (318-752-1455, www.louisianaboardwalk.com), 540 Boardwalk Blvd., Bossier City. The boardwalk is a premier outdoor shopping and entertainment destination just across the Texas Street Bridge from downtown Shreveport. Check out the nifty boutiques and cafes, and then see a first-run movie at **Regal Cinemas Louisiana Boardwalk 14,** which includes a newly installed IMAX screen. A short walk away is **GloPuttz,** indoor golf. End the evening at

Chocolate Crocodile, a locally owned chocolatier. It's a lot of fun to bite the head off a chocolate alligator.

Minicine (www.facebook.com /minicine), 846 Texas Ave., Shreveport. Minicine is an underground, experimental movie house that frequently hosts live musical performances, art shows, and installations of the more bizarre and unpredictable variety. Here, you're likely to catch a traveling film festival or a punk rock showcase, a new music or dance performance, or a blues jam performed from the bed of a truck parked on the sidewalk outside. Local film and media makers flock to the place, but its Facebook page is often the only place to find out about events.

Robinson Film Center (318-459-4122, www.robinsonfilmcenter.org), 617 Texas St., Shreveport. The film center in downtown Shreveport is a two-screen, independent art house cinema. It showcases the best in foreign, independent, classic, and cult films to a die-hard base of fans. The venue is also home to about a half-dozen film festivals throughout the year, including a French film festival in April and a gay and lesbian film festival in September. The center frequently hosts screenings with celebrity guests, including Val Kilmer, Oliver Stone, Matthew Broderick, Nicolas Cage, Treat Williams, and John Waters. Abby Singer's Bistro, on the second floor, is a hidden treasure. The contemporary menu has just the right touch of Louisiana cuisine and you can dine casually indoors or outside on the balcony overlooking Texas Street. P.S. You can take cocktails and wine into the theaters!

✍ **Strand Theatre** (318-226-8555, www.thestrandtheatre.com), 619 Louisiana Ave., No. 200, Shreveport. Built in 1925, the Strand is listed on

Cynthia V. Campbell

SHREVEPORT'S ROBINSON FILM CENTER FEATURES CLASSIC AND ART FILMS AND AN INTIMATE RESTAURANT UPSTAIRS.

the National Register of Historic Places. The beautifully restored theatre presents top touring Broadway shows, such as *The Wizard of Oz, Damn Yankees,* and *Young Frankenstein.* The theater also offers performances for children. In addition, the Strand has a children's series, which brings 12,000 kids to the theater for school performances.

✳ Selective Shopping

Shoppers will love exploring Shreveport's boutiques, malls and specialty shops. Since this is the largest metropolitan center in the Ark-La-Tex region, people make special trips here to find world-class, one-of-a-kind items as well as bargains. Before leaving home, get a copy of the official guide to Shreveport-Bossier by contacting www.shreveport-bossier.org.

Absolutely Abigail's (318-219-0788, www.absolutelyabigails.com), 3795 Youree Dr., Shreveport. Gals planning a day or a weekend trip love stepping into this delightful boutique. The owner, Donna Phillips, combines the fashions of Bleecker Street in New York's West Village with those of Magazine Street in New Orleans. Check out the art-driven apparel and walk out feeling dressed to kill.

American Rose Center Gift Shop (318-938-5402, www.ars.org), 8877 Jefferson-Paige Rd., Shreveport. This is a garden lover's fantasy boutique, with rose water and glycerin hand-care products, porcelain roses, note cards embossed with roses, and garden and patio accessories. This store participates in the Louisiana Tax Free Shopping program.

Antiques on Gladstone (318-868-2940), 755 Gladstone Blvd., Shreveport. Don't be surprised if you run into antiques shoppers from Oklahoma and Texas in this shop, which has been in business for more than 20 years. The primary focus is furniture, but it's also a good place to find dolls, toys, and linens.

Barnwell Center Store (318-673-7703, www.barnwellcenter.com), 601 Clyde Fant Parkway, Shreveport. This store specializes in handmade arts and crafts from highly skilled local and regional artisans. Pieces of pottery and jewelry, many created by members of the Louisiana Craft Guild, are unusual and especially attractive.

Big Mama's Antiques and Restoration (318-573-2127), 6521 Bostwick Rd., Shreveport. You never know what you're going to find in this shop's eclectic mix. The three-bedroom cottage that serves as the store was once the owner's great-grandmother's home. Expect to be greeted by chickens and peacocks. Movie makers sometimes come to Big Mama's looking for props. Check out the vintage glassware, dishes, and linens.

Caboose Antiques (318-865-5376, www.cabooseantiques.com), 855 Pierremont Rd., No.152, Shreveport. Looking for fine antiques from France and England? Caboose Antiques may have just what you're seeking. In business for more than 30 years, the store has a large array of decorative and functional furniture, Staffordshire and Imari china, clocks, candlesticks, and lamps.

Discoveries Unlimited Gift Shop (318-424-3466, www.sciport.org), 820 Clyde Fant Parkway, Shreveport. This delightful shop is located inside Sci-Port Louisiana Science Center. Pick up a toy or two that will make you think, or go for souvenir T-shirts, caps, messenger bags, totes, and items of a scientific bent.

Enchanted Garden (318-227-1213, www.enchantedgarden.com), 2429 Line Ave., Shreveport. Browsers are likely to find just the right thing for Aunt Suzy or the family chef in this shop. Gift items includes jewelry, spa specialties, Boyds Bears, Pocket Dragons, Roman Seraphim figurines, Shreveport-Bossier afghans, and Louisiana food, books, and souvenirs.

Libbey Glass Factory Outlet (318-621-0265, www.libbey.com), 4302 Jewella Ave., Shreveport. Located at the plant itself, the outlet has more than 14,000 square feet of glassware, dinnerware, flatware, and more. It's a great place to find wedding and Christmas gifts. Locals suggest checking out the bargain room for extra deals. Tour buses are welcome.

✿ **Shreveport Farmers Market** (318-455-5788, www.localharvest.org), 101 Crocket St., Suite C, Shreveport. Fresh fruits and vegetables are offered for sale by area farmers, who also bring in herbs, plants, cut flowers, along with homemade jellies and jam, handmade soaps, and primitive paintings. There's on-site parking and public restrooms. The market is family friendly. Open 7 A.M.–noon, Sat. June–September; and 3–6 P.M. Tues., June and July.

Timeline Antiques & Collectibles (318-861-0808, www.timelineanc.com), 3323 Line Ave., Shreveport. If your particular timeline for vintage items is somewhere between 1835 and 2005, you're likely to love this shop. The store's extensive collection of vintage cookbooks is regularly updated, and you can find antique chairs, desks, cabinets, and more. There are also collections from Mark Roberts, Cameo Girls lady head vases, and Clementine Hunter prints.

✳ Special Events

February: **Mardi Gras** (800-454-VISIT, www.shreveport-bosser.org). Although the dates change according to the liturgical calendar, Mardi Gras is always about pageantry. In the Shreveport-Bossier area, it's celebrated over the course of two parade weekends. Floats are crafted to reflect various themes. Millions of "throws" (cheap bead necklaces) and trinkets are tossed to parade goers. Two major parades offer a no-alcohol family zone. The Krewe of Gemini and the Krewe of Centaur host the largest parades. The Krewe of Aesclepius welcomes members of the medical community, and members of the legal community make up the Krewe of Justinian. Organizations working toward curing HIV/AIDS make up the all-male Krewe of Apollo. Pet owners form the Krewe of Barkus and Meoux; the group sponsors a free event featuring animal-costumed revelers at a local park. Many events are open to anyone who can afford tickets. Out-of-towners can purchase a spot on a float for a set fee plus the cost of beads and trinkets.

March: **Louisiana Redbud Festival** (318-375-3893, www.laredbud.com), Vivian Townsquare, Vivian. The festival is always held the third Saturday in March. Join the 5K run, or just enjoy the parade, live music, food, and craft booths.

April: **Holiday in Dixie** (318-865-5555), Festival Plaza, downtown Shreveport. Holiday in Dixie celebrates the 1803 Louisiana Purchase. The family oriented, 10-day event features a treasure hunt, Neighborhood Block Party Day at the Carnival, a classic parade, and more.

Spring Bloom Celebration/American Rose Center (318-938-5534, www.ars.org), 8877 Jefferson-Paige Rd., Shreveport. During April, a spectacular canvas of roses unfolds into a grand landscape. Stroll through the meandering garden paths and more than 20,000 roses. Special features include the playground and picnic areas.

May: **Barksdale Air Show** (318-456-5650, www.barksdaleafbairshow.com), Barksdale Air Force Base, 555 Davis Avenue West, Bossier City. This spectacular air show allows the U.S. Air Force to showcase the home of the B-52 and grant access to tour the military base. Visitors and their families can view military and aerobatic performers, and show support for the country's armed forces. See America's top-gun pilots in action. Watch dramatic flybys and performances by Tora! Tora! Tora!, Vintage Warbirds, Jacquie B. and Greg Poie, among others. Static displays focus on airplanes that have played roles in U.S. military actions, including the F-22A Raptor, 2xF-15C Eagle, B2A Spirit, and B-52H Stratofortress. Safety and security are always of primary concern at air shows. Containers, such as backpacks and coolers, are prohibited on the airfield. Weapons of any type are strictly prohibited. Safety concerns related to the presence of jet fuel restrict where people can smoke on base. Pets are not allowed unless they are assistance animals. For complete details visit the website.

Hot Jazz on the Red (318-673-7703), Clyde Fant Parkway, The Barnwell Garden and Art Center on the riverfront, Shreveport. The Shreveport Riverfront is the hottest spot in town when the Friends of the Barnwell present the annual Hot Jazz on the Red concert series, sponsored by Eldorado Resort Casino. Bring your lawn chair, blanket, and picnic basket, or sit with friends at one of the pre-set tables while relaxing on the patio of the Barnwell Garden and Art Center to the swinging sounds. A cash bar is available. Thursdays 6–8 P.M., May–June.

Mudbug Madness (www.mudbug madness.com), Festival Plaza, Shreveport. Always the third Saturday in May, the four-day Mudbug Madness is a giant crawfish festival where highly seasoned mudbugs (a.k.a. crawfish) are the stars of the plate. Other foods include shrimp, alligator, red beans, jambalaya, and meat pies, and there's plenty of music and good times to go with. Be prepared for three entertainment stages with plenty of foot-stompin,' two-steppin' music. Past entertainers have included Lil Nate and the Zydeco Big Timers, Wayne Toups and ZyDeCajun, Jamie Bergeron and the Kickin' Cajuns, and Geno Delafose and French Rockin' Boogie. Stick around for the women's crawfish eating contest and the children's crawfish eating contest. Everyone gets a kick out of the celebrity crawfish eating contest.

Poke Salad Festival (318-309-2647, www.pokesaladfestival.com), Pinehills Rd., Blanchard. The second Saturday of May. Festival-goers celebrate the Pokeweed plant, which has been used as a substitute for greens and spinach. Young shoots, properly prepared, taste like asparagus. The entire plant, especially the berries, is poisonous when eaten raw. Cooked, it has some medicinal properties. The festival website has an excellent description of pokeweed. Locals and visitors turn out for a parade, craft booths, food, carnival, and children's activities Highlights include the live entertainment by country, pop, rock, and gospel groups, and a street dance.

June: **Sunflower Trail Festival** (318-296-4303), LA 3049 and Gilliam Library, Gilliam. Brighten your spirits in the first week of June and follow LA 3049 north leaving Shreveport from Grimmet Drive. View fields of big yellow sunflowers grown by farms along the roadway. From 9 A.M. to 4 P.M., people gather in Gilliam under shade trees behind the Crossroads Museum and Library, where craft and food vendors set up for business. A variety of artisans display crafts, pottery, jewelry, as well as plants, antiques, glassware, and numerous other wares. The festi-

THE RED RIVER REFLECTS THE LIGHTS OF DOWNTOWN SHREVEPORT AT NIGHT.
Cynthia V. Campbell

val is a family event with hands-on children's activities, face painting, a children's art display, and a clown. Crossroads hosts special music and provides cold lemonade to sip while you tour the historical museum. The sunflowers are in bloom for about a month, so make the drive and enjoy the countryside.

September: **Dragonboat Race on the Red River** (318-459-3000, www.hays @oilbank.com)**,** RiverView Park, Shreveport. Paddlers race colorful canoes along the Red River in a competition whose proceeds support educational endeavors in the community.

October: **Red River Revel Arts Festival** (318-424-4000, www.redriver revel.com), 101 Crocket St., No. 3, Shreveport. The Red River Revel Arts Festival, the largest outdoor arts festival in North Louisiana, attracts more than 180,000 people to the Shreveport riverfront in October with over 140 visual artists from throughout the country displaying their ceramics, watercolors, oils, acrylics, and metals. There is a children's area to delight young and old with art projects, face painting, and much more. Music or dance more your style? Check out all the exciting performing artists, who in past years have included George Clinton and Parliament Funkadelic, Keith Urban, and The Band Perry, on three outdoor stages.

November: **Christmas in Roseland** (318-938-5402, www.christmasin roseland.everbrite.com), 8877 Jefferson Paige Rd., Shreveport. Each Christmas season the gardens of the American Rose Center are transformed into a wonderland with more than a million twinkling lights and dozens of lighting displays. Families turn out to enjoy giant Christmas cards to the community created by area schoolchildren, photos with Santa, and rides on the Roseland Express. Visitors can also enjoy nightly entertainment by local school groups and choirs, Santa's Candy Shop, and a model train display. Open 5:30–10:30 P.M., Fri.–Sun., November 27–December 20.

The Holiday Trail of Lights (318-222-9391, www.holidaytrailoflights .com), Shreveport. Shreveport joins seven other cities in Louisiana's Holiday Trail of Lights with millions of lights, fireworks, great food, live entertainment, Christmas music, and parades. The lights illuminate the skies from Thanksgiving until after New Year's Eve. It's quite a thrill.

MONROE-RUSTON AREA

Conveniently located on I-20 between Shreveport and Jackson, Mississippi, this section of north Louisiana invites people to enjoy the warmth and hospitality of the agricultural South. The twin cities of Monroe and West Monroe sit on either side of the Ouachita River.

The food here is real Southern comfort. More than 70 local restaurants offer dishes such as crispy fried chicken, smothered pork chops, black-eyed peas, candied sweet potatoes, catfish, po-boys, hot-water cornbread, cakes, and pies. Choose a plate lunch with sides or a satisfying steak dinner with salad.

Monroe was formed in 1785 by French settlers under the lead of Don Juan Filhiol, a Frenchman in Spanish service, who established Fort Miro as a trading post on the Ouachita River. It was renamed in 1819 to honor the arrival of the James Monroe, the first steamboat to ascend the Ouachita. West Monroe received its name in 1880 from railroad workers who needed to christen a new city that developed just to the west. The twin cities became the commercial hub for the surrounding rural parishes. In 1925 the world's first aerial crop-dusting organization, Huff Daland Dusters, was formed in Monroe; it eventually became Delta Airlines. Today the area remains a commercial center for north-central Louisiana and is the home of the University of Louisiana at Monroe.

Ruston, between Shreveport and Monroe-West Monroe, anchors the agricultural economy of central North Louisiana. It was named after Robert E. Russ, who donated 640 acres to the town in 1883. Two universities give the city a touch of young bravado. Adults and children are welcomed to Idea Place, a math and science museum filled with exhibits. Visitors can see how wind affects the patterns of sand dunes and show drifts, and learn about the formation of tornados and dust storms or about dew points. You can also visit the 120-seat Louisiana Tech University Planetarium, where a Spitz A-4 instrument projects the Milky Way, including the Sun, Moon, planets and about 3,000 stars on a huge dome. Louisiana Tech's sports teams bring in the crowds, and so do the teams at Grambling State University, a historically black school with more than 75 degree programs and a dynamic athletic program. The Eddie G. Robinson Museum on the Grambling campus honors the coach's outstanding contributions to the state of Louisiana, the nation, and the game of football. Objects of art, documents, and archives reflect the life and coaching of Coach Robinson, who won 408 games at Grambling during a career that stretched from 1941–1997.

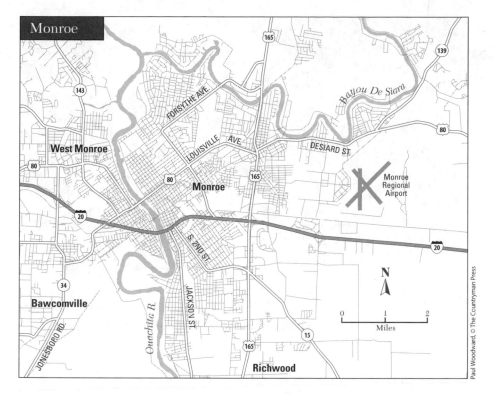

Ruston's cultural attractions include a number of art studios and the Piney Hills Art Gallery, which features works from 30 regional artists. Visit the Louisiana Military Museum, containing military artifacts and displays dating from the Civil War. Outdoor enthusiasts will find the Lincoln Parish Park a hidden treasure. Clean and scenic, the park is recognized as one of the best mountain bike trails in the South.

In West Monroe, stroll along Antique Alley and downtown, where you'll find everything from vintage clothing and jewelry to Victorian antiques and regional art. Check out the original T-shirt designs at Mojo Boutique. In Monroe, continue shopping at Pecanland Mall with familiar stores such as Belk, Dillard's, and Forever 21. Join the kids for fun on the two-story carousel. Additional brand-name stores are found in Pecanland Plaza.

You won't regret making a special stop at the Biedenharn Museum and Gardens. Tour the eclectic home of Emmy-Lou Biedenharn, daughter of Joseph Biedenharn, the first bottler of Coca-Cola. The beautiful home is furnished with antiques and unusual items she picked up on her travels in Europe. View the incredible collection of memorabilia in the Coke Museum and enjoy an ice cold, glass-bottle Coke for just a nickel. On another level, take time to tour the Bible Museum, full of rare Bibles and religious artifacts. Allow time to enjoy tranquil moments in the gardens.

In Monroe, zip through down to the east side where you'll find the airport and the Chennault Aviation Museum of Louisiana, housed in the last standing building

Louisiana Office of Tourism

GRAMBLING UNIVERSITY NEAR RUSTON IS HOME TO THE EDDIE ROBINSON MUSEUM, HONORING THE LEGENDARY AWARD-WINNING FOOTBALL COACH.

of the Selman Field Army Corps Navigation School. The school trained more than 150,000 navigators during World War II. The museum also tells the story of General Claire Chennault and his Flying Tigers.

Just north of Monroe, you'll find the pristine Black Bayou Lake National Wildlife Refuge. Walk out on the pier over the bayou or along well-defined trails that bring you into the woods where wildlife roams. Bird lovers will find numerous species here. The beautiful lake is studded with tupelo and cypress trees. Further north in Morehouse Parish, you can spend a weekend at Chemin-A-Haut State Park, where cabins overlook Bayou Bartholomew. Feel comfortable letting the kids have fun in the playground area or ride bikes on the nature trails. The site's swimming pool is perfect for cooling off on hot summer days.

Nearby in Bastrop, sportsmen will find just about anything they need at the 70,000-square-foot Simmons Sporting Goods, the largest independently owned sporting-goods store in the South. Not only can hunters find special equipment, the store also features home furnishings, clothing, and gifts. Drive by Bastrop Courthouse Square and tour the stunning Rose Theatre, built in 1927 for vaudeville shows and silent movies. Seven miles away, Mer Rouge is a small community that makes a big impact with ice cream and hot dogs at Country Cream. South of Bastrop, visit Handy Brake National Wildlife Refuge. Walk out on the observation deck for a view of some 20,000 acres of hills and valleys full of wildlife.

Travel east of Bastrop via LA 2 to Lake Providence in East Carroll Parish, where summer and early fall put on a show of miles of crops along every byway. Thousands of acres are planted with cotton, corn, rice, and soybeans on farmlands that spread to the horizon. If you're traveling with children, help them identify crops that provide such bounty. In Lake Providence, stop at Jehovah Java Gourmet Coffee Bar or The Dock for Louisiana cuisine. For local points of interest, start on

US 65 at Byerley House and Grant's Canal. Two miles north you'll find the Louisiana State Cotton Museum. Another stop is the Panola Pepper plant, home of Cajun sauces, relishes, and Creole foods. A tour will show you how peppers are processed into spicy sauces and condiments. Drive due south of Lake Providence on US 65, and you'll arrive at one of the state's most unusual villages, Transylvania. You can't miss it: The town paints a huge bat on its water tower. Apparently the town was named in the early 19th century by Dr. W. L. Richards, a Transylvania University alumnus and a wealthy landowner. A sign at the General Store proclaims, "We're always glad to have new blood in town." Stop for a snack at Dupuy's, where you can buy a sandwich, hardware and items including rubber bats and T-shirts emblazoned with TRANSYLVANIA, LOUISIANA.

From Lake Providence, follow LA 134 south to Poverty Point, where you'll find the oldest mounds in the Western hemisphere. The prehistoric earthworks are a National Monument and a Louisiana State Historic Site. The site is a complex of mounds built between 1700 and 1100 B.C. Archaeologists from around the world have used the mounds to better understand ancient hunter-gatherer societies. Poverty Point was the center of a culture that developed in the Delta region of northeast Louisiana centuries before the first stones were laid for the Mayan pyramids. When walking the site, you will see the enormous Mound A, which takes the shape of a giant bird, towering 72 feet above the rest of the site. Below it is an amazing complex of smaller mounds and ridges that once overlooked the Mississippi River floodplain.

In the Visitors' Center you can view an excellent film explaining what scientists have learned about this ancient culture. Displays contain artifacts unearthed at the site, including quartz and crystals from the Ouachita and Ozark Mountains in Arkansas, copper from the Great Lakes, and shells from the Gulf of Mexico. More than 8,000 complete spear points have been recovered, along with an array of artistic items. (A more detailed description is contained in the To See listings.)

✳ Cities, Towns, and Villages

Taking the roads less traveled in northeastern Louisiana, you'll come to small rural towns with interesting stories to tell. Many look much as they did in the 1950s and '60s. Using I-20 as your base line, you can take any number of side trips to smaller communities offering quaint town squares, nifty museums, and access to lakes, parks, and wildlife areas.

Arcadia. East of Shreveport you'll find **Arcadia**. The town's Railroad Depot and Museum is the focal point for special events. Bluegrass pickers gather here the second Saturday of each month to play music and swap stories. The fourth Saturday of each month features the *Louisiana Hayride* road show featuring "Homemade Jam" with an occasional guest from Branson, Missouri, or Nashville. A marker just south of town is a reminder that outlaws Bonnie Parker and Clyde Barrow met their ends here. Their bodies, still in the bullet-riddled car, were brought to the coroner downtown for autopsies. Folks stop here frequently at the Bonnie and Clyde Trade Days and RV Park.

Bernice is North of Arcadia on LA 2 where you'll find the Bernice Depot Museum and Captain Henderson Caboose. The town is the heart of a recreational area bounded by Lake D'Arbonne State Park, Lake Claiborne, and Corney Lake.

MADAM C. J. WALKER
THE FIRST AFRICAN AMERICAN FEMALE MILLIONAIRE

Sarah Breedlove was born December 23, 1867, to sharecropper parents in Delta. Orphaned at 7, she started working at 10, married at 14, and by 20 she was a widow with an infant daughter. She moved to St. Louis, Missouri, where for the next 18 years she supported herself as a washerwoman. In 1905, she had an idea to begin a cosmetics business. She developed a hair-care and grooming system for African American women, creating an ointment that helped stop hair loss and made hair smooth and shiny, and within a few years, her cosmetic empire was worth a fortune. In 1906 she married the newspaperman Charles J. Walker. Although they divorced six years later, she retained the name Madam C. J. Walker. In 1910, she built a plant in Indianapolis, Indiana, and provided employment for more than 3,000 people. She became known as the wealthiest African American woman of her time. Madam C. J. Walker was a generous donor to black charities and endowed a number of educational institutions.

THE MADAM C.J. WALKER EXHIBIT IN THE HERMIONE MUSEUM HONORS THE FIRST AFRICAN AMERICAN FEMALE MILLIONAIRE.
Louisiana Office of Tourism

Homer, north of Ruston, is the county seat of Claiborne Parish and has a Greek revival courthouse—one of Louisiana's four remaining antebellum courthouses. Also on the square is the Herbert S. Ford Memorial Museum filled with displays on the history and culture of north Louisiana's hill country. South of Ruston just off US 167, you'll find Jonesboro, home of Jimmie Davis, Louisiana's singing governor, famed for "You Are My Sunshine." Nearby is the Jimmie Davis State Park at Caney Lake, a premier trophy bass-fishing lake. The park offers cabins, lodges, boating, fishing, and biking trails.

Columbia, south of Monroe on US 165, is a quaint village on the Ouachita River. A Main Street community, Columbia has been meticulously restored to its early 20th century beginnings. The focal points are the Schepis Museum, circa 1916, built like an Italian opera house, and the First Methodist Church, modeled after a

Louisiana Office of Tourism

THE CLAIBORNE PARISH COURTHOUSE
IN HOMER IS ONE OF LOUISIANA'S
FOUR REMAINING ANTEBELLUM
COURTHOUSES.

Scandinavian chapel. Riverview Park on the Ouachita River is a wonderful place, with walks and benches where you can sit and relax any time of day.

In **Winnsboro**, you find patriotism and beauty on LA 15, the Veteran's Memorial Highway. Known as the Stars and Stripes Capital of Louisiana, the town displays more than 400 American flags during patriotic holidays.

The **Newellton/St. Joseph** area is farther east, just off US 65. Here, two natural oxbow lakes, Lake Bruin and Lake St. Joseph, created when the Mississippi River changed course more than 3,000 years ago, offer numerous recreational opportunities. The village of St. Joseph has a historic district. About 8 miles from Newellton is Winter Quarters, a State Historic Site, one of the few remaining plantation homes built in a simple style before planters amassed great wealth in the 1850s.

From here, you can drive US 65 north connecting with I-20 at **Tallulah**, the parish seat of Madison Parish. Take a look at the parish courthouse, and then visit the Hermione Museum to learn more about the parish. Tallulah is the site of the first agricultural experiment stations to use airplanes to control cotton pests.

Nearby in **Delta**, the birthplace of Madam C. J. Walker, the world's first female African American millionaire, is used as City Hall. Madison Parish considers itself the home of Delta Air Lines. The original airport building at Scott's Field still stands near Tallulah and is on the National Register of Historic Buildings. Just east

TALLULAH'S HERMIONE MUSEUM CONTAINS DISPLAYS ON MADISON PARISH AND THE CIVIL WAR.

Louisiana Office of Tourism

of Tallulah on I-20, there's a Louisiana Welcome Center at Mound, a perfect spot to pick up info on north Louisiana. If you continuing heading east, you'll cross the Mississippi River into Vicksburg, Mississippi.

✳ To See

✄ ♂ **Biedenharn Museum** (800-362-0983 or 318-387-5281, www.bmuseum .org), 2000 Riverside Dr., Monroe. This complex includes ELsong garden and conservatory and the home of Emy-Lou Biedenharn, an opera singer during the pre–World War II years. The property includes the Coca-Cola Museum, with Coke memorabilia including a delivery truck, signs, posters and machines, and the Bible Museum, with an extensive collection of rare Bibles and an exhibition of Russian icons. Open 10 A.M.–5 P.M. Tues–Sat. Last tour begins at 3:30 P.M. Admission $6, adults; $4, children ages 2–11.

✄ & ♞ **Chennault Aviation & Military Museum** (318-362-5540, www.chennault museum.org), 701 Kansas Lane, Monroe. Visitors here can view exhibits on Louisiana's aviation pioneers, learn about the World War II Selman Field Army Air Corps Navigation School, the birth of Delta Air Lines as a regional crop dusting service, and all about native son General Claire Lee Chennault and his Flying Tigers fighter squadron. The museum also houses personal artifacts and an abundance of weaponry, uniforms, photographs, and documents from World War I to the present. Individuals from northeast Louisiana who have served in the U.S. military are profiled in a number of exhibits. You'll also see an impressive collection of Nazi artifacts and an outdoor display of World War II aircraft and vehicles. Open 9 a.m.–4 p.m. Tues.–Sat. Free.

A ROMANTIC FOUNTAIN ANCHORS THE BALLET GARDEN AT BIEDENHARN MUSEUM AND GARDENS IN MONROE.

Monroe-West Monroe CVB

Monroe-West Monroe CVB

VINTAGE PLANES AND MILITARY DISPLAYS ARE OUTSTANDING AT THE CHENNAULT AVIATION AND MILITARY MUSEUM IN MONROE.

Eddie G. Robinson Museum (318-274-2210, www.robinsonmuseum.com), 126 Jones St., Grambling. Eddie G. Robinson, football's "most winningest coach," is honored in the museum on the Grambling University campus. Exhibits spotlight Robinson's career, his players, and the university. Open 10 a.m.–4 p.m. Thurs.–Sat. Free.

Landry Vineyards (318-557-9051, www.landryvineyards.com), 5699 New Natchitoches Rd., West Monroe. Overlooking hillside vineyards, the family-owned and -operated vineyard and winery produces wines ranging from dry to semi-sweet. The winery offers tours and harvest festivals, and hosts a concert series with music on its beautiful grounds. Tasting room open 11 a.m.–5 p.m. every Saturday.

Louisiana Purchase Gardens and Zoo (318-329-2400, www.monroezoo.org), 1405 Bernstein Park Dr., Monroe. This delightful zoo has an unusual design that includes a waterway with boat rides winding through animal habitats. The zoo features more than 450 animals from all over the world and a variety of exotic plants. The Hall of Small gives visitors a look at insects of all sizes. The Louisiana Purchase Exhibit contains animals indigenous at the time of the 1803 Louisiana Purchase, including the black bear, bison, mountain lion, and American bald eagle. Open 10 a.m.–5 p.m. daily. Admission $4.50 adults; $3, children and seniors.

A TOUR BOAT FLOATS PAST ANIMAL HABITATS IN LOUISIANA PURCHASE GARDENS AND ZOO IN MONROE.

Monroe-West Monroe CVB

⚓ **Louisiana State Cotton Museum** (318-559-2041, www.sos.la.gov), 7162 US 65 North, Lake Providence. Three miles north of Lake Providence, the Cotton Museum explores the economic and cultural impact cotton farming and production had on Louisiana and the Mississippi Delta. The 30-acre complex focuses on cotton's impact on African American history, the Civil War, and the Great Depression. Visitors can see a planter's house original to the site, an original sharecropper's cabin, a plantation chapel, commissary, and other buildings. You also can view the historic Homer Cotton Gin, Louisiana's first electric-power gin, and strings on the Diddley bow and other musical instruments allow visitors to pluck and strum along with blues music. An old Wurlitzer plays sons by famous bluesmen. Open daily 9 a.m.–4:30 p.m. April–October, and 9 a.m.–4 p.m. November–March. Free.

Louisiana State Oil and Gas Museum (318-995-6845, www.sos.la.gov), 200 South Land Ave., Oil City. About 20 minutes from Shreveport, this museum interprets the drama of the state's early oil industry. Photographs, films, and life-size dioramas interpret early explorations and drilling. Across the street and next to the old train depot, you can view a collection of machinery, oil rigs, and equipment.

Masur Museum of Art (318-329-2237, www.masurmuseum.org), 1400 South Grand St., Monroe. Set in a 1920s Tudor-style structure, the museum is listed on the National Register of Historic Places. Visitors will find charming open spaces and hardwood floors that make viewing art truly pleasurable. Inviting, year-round displays of a wide spectrum of art encourage return visits. The Masur Museum features a permanent collection of paintings, prints, and sculpture, as well as six to eight exhibitions each year of art from museums and artists across the country. An annual national juried exhibition is also held. Open 9 A.M.–5 P.M. Tues.–Fri. and noon–5 P.M. Sat.

A RUSTED PUMP TESTIFIES TO THE IMPORTANCE OF OIL IN NORTHWEST LOUISIANA'S HISTORY.

Louisiana Office of Tourism

♂ ⚘ **Northeast Louisiana Children's Museum** (318-361-9611, www.nelcm.org), 323 Walnut St., Monroe. It's so much fun they'll never know it's a museum! This is a joyful place where adults and kids can learn and grow together. Permanent exhibits include the Firehouse (a replica with its own pole), Health Hall (be a paramedic, listen to your heart), Toddlertown (a cool, whimsical area for those under 4), Kids' Cafe (be a server, cashier, chef), Bubbleworks (a giant bubble!), and The Big Mouth (walk in and explore). Great traveling exhibits from across the United States are featured throughout the year, too. Open 9 a.m.–2 p.m. Tues.–Fri. and 10 a.m.–5 p.m., Sat. Admission is $5 per person age 1 and over; $3 per person for groups of 15 or more.

♂ ⚘ **North Louisiana Military Museum** (318-251-5156, www.sos.la.gov), 201 Memorial Dr., Ruston. Exhibits here focus on U.S. conflicts from the Spanish American War to today's war on terror. View personal items from soldiers and sailors who served through many conflicts. Open 10 a.m.–6:30 p.m. Mon.–Fri., 10 a.m.–5 p.m. Sat., and 1–5 p.m. Sun.

Panola Pepper Company (318-559-1774 or 800-256-3013, www.panolapepper .com), Holland Delta Rd., Lake Providence. Panola Pepper Company, located on the outskirts of Lake Providence, welcomes tours of the plant where it bottles more than 30 sauces, seasonings, and condiments. Products include hot wing sauce, barbeque sauce, olives, steak sauces, crab and shrimp boil, and more. The company also does a "private label," so you can have your own name put on a label. Tours educate visitors about different types of peppers and what it takes to get sauces from the farm to your table. Open for tours 8 A.M.–4 P.M., Mon.–Fri.

♂ ⚘ **Poverty Point State Historic Site** (318-926-5492, www.crt.state.la.us /parks), 6859 LA 577, near Epps. Designated a state historic site, a National Monument and a National Landmark, the mounds here are astounding. The people who built them were a highly civilized group who left behind one of the most important archaeological sites in North America. View the film and exhibits in the Visitors' Center, then walk among the earthworks and imagine what life was like here in the centuries before pyramids were built in Egypt. Interpretive rangers conduct programs throughout the year. Tram tours are given daily at 9:30 A.M., 11 A.M., 12:30 P.M., 2 P.M., and 3:30 P.M. from March 1 through Oct. 31.

Schepis Museum (318-649-9931), 106 Main St., Columbia. Built by John Schepis around 1916, the museum is famous for its unusual Italian architecture. Well-planned rotating exhibits showcase Louisiana artists. Admission is $4 per person; free to those 62 and over and 12 and under.

Simmons Sporting Goods (800-726-9930, www.simmonssportinggoods.com), 918 North Washington, Bastrop. Considered one of the South's largest sporting goods stores, Simmons specializes in advanced hunting equipment. Look for archery, cooking, cutlery, rods and reels, bait and camping equipment among the 70,000 square feet of sporting goods.

✳ Green Spaces

Black Bayou Lake National Wildlife Refuge (318-387-1114, www.fws.gov /refuges/profiles), LA 165 North, Monroe. Discover the beauty of herons, egrets, orioles, and red-winged blackbirds from a bird blind or fishing pier. Meander along a trail in a forested area with bottomland hardwoods and pines. Paddle a rented canoe for an excursion along the 1,600-acre lake. The semi-urban refuge is ideally situated. The Visitors' Center, a restored 1880s Acadian house, contains interactive exhibits and a nature shop. You can visit the Aquarium Room to see exhibits of live fish, reptiles, and frogs. Facilities also include a milelong raised asphalt/boardwalk nature trail, a 400-foot wildlife pier, and a raised observation deck with spotting scope and several informational kiosks. There's also an arboretum with 150 labeled species of native trees and wood shrubs, a photo blind, and a large windowed bird blind. Year-round fishing and seasonal hunting are also available.

Caney Ranger District (318-927-2061), 3288 LA 79, Homer. Today a forest restored from sugar cane and cotton fields, the Caney Lakes Recreation Area is easily accessed. Recreational opportunities include water skiing as well as hiking and biking on the Sugar Cane Trail, which has been designated a National Recreation Trail because of its outstanding lake views and challenging terrain. There's a ski beach area for boaters to park their craft and enjoy picnicking in the grass. Caney Lake's Beaver Dam Campground can accommodate large RVs. A popular destination, the campground has plenty of sites with electric and water hookups, showers, and a nearby dump station. Turtle Slide Campground is designed for campers with tents or small campers and is primitive and scenic. On Corney Lake, you'll find primitive camping on both the north and south shores. The north shore also offers sites strictly for tent campers.

✔ ⤵ ✿ **Chemin-A-Haut State Park** (318-283-0812 or 888-677-2436, www.crt .state.la.us/parks), 14656 State Park Rd., Bastrop. Designed with children in mind, the park has two playgrounds in the day-use area. Youngsters also can have fun in the wading pool in the swimming complex, which is usually open Memorial Day weekend to Labor Day. The picnic area has more than 30 family sites with grills and tables. A hard-surfaced trail runs through the picnic area and along the high scenic banks of Bayou Bartholomew. Big Slough Lake near the edge of the park is perfect for people who like to fish from the shore. Check with the park about camping facilities and overnight cabins. Entrance station is open 6 A.M.–7 P.M. April–September, and 8 A.M.–5 P.M. October–March. Admission is $1 per adult, free for seniors 62 and over and children 3 and under.

⤵ **Handy Brake National Wildlife Refuge** (www.fws.gov/handybrake, 318-726-4400). Follow US 165 into Bastrop, then east of Courthouse Square and after the divided lanes merge, turn north onto Cooper Lake Road. Travel about 6 miles and look for the refuge sign on the east side of road. Established in 1988, the primitive 501-acre refuge harbors wintering waterfowl, wading birds, and other wetland-dependant species. The refuge has a wood duck nest box project to provide optimal habitat for nesting and wintering ducks. Prairie grasses between the water and the observation tower are maintained to provide a habitat for grassland birds and other wildlife. Walk out on the observation platform, and don't forget your camera.

✔ ⤵ ✿ **Jimmie Davis State Park** (318-249-2595 or 888-677-2263, www.crt.state .la.us/parks), 1209 State Park Rd., Chatham. About 13 miles east of Jonesboro, the park on Caney Lake is named for the songwriter, performer, and politician, who served as Louisiana's governor 1944–1948 and 1960–1964. After a day of fishing and exploring the outdoors, enjoy an evening camping out or sleeping in a cabin. Park facilities include two boat launches, a pier, and a beach with swimming. Entrance station is open 6 A.M.–7 P.M. April–September and 8 A.M.–5 P.M.,

October–March. Admission is $1 per person; free for seniors age 62 and over and children age 3 and under.

☞ **Kalorama Nature Preserve** (318-874-7777), 7197 Collinston Rd., Collinston. Kalorama Nature Preserve is located approximately 30 minutes north of Monroe, on the Bastrop Ridge that has steep ridges attracting a rich variety of plant and animal life. There are upland pines and hardwoods, open prairie meadows, centuries-old bottomland hardwoods, pawpaw stands, and abundant plant species. Kalorama places emphasis on the relationship between plants, animals, and their natural habitats. The old forest area is extremely beautiful in spring when flowering shrubs bloom and in fall when the trees turn red and gold. Open seasonally on weekends or year-round by appointment.

♂ & ☞ ❀ **Lake Bruin State Park** (318-766-3530 or 888-677-2784, www.crt.state .la.us), 201 State Park Rd., St. Joseph. With more than 3,000 acres of water surface, there's no doubt about the quality of fishing and superb water sports to be enjoyed at this park. It has three large fishing piers, a year-round boat launch, and a boat shed. Rental boats are available. Largemouth bass fishing is popular year-round. Crappie is found around piers in early spring and bluegill fishing is best in shallower waters at both ends of the lake. There are picnic tables and grills near the lake and adjacent to two fishing piers, as well as restrooms and playgrounds. Most facilities are wheelchair-accessible. Entrance gates open 6 A.M.–7 P.M. April–September and 8 A.M.–5 P.M. October–March. Admission is $1 per person; free for seniors 62 and over and children 3 and under.

♂ ☞ ❀ **Lake D'Arbonne State Park** (318-368-2086 or 888-677-5200, www.crt .state.la.us), 3628 Evergreen Rd., Farmerville. Piney forests, rolling hills, five fishing piers, and a beautiful lake draw visitors to this quiet, majestic state park. Designed to keep the focus on nature, the facilities blend with the natural landscape to enhance the outdoor experience of this 655-acre park. The lake is the centerpieces of the park. Locals and visitors enjoy record freshwater catches of bass, crappie, and catfish. Tree stands in the lake captivate photographers, as do the towering pines on land and the rich diversity of wildlife and birds that make the park their home. Cyclists can enjoy the rolling hills as a starting point for biking into the steep inclines. Bring your binoculars and camera to capture the wonders along the beautiful trails. Entrance gates are open 6 A.M.–7 P.M. April–September and 8 A.M.–5 P.M. October–March. Admission is $1 per person; free for seniors 62 and over and children 3 and under.

♂ & ❀ **Lincoln Parish Park** (318-251-5156, www.park.lincolnparish.org), 211 Lincoln Parish Park Rd., Ruston. Rated one of the best mountain bike trails in America, Lincoln Parish Park is a treasure for residents and mountain bike lovers alike. The 10-mile trail offers a challenging and exciting course for not only the advanced rider, but beginners as well. A campground for RVs provides full hookups to water, sewage, and electricity for $20 a night; primitive camping for tents only is $15 a night. The beach, staffed by lifeguards, is open from Memorial Day to Labor Day. No alcohol or hunting is allowed in the park.

♂ & **Tensas River National Wildlife Refuge** (318-574-2664, www.fws.gov /tensasriver), near Tallulah, 2312 Quebec Rd., Monroe. Visitors' Center and headquarters are about 60 miles east of Monroe, off eastbound I-20. Exit at Waverly (Exit 157), make a left onto LA 577. A mile or two in, turn right onto US 80 East toward Tallulah. Make a right onto Fred Morgan Sr. Road and drive about 6 miles of gravel road and 4.5 miles of paved road. This refuge was created in 1980 to preserve one of the largest privately owned tracts of bottomland hardwoods remaining in the Mississippi Delta. The forest contains more than 400 species of mammals, birds, reptiles, amphibians, and fish. There are nearly 80,000 acres of land and oxbow lakes. It is a habitat for the threatened Louisiana black bear. The last sighting of the ivory-billed woodpecker, which is thought to be extinct by most scientists, occurred in the 1940s adjacent to what is now the refuge. Public-use areas include an auto tour route and two interpreted hiking trails: the quarter-mile Hollow Cypress Wildlife Trail and the 3.5-mile Rainey Lake Hiking Trail, both fully handicapped-accessible. There are also about 30 miles of ATV trail open to hikers, as well as fishing, several observation towers, and designated hunting areas. Be ready for great photo ops. In September, the Visitors' Center observes National Hunting and Fishing Day with wildlife exhibits, rock climbing, a bounce area, puppet show, bear maze, bird identification demonstrations, forestry information booths, calling contests, games and activities for children, and food and craft vendors.

✳ To Do

AUTO RACES Twin City Dragway (318-388-1612), 3695 Prairie Rd., Monroe. You'll find bleachers, a concession stand, and plenty of parking. Get those RPMs revving at this super quarter-mile asphalt drag strip. Open Saturday and Sunday and Friday evenings during holiday weekends from February through October. Admission: Spectators $15–$20; free for children under 10. Entry fees apply.

✔ **West Monroe Motocross** (318-396-3478), 280 Tinsley Rd., West Monroe. This is a family friendly facility where you can ride, practice, and race. There's a mile-long dirt track for bikes and quads, plus a pee-wee track, a mud track for four-wheelers, and a remote-control car track, as well as year-round racing and events. The track is excellently maintained. There is night lighting, a concession stand that's open on weekends, parking, camping, and RV parking. Open daily (weather permitting) from dawn to dusk. Daily, monthly, and yearly rates are available.

FISHING AND HUNTING Visitors will find extensive wildlife refuges, state parks, and rivers in northeast Louisiana. Fishing is permitted year-long. Along with a few places mentioned here, see the Green Spaces listing.

✔ **Black Bayou Lake** (318-387-2628, www.friendsofblackbayou.org), 140 Richland Place, Monroe. The 4,600-acre refuge contains a 1,700-acre lake teeming with fish. Take advantage of the year-round boating, fishing, hiking, and birding.

✔ 🐾 **James Lake** (318-777-3331, www.rustonlincoln.com), off Wynn St., east of the Dubach Post Office, Dubach. Off the tourist path, the lake offers fishing and a birding trail that is one of the best in north Louisiana. Enjoy the viewing platform, the bridge, or the wooded walking trail. Free.

✔ 🐾 **Poverty Point Reservoir State Park** (800-474-0392, www.crt.louisiana.gov), 1500 Poverty Point Parkway, Delhi. Anglers can fish in the man-made lake for largemouth bass, black crappie, blue gill, and channel catfish. The park area offers camping, a swimming beach area, and a marina. The eastern edge of the park, along Bayou Macon, contains an active bear habitat. Bear-proof containers are provided for waste disposal throughout the park.

GOLF **Black Bear Golf Course** (318-878-2162, www.crt.la.gov/parks/blackbear), 253 Black Bear Dr., Delhi. Just off I-20, Exit 153, and north on LA 17 for 6.7 miles; look for the Audubon Golf Trail sign. The 7,200-yard championship course has varied topography. Lush fairways and native grasses in nonplay areas make Black Bear a pleasure. The property, close to the Poverty Point State Historic Site, includes the 17-room Black Bear Lodge, with swimming pool and tennis courts, for those who want to stay overnight, as well as a clubhouse, pro shop, and the Waterfront Grill.

Chennault Park Golf Course (318-329-2454), 8475 Mill Haven Rd., Monroe. This 18-hole, par-72, 7,042-yard course features a flat, wooded landscape, a driving range, and carts with GPS systems. Check out the 2007 Buick Open winner Brian Bateman's trophy display. The championship course, with lush fairways, is designed to appeal to golfers of all skill levels. Hint: Look out for the 18th hole—it's a par-4 with water all the way down the right side.

Frenchman's Bend Golf Course (318-387-2363, www.frenchmansbend.com), 1484 Frenchman's Bend Rd., Monroe. With its soft, rolling hills, this beautiful, semi-private, championship 18-hole, par-72 golf course was designed by Dave Marr and Jay Riviere. It features undulating greens, three sets of tees, a driving range, and restaurant.

Trails End Golf Course (318-263-7420), 400 Trails End Rd., Arcadia. The municipal 18-hole golf course at the Trails End Golf Club in Arcadia features 6,775 yards of golf from the longest tees for a par of 72. Designed by R.T. Anderson, the course is rated 72.3 and has a slope rating of 126.

✳ Lodging

The Atrium (318-410-4000 or 800-428-7486, www.theatrium.biz), 2001 Louisiana Ave., Monroe. Just a mile from downtown, this recently renovated, full-service hotel is convenient and comfortable for both the business and pleasure traveler. The large atrium lobby is a good place to meet friends or just relax. Guest rooms are large and feature very comfortable beds, and range from standard doubles to plush suites designed for conducting business and entertaining. Tip: Choose a room away from the atrium if you want a really quiet place for sleeping, because groups tend to gather here at all hours. Facilities include an outdoor pool, whirlpool spa, fitness room, and the Brandy House Restaurant, which serves lunch and dinner. Ask for a truly ice-cold drink from the ice bar. Moderate.

Black Bear Lodge (318-878-2681, www.crt.state.la.us/parks), 2131 Black Bear Dr., Delhi. This 17-room hotel designed is designed for visitors to Black Bear Golf Club. The hotel and golf course are operated by the Louisiana State Parks. Guest rooms have views of the course. The Waterfront Grill in the clubhouse is open daily (318-878-5941). The lodge and course are adjacent to Poverty Point Reservoir State Park, which has cabins and an RV complex. Make reservations early, as these sites fill early in the spring, summer, and fall. Moderate–expensive.

Days Inn Tallulah (800-329-7466 or 318-574-5200, www.daysinn.com), 143 US 65 South, Tallulah. This is a clean, small hotel near the intersection of US 65 and I-20. It doesn't compare to boutique hotels but it's kept in good repair.

The breakfast offering is limited. The hotel has a reputation for a friendly staff. Moderate.

Hampton Inn Ruston (318-251-3090, www.hamptoninn.com), 1315 North Trenton St., Ruston. While conveniently located by I-20, the inn is somewhat tricky to reach from the I-20/US 167 exit. The rooms are well-appointed, with comfy beds and clean, modern bathrooms. There's an outdoor pool and fitness facility and business center. The complimentary breakfast buffet is excellent and well worth the stay. Moderate.

((ᵧ)) **Hilton Garden Inn** (888-370-0984, www.hiltongardeninn.hilton.com), 400 Maine St., West Monroe. Just off I-20 on the western outskirts of West Monroe, the new hotel has large rooms with excellent beds and Wi-Fi. The dining area offers wonderful breakfast buffet or you can order from the menu. Service is exceptionally friendly. The only problem is getting to the hotel from the freeway. You can see it, but there are few directional signs, and roads are not well lighted at night. Moderate.

Residence Inn Monroe (318-387-0210, www.marriott.com), 4960 Mill-haven Rd., Monroe. The inn is close to I-20 and the Pecanland Mall. Guest rooms are spacious with excellent beds. Suites have a full refrigerator—a plus for guests with lengthy stays. While a railroad runs across the street, the inn's construction is sturdy and night sounds are minimal. There's a free breakfast buffet with friendly service. Facilities include a great swimming pool. The hotel is near numerous restaurants and shops. Moderate.

((ᵧ)) **Wingate by Wyndham** (318-387-7395), 114 North Thomas Rd., West Monroe. Designed for business travelers, the Wingate is just off I-20 and offers free wired and wireless high-speed Internet. The larger-than-average guest rooms have a separate work area with desk and adjustable swivel chair. Amenities include a microwave, refrigerator, coffeemaker, and iron. There's a 24-hour, self-serve business center with free faxes, copies, and printing. Guests enjoy a happy hour and free hot deluxe Continental breakfast. Moderate.

BED & BREAKFASTS Lewis House (318-255-3848, www.thevictorianlewishouse.com), 210 East Alabama Ave., Ruston. Lewis House is a two-story Queen Anne/Colonial Revival home built in 1900. The property contains beautiful Victorian furnishings and several rooms include large four-poster beds. An excellent country breakfast is served in the formal dining room. Amenities include gift bags and afternoon tea and treats. The gift shop is an added bonus. Moderate–expensive.

The Fowler House (318-435-6845, www.thefowlerhouse.com), 203 Newt Winters Rd., Winnsboro. Discover the joy of rural life in this country farmhouse with front porch rockers and shade trees. Guests enjoy the use of the entire home, including the fully equipped kitchen and washer and dryer. There's a charcoal BBQ grill and a butane fish fryer. Relax by the outdoor fire pit on cool evenings. Your stay includes a complimentary Continental country breakfast with homemade jams and jellies. Moderate.

Jackson Street Guest House (318-435-4105, 318-435-9331, www.jacksonstreetguesthouse.com), 803 Jackson St., Winnsboro. This B&B is a 1900 cottage adjacent to the Franklin Parish courthouse. Furnishings are simple, yet elegant. Enjoy the king-size bed and whirlpool tub or relax on the cozy, screened back porch. Moderate.

Rose Lee Bed & Breakfast (318-366-2412), 318 Trenton St., West Monroe. Spend the evening in a restored 1905 hotel. Situated right in the heart of the city's antiques district, this quaint spot is within walking distance of outstanding antiques shops. Enjoy the décor and antique clawfoot tubs. Children are welcomed. Moderate–expensive.

CAMPGROUNDS There are a number of excellent RV campgrounds in Louisiana State Parks in north Louisiana; see the parks listed in this guide's Green Spaces sections for details. Reservations can be made 11 months to the day in advance online at www.reserveamerica.com or by calling the reservation center at 877-226-7652, Mon.–Fri. The center is closed weekends and state holidays. Also, Sportsman's Paradise contains units of the Kisatchie National Forest as well as national and state wildlife refuges. Some designate campgrounds with RV hookups and primitive camping. Contact information is listed in Green Spaces for each area and in the What's Where section. The campgrounds below were selected for their accessibility and well-earned good reputations.

Lincoln Parish Park (318-251-5156, www.park.lincolnparish.org), 211 Parish Park Rd., Ruston. This is a lovely park, beautifully planned and maintained by Lincoln Parish. There's a tranquil lake for swimming, boating, and fishing. A 1.25-mile walking path is also accessible to the handicapped. The mountain biking trail is rated one of the best in the country for advanced riders, and there is a 4-mile beginners' biking trail. RV camping in specially designed areas includes full hookups to water, sewage, and electricity. Primitive camping for tents only is $15 per

night. No alcohol is allowed. Quiet time starts at 10 P.M. Pets must be kept on a leash, and all campers must be in the campground at closing time. Inexpensive.

Pavilion RV Park (318-322-4216 or 888-322-4216, www.pavrv.com), 309 Well Rd., West Monroe. Family friendly Pavilion Park has full hookups with cable and Wi-Fi, and 10 cabins with kitchens. The campground features include a large activity room, two laundromats, a bath house, swimming pool, catch-and-release fishing in Lake Katherine, and an RV supply shop. The nightly base rate is $40, including tax. Ask about RV hookup discounts (Good Sam, AAA, others). No discounts on cabins. Inexpensive-moderate.

✳ Where to Eat

Towns along I-20 in the central and eastern areas of north Louisiana have an excellent mix of restaurants. Louisiana's reputation as one of the best places in America to find exceptional cooking is in good standing in both Monroe and Ruston. Traditional Southern cookery is at its best here, but you also will find outstanding Creole and Cajun food. Fried and grilled catfish and hushpuppies are popular, as is Louisiana Gulf Coast seafood. Certainly, fast-food eateries are popular, and so are Mexican and Asian cafes.

EATING OUT Dawg House Sports Grill (318-513-1188, www.dawghousesportsgrill.com), 102 North Homer St., Ruston. Located next to Louisiana Tech University, Dawg House is understandably a collegiate hangout and it gets crowded on sports events weekends. Watch the action on the many TV screens, play a game of pool or darts, or listen to live entertainment from local musicians. The place is famous for its burgers, but there's a great full-service menu. Sandwiches and burgers are served on your choice of white, wheat, or jalapeno cheese bread. Try the onion strings or curly fries, but you can also get sweet potato chips or steak fries. Entrees take a bit longer, but they're worth the wait. Another option is to order baskets or large salads with homemade dressings. Moderate.

🖉 **Dowling's Smokehouse** (318-513-9966, www.dowlingsbbq.com), 1313 Cooktown Rd., Ruston. Dowling's is a family friendly restaurant serving a variety of smoked meats. The barbecue sandwich piles a quarter-pound of meat on your choice of sourdough, white, whole wheat sourdough, or jalapeno cheese sourdough bun. Meats include pulled pork, beef brisket, pulled chicken, and spicy sausage. If you dare to try it, the "Scatterload" sandwich is made of minced ham, turkey, hot link, sausage, brisket, and cheese, all mixed together. Try one of the meat platters with Texas toast and a choice of two sides, which include baked beans, yellow potato salad, and coleslaw. The restaurant serves homemade apple or peach pies for dessert. Open 10 A.M.–8 P.M. Mon.–Sat. Moderate.

((ɢ)) **Jehovah Java Gourmet Coffee** (318-559-7430), 218 North Hood St., Lake Providence. When traveling along US 65 North toward Arkansas, here's the spot to stop for a great pick-me-up. The coffee house has a cozy atmosphere. Order your favorite latte or just get a mug of really good coffee. Take advantage of the Wi-Fi and browse in the gift shop. Inexpensive.

🖉 **Johnny's Pizza House** (318-387-8668), 1707 Mckeen Place, Monroe. Popular with locals and visitors, Johnny's is a casual spot for pizza lovers. The pizza is made with sour-dough bread and cut in squares. The locals go for the Sweep the Kitchen, with Italian sausage, pepperoni, Canadian bacon, onions, jalapenos, and anchovies, and Sweep the Swamp, with onions, bell peppers, crab, crawfish, shrimp, andouille sausage, and jalapenos. Moderate.

🖉 **Not Just Pie Inc.** (318-322-9928), 2117 Forsythe Ave., Monroe. This is a delightful place to stop for a light meal, with a menu that includes soups, salads, and sandwiches. Best of all are the yummy homemade pies and cakes. Forget the calories and indulge. The lemon meringue will melt in your mouth and the apple pie with vanilla ice cream will create new memories. Inexpensive–moderate.

Pickle Barrel (318-325-5996), 1827 Avenue of America, Monroe. Pickles are served in a bowl on every table at this casual spot offering a big variety of sandwiches. The sandwiches come with French fries. The eatery has more than 100 different beers from American and international breweries, including Russian, Chinese and Japanese. Moderate.

Ponchatoulas (318-254-5200, www .ponchatoulas.com), 109 East Park Ave., Ruston. Authentic Louisiana cuisine is served at Ponchatoulas. The seafood platters are large (they can easily be shared by two, maybe three people). Try the crawfish entrees in season. Seafood gumbo is made with a dark roux and features Gulf shrimp and blue crab meat. There's a full bar with mixed cocktails, frozen drinks, and beer. It's a good place to rub shoulders with locals, including Louisiana Tech faculty and students. Open 11 A.M.–9 P.M. Mon.–Sat. and 11 A.M.–3 P.M. Sun. Inexpensive-moderate.

Scott's Catfish and Seafood (318-387-6700, www.scottscatfish.com), 305

West Constitution Dr., West Monroe. This family restaurant specializes in Louisiana seafood and American farm-raised catfish. The cafe, a converted Dairy Queen, draws big crowds for lunch and dinner. In addition, Scott's serves pastas and cheese, chicken and shrimp quesadillas, and seafood, hickory smoked brisket, ham, and turkey po-boys. Open 10:30 A.M.–9 P.M. Mon.–Sat. Inexpensive-moderate.

Waterfront Grill (318-322-1340, www.waterfrontgrill.com), 5201 DeSiard St., Monroe. Located on tranquil Bayou DeSiard, the restaurant is known for its grilled catfish, seafood, and steaks. Nothing is fried. Everything is grilled or baked. Portions are generous. If you're not in the mood for a huge meal, try the steak sandwich on grilled bread or the grilled shrimp po-boy. Also, you can ask for lunch portions at dinner. The kids' menu includes hot dogs, hamburgers, chicken sandwiches, and macaroni and cheese. Moderate.

DINING OUT 102 A Bistro (318-254-1102, www.102abistro.com), 102 North Monroe St., Ruston. This upscale restaurant serves contemporary Louisiana cuisine as well as excellent sushi. It's also known for its pleasant décor, white tablecloths, and courteous wait staff. We suggest the pepper-crusted duck breast served with cranberry wild rice for dinner and the Louisiana shrimp remoulade salad for a light but delicious lunch. Open for lunch, 11 A.M.–2 P.M. Mon.–Fri.; dinner, 5–9 P.M. Mon.–Thurs. and 4–10 P.M. Fri.–Sat. Expensive.

Rabbs Steakhouse (318-255-1008, www.rabbssteakhouse.com), 2647 South Service Rd. West, Ruston. This is where the locals hang out for food, drinks, and live bands. The steakhouse serves all major cuts of prime and

choice beef, from filet mignon to New York strip. The large dinner menu includes salmon, shrimp, and a seafood platter. Entrees are served with a house salad and a choice of baked potato, steak fries, stuffed potato, or grilled vegetables. The lunch menu features a variety of burgers and po-boys. Open for lunch, 11 A.M.–2 P.M. Mon.–Fri.; dinner, 5–10 P.M. Mon.–Sat. Moderate–expensive.

Sage (318-410-9400, www.restaurant-sage.com), 1301 North 19th St., Monroe. Sage presents contemporary cuisine with a definite Southern touch. Guests can dine in the restaurant or try cocktails and appetizers in the Red Oak Bar. The restaurant draws upon the cuisines of New Orleans and Atlanta to present seafood and steak dishes that delight patrons. Try the char-grilled oysters or marinated or classic turtle soup with lots of sherry. Patrons rave about the signature braised sea bass served with an avocado and jumbo crab salad. The dishes are noted for their delicate combinations of flavors and textures. If you have room for dessert, go for the raspberry bread pudding or pecan pie. Moderate–expensive.

Warehouse No. 1 Restaurant (318-322-1340, www.warehouseno1.com), 1 Olive St., Monroe. You can expect casual fine dining at the Warehouse. We suggest an early evening meal on the deck, where you can enjoy sunset on the Ouachita River. The atmosphere sets the mood for relaxed dining. Start with an appetizer of bite-sized crispy fried catfish strips served with tartar and cocktail sauces. The menu features a wide variety of seafood dishes, from stuffed shrimp to grilled ahi tuna steak served with Thai fried rice. Steak lovers can choose rib eyes or filets cooked to order. Open for lunch, 11 A.M.–2 P.M. Tues.–Fri.;

dinner, 5–9 P.M. Tues.–Thurs. and 5–9:30 P.M. Fri.–Sat. Moderate–expensive.

✴ Entertainment

THE ARTS Downtown Gallery
(www.monroe-westmonroe.org), Monroe and West Monroe. The Crawl is held on the first Thursday of February, April, June, August, October, and December. Discover works by North Louisiana artists while you stroll from one gallery to another on streets running along the Ouachita River while sampling local cuisine.

Impresario's Choice (318-361-574-0440, www.impresarioschoice.com), Monroe Civic Center, 401 Lea Joiner Expressway, Monroe. The nonprofit organization presents high-quality Broadway musicals on national tour. Call for series schedule.

Monroe Symphony Orchestra (318-435-0029 or 318-338-1501, www.bayou .com/symphony), West Monroe Convention Center, 901 Ridge Ave., West Monroe, and Monroe Civic Center, 401 Lea Joiner Expressway, Monroe. The Community Orchestra's season, presented October through May, consists of three classical concerts, a family concert in November, and a Patriotic Pops in April. An educational concert, Sound Safari, is presented during the year to third, fourth, and fifth graders. Performance venues vary.

Strauss Theatre Center (318-323-6681, www.strausstheatre.com), 1300 Lamy Lane, Monroe. This private community theater was established in 1932. It offers Mainstage and Youngstage productions featuring regional actors and children.

ULM Visual and Performing Arts (318-342-3811, www.ulm.edu/vapa), 700 University Ave., Monroe. The University of Louisiana at Monroe offers a wide array of performances in dance, lyric opera, music, and theater, all open to the university community, area patrons, and residents of the region. Stop by Biedenharn Hall on the campus or call for information.

MOVIES Cinema 10 (318-325-4697), 4700 Millhaven Rd., Monroe.
Take a break from shopping in Pecanland Mall and catch a film in this 10-screen complex.

Tinseltown (318-398-0600, www .cinemark.com), 220 Blanchard St., West Monroe. Check out the hottest new films in the 17-screen complex.

NIGHTLIFE AND CONCERTS 3
Docs Brewhouse (318-251-3367, www.3docsbrewhouse.com), 2550 West Alabama, Ruston. This is just the place to hear plenty of live music from upcoming Louisiana entertainers. Listen to country, rock, funk, and bayou blues Thursday, Friday, and Saturday. Among those who have performed here are Kyle Turley, the former New Orleans Saints tackle turned recording artist; the Stiff Necked Fools; and the Super Water Sympathy, a popular rock band from Shreveport. Open 3 P.M.–midnight Mon.–Wed., 3 P.M.–2 A.M. Thurs.–Fri., noon–2 A.M. Sat., and noon–midnight Sunday.

Blue Monkey Tavern (318-324-9864), 819 North Third St., Monroe. Stop by for live bands Tuesday, Friday and Saturday, and there's karaoke on Thursday. The tavern offers pool and bowling. Open 5 P.M.–2 A.M. Tues.–Sat.

Coda Bar & Grill/Rising Sun (318-512-0236, www.codagrill.moonfruit .com), 101 North Grand, Monroe. A hangout for folks with sophisticated tastes. Open 11 A.M.–10 P.M. Mon.–Thurs., 11 A.M.–2 A.M. Fri.–Sat., and

11 A.M.–10 P.M. Sun. The upstairs martini bar in the Rising Sun stays open Saturdays until 2 A.M.

Enoch's Pub & Grill (318-388-3662, www.enochsirishpub.com), 507 Louisville Ave., Monroe. Enoch's considers itself an Irish pub with a Louisiana attitude! Established in 1980 and now a local landmark, the pub features live music throughout the week. Bands may come from Ireland, Scotland, or bayou country. Listen to traditional Irish melodies and other music. A bluegrass session is held on Thursdays. The pub menu includes burgers with Guinness gravy, and there are also sandwiches, salads and vegetarian offerings. The pub is the founder of the Northeast Louisiana Celtic Festival.

♪ **Harvey's Dance Hall** (318-325-5026), 500 DeSard St., Monroe. The dance hall offers lessons in ballroom, country, line dancing, and salsa. It's a family friendly place with a no-smoking policy and no alcohol. Open Thursday at 7 P.M. and Friday at 6:30 P.M. There's a $6 cover charge.

Landry Vineyards (381-557-9050, www.landryvineyards.com), 5699 New Natchitoches Rd., West Monroe. Sip wine and listen to a celebratory mix of music on the vineyard's grounds. The winery's tasting room is open Saturday 11 A.M.–5 P.M. Concerts, ranging from blues to country to jazz, are held at various times from March to October. Visit the website for a schedule.

Riverside Coney Island (318-388-3644), 710 Walnut St., Monroe. Rub shoulders with Monroe's "in-the-know" crowd while enjoying shrimp and crawfish dishes, cold beer and drinks, and karaoke music. Occasional live bands.

LANDRY VINEYARDS IN WEST MONROE WELCOME VISITORS WITH A TASTING ROOM AND POPULAR SEASONAL CONCERTS.

Monroe-West Monroe CVB

✳ Selective Shopping

Monroe and West Monroe attract travelers looking for antiques, collectibles, and that unusual find. In addition to the numerous individually owned shops, there are several antiques malls where credible dealers have consignment areas. For the contemporary shopper, the Pecanland Mall, 4700 Millhaven Rd. just off I-20 in east Monroe, is North Louisiana's largest mall, with more than 100 stores, a food court, a carousel for kids, and Cinema 10. Farther afield in the Ruston area and in smaller communities, you'll find shops featuring local art, crafts, and collectibles.

Antique Alley (318-737-7207, www.antique-alley.org), 100–300 block of Trenton St., West Monroe. Southern Living calls this "a shopaholic's delight" that "has pretty much anything a shopper with eclectic tastes could want." Discover multiple blocks of unique stores downtown in West Monroe's Cotton Port Historic District selling everything from home decor, jewelry, and clothing to European and American antiques, art, and more. Stores are open Tuesday–Saturday, unless noted otherwise in each store's description.

Antiques and More (318-388-3681), 101 Trenton St., West Monroe. The shop specializes in Hummel figurines from Germany and American Art Pottery. It's a good place to browse for miscellaneous collectibles of all types.

Bayou Crafters Mall (318-325-6519, www.bayoucraftersmall.com), 2400 Cypress St., West Monroe. In operation for more than 20 years, the mall contains handmade furniture, personalized signs, ceramics, children's clothing, purses, jewelry, and more, all made by local artists and craftsman.

Cotton Port Antique Mall (318-323-0090, www.antique-alley.org), 323 Trenton St., West Monroe. The mall has more than 20 dealers. It's a good place to look for collectibles, Coca-Cola memorabilia, coins, books, primitive art, records, glassware, giftware, vintage sterling, baseball cards, and home décor. Open 10 A.M.–5 P.M. Tues.–Sat.

Follette Pottery (318-513-9121, www.follettepottery.com), 1991 Pea Ridge Rd., Dubach. You'll find one of Louisiana's oldest pottery producers in the wooded hills a few miles north of Ruston. The artist's whimsical spirit captures your attention as you walk about this studio and shop. View the studio where clay is shaped into beautiful dishes that are practical enough to go in your oven or on the dinner table. Feed the fish, sit on the porch, and listen to the wind chimes. Browse in the shop filled with Follette creations, from small Christmas ornaments to giant pots.

Hooshang Studio (318-255-9368), 1001 Cedar Creek Rd., Ruston. This is the studio of the artist Hooshang Khorasani, whose works have appeared in exhibits and galleries throughout the United States. Call to make an appointment to see his abstract and contemporary works.

Martha's Unfinished Furniture (318-323-1454), 311 Trenton St., Monroe. Browse for unfinished furniture, antiques, jewelry, linens, candles, and new and vintage clothing. Open 10 A.M.–5 P.M. Tues.–Sat.

Memory Lane Antiques (318-323-3188), 301 Trenton St., West Monroe. This store offers New England antiques, furniture, collectible glassware, a large selection of old books, and sports memorabilia.

Minsky Pecan Market (800-646-7597, www.minskywearenuts.com), 1214 Sparrow St., Lake Providence.

The market started in1950 as a family business. Look for pecans and other nuts as well as additional specialty foods. You'll find whole, cracked, and shelled pecans, pecan brittle, pecan pralines, cinnamon pecans, and key lime pecans. Regional specialties include candied jalapenos, Bat's Brew Hot Sauce, and an entire array of Panola sauces and seasonings.

Mojo Boutique (318-387-7823, www.shopmojo.com), 206 Trenton St., West Monroe. You'll love the original T-shirts with fanciful designs by twin brothers John and Doug Kennedy. Natives of West Monroe, their business is growing, but this hometown store is a great shopping experience. The bags are to die for. It's hard to pass up the jewelry, hats, and offbeat clothing, too.

Potpourri de Tante Marie (318-325-0103), 312 Trenton St., West Monroe. This multidealer store includes antique furniture, collectibles, and home décor items. Pat's Emporium, a booth located inside, also features Fenton Art Glass, fragrance lamps and oil refills, reed diffusers, and fashion jewelry.

Rustic Rose (318-323-2586), 320 Trenton St., West Monroe. OK, gals! This is a store for real women with real budgets. The Rustic Rose features everything from jeans and boots to that special little black dress. Shop for business or casual clothing in a variety of sizes and styles. You'll also find shirts and boots for men. Open 10 A.M.–5:30 P.M. Tues.–Sat.

Simmons Sporting Goods (318-283-2688, www.simmonssportinggoods .com), 918 North Washington St., Bastrop. Even if you're not inclined to spend a vacation fishing and hunting, you'll find this huge store amazing. Outdoorsmen and -women can find the latest gear for their sport.

✳ Special Events

January: **Ag Expo** (318-355-2495, www.agexpo.org), Ike Hamilton Expo

DISTINCTIVE T-SHIRT DESIGNS DRAW CUSTOMERS TO MOJO BOUTIQUE IN WEST MONROE.
Monroe-West Monroe CVB

Center, West Monroe. The family event takes place over two days in mid-January and features a livestock show, sanctioned rabbit show, miniature cow show, Elsie the Cow, and a trade show. Admission $6. Children under 6 free.

Antique Show (318-323-3188 or 318-396-9143), Monroe Civic Center, 401 Lea Joiner Expressway, Monroe. Mid-January. The two-day annual antiques show features dealers from all over the United States offering glassware, jewelry, silver, furniture, linens, old books, and crystal restoration. Admission $5. Children under 12 free.

February: **Mardi Gras** (318-338-3172, www.kreweofjanus.org), Monroe-West Monroe. Mardi Gras falls at a different time each year, but most often in mid-February. The Krewe of Janus Mardi Gras Parade along Natchitoches Street in West Monroe and Louisville Avenue in Monroe is a major event with lighted floats and marching bands parading through both of the twin cities.

April: **DeltaFest** (800-843-1872, www.ladeltafest.com), Monroe Civic Center, 401 Lea Joiner Expressway, Monroe. Northeast Louisiana's premier music festival takes place over two days in downtown Monroe. The event, formerly known as the Louisiana Folk Life Festival, has a huge lineup with a diverse range of musical genres, including pop, country, and urban contemporary. Artists share the Monroe Civic Center stage with a leading comedy performer. Past performers have included the Grammy-nominated singer/songwriter Keyshia Cole, the country singer Colt Ford, the modern soul singer-songwriter Avant, and the comedian Bruce Bruce. In addition to music and comedy acts, crowds attending DeltaFest enjoy food, fun, and activities for the entire families. Two outdoor stages feature local and regional entertainers as well as demonstrations of martial arts, tumbling and cheerleading. The DeltaFest Classic Car and Truck Show is among the activities that bring people to town.

Franklin Parish Catfish Festival (318-435-7607, www.franklinparish catfishfestival.com), 805 Jackson St., Winnsboro. Residents claim this is the largest one-day festival in Louisiana. The festival salutes the area's farm-raised catfish industry. Yes, there's plenty of catfish for everyone, as well as vendor booths. Live performances are presented by nationally known American country music artists as well as leading Cajun, zydeco, and pop bands. You'll hear headliners such as Grammy winners Chubby Carrier and the Bayou Swamp Band and Christian artists the Isaacs. An antique car show is part of the fun.

May: **Louisiana Southern Fried Festival** (318-325-9160, www.la southernfriedfestival.com), Ike Hamilton Expo Center, West Monroe. Last part of May. Be on hand to see country music stars line up to entertain your clan. Past performers have included Cody McCarver, Joe Diffie, the Swamp Hippies, and the Bard of the South Rickey Pittman. Special events include a rodeo, a steak cook-off, a classic car show, Kids Western Show, and the Miss Southern Fried Beauty Pageant.

June: **SquireCreek Louisiana Peach Festival** (318-255-2031 or 800-392-9032, www.louisianapeachfestival.org), Ruston Railroad Park, West Park Ave., Ruston. An annual celebration in the fourth week of June, this great festival dates from 1951 when the town decided to fete the area's famous peaches grown for commercial consumption. The Chamber of Commerce, civic clubs, garden clubs, and hundreds of individuals are involved in the event. More than 200 artisans and vendors of all types display their wares at the railroad marketplace and at the Ruston Civic Center. Activities include a parade, antique cars, a rodeo, tennis tournament, 5K run, cooking contest, and a fine arts show presented by the North Central Louisiana Arts Council. Live music takes place nightly and features national and regional headliners. Admission is $5 Friday after 5 P.M. and $5 Saturday daytime, and $10 Saturday after 6 P.M.

October: **Teddy Bear Festival** (888-744-8410, www.ladelta65.org), Tallulah Courthouse Square, Tallulah. In October 1897, President Theodore Roosevelt killed a black bear near Tallulah. Consequently, this annual event celebrates his successful hunt with this festival on the grounds of Courthouse Square. A highlight is always the parade with floats and bands. Musical entertainment includes country and Western, gospel, rhythm and blues, rock, and bluegrass. Often the Tensas National Refuge and Poverty Point State Historic Site offers exhibits on wildlife, hunting, and fishing.

Louisiana Art and Folk Festival (318-649-0726, www.chamberof commercecaldwellparish.com), 103 Main St., Columbia. For a small town, Columbia throws a great party during this annual event. View an art exhibit in the historic Schepis Museum and check out the works at the adult and children's art contest. The Folkways area features woodstove cooking, chair caning, net making, quilting, and other demonstrations. You can sample local cooks' famous biscuits and sausages and tea cakes as well as the usual festival fare. Entertainment includes country, bluegrass, and gospel music groups, cloggers, and choirs.

December: **Christmas on the River** (www.christmasontheriver.org), Monroe and West Monroe. The twin cities of Monroe-West Monroe celebrate

COURTHOUSE SQUARE IN TALLULAH IS THE SITE OF THE ANNUAL TEDDY BEAR FESTIVAL, CELEBRATING THE GREAT OUTDOORS.

Louisiana Office of Tourism

with Christmas on the River the first three weekends in December every year. Festivities along the Ouachita River start after Thanksgiving and every weekend you'll find extended shopping hours, entertainment, carriage rides, and more. In addition to the millions of lights, the schedule includes ice skating, carolers, carriage rides, the Children Museum's, Santa's Village, and other entertainment. The event joins towns in north and central Louisiana for the Holiday Trail of Lights, which encourages people to drive the state's scenic byways during the holidays.

Central Crossroads 2

NATCHITOCHES AREA

TOLEDO BEND/LEESVILLE AREA

ALEXANDRIA/VIDALIA/
MARKSVILLE AREA

INTRODUCTION

In some ways, central Louisiana is a land less traveled. It is the heart of the state, where early explorers staked out claims along rivers teeming with fish and rolling prairies. They came on horseback and in boats—trappers, soldiers; homesteaders—crossing the mighty Mississippi where they found the rich Delta soil. Traveling westward they met with meandering bayous and the unpredictable Red River, rolling hills and deep green pine and hardwood forests. Eventually they arrived at the Sabine River and the unknown place called Texas beyond. The earliest Europeans to settle here dealt not only with Native American clashes and harsh living conditions, but with shifting policies dictated by France and Spain. Yet, they survived. Residents of the Crossroads region today have a deep attachment to their heritage. They call their region CENLA, short for Central Louisiana, with pride. If you have a chance to chat with a local, let him or her share a tale or two about their homeland.

A number of Native American tribes occupied the region, and today visitors find rivers, parishes, and towns bearing their names, such as Avoyelles and Catahoula parishes. Caddo Nation tribes, including the Adai and Natchitoches, were found in north and central Louisiana as well as the Avoyel and Tensa, members of the Natchez Nation, and the Tunica. Known as farmers and mound builders, these tribes were assimilated into the local culture. In some cases, tribes like the Tunica-Biloxi thrived as entrepreneurs and casino owners.

In 1682, the explorer Robert Cavelier de La Salle named the region Louisiana after King Louis XIV. La Salle claimed all lands along the Mississippi River for France. In 1714, Louis Juchereau de St. Denis established a French outpost on the Red River. This became the first European settlement in the territory that later made up the Louisiana Purchase. The community that developed was named after the Natchitoches tribe. France intended the settlement to establish trade with the Spanish in Texas and to limit Spanish advances into the Louisiana colony. During this period, the old San Antonio Road, or El Camino Real, ended near Natchitoches.

By the late 1700s, settlement in the region was growing. Bordering the Mississippi River, the eastern section of the Crossroads region was a natural draw to Europeans seeking business opportunities and adventures. Vidalia was established in 1798 by the Spanish commandant Don Jose Vidal as the Post of Concord. Nearby, the community of Ferriday began with Benjamin Smith, a congregational minister, who settled in New Orleans in 1776. One of his sons, Calvin Smith, made

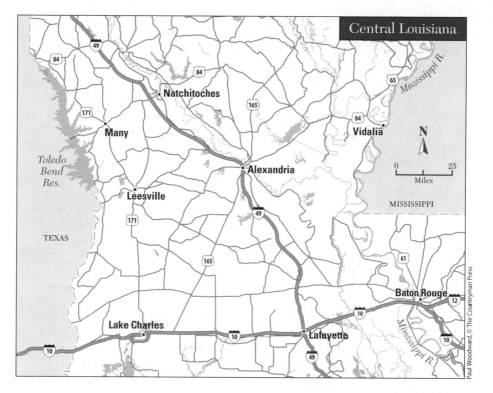

Paul Woodward, © The Countryman Press

his way to Adams County, Mississippi, which was across from what became Concordia Parish. Calvin Smith's two daughters married two Ferridays, Joe and William. By 1827 a plantation in the Vidalia area was being operated by J. C. Ferriday.

An American from Pittsburg, Alexander Fulton received a land grant from Spain. In 1805, he and a partner, Thomas Harris Maddox, founded the town of Alexandria on the Red River in the center of the region. Farther south, Marc Eliche, a Jewish Italian trader, established a trading post about 1794, which became Marksville. He later donated land that became Courthouse Square, still the center of the town. French, French Acadians and Americans settled here. Today, the city is the home of the Tunica-Biloxi Tribe, which operates the successful Paragon Casino Resort. Plantations in this eastern area thrived and today agriculture and tourism are major factors in the economy.

In 1803, a dispute arose between the United States and Spain over the newly purchased Louisiana Territory. Neither side wanted to go to war. So the American General James Wilkinson and the Spanish Lieutenant Colonel Simon de Herrera, the two military commanders in the region, signed an agreement in 1806 declaring the disputed territory a judicial neutral ground until their governments established a boundary. Although the agreement was not ratified by either government, it was mostly respected by the local authorities. However, the agreement was vague. The Calcasieu River, then known as the Arroyo Hondo, and the Sabine River were named the eastern and western boundaries, respectively. The area was declared off-limits to soldiers of both countries and it was stipulated that no settlers would be permitted in the no-man's land of the neutral ground. But it didn't take long for people to move in; some simply squatted on unclaimed land. Wild and lawless, the area also attracted an array of ne'er-do-wells, including military deserters, exiles, and an assortment of outlaws. The area became notorious and dangerous to travelers. Finally, in 1810 and 1812, the two governments sent military expeditions in to get rid of the outlaws. The Adams-Onis Treaty of 1819, ratified in 1821, recognized the U.S. claim and things became more orderly. Now, the spectacular Toledo Bend Reservoir forms a magnificent lake and recreational area in the once-disputed territory. It remains rural, a haven for fishermen, golfers, and outdoorsmen. Just southeast of the lake, Fort Polk at Leesville is a major U.S. Army installation with an impressive history that's linked to local communities.

Within a short drive of Toledo Bend Reservoir and Fort Polk are several units of the Kisatchie National Forest. Outdoor enthusiasts can enjoy any number of day-use and overnight camping sites that are open to the public, making this a recreational haven. Hidden in the bayous beneath the bald cypress groves and old-growth pine lies a world of natural beauty, excitement, learning, recreation, resources, and wildlife in its purest form. Travel through the Crossroads of Louisiana and you will come to love this remarkable landscape.

A YOUNGSTER SWINGS OUT OVER A CREEK IN KISATCHIE NATIONAL FOREST NEAR NATCHITOCHES.
Louisiana Office of Tourism

GUIDANCE Alexandria/Pineville Convention and Visitors Bureau (318-442-9546, 800-551-9546, www.theheartoflouisiana.com), 707 Main St., Alexandria. The Visitors' Center is downtown within walking distance of beautiful overlook of the Red River. Open daily 9 A.M.–5 P.M.

Avoyelles Parish Tourist Commission (318-964-2025, 800-833-4195, www.travelavoyelles.com), 8592 LA 1, Ste. 3, Mansura. The center provides details on parish attractions in Marksville, Paragon Casino Resort, other villages and attractions.

Beauregard Tourist Commission (800-738-5534, www.beauregard tourism.com), 113 South Washington Ave., DeRidder.

Concordia Parish Tourist Commission (318-336-8223, www.seevidalia .com), 1401 Carter St., Vidalia.

Sabine Parish Tourist Commission (800-358-7802 or 318-256-5880), 1601 Texas Highway, Many, or the **Toledo**

Bend Reservoir and Tourist Center (318-256-4114 or 800-259-5253, www.srala-toledo.com) 15091 TX, Many.

Vernon Parish Tourism Commission (337-238-0783 or 800-349-6287, www .venturevernon.com), 201 South Third St., Leesville.

Vidalia Welcome Center (318-336-7008, www.crt.state.la.us), 112 Front St, Vidalia. This state-run Visitors' Welcome Center fronts the Mississippi River, just as you cross the bridge on US 84 to and from Natchez, Mississippi. You'll find maps, brochures, and advice from expert counselors here. The staff is well-informed about local area events and attractions as well as the entire state. Open daily 9 A.M.–5 P.M.

AREA CODES 317 and 337.

MEDICAL EMERGENCIES Byrd Regional Hospital (337-239-9041, www .byrdregional.com), 1020 Fetita Blvd., Leesville.

Franklin Medical Center (318-435-9411, www.fmc-cares.com), 2106 Loop Rd., Winnsboro.

Natchitoches Regional Medical Center (318-214-4200, www.natchitoches hospital.org), 501 Keyser Ave., Natchitoches. The hospital has a 24-hour emergency department.

NATCHITOCHES AREA

Spend a few hours in Natchitoches and you may never want to leave. The town's historic landmark district, fronting onto the Cane River Lake, takes you make to another time. The town and its inhabitants were the inspiration for the novel *Steel Magnolias* and the romantic film of the same name.

Natchitoches dates from 1714, when Louis Juchereau de St. Denis established a French outpost here. Juchereau de St. Denis, a French explorer born in Canada, befriended the Natchitoches Indians, married a Spanish woman named Manuela Sainchez, and represented France in its dealings with the Spanish. Among his other accomplishments, he helped to establish six missions and a presidio in east Texas. His story, like others of his era, begins to explain the early blending of nationalities and cultures in the region. The amazing mix of French and Spanish Creoles, African Creoles, and American Indians formed the culture you find in Natchitoches today.

A HORSE AND BUGGY RIDE MAKES A NICE EXCURSION THROUGH HISTORIC NATCHITOCHES.
Natchitoches CVB

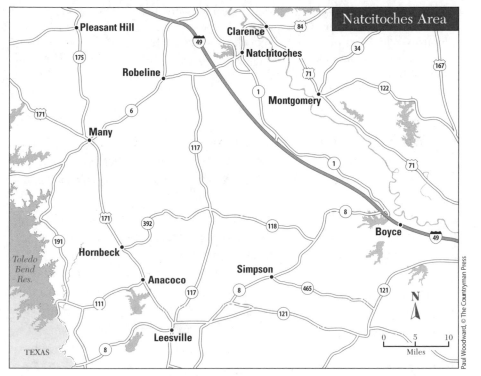

Natcitoches Area

Paul Woodward, © The Countryman Press

The town was named after the Natchitoches Indians, and you pronounce it "na-ka-tosh." But locals will smile however you say the name and graciously invite you to explore the area. The original French settlement lay south of the current town center. The Louisiana territory became Spanish and eventually American following the Louisiana Purchase, and the town moved north to Front Street. Much of the historic architecture has been preserved. The shifting Red River left Natchitoches behind, protecting it from 20th-century development but leaving an old channel that became beautiful Cane River Lake. The long, narrow lake has the characteristics of a stream and creates a serene, romantic setting for the town center and the homes on either side of its banks. Houses along Front and Jefferson streets and others nearby still have wonderful architectural features from the 1800s and early 1900s. Many are surrounded by lovely lawns landscaped with old roses, azaleas, and other heritage shrubs. If you choose to stay in a bed & breakfast in this area, you can enjoy evening or morning strolls to the Lakefront Park. It's an asset that has served the town well, attracting new residents as well as tourists who almost always return. Adding youthful energy to the community are students from Northwestern State University, founded in 1884 as the Louisiana State Normal School. The campus, not far from the historic district, is also home of the Louisiana School for Math, Science and the Arts, a residential high school for sophomores, juniors, and seniors. The scenic beauty of the community and the fascinating sites in and around it have attracted the film industry. In addition to *Steel Magnolias, The Horse Soldiers,* and *Man on the Moon* were filmed here.

Don't worry about finding the "right" meal in Natchitoches. Dining options here range from Southern to Creole to Cajun to all ethnic groups. Bite into a famous Natchitoches meat pie to enjoy the town's signature dish. If you're looking for an authentic Louisiana souvenir, head to a shop like the Gingerbread House or Fancy Stitches.

CREOLE

The term *Creole* can be confusing because it is used in various ways. Search for an accurate description and you'll find any number of answers. The website for the Cane River Creole National Historical Site explains the term this way:

"The term 'Creole' means many things to many people. Creole, used in its original sense, is derived from the Portuguese *crioulo,* meaning 'native to this place.' In 18th-century Louisiana, Creole referred to locally born Spaniards, French and enslaved people. After the Louisiana Purchase, Creole was used to differentiate between those native to Louisiana and those who were Anglo-American. Consequently, French-speaking white residents of Louisiana were also considered Creole. Today, the term Creole commonly refers to a mixture of predominantly French, African and Spanish traits with traces of American Indian culture. It is the intense pride in and attachment to one's ancestry and culture that is key to understanding what it means to be Creole. This manifests itself in architecture, religious practices, food, and language."

OAKLAND PLANTATION, PART OF CANE RIVER CREOLE NATIONAL HISTORICAL PARK, INTERPRETS THE LIFE AND CULTURE OF PEOPLE IN THE CANE RIVER AREA.
Natchitoches CVB

In discussing food, you'll discover that Creole takes on an additional meaning. Creole dishes are more sophisticated (often with delicate sauces), while Cajun cuisine is often described as country cooking with locally grown and caught ingredients like crawfish or alligator. Louisiana restaurants often serve dishes of both styles, or blend the flavors in newly created dishes.

You must plan to wander about. Numerous Creole plantation homes are open daily for tours and the Cane River National Heritage Area has outdoor activities including fishing, hiking, and walking. For something really different, visit a fish hatchery or an alligator park. If you come for a festival, be prepared for music, laughter, and brilliant lights. The monthlong Christmas festival is famed, and here's a tip: Skip the opening week and come a week or two later, when it's every bit as much fun and less crowded.

GUIDANCE **Natchitoches Convention and Visitors Bureau** (800-259-1714 or 318-352-8072, www.natchitoches.net), 781 Front St., Natchitoches. The Visitors' Welcome Center, where you can pick up maps, advice on lodging and attractions, is right on Front Street. Open daily 9 A.M.–5 P.M.

GETTING THERE Natchitoches is 71 miles southeast of Shreveport via I-49. There's just one exit to the city via LA 3228. LA 1 runs through town. The major east-west highway, US 84, connects Natchitoches with Logansport and Texas to the west and with Winnfield and eventually Natchez, Mississippi, to the east.

✳ Cities, Towns, and Villages

Visiting **Winnfield** (US 164 and US 84, www.cityof winnfield.com) is taking a step back in time. Rich in stories about outlaws, Indians, railroad men, oil men, and above all politicians, the town has been home to three governors: Huey P. Long, Earl K. Long, and O. K. Allen. The Louisiana Political Museum (in the Old L & A Depot) contains the Louisiana Political Hall of Fame, where you can hear speeches made by the Long brothers. In March, the city hosts Uncle Earl's Hog Dog Trials, the Super Bowl of hog dog baying. The Louisiana Forest Festival in April is a three-day event with timber-related activities including log loading, log

MELROSE PLANTATION NEAR NATCHITOCHES WAS DEVELOPED IN THE EARLY 1800S BY A FRANCO-AFRICAN CREOLE FAMILY

Natchitoches CVB

rolling, bow-sawing, and rope climbing. Check out the food booths, family oriented activities, and children's rides.

Isle Brevelle (2250 LA 484) is a community made up of descendants of French and Spanish Colonials, Africans, Native Americans, and Anglo Americans who lived in an isolated area between Cane River and Bayou Brevelle. St. Augustine Catholic Church is believed to be the oldest church built by free people of color for their own use. It was established by Augustin Metoyer, the owner of Melrose Plantation, with the aid of his brother Louis. The annual church festival in October features self-guided tours of the church and cemetery. Authentic Creole cuisine includes chicken gumbo, meat pies, boudin balls, and homemade cakes. The event serves as a reunion for area families.

Goldonna (LA 156 and LA 479) was once the site of large salt licks, and the community was a major salt supplier for Confederate forces during the Civil War. The Rails to Trails project publicizes outdoor recreational trails, and the area is also popular for hiking, biking, and ATV riding. The Drake Salt Works Festival and Trail Ride the first Saturday in September is popular for its homemade ice cream contest and food.

✴ To See

✄ **Adai Indian Nation Cultural Center** (318-472-1007 or 877-472-1007, www.adaiindiannation.com), 4460 LA 485, Robeline. Experience a day in the life of the Adai Caddo Indians. Visit historic dwellings, traditional dances, and crafts. There's a gift shop and food court. Open 9 A.M.–5 P.M. daily.

ST. AUGUSTINE CATHOLIC CHURCH AT ISLE BREVELLE WAS FOUNDED BY IN 1803 BY NICHOLAS AUGUSTIN METOYER, A FREED SLAVE.
Natchitoches CVB

✄ ✎ **Bayou Pierre Alligator Park** (318- 354-0001, www.alligatorpark.net), 380 Old Bayou Pierre Rd., Natchitoches. Really fun. The family oriented park features Cajun music and cuisine along with lots of hungry alligators. Covered walkways and platforms are perfect for watching and feeding the gators. Children also love Jungle Town, Turtle Town, Reptile Town and the feeding zoo. After feeding the gators, head for the snack shop for gator kabobs and "swamp water" (fruit punch). The gift shop offers alligator boots, belts, jewelry, and novelties.

✄ ✎ **Cane River Creole National Historical Park** (318-352-0383, www.nps.gov/cari), Oakland Plantation, 4386 LA 494, Bermuda, and Magnolia Plantation, 5549 LA 119, Derry. Dedicated to the distinct Creole culture of the Cane River Lake area, this is a

Natchitoches CVB

A COSTUMED INTERPRETER PLAYS A
MERCENERY AT FORT ST. JEAN BAPTISTE
STATE HISTORIC SITE IN NATCHITOCHES.

remarkable site. Wander through the grounds of Oakland and Magnolia plantations, both of which still have many original structures. See hand-hewn cypress beams, ancient bousillage walls and weathered fencerows, carpenter and blacksmith shops, pigeonniers, and tenant houses. You can pick up a map to reach these sites, but a GPS navigational system will serve you better. To reach Oakland Plantation, take I-49 to Exit 127, Flora/Cypress. Head east on LA 120 toward Cypress. Cross LA 1 onto LA 494. The parking lot and entrance pavilion for Oakland is 4.5 miles east of LA 1 on the left. To reach Magnolia Plantation, take I-49 to Exit 119, Derry. Head east on LA 119. Cross over LA 1 and proceed for 2 miles. The plantation grounds are on the right. The main house at Magnolia is privately owned and closed to the public.

✎ ⚬ **Fort St. Jean Baptiste State Historic Site** (318-357-3101 or 888-677-7853, www.lastateparks.com), 155 Rue Jefferson, Natchitoches. Situated on Cane River Lake near the location of the original fort, this site is absolutely fascinating. Based on authentic plans and archival research, 18th-century building techniques were used in replicating the fort. All the hinges and latches were handmade at a nearby foundry. Site interpreters regale visitors with stories of life here in the late 1700s and early 1800s. Periodically, the site hosts living history programs and encampments. Open 9 A.M.–5 P.M.

Historic Cemeteries (318-352-8072), 321 Second St., Natchitoches. Believed to be the oldest cemetery in the Louisiana Purchase Territory, the **American Cemetery** contains graves dating from Colonial times. Visitors will find the names of Natchitoches's pioneer families, including Prud'homme, Cloutier, Roquier, DeBlieux, and others. Equally interesting are the **Catholic Cemetery** on Fifth St. and the **Jewish Cemetery** on Martin Luther King Dr., formerly Lee St.

Immaculate Conception Catholic Church (318-352-3422), 613 Second St., Natchitoches. The history of the church begins in 1716 or 1717 when the Franciscan priest Antonio Margil de Jesus walked 21 miles from the Spanish mission at Los Adaes to say Mass at the French Fort St. Jean Baptiste in Natchitoches. The first chapel was called St. Francis and numerous churches were built over the years. The church was renamed Immaculate Conception in 1856. Construction began on the present structure in 1857 and finished in 1892. All the interior fittings and furnishings, except the pews, were imported from France, and the twin stained-glass windows in the rear of the church came from Austria. An extensive restoration was completed in 1996. Across the street are the Rectory and the Bishop Martin Museum containing records dating from 1724 and church artifacts. Call for information on services.

Louisiana Political Museum (318-628-5928, www.lapoliticalmuseum), 499 East Main St., Winnfield. When some people think about Louisiana, the first thing that comes to mind is its colorful politicians. Winnfield, north of Natchitoches via US

84, is the birthplace of three Louisiana governors, Huey P. Long, Earl K. Long, and O. K. Allen. The Louisiana Political Museum and Hall of Fame highlights the careers of more than a hundred of the state's leading political figures. You can find newspapers, magazines, portraits, and personal artifacts relating to politicians and political pundits, including Zachary Taylor, Edward Douglass White, James "Jimmie" Davis, Lindy Boggs, Jimmy Fitzmorris, W. Fox McKeithen, Edwin Edwards, James Carville, Kathleen Babineaux Blanco, Mary Landrieu, and Melvin "Kip" Holden. In January, the museum hosts its annual Hall of Fame induction ceremony in the Winnfield Civic Center. Open 9 A.M.–5 P.M. Mon.–Fri., Saturday by appointment. Free.

Melrose Plantation (318-379-0055, www.aphnatchitoches.net), 533 LA 119, Melrose. The story of Melrose Plantation begins with Marie Therese Coincoin, an enslaved African American woman who was sold to Claude Thomas Pierre Metoyer, who eventually freed her and many of her children. She was head of a family of 14 children, four of whom were black and 10 of Franco-African blood. Coincoin and her sons acquired land grants, cleared the property, and developed a successful and wealthy plantation operation. They built Yucca House (circa 1800), and the African House, perhaps the only Congo-style structure left in the United States. The Big House was constructed about 1833. In the economic upheaval of the 1840s, the property passed to white ownership. Under the ownership of John Hampton and Cammie Garrett Henry, Melrose became an artists' and writers' colony. If you tour the structures you'll see wonderful original paintings by Clementine Hunter, a one-time Melrose cook who in the late 20th century emerged as Louisiana's most celebrated primitive artist.

✍ ↝ **Natchitoches National Fish Hatchery** (318-352-5324), 615 South Dr., Natchitoches. Anglers of all ages will enjoy seeing the hatchery, with its 16 tanks of fish species native to the southeastern United States. The Hatchery is a warm-water center devoted to spawning, hatching, and rearing young fish, called fingerlings. The fingerlings are raised to a size and age that gives them the best chance at survival in the wild. In addition to fish, you can see alligators and turtles, including the rare albino snapping turtle. The Hatchery houses an aquarium and a classroom used for grades K-12, and is equipped with microscopes and video teaching capabilities.

✍ ❀ **Rebel State Historic Site** (888-677-34600 or 318-357-3101, www.lastate parks.com), 1260 LA 1221, Marthaville. People in this rural area love country and gospel music, making it the ideal site for the Louisiana Country Music Museum. The museum's design resembles the shape of a treble cleff, and its displays focus on folk music traditions. Visitors can see costumes, instruments, and photos donated by many performers. The amphitheater is a showplace for concerts. The park has a picnic area with barbeque pits and a pavilion with kitchen facilities for groups that is available on a first-come, first-served basis. The site is 25 miles west of Natchitoches and I-49 and 3 miles northwest of Marthaville.

Roque House (318-352-8072, www.natchitoches.net), Rue Beauport on Cane River bank. This historic home is one of the best examples of the Creole style of French architecture in the Cane River area. Constructed in typical French Colonial fashion with hand-hewn cypress and bousillage fill (a mix of Spanish moss, animal hair, and mud), the structure is topped with an overhanging hipped roof of cypress shingles. The house has three original rooms and a plank lean-to in the rear. The double fireplace contains some of the original bricks, but many were broken when the house was moved from its original site in 1967. The house is currently owned by the Natchitoches Historic Foundation.

Trinity Episcopal Church (318-352-3113, www.trinityparish.info), 533 Second St., Natchitoches. Trinity Episcopal Church predates the Civil War. Regular services in the current edifice began on Ash Wednesday, 1858. The Gothic-Norman building features laminated wood arches that resemble a wagon vault. The wood flooring is of hand-cut timber. General John Watts de Peyster of Tivoli, New York, who commanded Federal troops at Grand Ecore on the Red River before the Civil War, gave a large amount of money for the building in memory of his daughter Maria, who died of yellow fever. His other gifts to the church, which are still in use, were an organ, tower bell, and communion vessels. Check the website for service times.

✱ Green Spaces

↦ **Beau Jardin Park** (318-352-2746, www.natchitochesla.gov), Front St., Natchitoches. Located on the north end of Natchitoches Riverfront Park, Beau Jardin, also known as the Virginia Baker Park, is a picturesque new park with a delightful garden and water feature. The idyllic setting is a perfect spot for simply contemplating the town's beauty or even planning a wedding.

✎ ↦ **Cane River National Heritage Area** (318-356-5555, www.nps.gov/crha /index.htm), 452 Jefferson St., Natchitoches. Established by Congress in 1994, the Cane River Heritage Area is a largely rural, agricultural area between I-49 and the Red River. Roads within the central corridor begin just south of Natchitoches and extend on both sides of Cane River Lake for about 35 miles. The heritage area includes the Cane River Creole National Historical Park, where visitors can roam the spacious grounds for hours and where programs vary from history to agriculture and science. The area includes three state historic sites and other historic plantations, homes, and churches. Keep in mind that Louisiana's climate is hot and humid in summer and usually wet and cold in winter and dress appropriately for the seasons, with comfortable walking shoes in any weather.

✎ ↦ **Longleaf Scenic Byway** (318-352-2568, www.byways.org/explore/byways). From I-49 take Exit 119 toward Derry. Follow LA 119 about 5.5 miles south to FH 59 (Longleaf Trail). The 17-mile byway takes motorists through part of the Kisatchie Ranger District of the Kisatchie National Forest. The route follows a high ridge through a rugged hills area, connecting with LA 117. Along the way, you'll find access to several recreation spots. The trail crosses Kisatchie Bayou, designated a Louisiana Natural and Scenic stream. Be sure to stop at Longleaf Vista, where you'll find great views and a picnic area. In spring, you'll see an abundance of flowers in bloom. While the trees don't turn brilliant colors in Louisiana during fall, you will see muted shades of yellow, amber, and red in parts of the Kisatchie forest.

✎ **Riverfront Park** (318-352-8072, www.explorenatchitoches.com), Front St., downtown Natchitoches on Cane River Lake. One of the most delightful city parks in Louisiana, Riverfront follows the gentle slope from the top of Front Street to the edge of the lake. Carefully maintained lawns and old oaks with spreading limbs provide a perfect place for community gatherings from art shows to rollicking music festivals and fireworks displays. People of all ages gather here to watch fireworks on the Fourth of July and during weekends during the annual Christmas Festival of Lights. In between, you'll see visitors strolling along the lake and students from Northwestern State University taking a break from their studies.

✳ To Do

FISHING There are numerous fishing areas in Natchitoches and the outer areas of the parish. Trapping, fishing, and hunting are possible in many rivers, streams, bayous, and lakes. There are 129,174 acres of Kisatchie National Forest in Natchitoches and Winn parishes. Fishing spots in Natchitoches include Cane River Lake, Sibley Lake, and the Red River. Spots in outlying areas of the parish are Kisatchie National Park, Black Lake, Clear Lake, Saline Lake, and Saline Bayou.

Fishing and hunting licenses may be purchased at certain retail establishments or parish sheriff's offices. For details, contact the Louisiana Wildlife and Fisheries at 888-765-2602 or www.wlf.louisiana.gov.

GOLF ♂ ↝ **Cypress Bend Resort** (318-352-5532, www.cypressbend.com), 2000 Cypress Bend Parkway, LA 191, Many. The golf course and conference center on Toledo Bend Lake is 45 minutes from Natchitoches. The course, with breathtaking views, is designed to challenge all playing levels. Because it is curled around one of the lake's many inlets, the 18-hole course features 10 holes along the water and six with shots across the water. Surrounding forests and undulating greens add to the challenge. The facility includes a hotel, pro shop, spa, and restaurant (see also the Lodging listings for the Toledo Bend area). Open 7 A.M.–9 P.M. daily.

Northwestern Hills Golf Course (318-357-3207, www.thegolfcourses.net), 6604 LA 1, Natchitoches. The layout of this 18-hole regulation public course is good, but it needs better grooming. It's a fun way to spend a few hours outdoors. Inexpensive green fees run about $25. Open 8 A.M.–dusk.

HIKING/HORSEBACK RIDING ♂ ↝ 🐎 **Caroline Dorman Trail** (318-472-1840), Kisatchie Ranger District, National Kisatchie Forest, off Longleaf Scenic Byway, Forest LA 59. The Caroline Dorman Trail is named for the first woman employed in forestry in the United States. Born at Briarwood, the family home in Natchitoches Parish, she became a renowned horticulturist, naturalist, preservationist, and author. The trail provides 10.5 miles of hiking, biking, and horseback riding. It's not a loop trail, but ends just short of the Kisatchie Bayou Recreation Complex. Visitors can park at the trailhead just off the Longleaf scenic byway. The trail passes a forest thick with beeches, oaks, hickories, gums, and magnolias mixed with loblolly pine. The best time to see wild azaleas and dogwoods is late March and early April. Among the wildlife you might see are squirrels, nutria, raccoons, foxes, deer, armadillos, and owls.

Gum Springs Horse Trail (318-628-4664), 9671 US 84 West, Winnfield. Enjoy a horseback ride through the forest on two developed trails about 8 miles west of Winnfield in Winnfield Parish. Sections of both trails pass through Keiffer Prairies, where native grasses and cedar trees predominate. Primitive camp sites with fire rings, three corrals, hitching posts, a pond for watering animals, and drinking water are available. Contact Winn Ranger District for more information.

SPORTS National Shooting Range (318-356-9457), near the Red River and Grand Ecore Bridge on LA 6. Affiliated with the National Rifle Association, the National Sporting Clays Association, and the National Skeet Shooting Association, this is a rifle, pistol, and archery range. It is designed for sporting clays, lighted skeet, and trap shooting. Shotgun practice and instruction are available.

Northwestern State University (318-357-6467, www.nsudemons.com), 715 University Parkway, Natchitoches. The Demons compete in Division 1-AA football as a member of the southland Conference. Fielding 15 intercollegiate sports teams, NSU is home to the Louisiana Sports Hall of Fame, which honors a long list of athletes who have excelled in competitive sports throughout Louisiana and the world.

✳ Lodging

Natchitoches is famous for its attractive, romantic bed & breakfasts. Choose between spacious antebellum mansions and beautiful, cozy cottages from an even earlier era. The city is fortunate to have a number of chain hotels that cater to businessmen and travelers seeking clean, competent, and fast service. Those situated at the junction of LA 6 and I-49 are particularly convenient for people traveling through.

GUESTS ENJOY THE ROMANTIC BALCONY AT A B&B IN NATCHITOCHES, THE HOME OF "STEEL MAGNOLIAS."

Natchitoches CVB

Cane River Cottage & Guesthouse (318-663-8239, www.canerivercottage .com), 228 Pratt Lane, Natchitoches. Situated on scenic Cane River Lake, this B&B is 15 minutes from downtown. Each of the two buildings offers three bedrooms. The Cottage features a fully equipped kitchen and a large master bedroom with a king bed and private bath. Two other bedrooms upstairs share a bath and shower. The Guesthouse is fully equipped and includes a medium room. Each of the three bedrooms has a private bath. You can bring your boat to private docks. Expensive.

Chez des Amis (318-352-2647, www.chezdesamis.com), 910 Rue Washington, Natchitoches. When it was built in 1923, the Iglehart residence, an arts and crafts bungalow, was the latest style in Natchitoches. Visit with the resident innkeepers to learn about local architecture, cuisine, and art. Guests have access to the parlor, sitting room, a library of movies on video, a baby grand piano, and the original house library. High-speed wireless Internet is available throughout. No smoking. Low season rates $110 per night and high season. Moderate.

Church Street Inn (318-238-8888 or 800-668-9298, www.churchstinn.com), 120 Church St., Natchitoches. This inn has 20 rooms, each with its own view and personality. Rooms are decorated with hand-carved mahogany furniture and accented with themes taken from the history and culture of Natchitoches. Sit back and relax in the private courtyard with a continental breakfast, and later return for an aperitif before walking a short distance for dinner. Moderate–expensive.

Judge Porter House Bed and Breakfast (318-352-9206 or 800-441-8343, www.judgeporterhouse.com), 321 Second St., Natchitoches. Built in 1912 by Thomas Fitzgerald Porter, the house features 19th-century antiques and cut-crystal chandeliers, queen-sized full tester beds, and private gardens. There are five rooms, each with a private bath. Moderate–expensive.

Log Cabin on Cane River (318-357-0520 and 318-352-6494, www.cabin oncaneriver.com), 614 Williams Ave., Natchitoches. Built in 1935 as a writer's cottage, the log cabin is now a private guest house. It is whimsically decorated, with modern conveniences. It is directly across the river from Front Street and the Riverbank Park. The cabin features a completely equipped kitchen and accommodates four. Children and pets with prior approval. Expensive.

Steel Magnolia House (318-238-2585 or 888-346-4095, www.steel magnoliahouse.com), 320 Jefferson St, Natchitoches. From its involvement in the Civil War, the home is a piece of Southern history and romance. It's primarily known for the on-site filming of the 1989 award-winning classic movie *Steel Magnolias*. The Shelby Room is original to the movie, with pink décor and an antique French bed. A tour of the house includes insight into the filming of the movie. Guests can relax and enjoy rare antiques, peaceful gardens, large guest rooms, and a gourmet breakfast. Expensive.

Violet Hill Bed & Breakfast (866-357-0858, www.violethillbandb.com), 917 Washington St., Natchitoches. The house, built in 1888, is handsomely appointed in cool, relaxing shades. Enjoy the gourmet breakfast by candlelight, porch swings on the veranda, and the gazebo and dock on the riverfront. Moderate.

✳ Where to Eat

EATING OUT Cane River BBQ Bar and Grill (318-352-2600), 1125 Washington St., Natchitoches. This spot specializes in St. Louis–style ribs, steaks, potato salad, fried fish, and burgers. Not far from Front Street, the restaurant attracts the college crowd with a great rear deck overlooking Cane River Lake. Zoning laws don't allow liquor here, but beer is served on tap. Moderate.

🍽 **Lasyone's Meat Pie Kitchen & Restaurant** (318-352-3353, www .lasyones.com), 622 Second St., Natchitoches. The landmark eatery is famous for its meat pies. People from all over the world have stopped here, including Charles Kuralt, Vanna White, and Daryl Hannah. It's been featured in newspapers and magazines in the United States and Europe. The fare is simple. In addition to a meat pie, try the local version of red beans and sausage or chicken and dumplings, both staples in the Louisiana diet. Open for breakfast and lunch, 7 A.M.– 3 P.M. Inexpensive.

🍽 **Mariner's Restaurant** (318-357-1220, www.marinersrestaurant.com), 5948 LA 1, North Pass, Natchitoches. Operated by the Nichols family, this restaurant offers a varied menu of

Natchitoches CVB

DON'T MISS THE ICED TEA AND FAMOUS
NATCHITOCHES MEAT PIE AT LASOYNE'S
RESTAURANT.

seafood, steak, chicken, and lamb.
Local favorites include Black Bayou
shrimp served with crawfish and
pancetta-stuffed chicken. The Cove
Bar and Grill has more than 50 wine
selections. Open 4:30–9:30 P.M.
Mon.–Thurs., and 4:30–10 P.M.
Fri.–Sat. Moderate.

Merci Beaucoup Restaurant (318-
352-1538, www.mercibeaucoup
restaurant.com), 127 Church St., Natchitoches. A delightful atmosphere and
top-flight service make this lunch spot
a great place for a tete-a-tete. The
chicken salad sandwich on a croissant
is well worth trying, and so is the luscious bread pudding. Open 11 A.M.–3
P.M. Pricey, but delicious.

**Papa's Bar & Grill and Mama's
Oyster House** (318-356-5850 or 318-
356-7874, www.mamasoysterhouse
.com), 608 Front St., Natchitoches.
You may want to start with a beer or
chilled drink at Papa's and then walk
next door to Mama's, where someone
will be shucking ice-cold, briny oysters
to order. Papa's has filling hamburgers
and po-boys. Mama's concentrates on
seafood dishes, fried frog legs, and
blackened alligator. Mama's has live
music on weekend nights. Papa's

hours: 11 A.M.–10 P.M., Mon.–Sat.
Mama's hours 11 A.M.–10 P.M.
Mon.–Sat. and 11 A.M.–3 P.M. Sun.
Moderate.

**DINING OUT The Landing
Restaurant & Bar** (318-352-1579,
www.thelandingrestaurantandbar.com),
530 Front St., Natchitoches. This New
Orleans style–restaurant is a premier
dining destination for locals as well as
visitors. Start with fried green tomatoes or crab cake remoulade as an
appetizer. For lunch, you might like
the hot turkey and cheese sandwich
with some sweet potato fries. For a
grand dinner, go for the 14-ounce rib
eye steak with grilled shrimp or the
Ahi Tuna Ruby—grilled tuna with
lump crabmeat, baby shrimp, and
Hollandaise sauce. Hours are 11 A.M.–
10 P.M. Moderate.

❋ Entertainment

The Cove, Mariner's Restaurant
(318-357-1220), LA 1 Bypass, Natchitoches. The Cove at Mariner's is a
warm, traditional bar that attracts an
upscale crowd. It's a perfect place to
relax in the evening with domestic or
imported beer, or mojitos made with
the mariner's own fresh grown mint. If
you're hungry, the bar menu includes
appetizers, sandwiches, and baskets
from the restaurant. There's live entertainment every Friday and Saturday
beginning at 9 P.M.

JJ's Bar and Lounge (318-352-4899),
9501 LA 1, Natchitoches. Entertainment features artists such as the Luke-
jazz Duo.

The Landing Restaurant & Bar
(318-352-1579), 530 Front St., Natchitoches. The Landing is a fun place to
relax for tourists and locals alike. Live
entertainment every Wednesday by
local performers including Steve Wells

and Friends. Open 11 A.M.–10 P.M. Tues.–Sat., 11 A.M.–9 P.M. Sun.

NSU Music & Theater (318-357-6011, www.nsula.edu), 715 University Parkway, Natchitoches. Northwestern State University's Department of Theater and Dance presents student and faculty productions in the 1,400 seat A.A. Fredericks Auditorium, the 125-seat Theatre West, and the Loft Theater, a black box theater. Productions also include Summer Mystery Dinner Theater.

Pioneer Pub (318-352-4884), 812 Washington St., Natchitoches. The pub offers live music by local musicians every Thursday, Friday, and Saturday night. The pub has a great selection of domestic and international beers on tap. The crowd is an interesting mix of

VISITORS ENJOY SHOPPING ON FRONT STREET IN NATCHITOCHES.

Natchitoches CVB

locals. Try burgers, pizza, seafood, and steaks, and enjoy free wireless internet access.

✳ Selective Shopping

Cane River Kitchenware (318-238-3600), 732 Front St., Natchitoches. You'll be drawn into this shop by the aroma of good things cooking inside. You don't have to be a gourmet cook to enjoy shopping for kitchen gadgets and food items. Saleswomen will help you find seasonings and sauces to make dinners extra delicious.

Dickens & Co. (318-352-1993), 524 Front St., Natchitoches. Find furniture, fleur de lis–themed items, fragrance lamps, seasonal gifts, sugared pecans, pralines, and baked goods here. Open 8 A.M.–6 P.M. Mon.–Sat. and 11 A.M.–3 P.M. Sun.

Fancy Stitches (318-354-8864, www.fancystitchesonline.com), 902 East Fifth St., Natchitoches. This shop specializes in custom embroidery, monograms, totes, and handbags. It's a handy spot for picking up something special for grandma or a coworker. Open 10 A.M.–5:30 P.M. Tues.–Fri. and 10 A.M.–2 P.M. Sat.

The Gingerbread House (318-354-6009), 520 Keyser Ave, Natchitoches. A nifty spot to pick up decorative items for the house, baby gifts, and Christmas items. Open 10 A.M.–6 P.M. Mon.–Sat.

Kaffie-Frederick General Mercantile (318-352-2525, www.oldhardware store.com), 516 Front St., Natchitoches. As Louisiana's oldest general store, this place features everything you can remember from the good old days, including hardware, housewares, cookware, and kitchen supplies. You'll find classic toys like Radio Flyer, cast-iron cookware, and copper weather vanes.

Natchitoches Pecans (800-572-5925, www.natchitochespecans.com), 439 Little Eva Rd., Cloutierville. The Pecan Store, owned by the Swanson family, is located on Little Eva Plantation. It gives people a chance to visit a regional agricultural enterprise and to obtain fresh nuts directly from the orchard. You'll find a variety of items, including pecans in the shell, glazed pecans, gift baskets, and pecan cookbooks.

Plantation Treasures, 746 Front St., Natchitoches (318-354-1714, www .plantationtreasures.com). This gift shop in the historic Prudhomme Hughes building carries an array of beautiful items including fleur de lis plates and trays and Clementine Hunter prints.

✷ Special Events

February: **Mardi Gras** in Natchitoches includes the Krewe Dionysus and a parade traveling both sides of Cane River Lake and winding through the historic district. The Krewe of Wag-uns parade is for pet owners and children are invited to participate. Dates and times are announced as Carnival season approaches.

March: **Bloomin' on the Bricks** (866-941-6246, www.natchitoches.net), downtown along Cane River Lake. Sponsored by the Natchitoches Main Street Program, the colorful spring festival gives you a chance to see the beauty of springtime here, with hanging flower baskets and thousands of daffodils and tulips planted along the riverbank. Merchants sell plants, trees, patio furniture, and garden accessories. Other activities include musical entertainment, a children's activity tent, and gardening demonstrations. On the same day, **Art Along the Bricks** on Front St. showcases work by regional artists 9 A.M.–4 P.M.

June: **Melrose Arts & Crafts Festival** (800-259-1714, www.aph natchitoches.net), Melrose Plantation, Natchitoches. One of Louisiana's largest fine arts and crafts fairs, the festival has been in existence for more than 40 years. The two-day event takes place on the grounds of the Big House. People in booths sell local foods and offer respite from the heat with cool liquid refreshments.

July: **Natchitoches/NSU Folk Festival** (318-357-4332, www.nsula.edu /folklife), Prather Coliseum, Northwestern State University. Without doubt, this is one of Louisiana's best folklife festivals. Each year, the two-day event focuses on a different aspect of the state's culture. For example, the 2011 festival highlighted Contemporary Southeastern Indian Culture, and how Louisiana tribes have maintained their arts, music, and lore. In addition to special seminars, the event always salutes Louisiana's legendary folk artists. Part of the program is the Louisiana State Fiddle Championship. Musical entertainment includes bluegrass, gospel, Cajun, rock, and jazz. Admission is $5, 4:30–11:15 A.M. Fri., and $8, Sat. 8 A.M.–11 P.M. No admission for children under age 12.

September: **Cane River Zydeco Festival & Poker Run** (318-652-0079 or 354-1077), Downtown Stage in the historic district. Held the first weekend in September, this two-day event features zydeco bands, a dance contest, and a poker run through Natchitoches Parish. The event is sponsored by the Magnolia State Police Officers Association and the Magnolia State Peace Officers Association. Proceeds benefit community functions.

Natchitoches Meat Pie Festival (www.meatpiefestival.com), downtown riverbank along Cane River Lake. The festival celebrates the town's famous dish with two days of festivities. Activities begin on Friday with performances by regional bands. The fun continues Saturday beginning at 10 A.M. with a Motorcycle River Run. There is a large children's activity area with games, arts and crafts, inflatable jumps, and more. The public is invited to bring lawn chairs and enjoy the free event.

October: **Fall Pilgrimage/Tour of Homes** (800-259-1714, www.aph natchitoches.net), tickets sold at 781 Front St., Natchitoches. In 1954, the Association for the Preservation of Historic Natchitoches began the Fall Pilgrimage to raise money for preservation projects. The association owns Melrose Plantation and the Lemee House in Natchitoches. Exceptionally well-organized, the event, usually held in early October, includes a plantation tour, a city tour, and an evening candlelight tour. Visitors are welcomed into a number of private homes and get to see exceptional preservation projects as well as family antiques and memorabilia.

December: **Christmas Festival of Lights** (800-259-1714, www.christmas festival.com), on Cane River Lake and throughout the Downtown Historic District. Get ready. This is the most amazing Christmas festival you can imagine. It begins November 19 and lasts until January 6 and involves the entire town. Sponsors include the Natchitoches Area Chamber of Commerce, the Natchitoches Convention and Visitors Bureau, and numerous businesses. The event draws more than 500,000 visitors each year for the parade, live entertainment, and fireworks every Saturday and on New Year's Eve. The festival started in 1927 with the display of holiday lights downtown. Through the years, it has expanded to include elaborate lighted set pieces along the riverfront. Fireworks were added in the late 1930s. In the 1950s came the addition of a contest to select a theme and the selection of Miss Merry Christmas and the Christmas Belles. Today there is literally a festival every weekend throughout the holiday season, with live entertainment, carolers, a food fair, an arts and crafts show, and nightly tours by streetcar or carriages. If you plan on going, a schedule is posted on the website. Make your lodgings reservations months in advance.

TOLEDO BEND/LEESVILLE AREA

With towering pine trees and hardwood forests, the western part of central Louisiana is one of the most scenic areas of the state. US 171 running between I-20 and I-10 takes travelers to one of the nation's largest lakes, small rural villages, and a major U.S. military base. The Kisatchie National Forest operates two ranger districts in the area: Kisatchie Ranger District and Calcasieu Ranger District. Numerous camping and day-use areas attract outdoorsmen year-round. Spectacular Toledo Bend Reservoir and Sabine River form the shared boundary between Louisiana and Texas. Barely tamed, with acres and acres of woodlands and a massive man-made lake, the region is a place to commune with nature, search for birds, hike for hours, or just get away from humanity for a while. Here, outlaws once hid out and brave pioneer families dared to settle in no man's land. Now, it welcomes all who want to share in its beauty and bounty.

GETTING THERE When Toledo Bend Reservoir was created by building a dam across the Sabine River, thousands of acres of farm and timberlands were flooded, creating innumerable inlets and coves. You need a four-wheel vehicle to reach the lake itself, and a current global positioning system is a must. A GPS is also invaluable if you plan to camp or enjoy outdoor activities in any of Kisatchie National Forest's seven ranger districts in Louisiana. Along the way, pick up current maps at welcome centers and service stations.

By car: If driving from Shreveport, the northern point of Toledo Bend Reservoir can be reached by driving US 171 south and taking US 84 west to Logansport. Further south, US 171 crosses LA 6 at Many. If you follow LA 6 west it becomes TX 21 when it crosses the bridge at Toledo Bend Lake. If driving from I-10 at Lake Charles, take US 171 north through Leesville and follow back roads to fishing resorts along Toledo Bend Reservoir. At Leesville, you can follow LA 28 east to reach I-49 at Alexandria.

By air: If you are flying to western central Louisiana for business or recreational purposes, we recommend **Alexandria International Airport**, about 44 miles from the center of Leesville. The **Lake Charles Regional Airport** is 70 miles from Leesville. The **Leesville City Airport** (337-238-5968 or 337-208-2219, www.leesvilleairport.com) is a general aviation, uncontrolled airport for use by small planes. Services and facilities include a pilot's lounge, terminal, aircraft parking ramp and tie downs, restrooms, and public telephones. **Beauregard Regional**

TOLEDO BEND RESERVOIR: A TWO-STATE PROJECT

In 1949, the Texas State Legislature created the Sabine River Authority of Texas. One year later, the Louisiana State Legislature created the Sabine River Authority, State of Louisiana. Together, these two bodies were given the duties of conserving and developing the waters of the Sabine River Basin for beneficial purposes.

In 1955, the seeds of Toledo Bend as we enjoy it today were sown by both authorities cooperating under a memorandum of agreement. Studies were undertaken and the results clearly indicated the feasibility of such a project.

Toledo Bend is the largest man-made body of water in the South, and the fifth largest in surface acres in the United States. From the dam site, the reservoir extends 65 miles upriver to Logansport, Louisiana, and inundates land in Sabine, Shelby, Panola, and Newton counties in Texas, and Sabine and DeSoto parishes in Louisiana. It was constructed for the purposes of water supply, hydroelectric power generation, and recreation. In all, the lake normally covers an area of 185,000 acres.

Airport (337-463-8250) 1220 First Ave., DeRidder, open 7:30 A.M.–5 P.M. Mon.–Fri. and 7 A.M.–5 P.M. Sat.–Sun., has a colorful history. The property was the site of the Galloway Sawmill in 1912. In the 1930s, two earthen runways were built as a WPA project and Beauregard Field was used occasionally by barnstorming pilots. In the summer of 1940, the field was used extensively during the Louisiana Maneuvers. A general aviation airport, the former Army air base serves private, corporate, agricultural, and military aircraft. There is no commercial airline service. A concrete airplane parking ramp is adjacent to the main hangar and has tie downs for 200 aircraft. Fuel and courtesy vehicles are available. These regional airports are particularly useful during hurricane season, when many aircraft use them as an evacuation location.

✷ Towns and Villages

Beyond the shores of Toledo Bend Lake you'll find rural Louisiana, where small communities celebrate their heritage with lively festivals. The area contains two outstanding state parks and a remarkable botanical garden. Follow trails through units of Kisatchie Forest. Take a day trip to Natchitoches or to the Texas towns of Hemphill and Milam. An antiquing trail 30 miles west and north may lead to special finds. When you see Hodges Garden State Park, you may want to stay overnight. Villages in the area include Zwolle, Fisher, Florien, and Ebarb, each of which becomes a hotbed of activity during annual festivals.

Leesville, named for Robert E. Lee, is the seat of Vernon Parish and the home of Fort Polk, one of the largest military installations in the United States. The U.S. Army base takes its name from Leonidas Polk, the first Episcopal bishop in

On October 5, 1961, two state governors, Jimmie Davis of Louisiana and Price Daniel of Texas, officially launched construction on the dam and reservoir that link the two states. The massive project was 12 years in making. Land was acquired and by 1969, the Toledo Bend Dam Spillway and power plant were complete. The states built the dam without any assistance from the federal government.

With 186,000 acres and some of the best fishing in Louisiana, the lake provides incredible recreational opportunities. Whether you're a sportsman looking for a trophy or you just want a family getaway, Toledo Bend is a great choice. It's known for its large bass as well as other fish. The reservoir is extremely popular for freshwater fishing and many clubs host tournaments.

Private and public facilities are available, as are boating, fishing, swimming, camping, hunting, and sightseeing. The lake is best suited to shallow draft powerboats because there are still many trees and stumps in the bed. Although there are a number of well-marked boat lanes that have been cleared, boaters must be cautious even there. Use extreme caution when off the lanes and watch for stumps and trees as well as floating logs.

Louisiana and a Confederate general. Thousands of soldiers learned the basics of combat at the base during the World War II Louisiana Maneuvers in 1939–40. The fort was used by the military during the Korean War and then closed, but it was reactivated during the 1961 Berlin Crisis. It became an infantry training center in 1962. Currently Fort Polk, which encompasses more than 200,000 acres, provides contingency training for the Army's light infantry and special operations forces and deploys home station and reserve forces. It's easy to understand why the fort is called the Home of Heroes. With the constant movement of soldiers and their dependents in and out of Leesville and Vernon Parish, local residents pride themselves on welcoming strangers. Leesville's Downtown Historic District contains a number of buildings dating from the early 1900s. Take a short drive to see the Benson H. Lyons House, circa 1900, with its wraparound gallery and elaborate woodwork, and the Beaux-Arts Vernon Parish Courthouse, designed with Corinthian columns and a gazebo on the north side. Stop by the Museum of West Louisiana to learn more about the culture of west central Louisiana.

DeRidder, south of Leesville, also has connections to Fort Polk and the Louisiana Maneuvers. The first peacetime draft had barely passed Congress when the need arose for a place where soldiers could feel at home. DeRidder became the site of the War Memorial Civic Center, the first building constructed for and donated to the United Services Organization in 1941. Dozens of volunteers from the city flocked to man the kitchen, help write letters, and provide dancing partners for the horde of displaced servicemen. The U.S.O. was open to any enlisted man in good standing, and no drinking or fighting was allowed. Local girls were carefully chaperoned to and from each event. The building, located at the corner of LA 27 and 7th Street, is now used as a Civic Center. DeRidder also boasts a collection of historic homes, including the famous Gothic revival building known as the Hanging Jail (check the To See listings).

The **Toledo Bend area**, which includes Sabine and Vernon Parishes, is extremely rural. Toledo Bend Lake on the western border is mostly surrounded by undeveloped land, much of which is the Sabine National Forrest. **Many**, the Sabine Parish seat, serves as a handy center for area residents and travelers seeking supplies. The nearby town of **Zwolle** received its name from a Dutch investor, Jan De Goeijen, who named the town after his hometown in Holland. Its claim to fame is the Zwolle Tamale Fiesta, which celebrates the area's Spanish and Indian heritage. **Fisher**, created by the Long Leaf Lumber Company in 1899, is what remains of a sawmill town built in the heyday of lumbering in Louisiana. The community comes to life in May during Fisher Sawmill Days. **Florien**, established in the late 1800s, was a whistle-stop community on the Kansas City Southern Railroad. Each year, the village hosts the Sabine Free State Festival with food dancing and an operational grist mill. Nearby is Hodges Gardens State Park, with magnificent landscapes and camping facilities.

✳ To See

✐ ❦ **Beauregard Parish Jail** (377-463-5534 or 800-738-5534, www.beauregard tourism.com), 201 West First St., DeRidder. Built in 1915, this imposing Gothic jail is celebrated in tradition and song as "The Hangman's Jail." Architecturally innovative for its time, it was designed with a shower, toilet, and window in each cell. The jail could house more than 50 prisoners. The lockup was the location of a double execution in 1928, and it's little wonder that the place is supposed to be haunted. There is a tunnel leading from the courthouse to the jail. Open 1–5 P.M. Tues.–Sun.

✐ ❦ **Fort Jesup State Historic Site** (318-256-4117 or 888-677-5378, www.crt .state.la.us), 32 Geohagan Rd., Many. Imagine being here when the nation was young and raw and Fort Jesup was on the frontier. After the territorial boundary between Louisiana and Texas was finally fixed at the Sabine River in 1819, the United States built Fort Jesup in 1822. As a lieutenant colonel, Zachary Taylor established a post here and named it for his friend Brigadier General Thomas Sidney Jesup. Taylor's troops established law and order in the Neutral Ground. In 1845, half the U.S. Army traveled through the fort en route to war with Mexico. The fort was abandoned in 1846 when it was no longer needed as a border outpost. The only original structure still standing is the kitchen, where army cooks prepared the troops' meals. You can see their cooking implements and imagine what a meal was like for the soldiers stationed here, then tour the reconstructed officers' quarters to see exhibits explaining what life was like in the early 1800s. The building was constructed with the assistance of historians from the Army Quartermasters General Office and the National Trust for Historic Preservation. From here, officers formally courted young ladies in Natchitoches, honed their fighting skills in drills, and prepared to lead troops into battle in far-away Mexico. Later some of these same men fought on both sides of the Civil War. Admission is $4 per person; free to those 62 and over and 12 and under. Open 9 A.M.–5 P.M. Tues.–Sat.

Gaines-Oliphint House (www.toledo-bend.com), 10 North Ensign Dr., Milam, Texas. Drive west across Pendleton Bridge on LA 6 to the point where it becomes

Larry B. Campbell

VISITORS IN ALEXANDRIA CAN VIEW THE ORIGINAL BRICKS AND CONSTRUCTION ON
TYRONE PLANTATION'S GROUND-LEVEL GALLERY.

TX 21, then follow signs to the Pendleton Harbor subdivision near the bridge. The
Gaines-Oliphint House, built about 1818, has been acknowledged by the Texas
Historical Commission as the oldest standing log structure in the state. The building is a double pen planked log story and a half building, and features a dog trot.
The house is owned by the Sabine District Chapter 33 of the Sons of the Republic
of Texas. It was built by James Taylor Gaines, one of the signers of the Texas Dec-
laration of Independence. The Gaines-Oliphint house provided lodging for Sam
Houston, Davy Crockett, and Stephen F. Austin, among others. According to legend, it is the site where the pirate Jean Lafitte held his auctions to sell slaves and
goods he had taken from captive ships. A Pioneer Trade Day is held at the house
the third Saturday in April.

Los Adaes State Historic Site (888-677-7853 or 318-357-3101, www.crt.state
.la.us), 6354 LA 485, Robeline. Los Adaes dates from the early 1700s when a Franciscan missionary, Father Antonio Margil de Jesus, established the San Miguel de
Linares de los Adaes Mission at the end of El Camino Real near Robeline. The
mission lay within the territory of the Adaes Indians, a small, peaceful group. The
small Spanish outpost was manned by a few soldiers and several padres. In 1721,
the soldiers built Presidio Nuestra Senora del Pilar de los Adaes. Lacking stone,
the presidio and mission were built of pine and hardwood timber, but the wood
deteriorated rapidly in the humid climate and repair and rebuilding were constant
features of life at the post. In 1721, Los Adaes was officially designated the capital
of the Province of Texas, and it remained the provincial capital until 1770. Life was
extremely harsh here. Unsuccessful maize crops and isolation because of extreme
flooding led to the mission's failure. The mission and presidio at Los Adaes were

closed in 1772–73 and its citizens were ordered to move to San Antonio. However, a number of Adaesenos remained in the outlying area, and some of their descendants still live in the region. There are no historic structures left on the site, but visitors can see artifacts related to the mission at the archaeology workshop/interpretive building. People can walk the outline of the old stockade, which has been determined by archaeological studies. Free. Call before going; open by appointment.

Mission Nuestra Senora de los Dolores de los Ais (936-275-3815, www .missionrv.sanaugustinetx.com) 701 South Broadway St., San Augustine, Texas. Sixth in a string of Spanish missions, Mission Dolores was established in 1717. View the million-dollar visitor center with interpretation exhibits and enjoy the walking trail along Ayish Bayou. A landscaped RV park is across the street, surrounded by trees. The mission is in San Augustine County, 30 miles from Toledo Bend Lake. Open 9 A.M.–5 P.M. Mon.–Fri and 9 A.M.–4 P.M. Sat.

✐ ❦ **Museum of West Louisiana** (337-239-0927, www.louisianatravel.com /museum-west-louisiana), 803 South Third St., Leesville. Listed on the National Register of Historic Places, the museum is housed in the old Leesville Kansas City Southern Railroad. The last passenger train departed Leesville on May 19, 1968. The museum has a model of the old roundhouse and train yard along with many railroad photos and memorabilia. Other buildings include a dogtrot cabin and shotgun house. The museum interprets life in early Vernon Parish. You can see logging artifacts, clothing and household items from the 1800s and early 1900s. It also houses the Lois Loftin Doll Collection. Recent additions include The P.O.W. Paintings, a group of scenes painted by German prisoners of war who were housed at Fort Polk during World War II. A gift shop features handmade items.

Talbert-Pierson Cemetery (www.venturevernon.com), LA 277 next to Pine Grove Methodist Church, Cravens. The cemetery contains unusual wooden grave houses. The covered graves, an Upland South tradition, were thought to protect the deceased from hungry animals. Part of the tradition was to decorate the graves with shells. Although modern burial practices have made this unnecessary, some families continue the tradition today.

✳ Green Spaces

✐ ✧ **Anacoco Spillway Park** (337-392-0018), 171 Anacoco Lake Rd., Leesville. The park is a gated campground with a grocery. It's available for horseback riding, ATVs, fishing, boating, and swimming. Campers are welcomed to use the primitive trails located beneath the spillway, along lovely Anacoco Creek. After the dam was built in 1951, the lake was stocked with largemouth bass, bluegill, crappie and channel fish.

✐ ✧ **Blue Hole, Kisatchie Forest** (318-473-7160, www.fs.usda.gov/kisatchie), FR 405 in Vernon Parish. The compact area has a lot to offer visitors. Walk the nature trail that circles the Blue Hole and stop near the midpoint at the observation pier where you can overlook an isolated pond. Bring binoculars. The Forest Service has placed a number of nests, including a bat box, along the trail to enhance your chance of seeing wildlife. The complex has a pleasant picnic area near the water's edge under shade trees. The group-use shelter includes picnic tables and a barbeque pit. The area has vault restrooms and trash receptacles. In the past, the Blue Hole has been the Vernon Unit's choice for its annual fishing derby. The Blue Hole Recreation Complex is free for day users.

↪ 🐾 **Enduro Multi-Use Trail, Kisatchie National Forest** (318-793-9427 or 800-225-9733), junction of Forest Rd. 440 and LA 442 near Cravens. This multi-use trail offers grand views of open longleaf pine savannahs. It is the only unit of the Kisatchie National Forest that has been approved off-highway vehicles. Louisiana requires OHV registration and riders 18 years or older must have a valid driver's license. No vehicle can exceed an overall width of 50 inches. Tires can't exceed 1-inch lug depth. Forest service approved spark arresters are required on all Kisatchie National Forest lands. The day-use area costs $5 per operator, which can be paid at a self-service fee station. The Trailhead Camp is a primitive tent camping area with vault toilets. From the intersection of LA 10 and LA 399 North in Cravens, take LA 399 North 1.9 miles and turn left on road No. 440. Proceed 1.2 miles and turn left on road 442 into the Enduro Camp and Trailhead.

✎ ↪ 🐾 **Fullerton Lake Campground, Kisatchie Forest** (318-473-7160, www.fs.fed.us/r8/kisatchie/calcasieu-rd/vernon), near Craven. The Fullerton Lake Campground is a designated fees campground at the Fullerton Lake shore. The recreation complex was once the site of the Fullerton Sawmill, once one of the largest such operations in the South, and its community was placed on the National Register of Historic Places in 1968. An interpretive bulletin board at the trailhead has historic pictures and information about the community that existed here. The ruins and foundations can be seen on the 1.6-mile Fullerton Mill Trail. The Fullerton Recreation Complex has day-use picnic facilities, a nonmotorized boat launch, hiking and biking trails, flush restrooms, water, and trash receptacles. Visitors will find camp areas for trailers, campers, and tents, fire rings, bank fishing. From Leesville take US 171 south 7 miles to LA 10, turn left and proceed 18 miles to LA 399. Turn left on LA 399 and proceed 5 miles to the signed entrance road on the left to Fullerton Lake Recreation area. There is a $5 per night camping fee. Hikers and bikers will find the Ouiska Chitto Trail passes near Fullerton Lake.

✎ ↪ 🐾 **North Toledo Bend State Park** (318-645-4715 or 888-677-6400), 2907 North Toledo Park Rd., Zwolle. If you want to have a Daniel Boone weekend and play frontiersman, why not do it here? With more than 900 acres in which to hike and set up a tent, you can commune with nature for hours at a time. This park combines land and water activities. For hikers, Trail A is 1.5 miles long and Trail B, 4 miles. There's a boat launch area with a spacious ramp, a large parking lot, and a fish cleaning station. You can rent a boat with two paddles and three life jackets for $15 a day; canoes for $5 an hour or $20 per day; and paddle boats for $5 an hour. A spacious Visitors' Center complex includes a meeting room for group functions, an Olympic-size swimming pool, and a bathhouse. A concession area and laundry provide conveniences for long or short stays in the park. North Toledo Bend Park has 55 improved campsites with water and electrical hookup ($16 per night), 8 premium campsites on prime locations ($18 a night); and 10 deluxe cabins ($120 a night October–March, and $150 a night weekends April–September). Cabins are equipped with cookware, cooking utensils, dinnerware, silverware, towels, and linens. Bring your own food and personal supplies (soap, tissues, toilet paper). The park entrance station is open 6 A.M.–7 P.M. April–September, and 8 A.M.–5 P.M. October–March. Admission is $1 per person; free to seniors age 62 and older and children age 3 and under.

South Toledo Bend State Park (337-286-9075 or 888-398-4770, www.crt.state
.la.us/parks), 120 Bald Eagle Rd., Anacoco. Use 648 Bass Haven Resort Dr. for GPS
and navigational units. Located on small bluffs that extend over and into the Toledo
Bend Reservoir, South Toledo Bend Reservoir State Park is relatively easy to reach
from I-10. Visitors enjoy scenic water views from many vantage points. While the
lake is nationally recognized as a destination for bass fishing tournaments, visitors
can also enjoy hiking, cycling, birding, camping, and wildlife viewing. The Lakeview
Nature Trail is a half-mile long and the Hippie Point Trail is three times that length.
The area is a popular nesting ground for the American bald eagle, which feeds from
the reservoir's plentiful supply of largemouth bass, catfish, bream, and white perch.
Learn more about local animal and plant life at the Visitors' Center, with exhibits
designed to increase awareness of the species and their role in the environment. An
open-air breezeway leads to an observation deck with an expansive view of the lake
and islands. A 3,000-foot surfaced nature trail gives visitors a chance to explore the
area around the center. You'll also find picnic tables nearby. The park has 42
improved campsites with hookups ($16 a night October–March and $20 a night
April–September; 13 premium campsites (four pull-through and nine prime location sites that cost $18 a night October–March and $26 a night April–September).
Five campsites without a hookup run $12 a night. Cabins are equipped with cook-
ware, cooking utensils, dinnerware, silverware, towels, and linens. Bring your own
food and personal supplies (soap, tissues, toilet paper). Park hours and fees are subject to change. Call for information.

✍ **Vernon Lake** (337-238-0324, www.vppjla.com), off LA 392 near Anacoco. Vernon Lake is a 4,600-acre lake designated as a Louisiana quality lake that attracts
largemouth bass anglers. The lake is partially wooded with lots of dead timber in
its upper end. Open water is located near the dam. Fishing for crappie and bluegill
is usually excellent in spring, early summer, and fall. Hickory Ridge Recreation
Park on Vernon Lake is maintained and operated by the Vernon Parish Police Jury
(an elective governing body similar to a council). The park has eight campsites
with electricity, a gated campground with tent and RV camping, bathroom, and
showers, an enclosed public boat ramp, fishing and swimming areas, tables, charcoal grills, and a dock area, and aims to create a family friendly atmosphere. For
rental information, call 337-238-0324.

✳ To Do

FISHING Toledo Bend Reservoir (318-256-5880 or 800-358-7802, www.toledo
bendlakecountry.com), Sabine Parish Tourist and Recreation Commission, Many.
With more than 186,000 acres of lake, freshwater fishing is the major attraction here.
Two state parks and countless licensed guides make it easy to find that one perfect
spot for your catch of a lifetime. The website above maintains a comprehensive list
of fishing guides, public and private launches and piers, fishing reports, fishing regulations, tournaments, and more. The lakes and bayous in forests and wilderness areas
listed in the Green Spaces sections also provide numerous fishing opportunities.

GOLF Cypress Bend Golf Resort (318-590-1500, www.cypressbend.com), 2000
Cypress Bend Blvd., near Many. This beautiful course is strategically designed to challenge all golfers. It is curled around one of Toledo Bend Lake's many inlets. The 18-
hole course has 10 holes along the water and six with shots across water. The course is
open daily all year. Tee times begin at 11:30 A.M. Mon., and 7 A.M. Tues.–Sun.

Emerald Hills Golf Course (318-586-4661), 42168 US 171, Florien. The 18-hole course at Emerald Hills features 6,548 yards from the longest tees for a par of 72. It has a slope rating of 125. Fairways are narrow and hilly. Water hazards come into play on four holes. Golf cart rentals are available. No caddies are available.

HISTORIC SITES AND GARDENS El Camino Real Tour LA 6 in Louisiana and TX 21 in Texas. El Camino Real—the Old Texas Road—has existed for more than 300 years. The Spanish and French missionaries and soldiers who marked the trail were followed by such adventurers as Moses Austin and his son Stephen Fuller Austin, Jim Bowie, Davy Crockett, Sam Houston, and others. A number of historic sites are along the trail. Take a road trip through the rolling piney woods to San Augustine, Texas, and stop at the communities along the way. It's especially lovely in the fall.

✦ ✦ ❀ **Hodges Garden State Park** (318-586-4020, 800-354-3523), 1000 Hodges Loop, Florien. Be prepared. Hodges Gardens is stunning. More than 700 acres of wild and cultivated landscape capture your heart. Stroll through formal gardens where something is blooming every season, explore nature trails, boat on the lake, and sit on a rock bench and listen to the waterfall gurgling. The site is a testament to one family's contribution to preservation. Hodges Gardens was donated to Louisiana by the A. J. and Nona Trigg Hodges Foundation in 2007. Recognizing the potential of an abandoned quarry, the Hodgeses created the gardens using the natural rock formations. Flowers were planted on one level above another, creating a terraced effect. Walkways and footbridges allow you to stroll through an abundance of beauty. Water from the 225-acre lake, built in 1954, is pumped to the waterfalls, pools, geyser, fountains, and the watering system before it is recycled back into the lake. In spring, walk the wild azalea trail to see the feathery hoary azaleas and fringetrees. Schedule your visit so you can take a Full Moon Garden Tour to see spider webs and water lilies glistening in moonlight. There are boat and canoe rentals. (Only boats rented at the site are allowed on the lake.) The park has limited overnight facilities. There are nine standard cabins, each sleeping up to four people, and two deluxe cabins, each sleeping up to six. The park also has 20 equestrian campsites with no hookups and nine tent campsites with no hookups. There's also a primitive camping area. The Emerald Hills Golf Resort is across the street from the park, with an 18-hole course, overnight accommodations, and a restaurant. Entrance station is open 8 A.M.–7 P.M., April–September; 8 A.M.–5 P.M., October–March. Admission is $5 per person; $4, seniors 62 and over; free to children age 3 and under.

Old Mill Store (318-544-8898 or 318-256-5047), LA 171, Fisher, 6 miles south of Many. Near Hodges Gardens State Park. In the last of the old sawmill towns founded by Captain John Barber White and Oliver Williams Fisher, this store is filled with glassware, furniture, and other collectibles. Refreshments include Coca-Cola and ice cream. The old village here includes an opera house, depot, city hall, and church in the park. Most buildings are only open for special events. Talk with the store owners and sisters Ann Anderson and Gayle Lewing. They have a key to the opera house, and will keep the store open if you plan to linger. They also will open outside regular hours for groups such as garden clubs or church organizations. Bus parking is available. Open 10 A.M–4:30 P.M. Thurs.–Sat. and 1–4 P.M. Sun.

✱ Lodging

Allen Acres B&B (337-328-2252, www.allenacresbandb.com), 5070 LA 399, Pitkin. About 14 miles from Fort Polk, this bed & breakfast offers a country retreat near Ouiska Chitto Creek. The Allens have spent years developing gardens designed to attract butterflies and hummingbirds. An authority on native plants, Dr. Charles Allen can provide tours of some of the rarest ecosystems in the Kisatchie National Forest, Louisiana prairies, spring-fed bay galls, or pitcher plant bogs. Each guest room has its own theme: butterflies, birds, wildflowers, trees, and chickens. Take a moonlight walk in the night-blooming garden or count the fireflies. Enjoy your choice of a full breakfast, but a popular choice is fresh eggs from different variety of chickens and guinea fowl. No pets. Moderate.

Americas Best Value Inn (337-460-7747, www.americasbestvalueinn .com), 1515 North Pine St., DeRidder. The motel offers free high-speed Internet access and free breakfast. Expect a small, clean room with mini fridge, microwave, and coffee maker. Inexpensive–moderate.

(ᵗᵖ) **Best Western Stagecoach Inn** (866-538-0187, www.bestwestern.com), 1200 North Sixth St., Leesville. Conveniently located near Fort Polk, the motel offers fresh, clean comfortable rooms with fresh high-speed Internet access, microwave, refrigerator, and coffee maker. Coffee is always ready in the lobby, and continental breakfast is served each morning. The staff is friendly and welcoming to military families. Moderate.

Booker-Lewis House Bed and Breakfast (800-726-7090 or 337-239-8140, www.booker-lewishouse.com) 106 East North St., Leesville. Boutique-style lodging is unexpected in a tiny town. Enjoy comfortable rooms with old-fashioned quilts, the restaurant on the main floor with a casual-fine menu for breakfast, Sunday brunch and dinner, and Southern hospitality at its best. Moderate.

(ᵗᵖ) **Cypress Bend Resort and Conference Hotel** (318-256-4118, www .cypressbend.com), 2000 Cypress Bend Blvd., Many. Situated on Toledo Bend Lake, the resort makes a great getaway. The nationally recognized championship golf course is outstanding. The resort will make arrangements for fishing trips, lake cruises, and sightseeing. The Nature Trail for mountain bikers and hikers contains five loop paths ranging from 1 mile to more than 6. Rooms have views of water, woods, or the fairway and include a large desk, wireless high-speed Internet connection, and a full complement of amenities. The Cypress Dining Room is open for breakfast and lunch 7 A.M.–2 P.M. and dinner begins at 5 P.M. Closing times vary. The Cypress Cafe at the clubhouse serves breakfast and all-day casual fare, 7 A.M.–7 P.M., March–September, and 7 A.M.–2 P.M., October–February.

StarliteMotel (318-256-1200, www .hotelmany.com), 160 Fisher Rd., Many. This simple, updated court motel is clean and comfortable, but nothing fancy. Adjacent cafes come in handy. Inexpensive.

⚓ ↝ **Wildwood Resort** (800-341-3668 or 318-645-6438, www.wildwood-resort .com), 129 Wildwood Dr., Zwolle. An excellent rustic country getaway, Wildwood on Toledo Bend Lake treats guests like family. The discrete guest cottages, tucked beneath towering pines and hardwoods, were designed and constructed under the direction of expert craftsmen. Five luxury suites include a king-size bed, tub, shower, and a refreshment center in the sitting room. Guests can feed the ducks or meander down to the fishing pier to watch the sunset. The W. J. Brown Conference Center, designed like an old-fashioned lodge, is set up to handle any business meetings or social events. Attached to the center by a covered walkway is a lovely enclosed pavilion. The Junior Conference Center is designed for family meetings or corporate events. It features eight bedrooms and baths and a fully equipped kitchen. Most guests choose to pick up supplies at a local grocery and prepare their own meals, but Wildwood offers gourmet catering with anything from a fish fry to a prime rib dinner. Stop by the office for assistance or to browse in the gift area. Sit in rocking chairs on the front porch and soak up the peaceful atmosphere. Peacock and geese roam the grounds. Moderate–expensive.

CAMPGROUNDS ✐ ↝ ❦ **Cypress Bend Park and Pavilion** (318-256-4112 or 800-259-LAKE, www.toledo-bend.com), Cypress Bend Rd., off LA 191 between the 28- and 29-mile markers. The park is 1.5 miles beyond the entrance to Cypress Bend Golf Resort. Owned and operated by the Sabine River Authority, this park includes 114 acres of forested land and about 3 miles of shoreline on Toledo Bend Lake. Marked swimming areas have white, sandy beaches, and there's a nearby picnic area with tables and grills. Other features include a concession stand, restrooms, a children's playground area, and a paved, six-lane boat launch area with a large parking lot. You can fish from the jetty or the lighted fishing pier. There are 60 RV sites with full hookups and some cabin rentals. Inexpensive.

Pine Grove Estates (337-460-1800 or 337-460-1811, www.pinegroverv.com), 206 Louise St., DeRidder. This is a peaceful, family oriented RV park on the outskirts of DeRidder. There are 37 spacious sites with concrete or gravel pads and full hookup, 65 channels of free cable, and reliable wireless Internet. The site is near grocery stores, banks, shopping plazas, and historic sites. Shower, restroom, and laundry are available. The park is patrolled regularly for litter and to monitor the property. Inexpensive.

Pleasure Point Park (318-565-4810, www.srala-toledo.com), 1190 Pleasure Point Rd., Florien. The campground is situated on 195 wooded acres near the south end of Toledo Bend Lake, about 5 miles from the dam. There are several coves with playground facilities, picnic areas, and a swimming beach area. Tent and RV campers may stay overnight or by the month. Grills for BBQs are scattered around the park area. Inexpensive.

Turtle Beach Lodge (318-256-5595), 3017 Turtle Beach Rd., Many. To reach the property from LA 6, take LA 191 south to Turtle Beach Road. Situated about midway along Toledo Bend Lake, Turtle Beach Lodge is a clean, comfortable place to stay. Turtle Beach includes cabins, campgrounds and marina. The wide sea wall is ideal for fishing, and swimming is allowed with parental supervision. The lodge has a well-stocked grocery store, marine supplies, bait, tackle, gas and oil, a boat harbor, and fish-cleaning house. Rates start at $60 for a single motel unit and $65 for a double. Inexpensive.

✱ Where to Eat

EATING OUT Cecil's Cajun Cafe (337-460-2002), 120 West First St., DeRidder. The cafe serves excellent jambalaya and portions are large. Hamburgers, po-boys, and salads are very satisfying. Situated in an old downtown building, the atmosphere is pleasant. The outside seating area is relaxing and sometimes features live music. Moderate.

✐ **Down Home Dining** (318-256-9989, www.downhomedining.net), 12049 TX, Many. Across from Big Star at Toledo Town on Toledo Bend Lake, this cafe serves Texas-Louisiana com-

PINE TREES TOWER ABOVE BOARDWALK AT FORTS RANDOLPH AND BUHLOW STATE HISTORIC SITE AT PINEVILLE.

Larry B. Campbell

fort food: seafood platters, chicken-fried steak, hamburger steak, and rib eye. Appetizers include fried green tomatoes and fried pickles. There's always a giant baked "tater" and gumbo. Open 11 A.M.–9 P.M. Tues.–Sat., lunch buffet Tues.–Fri. Inexpensive.

✐ **Fatboy and Skinny's** (337-404-3933), 303 South Fifth St., Leesville. If you're a hamburger junkie, then make a point of stopping here. Order your burger they way you like it done and then select several or all of 20 items you can top it with. Amazing Cajun fries. All items are sold separately, so there's no meal-in-one (burger, fries, and drink) deal. Open 10:30 A.M.–8:30 P.M. Mon.–Sat. Inexpensive–moderate.

Hana Japanese Steakhouse (337-239-2886), 1404 South Fifth St., Leesville. The Japanese restaurant specializes in steak and sushi and offers a Hibachi grill, which provides plenty of entertainment as the knife-wielding chef prepares your meal. If you're not familiar with sushi ask your waiter about the rolls on the menu. Expect friendly service. Open daily 11 A.M.–10 P.M. Moderate.

Leesville Cafe (337-238-5168), 114 South Third St., Leesville. A good stop for Southern comfort food. The best bet is the lunch special with entrée and two sides. Outstanding fried chicken. Moderate.

Presley's Original Bar B Que (337-462-5968), 19632 Lake Charles Highway, DeRidder. Presley's wins over customers with its spicy BBQ sauce. Another specialty is the seafood buffet every Friday night. Open 11 A.M.–2 P.M. Mon., 11 A.M.–9 P.M. Tues.–Fri., and 4–9 P.M. Sat.

Thadapetch (337-239-6222), 1910 South Fifth St., No. C, Leesville. This authentic Thai restaurant serves non-Americanized spicy food, so unless you're really into hot foods, stick with mild or medium sauces. The mango with sweet sticky rice is a good choice. Moderate.

Thai Basil Restaurant (337-462-3885, thaibasilderidder.com), 1209 North Pine St., DeRidder. Thai food is seasoned with a well-balanced combination of flavors. The *pad kra-pao* (onions, basil leaves) with prawns is an excellent choice. Also try the *gaeng karee*, a yellow curry dish with chicken, potato, onion, carrot, and coconut milk. Ask for it to be served with jasmine rice. Prices are moderate. Open 11 A.M.–9 P.M. Tues.–Thurs., 11 A.M.–9:30 P.M. Fri., 11 A.M.–9:30 P.M. Sat., and 11 A.M.–9 P.M. Sun. Closed from 2–4 P.M. Tues.–Thurs. Moderate.

DINING OUT Booker-Lewis House Restaurant (337-239-8142, www.bookerlewisrestaurant.com), 102 East North St., Leesville. Reservations recommended but not required. The restaurant is known for its delightful cuisine. You can enjoy a meal in one of three dining rooms, on the wraparound porch, or in John Beck's Pub next door. Start dinner with silver-dollar mushroom caps stuffed with a blend of feta cheese and Cajun andouille sausage, or skewered chicken tandoori marinated in a savory blend of Indian spices. For an entrée you might want to try the pistachio breaded pork loin topped with a brandy apricot glaze and roasted red potatoes or the piquant jumbo shrimp in a spicy Creole sauce with white rice and salad. The restaurant's popular Sunday brunch buffet includes waffles, an assortment of rustic breads, a pasta station, beef stroganoff, and

lemon chicken. Prices are moderate. Breakfast only Mon., 6–10 A.M.; breakfast 6–10 A.M. and dinner 6–9 P.M., Tues.–Thurs.; breakfast 6–10 A.M. and dinner 6–9:30 P.M. Fri.; breakfast 8 A.M.–11 A.M. and dinner 6–9:30 P.M. Sat.; breakfast 8–10 A.M. and brunch buffet 10 A.M.–2 P.M. Sun. Expensive.

✳ Entertainment

Bon Temps Lounge (337-537-1000), 467 Entrance Rd., Leesville. The nightspot caters to a mature crowd with a mellow atmosphere. There's plenty of entertainment. Music includes rhythm and blues, hip-hop, and old school jams.

Sugar Shack Lounge (337-239-2448), 11494 Lake Charles Highway, Leesville. The lounge has wireless Broadband Internet access, so bring your laptops. Every Wednesday is karaoke night. Live bands perform on Friday and Saturday nights.

Vernon Parish Community Orchestra (337-239-7700, www.vpco.net). Conducted by Karen Gordy, the community orchestra gives live performances in Leesville, DeRidder, and Jasper. Programs feature a variety of music, including baroque, classical-romantic, popular, and light classics. Admission is free.

✳ Selective Shopping

The Louisiana Shoppe (337-460-9334), 113 South Washington, DeRidder. This is a one-stop shop for all things Louisiana. There's a lot of art by local artists, and many items decorated with fleurs de lis, from sunglasses to costume jewelry. You may want to pick up a Saints T-shirt, a comfy throw, a Cajun cookbook, or maybe an alligator head. Open 10 A.M.–5 P.M. Mon.–Fri. and 10 A.M.–4:30 P.M. Sat.

Nichols (318-256-6214, www.nichols
-stores.com), 252 Elizabeth St., Many.
This is a one-stop department store for
outdoorsmen and their families.
Nichols, founded in DeQuincy in
1914, is hunting and fishing central for
western central Louisiana. Check out
the latest in name brands, including
Browning, Winchester, Remington,
Colt, and others. The store also carries
muzzleloaders and crossbows. Anglers
will find a huge assortment of rods,
reels, and lures, as well as boating
accessories. The store carries a large
selection of casual and sportswear
along with gifts and decorative items
for the home. Check out the candles,
ceramics, and jewelry. Other stores are
located in Coushatta, DeQuincy, and
Winnfield. Hours are 8 A.M.–6 P.M.
Mon.–Sat. and noon–5:30 Sun.
Another Nichols, at 1110 Boone St.,
Leesville, is open 8 A.M.–6 P.M.
Mon.–Sat. and 12:30–5 P.M. Sun.

Two Sisters Pecan House & Deli
(337-460-9000), 1624 North Pine St.,
DeRidder. Two Sisters is famous for
their chicken salad sandwiches and
potato soup, and try the fresh pecans.
It's hard to say what you will like best,
the shopping or the food. The old-
fashioned décor is meant to look like
granny's, and gifts will please Auntie
Barbara.

✳ Special Events

April: **Battle of Pleasant Hill
Re-enactment** (318-686-8545, www
.battleofpleasanthill.com), three miles
north of Pleasant Hill at 23271 LA
175, Pelican. History buffs can step
back to the 1860s, as more than 400
people gather to re-enact the Civil War
battle that took place April 9, 1864.
The actual fight took place between
Confederate and Union forces the day
after the Battle of Mansfield, part of

the Red River Campaign. In addition
to the re-enactment, you can visit with
living history re-enactors, watch the
parade, see period dancers, listen to
gospel singing, and take part in open
camp activities.

Louisiana Doll Festival (337-463-
8014), West Park, DeRidder. Held the
third week of April, the festival spotlights the Lois Loftin Doll Collection
of more than 3,000 dolls that is housed
in the Beauregard Museum and
attracts dolls and traders. Other activities at the fair include antiques and
craft vendors, a car show, children's
games, music, and the Tour De Beauregard Bike Ride.

May: **Choctaw-Apache Pow Wow**
(318-654-2588, www.toledo-bend
.com), in the Zwolle Intermediate
School Gym, Zwolle. Join members of
the Choctaw-Apache tribe on the
banks of Toledo Bend in Ebarb for
their traditional pow wow. The tribe is
essentially 21 families strong, and
according to tribal records, 13 of them
were associated with the mission and
presidio of Los Adaes. After being
forced by the Spanish crown to move
from Los Adaes to San Antonio in
1778, the families made their way to
east Texas and resettled the abandoned
mission at Nacogdoches. It was only a
matter of time before they and eight
others resettled their ancestral lands
on the east side of the Sabine River.
Today, there are 1,100 enrolled members who still live within a 15-square-
mile area that has been home to many
since before European contact in the
1720s. Across the country, another
1,600 nonresident members live from
coast to coast and border to border.
The public is invited to attend the pow
wow. The site of the event may change
from year to year. No alcohol or drugs
allowed.

Loggers & Forestry Festival (318-645-6141, www.zwollela.net), Zwolle. Smaller than the Tamale Festival, this May event at the city festival grounds pays tribute to Zwolle's forestry and logging industry. The community's oldest living logger is honored each year. Families gather for the Blessing of the Fleet of logging trucks, a parade, logging activities, contests, and forestry exhibits. Expect food, arts and crafts, and music.

Fisher Sawmill Days (318-590-1212 or 318-256-2001, www.toledo-bend .com), Town Square and Park, Fisher. The event recaptures life in a sawmill village during the early days of lumbering in Louisiana. The old community comes alive the third weekend in May with an old-fashioned jamboree of country, Western, bluegrass, and gospel music. Browse through the flea market and displays of folk arts and crafts. You'll find horse and wagon rides, square dancing, food, horseshoe pitching, fiddlin,' and numerous games and contests with prizes. Sawmill Days also hosts the World Championship Southern Pine Wood Derby Races. The event serves as a homecoming for former residents of Fisher and extinct nearby sawmill towns. Call the Old Mill Store, stocked with an array of antiques, at 318-544-8898 or 318-256-5047 for more information.

MayFest (337-238-0783), Leesville Historic District, Leesville. Held the first full weekend in May, the event is a celebration of music and art—with food. Entertainment each year includes internationally known musicians such as Wayne Toups and ZyDe-Cajun, Tab Benoit, and Irma Thomas, as well as regional and local entertainers like Trout Fishing in America, Laurel and the Edge, and the Michael Foster Project. The festival includes the annual Lions Club pancake breakfast and a classic car show.

June: **Beauregard Watermelon Festival** (www.beauregardwatermelon festival.com), Beauregard Parish Fair Grounds, DeRidder. Because this is the home of the Sugartown watermelon, this is the sweetest three-day festival around, with a host of watermelon games and events in the last weekend of June. Favorite events include the watermelon carving contest and the Watermelon Idol talent contest. Don't miss the celebrity seed-spitting contest. Regional bands perform on the outdoor and indoor stages from morning until after dark all three days.

September: **Sabine Parish Fair** (318-586-7062 or 318-256-2349, www .toledobendlakecountry.com), Sabine Parish Fairgrounds, Fairgrounds Rd., Many. A parish-wide festival, the event takes place during the last full week of September. It's lots of fun for the entire family. Take your pick of carnival rides, games, rodeos, arts and crafts, a livestock show, and plenty of food and music.

October: **Four Winds Pow Wow** (337-825-8641, www.fourwinds cherokee.com), Beauregard Parish Fairgrounds. Learn about the Cherokee's culture and their history in Louisiana. Bring your lawn chairs and enjoy dances, entertainment. Native American arts and crafts as well as food will be available.

Zwolle Tamale Fiesta (318-645-6141), Zwolle Festival Grounds, Zwolle. Originally an Indian village, Zwolle was occupied by the Spanish Province of Texas, and eventually settled by the offspring of French and Spanish adventurers who intermarried with the Indians. Today, their descendants show off their family's tamale recipes at this October fiesta. Among the events are a tamale-making demonstration, a tamale-eating and tamale-judging contest, a Spanish costume contest, a treasure hunt, and a parade. Of course, there's live music, and more than 20,000 dozen tamales for sale.

November: **Florien Freestate Festival** (318-586-3521, www.toledo -bend.com), 3536 Anthony Rd., Florien. Held the first weekend in November, the event is also known as the Sabine Free State Festival. Be pre-pared to join in the fun and the comedy. The festival celebrates the era when this area was a Free State (1806–1822) between Spanish territory and the United States. It has a comedy of shoot-out skits (Free State Gang vs. the Law), trail rides, bull rides, kids' rides, a parade, a treasure hunt, and entertainment by local musicians.

ALEXANDRIA/VIDALIA/ MARKSVILLE AREA

Alexandria, the parish seat of Rapides Parish, is almost the exact geographic center of the state. Situated on the south banks of the Red River, it was originally a community supporting the adjacent Spanish outpost of Post du Rapides. Around 1796, the Kent Plantation House was established by Pierre Baillio II, whose family came from France. In 1805, Alexander Fulton, a merchant and planter from Washington County, near Pittsburgh, came to the region and built the first store in Rapides Parish, locating it beside the Red River. The same year he was appointed coroner by then-Territorial Governor William C.C. Claiborne. Also in 1805, Fulton and a business partner laid out the site of Alexandria, and it was incorporated in 1819. Fertile soils encouraged cotton and sugar cane agriculture, for which the area remains a hub today. During the Civil War, the Federal army took over the city during a long stay in Alexandria, foraging for lumber and building materials. They enclosed the city with fortifications. On May 13, 1864, when the Union decided to abandon Alexandria, the town was set afire in spite of General Nathaniel P. Banks's order to the contrary. Hundreds of people reportedly ran through the streets and fled to the levee. By noon, most of the town was destroyed. In the following years, Alexandria was rebuilt. The area recovered slowly, with the lumber industry boosting the economy. Only a year before the United States entered World War II, the U.S. Amy selected central Louisiana for its largest maneuvers, and several hundred thousand troops descended on the state to practice the strategy and tactics that lead to eventual victory. Among the command staff were David D. Eisenhower, George Patton, Omar Bradley, and George C. Marshall. The training camps, airfields, and military presence established during the early 1940s affected the area for decades. England Air Force Base, originally known as Alexandria Army Air Base, was a major Air Force center in operation from 1942–1992. The former base, now the Alexandria International Airport operated by England Authority, has been redeveloped into a vibrant commercial center and a community that includes a retirement community and general housing.

In recent years, the economy of the Alexandria and its sister city across the Red River, Pineville, have grown as new companies decided to locate facilities nearby. StarTek, a Denver-based company, has opened a technical support center in the

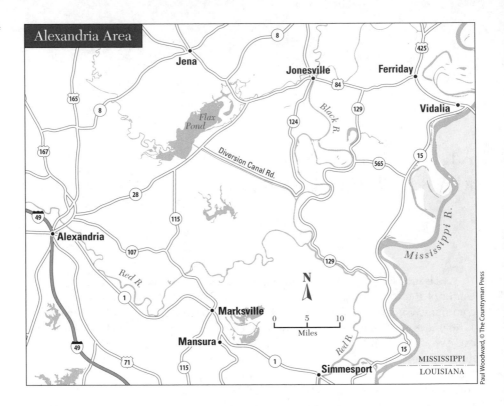

Alexandria Area

Jena

Jonesville
Ferriday

Vidalia

8

425

84

165

8

Flax
Pond

124

Black R.

129

167

Diversion Canal Rd.

565

15

28

115

49

Alexandria

107

Red R.

1

129

N

Marksville

0   5   10
Miles

Mansura

49

71

115

1

Simmesport

Red R.

15

Mississippi R.

MISSISSIPPI
LOUISIANA

Paul Woodward, © The Countryman Press

city. Union Tank Car Company chose Alexandria as the site for its new manufacturing facility.

Alexandria supports a lively arts community, with regular exhibitions at the
Alexandria Museum of Art housed in the historic Rapides Bank Building. The
Coughlin-Saunders Performing Arts Center on Third Street serves as the home of
the Rapides Symphony Orchestra. Plastipak and Integrated Packaging have set up
shop in the area to support Procter & Gamble's new liquid detergent line.

Travelers will find that much of downtown "Alex," as locals call it, is still suffer-
ing from residential flight to the suburbs. However, people still gather for festivals
and special events in the town square or in the spacious amphitheater on the Red
River levee.

Pineville, across the Red River, is the very picture of small-town America.
Established about the same time as Alexandria, the community dates from the
early 1700s. One glance at the towering pine trees shading homes and businesses,
and you immediately know how the town got its name. In 1856, a Rapides Parish
planter and businessman, George Mason Graham, was instrumental in establishing
a state university. The school was established in Rapides and named the Pineville
Seminary of Learning. Graham hired William Tecumseh Sherman as the school's
first superintendent. When the school building burned in 1869, Graham's friend-
ship with Sherman was instrumental in obtaining federal property (now known as
the Pentagon Barracks) in Baton Rouge as a new location for the seminary, which
became Louisiana State University.

Cynthia V. Campbell

A DISTINCTIVE SKYLINE SETS APART BUILDNGS IN DOWNTOWN ALEXANDRIA, ON THE
BANKS OF THE RED RIVER.

Pineville retains its reputation as a center for higher education. Louisiana College, a private Baptist liberal arts school just off Main Street, has beautifully landscaped walks and gardens. The four-year college offers degrees in business, education, fine arts and media, political science, human behavior, science and mathematics, nursing, and Christian studies. The Pineville Old Town Hall Museum on Main Street offers guided tours of the restored courtroom, jail cells, fire station, and library. The Louisiana Maneuvers & Military Museum is situated on Camp Beauregard, just off US 165 North. Don't miss the Forts Randolph & Buhlow State Historic Site (check the To See list), which interprets the area's role in the Red River campaign of the Civil War, a Union effort to control Louisiana's waterways.

GUIDANCE **Alexandria/Pineville Convention and Visitors Bureau** (318-442-9546, 800-551-9546, www.theheartoflouisiana.com). The visitors' center is downtown within walking distance of a beautiful overlook on the Red River. Open 9 A.M.–5 P.M. daily.

GETTING THERE *By air:* **Alexandria International Airport** (318-449-3504, www.ifly.com), 1499 Floyd Rogers Blvd., Alexandria. Located within the England Industrial Airpark, the airport is served by three regional air jet services with daily flights to Atlanta, Dallas–Fort Worth, Houston, and Memphis, with connections around the world. It's accessible via I-49 to Airport Road from exit 498 and North Bayou Rapides Road from exit 496. There's an attractive new terminal. Passengers should arrive one hour to 90 minutes before flight.

Cynthia V. Campbell

ALEXANDRIA CITY PARK FEATURES THE LOVELY BICENTENNIAL CLOCK, 1807-2007.

By car: Alexandria is in the heart of Louisiana and the hub of the crossroads region. The major highway, which runs through the city, connects with I-49 north at Shreveport and I-10 south at Lafayette. Other highways flow outward through the region in a wagon-wheel pattern, including US 71, US167, US 165, LA 1, and LA 28. The distance from Alexandria to Shreveport is 127 miles; to Lafayette, 86 miles; to Baton Rouge, 110 miles; and to New Orleans, 197 miles.

MEDICAL EMERGENCIES Christus St. Frances Cabrini Hospital (318-487-1122, www.cabrini.org), 3330 Masonic Dr., Alexandria.

Rapides Regional Medical Center (318-769-3000, www.rapidesregional.com), 211 Fourth St., Alexandria.

✳ Cities, Towns, and Villages

Vidalia, in the Crossroads' eastern area, is just across the Mississippi River from Natchez, Mississippi. As you'd expect, there are close economic and cultural bonds between the two cities. One claim to fame is the notorious 1827 Sandbar Duel involving James Bowie. The duel between Dr. Samuel Levi Wells III (with Bowie acting as his second) and Dr. Thomas Maddox turned into an all-out, bloody brawl that pulled in a number of bystanders. In defending himself, Bowie, who received multiple shots and stabbings, used a new hunting knife with great skill. Newspapers around the country picked up the story and Bowie and the knife became legends. The annual Jim Bowie Festival in September features a re-enactment of the famous fight. The number of contemporary lodgings and cafes make the town a convenient stopping point along US 84. If you're following the Louisiana Culinary Trail, then stop by Molly B's for catfish and get a panoramic view of Historic Natchez Under the Hill across the river. Stop first at the Vidalia Welcome Center (318-336-7008, www.crt.state.la.us), 112 Front St., which is open daily. Situated just off the US 84 bridge linking the two towns, the center is a great place to get the latest on local attractions and events. If you take a walk on the Riverfront next to the Mississippi River, the Sandbar Restaurant is not far away.

Lecompte and **Bunkie,** both on US 71, are located in the southern portion of the Cross roads region. The first was named for a race horse and is famous for Lea's restaurant. Bunkie's original name was Irion. In 1882, the Texas and Pacific Railway was seeking a right of way across land belonging to a local baron, Alexander M. Haas. In exchange for permission to build the railroad, Haas was given the privilege of naming the train station. Legend has it that Haas, returning from a trip to New Orleans, bought his small daughter a toy monkey, and Maccie Haas mispronounced it "bunkie." From then on she was her dad's little Bunkie. Given the chance to name the new depot, Haas suggested his daughter's nickname. Bunkie serves a large farming community, and it is home to the Louisiana Corn Festival, held the second full weekend in July.

✳ To See

Alexandria Museum of Art (318-443-3448, www.themuseum.org), 933 Main St., Alexandria. The area's primary source for exhibitions and collections of fine art. Housed in the restored, historic Rapides Bank Building, circa 1898, the museum presents works from antiquity to contemporary. There's an ever-changing array of collections from around the world as well the state's largest collection of North Louisiana folk art. Galleries are spacious and special programs emphasize education. Open 10 A.M.–5 P.M. Tues.–Fri., 10 A.M.–4 P.M. Sat. Admission is $4, adults; $3, seniors, students and military; $2, children 4–13; free under age 4.

✐ ✤ **Alexandria Zoological Park** (318-473-1143, www.thealexandriazoo.com), 3016 Masonic Dr., Alexandria. The zoo was founded in 1926, and it's still roaring. Here you can see more than 500 animals native to Africa, Asia, Australia, South America, and North America, and even get nose-to-nose with white tigers. The African Lion habitat features a safari jeep photo op. We like the Louisiana Habitat, with otters, alligators, and snapping turtles. Special events are held throughout the year. Open 9 A.M.–5 P.M. daily. Admission is $3, adults, and $2, children.

Arna Bontemps African American Museum (318-473-4692, www.arnabon tempsmuseum.com), 1327 Third St., Alexandria. Visit the birthplace of Arna Wendell Bontemps, a poet, author, anthologist and librarian. Bontemps was considered the leading authority of the Harlem Renaissance. The museum's mission is to spread Bontemps's work and promote awareness of African American history. Activities include a book fair, film screening, readings, theatrical presentations, and seminars. Open 10 A.M.–4 P.M. Tues.–Fri. 10 A.M.–2 P.M. Sat.

Big Bend Post Office Museum/Sarto Bridge (318-997-2465, www.travel avoyelles.com), 8554 LA 451, Moreauville. This off-the-beaten path spot is just perfect for bridge hunters and those who want a glimpse of Louisiana's past. About 14 miles from LA 1 at Moreau sits the Adam Ponthieu Grocery Store and Big Bend Post Office Museum. Artifacts and memorabilia include hardware, tools, kitchenware, medicine, and a time capsule showing old Avoyelles between 1900 and 1950. The Post Office memorabilia includes old ledger books documenting business and transactions. Directly across from the museum is the Old Sarto Iron Bridge. Prior to 1913, flood waters from the nearby Mississippi, Atchafalaya, and Red rivers frequently forced evacuations of people and livestock. The steel truss swing bridge over Bayou de la Glaise at Sarto Lane was completed in 1916. The bridge is a rare surviving example of its type and was the first in Louisiana listed on the National Register of Historic Places. You can see the bridge during daylight hours. Bring a camera. Tours are offered 8 A.M.–4 P.M. Tues.–Fri., but call if you want to tour after 3:30 P.M. Also open noon–5 P.M. Sun. Monday and Saturday tours available by appointment only.

Delta Music Museum (318-757-9999), 218 Louisiana Ave., Ferriday. The Delta Music Museum salutes the talents of performers from the Louisiana-Mississippi Delta. See exhibits on rock and roll and blues musicians, including Percy Sledge, Irma Thomas, and Leon "Pee Wee" Whittaker. The first exhibit you'll see is a sculpture of three Ferriday cousins at the piano: singers Jerry Lee Lewis, Mickey Gilley, and Jimmy Lee Swaggart (that's right, the TV evangelist). Next door is the Arcade Theater, with a concert hall and mini-recording studio. There's also a gift shop with autographed T-shirts and music memorabilia. The museum hosts the Delta Music Festival and Hall of Fame Induction Ceremonies the first Saturday in April. Donations accepted. Open 9 A.M.–4 P.M., Mon.–Fri. Free.

✿ 🐾 **Frogmore Cotton Plantation and Gins** (318-757-2453, www.frogmore plantation.com), 11054 LA 84, Frogmore. Frogmore's tour, one of the most comprehensive guides to plantation life in America's South, covers slave culture, share-

GUIDES DISCUSS AFRICAN AMERICAN GOSPEL MUSIC DURING A TOUR AT FROGMORE PLANTATION AT NEAR VIDELIA.

Louisiana North photo

cropping, a rare steam engine cotton gin, and a high-tech, computerized cotton gin. There are 19 historic buildings. You can choose from a variety of tours, but especially enlightening is the optional music tour for groups only: It's a journey through the South in song and a complete history of gospel music, with live vocalists and, as another option, an enactment of a slave wedding in costume. Winner of the 1999 Louisiana Tourism Award. Open seasonally. Hours vary. Call for information.

✇ ⚘ **Kent Plantation House** (318-487-5998, www.kenthouse.org), 3601 Bayou Rapides Rd., Alexandria. One of state's best home tours, this French Creole plantation house was completed in 1899 and is the oldest standing structure in central Louisiana. The tour explains how people lived, worked, and played on plantations between 1795 and 1855. Some furnishings and memorabilia belonging to original families remain in the home. Special programs during the year include open-hearth cooking and blacksmithing demonstrations. Open 9 A.M.–5 P.M. Mon.–Sat.; tours at 9, 10, and 11 A.M. and 1, 2, and 3 P.M. Admission $6 adults and $2 kids age 6–12.

✇ **Lewis House** (318-757-2563 or 318-757-4422, www.home.no/thelewismuseum), 712 Louisiana Ave., Ferriday. Goodness gracious, this is an unforgettable tour. The simple home where Jerry Lee Lewis was born and grew up fascinates music fans. The museum is operated by the rock 'n' roll legend's sister Frankie Jean Lewis Terrell. Visitors are invited to "just drop by" or call for a personal tour. View furnishings from the 1950s and '60s, family keepsakes, and memorabilia. Learn details about touring in the entertainment world and the tumultuous life of Jerry Lee and his sister Linda Gail Lewis, the singer and songwriter. For a different experience, check out the family-owned drive-through liquor store next door. Open noon–6 P.M. daily. Call ahead to make arrangements for a morning tour.

✇ ⚘ **Louisiana 4-H Museum** ((318-964-2245, www.lsuagcenter.com), 8592 LA 1, Suite 2, Mansura. This remarkable center is for and about kids. Enjoy the multimedia exhibits, a delightful "See Louisiana Parade" diorama and an animatronic puppet show. Experience the history of 4-H in Louisiana from its beginning as a boys' "corn club" to what it is today—an informal educational program reaching more than 225,000 boys and girls annually with activities in clubs, camps, and clinics. The museum includes the LSU AgCenter's Avoyelles Parish Office, Southern University Extension Service's Avoyelles Office, and the Avoyelles Commission of Tourism. Open 8:30 A.M.–3:30 P.M. Mon.–Fri. Call for weekend appointments and special programs.

✇ ⚘ **Louisiana Maneuvers & Military Museum** (318-641-8333), 409 F St., Camp Beauregard, Pineville. Housed in a replica of a WWII military barracks at Camp Beauregard and

THE TOWN NAMED FOR A RACEHORSE

The town of Lecompte was named for a famous stallion owned by Jefferson Wells, a breeder who lived on a plantation south of town. The chestnut colt won many races in the 1850s at the Fairgrounds Racetrack in New Orleans. One local story has it that the railroad painted a sign on the side of the train depot years ago, and a "p" was added to the name. The town has been Lecompte ever since.

Cynthia V. Campbell

THE LOUISIANA 4-H MUSEUM AT MANSURA GIVES VISITORS A CHANCE TO LEARN ABOUT THE TALENTS DISPLAYED AND CHALLENGES MET BY ITS BOYS AND GIRLS.

operated by the Louisiana National Guard, the museum is a partnership between the military and civilian community. Prior to and during World War II, thousands of soldiers trained at camps Beauregard and Polk during the Louisiana Maneuvers. The museum's exhibits include uniforms and equipment. Open 7:30 A.M.–3:30 P.M. Mon.–Fri.

♪ ♿ ✿ **Marksville State Historic Site** (318-253-8954 or 888-253-8954, www .crtstate.la.us), 837 Martin Luther King Dr., Marksville. This 42-acre site contains prehistoric Native American ceremonial earthen mounds dating from 1400 A.D. A museum displays artifacts and interprets the native culture of the region. Admission is $4 per person, free for seniors 62 and over and children 12 and under. Open 9 A.M.–5 P.M. Tues.–Sat.

Old Lecompte High School (318-776-9520), 2004 St. Charles St., Lecompte. Built in 1924, the restored high school and community center includes a Farm Museum, Veterans Museum, 19th- and 20th-century rooms, and a 12-ton Veterans Memorial on the lawn. The collections in the Old Books Museum were donated by owners of early plantations. Open 9 A.M.–5 P.M. Tues.–Fri., and 9 A.M.–1 P.M. Sat.

♪ ✿ **Southern Forest Heritage Museum** (318-748-8404, www.forestheritage museum.org), 77 Long Leaf Rd., Longleaf. Take a guided tour through a sawmill town representing the many small communities that once flourished in the South. The 57-acre museum gives visitors a good look at the golden age of lumbering and sawmilling. The museum displays rare equipment and buildings dating from the early 1900s. You can see three steam locomotives, a roundhouse, and a belt-and-shaft driven machine shop. Start in the commissary that serves as an entrance, gift shop, and exhibit space. Open 9 A.M.–4 P.M. daily. Admission is $8, adults; $7, seniors; $5, children.

St. Francis Xavier Cathedral (318-445-1451), 626 Front St., Alexandria. Established as a chapel in 1817, the first church was built in 1834, and it was the only church left standing after Alexandria was burned by the Union Army in 1864. The cornerstone of the present building was laid in 1895, just a few weeks before the original church was destroyed by a fire. A new Gothic Revival structure opened in 1899. Sand for mortar was dug from the Red River and the floors were made of native pine. The rose windows in the apex of the transept are the largest in the state, and the main altar is hand-carved walnut. The cathedral, the rectory, and the Academy, known as the Cathedral Complex, are on the National Register of Historic Places. Office hours are 8 A.M.–4:30 P.M. Mon.–Fri.

Tacony Plantation, a mile west of Vidalia on LA 84/US 65. Tacony Plantation is the last remaining brick antebellum house in the Vidalia area. The original portion of Tacony was built around 1845. Tacony is an Indian word meaning "big man," and the name referred to Alfred Vidal Davis, one of Louisiana's richest cotton planters in the 1860s. Call the Louisiana Welcome Center at 318-336-7008 to arrange a tour. Open by appointment to individuals and groups.

✳ Green Spaces

Louisiana has always been known as a paradise for outdoor adventures, and the Alexandria/Pineville area is certainly a good hub for getting out beneath the trees to hear the wind rustling leaves and songbirds calling. The wildlife, sports, recreation, and outdoor adventures make up a good portion of the area's tourism economy. The vast forests and recreation areas offer plenty of opportunity just to get out and commune with nature. Even small villages often have small parks where you can sit beneath shade trees and watch birds or take leisurely walks. Locals expect visitors to ask where they can spend a few hours hiking or fishing. Almost everyone has a favorite green space in Louisiana's Crossroads.

✎ ⇨ **Camp Livingston Off-road Vehicle Trails** (318-765-3545, www.fs.fed.us/r8/kisatchie). The Livingston Multiple Use Trails are easy to reach from Pineville and Ball. About 35 miles of designated off-road-vehicle trails are available for all ORV users. These trails loop through upland pine forest and sandy hardwood bottoms, including numerous creek and stream crossings. There are two connected loops. The Little Creek Trail is an easy-to-moderate 22.6 miles with a number of creek crossings. Very dense, hilly stretches will keep you alert, and yellow trail markers should keep you on track. The Hickman Trail is a moderately difficult, 12.5-mile trail that is predominately upland pine hills. To get to the trailhead from Ball, go north on US 165 to LA 3130 until it becomes a gravel road. Go left at the Y junction of Forest Rd. 129 and follow it to the trailhead sign on the left. Use caution while traveling on the paved portions of old Camp Livingston; adjusting soil humps have raised portions of the cement roads and created virtual speed bumps. The trail has a daily use fee of $5 per operator, which can be paid at the trailhead.

✎ ⇨ ❦ **Forts Randolph & Buhlow State Historic Site** (318-484-2390 or 877-677-7437), 135 Riverfront St., Pineville. Incredibly scenic, with majestic oaks and towering pine tree, the historic site sits where two strategic forts were constructed by Confederate troops on the Red River opposite Alexandria after retreating

Union forces burned the city. The forts were established in order to repel future Union attacks. Although armed and manned, they never saw action. The earthen forts used slave labor from local plantations and were fortified with cannon and more than 800 soldiers. The site also includes the remains of Bailey's Dam, which allowed Union forces to escape below the rapids on the Red River after the Battle of Mansfield. Inside the visitors' center, there's an outstanding film explaining the importance of the forts and exhibits on the Red River Campaign. Several easy-to-walk raised trails circle through the woods to give a look at the remains of the earth works, and there's a great overlook of the river. Interpretive rangers give guided tours. Bring your cameras and binoculars. Open 9 A.M.–5 P.M. Wed.–Sun. Admission $4 per person; free to seniors 62 and over and children 12 and under.

 **Kisatchie National Forest** (318-473-7160), Kisatchie Headquarters Office, 2500 Shreveport Highway, Pineville. Drive through the forest on well-tended roads. The Federal Land Management Agency offers outdoor recreation opportunities. The forest includes the Kincaid Recreation Lake Area, the Valentine Lake Recreation Area, and the Azalea Trail. Groups can view or stop at recreation sites throughout the forest. See endangered species or enjoy tree identification. Open 8 A.M.–4:30 P.M. daily. Guided tours are available and fees depend on the services required. Free to nature clubs.

The Kisatchie National Forest has 600,000 acres that are home to hiking and tree identification tours, endangered species, geological sites, horseback riding, and biking trails. The Louisiana Archery & Sports Center stands ready to assist the outdoor archery lover. The Wild Azalea Trail is Louisiana's longest, traveling 31 miles

FORTS RANDOLPH AND BUHLOW STATE HISTORIC SITE AT PINEVILLE FOCUS ON THE RED RIVER CAMPAIGN OF THE CIVIL WAR.

Cynthia V. Campbell

of wooded riding trails. For the high-spirited outdoorsman, central Louisiana is home to Bayou Balloon Adventures—hot-air balloons!

Indian Creek, Cotile Lake, and Kincaid Lake all offer water sports, fishing, camping, and hiking. If canoeing is more your idea of fun, be sure to visit Ouiska Chitto River and Kisatchie Bayou. River tours are available to help you relive the history of the area's majestic Red River. First-rate fishing organizations find the river a hot spot for state and national bass tournaments. If high-speed motorboat racing is what you like, try Lake Buhlow in Pineville, also known as the fastest lake in the world.

✔ ❧ **Red River/Three Rivers Wildlife Area Management Complex** (318-757-4571). Located in the southern tip of Concordia Parish about 50 miles south of Vidalia, the wildlife area is between the Mississippi and Red rivers. A wide variety of nongame wildlife is present. Hunters will find deer, turkey, squirrels, raccoon, and other fur bearers. Fish species include bass, bluegill, crappie, and catfish, and crawfishing and frogging are popular. A public lottery hunt for alligators is available. The camping areas are maintained by the Louisiana Department of Wildlife and Fisheries. One of the areas provides potable water and comfort stations. Primary access routes are LA 5 and LA 910.

✳ To Do

FAMILY FUN ✔ ❧ **Buhlow Fun Park** (318-442-5110, www.buhlowfunpark .com), 1715 Monroe Highway, Pineville. A perfect place for families and anyone young at heart. Enjoy the Cannonball splash, amusement rides, kiddie and adult go-cart rides, nine batting cages, arcade machines, 18-hole miniature golf, and the food court. Summer hours are 4–9 P.M. Fri.; noon–9 P.M. Saturday; and noon–8 P.M. Sun. Special haunted house weekends in October.

FISHING ✔ ❧ **Indian Creek Reservoir** (318-443-3903). Open year-round, this recreation area includes the 2,250-acre Indian Creek Lake. The camping area has 71 campsites with conventional hookups, a swimming area, bath houses, a boat launch, and 75 picnic sites.

✔ ❧ **Kincaid Recreation Area** (318-443-3903, www.waters-edge-outdoors.com), 9912 LA 28 West, Gardner. The forested recreation area set among piney woods offers fishing, boat launches, and toilet and shower facilities. The campground is operated by the USDA Forest Service and site assignments are first-come, first-served. No reservations.

❧ **Saline-Larto Complex** (318-487-5885, www.wlf.louisiana.gov), about 20 miles east of Alexandria via LA 28. The complex, including the Dewey Wills Wildlife Management Area, has some of the best crappie, white bass, and catfish fishing in the state. The area spans four parishes and includes 11,000 aces of cypress-studded fishing waters fed by the Catahoula Lake Diversion Channel in east-central Louisiana. Outdoors enthusiasts can enjoy fishing, boating, and swimming.

GAMING **Paragon Casino Resort** (318-253-2019, www.paragoncasinoresort .com), 711 Grand Blvd., Marksville. The land-based casino resort, operated by the Tunica-Biloxi tribe, features more than 2,000 slot machines, 70 game tables, four restaurants, and a supervised child-care center. The resort complex includes the

Mari Center showroom for concerts and special events, an 18-hole golf course and hotel tower (see golf and accommodations listings), three movie theaters, retail shops, a first-class spa, fitness room, an indoor pool with a tropical island design, and an RV park with cabins.

GOLF LSUA Golf Course (318-473-6507), 8100 LA 71 South, Alexandria. The Louisiana State University-Alexandria course is a great course for beginners and golfers on a strict budget. Open 7 A.M.–7 P.M. daily. Call for tee times.

OakWing Golf Course (318-742-0333, www.oakwinggolf.com), 2345 Vandenburg Dr., Alexandria. Situated on the former England Air Force Base, the Jim Lipe–designed course considers the natural beauty of bayous, lakes, and tree-lined fairways. Five different settings offer a challenge for professionals as well as amateurs. This Audubon Trail course requires every golfer to play his or her best.

Cynthia V. Campbell

THE TUNICA-BILOXI TRIBE RUNS THE PARAGON CASINO AND RESORT.

Tamahka Trails Golf Club (318-240-6300, www.paragoncasinoresort.com), 222 Slim Lemoine Rd., Marksville. The master golf course architect Steve Smyers drew on his appreciation of Scotland's legendary course to create 18 holes with massive bunkers and challenging greens. The Audubon Trail course offers GPS in all carts, a 10,000-square-foot putting green, and practice greens dedicated to bunker play, chipping, and putting.

✳ Lodging

Best Western Inn Suites and Conference Center Alexandria (318-445-8496, www.bestwestern.com), 2720 North MacArthur Dr., Alexandria. Because of its central location, the inn in is convenient to both business and leisure travelers. Ask for a suite with a fireplace, spa, microwave, and refrigerator. There are indoor and outdoor pools and complimentary breakfast. Moderate.

Comfort Inn (318-484-9155, www .comfortinn.com/hotel-alexandria),

2001 North Bolton Ave., Alexandria. Located near historic Kent Plantation House, this chain hotel is comfortable and convenient. There's an exercise room and a seasonal outdoor pool. Staff is friendly and accommodating. Enjoy the free breakfast in an airy dining area. Moderate.

Comfort Suites Riverfront (318-336-1655, www.choicehotels.com), 100 Front St., Vidalia. Rooms are clean and comfortable, and you can sit in front of your room's picture window and watch the boats on the Mississippi River. There's an indoor swimming pool. Breakfast features hot foods served cafeteria-style. Moderate.

Hampton Inn & Suites (318-253-7576, www.marksvillesuites.hampton inn.com), 6895 LA 1, Mansura. The inn appeals to both families and business travelers. It offers large, clean, comfortable rooms, a sparkling outdoor heated pool, and a fitness center. The breakfast is varied and delicious. You'll find a friendly staff willing to give pointers on things to do in the area. A complimentary shuttle service is available to the Paragon Casino in nearby Marksville.

Loyd Hall (318-776-5641, www.loyd hall.com), 292 Loyd Bridge Rd., Cheneyville. One of the region's most gracious bed & breakfasts, Loyd Hall is 16 miles south of Alexandria and the heart of a 640-acre working farm. The property includes five charming B&B cottages and two luxury suites. Enjoy a full plantation breakfast and great tour of the home. Ask about the ghosts. Moderate.

Maisonnette Dupuy (318-253-5223), 232 East Mark St., Marksville. This beautifully restored, 105-year-old home in downtown Marksville is a perfect retreat from the bustle of modern life. The two-bedroom, two-bath home serves guests a continental breakfast. The property is owned by the acclaimed Red River Grill, which is within walking distance. Moderate.

Paragon Casino Resort (318-253-1946, www.paragoncasinoresort.com), 711 Paragon Place, Marksville. Your best bet when staying in Marksville. Ask for a room in the Atrium Tower, with New Orleans–style balconies. These rooms are attractive, spacious, and clean. The hotel area is on the opposite side of complex from the casino, making it comfortable for fami-

lies. It is easy to access the indoor tropical pool, movie theater, spa, and gift shop. The casino buffet serves an excellent breakfast, with numerous choices. Enjoy the gator pond in the lobby (yes, they are real alligators). The front desk can be slow at check-out time. Moderate.

Parc England Hotel (318-445-7574, www.parcengland.com), 1321 Chappie James Ave., Alexandria. Just two minutes from the Alexandria International Airport, this boutique hotel offers luxury and comfort. Guest rooms are handsome, with pillow-top mattresses and large modern bathrooms. The hotel is known for its exceptional service, and it offers a complimentary shuttle service. It's adjacent to the upscale Bistro on the Bayou restaurant. A simple continental breakfast is included. Moderate–expensive.

Tyrone Plantation (318-442-8528, www.tyroneplantation.com), 6576 Bayou Rapides Rd., Alexandria. Tyrone Plantation was built in 1843 by George Mason Graham, a cotton planter who was instrumental in forming the first

AN ELEGANT SITTING ROOM AWAITS GUESTS AT TYRONE PLANTATION IN ALEXANDRIA.

Larry B. Campbell

Larry B. Campbell

TYRONE PLANTATION WAS THE HOME OF GEORGE MASON GRAHAM, INSTRUMENTAL IN ESTABLISHING LOUISIANA'S FIRST INSTITUTE OF HIGHER EDUCATION.

state college, the Pineville Seminary of Learning, and hiring William Tecumsah Sherman as its first superintendent. Sherman was a regular guest at the Graham residence. After the Civil War, the university was moved to Baton Rouge and became LSU. Bed & breakfast guest rooms are in the main house. Each room has a sitting room and a full bathroom. A plantation

NORTH TOLEDO BEND STATE PARK IS IDEAL FOR AVID RV CAMPERS

Louisiana Office of State Parks

breakfast is served on heirloom china in the formal dining room, or you can chose to have your meal served in your bedroom suite. Moderate.

CAMPGROUNDS 🖉 (🛜) **The River View RV Park and Resort** (318-336-1401 or 866-336-1402, www.riverview rvpark.com), 100 River View Parkway, Vidalia. The beautiful campground welcomes families. With 193 fully equipped sites, it is certainly big-rig friendly. It features Wi-Fi service, local television, a clubhouse, meeting facilities, group fire rings, and tables in the picnic area. It also has a primitive area for tent campers. Inexpensive.

✳ Where to Eat

EATING OUT Cajun Landing (318-487-4912, www.cajunlanding.com), 2728 North McArthur Dr., Alexandria. The restaurant, attached to the Best Western hotel, dishes up plenty of Louisiana seafood favorites like fried catfish, oysters, and thick, smoky gumbo with plenty of rice and vegetables. For something delicate, try the seafood crepes with shrimp and crawfish tails in an etouffee sauce topped with Hollandaise, asparagus, and Louisiana crabmeat. Open 11 A.M.–2 P.M. and 5–10 P.M. Mon.–Sat. Moderate.

✍ **Lea's Lunchroom** (318-776-5178, www.leaslunchroom.com), 1810 US 71 South, Lecompte. I have known people to miss the opening of a football game rather than skip stopping at Lea's for a slice of pie. One of the oldest family-run restaurants in Louisiana, Lea's is listed in the Louisiana Restaurant Hall of Fame. With a nod to the 1930s diner, locals often order the special-of-the-day lunch plate, which comes with three homemade side dishes and a meat of your choice. Always popular is the simple but filling ham sandwich, with lettuce, tomato, and pickle on a bun. If you eat one slice of pie, you'll likely order at least two whole pies for takeout. Try the chocolate, lemon, cherry, apple, or maybe the blueberry; there's also sweet potato or the famous pecan pie. Open 7 A.M.–5 P.M. Tues.–Sat. and 7 A.M.– 4 P.M. Sun. Inexpensive.

Sentry Grill (318-445-0952, www .sentrydrug.net), 3209 South MacArthur Dr., Alexandria. This grill inside a drugstore is famous for its burgers and patty melt. Stop by for the daily lunch specials—pork loin with baked sweet potatoes and green beans or meat loaf with macaroni and cheese and great northern beans. Open 8:30 A.M.– 5:30 P.M. Mon.–Fri. and 8:30 A.M.– noon Sat. Country-style breakfast is served daily until 11 A.M., lunch is served 11 A.M.–3 P.M. Inexpensive.

Spirits (318-445-4491, 318-445-4491), 1260-H Jackson St., Alexandria. Spirits is known for its excellent lunch menu featuring large, fresh salads. There's

live entertainment on Wednesday and some Saturday nights. Open for lunch, 11 A.M.–2:30 P.M. Mon.–Fri., and dinner, 5–10 P.M. Tues.–Fri. Moderate– expensive.

✍ ♿ **Tunk's Cypress Inn** (318-487-4014, www.tunkscypressinn.com), 9507 LA 28 West. Try the seafood gumbo and fried catfish, and of course you can always dig into a charbroiled steak. Tunk's has live nightly entertainment and beautiful lake views. Open 5– 10 P.M. Tues.–Sat. Oyster bar is open 4–11 P.M. Tues.–Sat. Moderate.

DINING OUT Bistro on the Bayou (318-445-7574, www.bistroonthebayou .com), 13211 Chappie James Ave., Alexandria. A fine dining establishment, the restaurant brings a touch of cosmopolitan sophistication to a small town. Entrees, served a la carte, range from rare pan-seared tuna to USDA Prime filet mignon with béarnaise sauce and Louisiana crabmeat. The lunch menu includes filet mignon po-boys and a Louisiana crabmeat enchilada with chipotle sour cream and avocado. Luscious desserts include bread pudding with almond sauce and crème brulee. Open for lunch 11:30 A.M.–1:30 P.M. Tues.–Fri., and dinner, 6–10 P.M. Mon.–Sat. Expensive.

Diamond Grill (318-448-8989, www .thediamondgrill.com), 924 Third St., Alexandria. The grill offers prime aged steaks, fresh Gulf seafood, homemade desserts, and a bar and wine vault. In 1931, this was a downtown jewelry store. Now it shines with a wide range of superb dishes. Patrons relax in the art nouveau/art deco setting and enjoy the new Creole cuisine. Try the crostini with melted blue cheese on toasted bread with peppered pears and toasted walnuts, drizzled with port wine syrup. For an entrée, select fish Creole (fish of the day topped with tomatoes, bell peppers, onions, and okra and lemon-thyme rice. There's always Southern shrimp and grits, y'all. Expensive.

Red River Grill (318-253-5252, www.redrivergrill.org), 313 North Washington St., Marksville. It's not unusual to find people planning a weekend outing in Marksville just to dine at the Red River Grill. It can easily stand up to any top restaurant in New Orleans. For an exceptional treat, select any of the dishes that are Louisiana favorites: pecan-crusted redfish Avoyelles, topped with crawfish, tasso, and mushrooms in a spicy cream sauce, or grilled lemon fish, topped with crabmeat and garlic *beurre blanc*. Finish up with white-chocolate mousse on an almond shell topped with raspberry sauce. The courtyard atmosphere, ample wine list, and soft lighting create the mood for a romantic outing. Guests have been known to linger for hours with an after-dinner drink or hot coffee. Hours are 5–10 P.M. Tues.–Sat.

Verona Italian Restorante (318-445-1500) McArthur Dr., Alexandria. Outstanding Italian dishes styled with a creative hand are the hallmark of this restaurant. Experience the exceptional service and the softly lit romantic atmosphere. You will most likely be met by the owner and the head chef, who will take time to ask about your favorite meats, sauces, and other foods. The wine list is more than ample and there are plenty of good vintages to pair with any entree. Open 11 A.M.–9 P.M. Mon.–Thur., 11 A.M.–10 P.M. Fri.–Sat., and 10 A.M.–8 P.M. Sun.

✳ Entertainment

Alexandria Symphony Orchestra (705-548-0885, www.alexsym.org), 3001 North Beauregard St., Alexandria. The orchestra, comprised of pro-fessional musicians, performs in the lovely Rachel M. Schlesinger Concert Hall and Arts Center. Currently the five-concert season features varied programs of classic pieces.

G.G.'s Club (318-473-4944, www.ggshinnclub.com), 7521 Coliseum Blvd., Alexandria. Owned by the swamp pop musician G.G. Shinn, this club truly rocks. The 2,500-square-foot dance floor features live music every night. Check out the dress code on the website. There's a $7 cover. The bar stays open until 3 A.M.

Paragon Casino Resort (318-253-2019, www.paragoncasino.com), 711 Grand Blvd., Marksville. In addition to 24-hour gaming, Paragon offers live shows in the Mari Center starring world-famed celebrities and live shows in the Pelican Club. Kids and families also can enjoy first-run films in the resort's movie theaters in a separate area from the gaming center.

River Oaks Square (318-473-2670, www.riveroaksartscenter.com), 1330 Main St., Alexandria. Check for lectures and special events. People can visit with visual artists while they work. The visual and crafts center has two facilities, the Bolton House, circa 1899, and the studio annex building. Hours are 10 A.M.–4 P.M. Tues.–Fri. and 10 A.M.–2 P.M. Sat.

Tunk's Oyster Bar (318-487-4014, www.tunkscypressinn.com), 9507 LA 28, Boyce. The restaurant and bar on Lake Kincaid is popular for its food and nightly live entertainment. Open 4–11 P.M. Tues.–Sat.

✳ Selective Shopping

Alexandria Antique Mall (318-449-4495), 5123 Masonic Dr., Alexandria. Made for folks who live to browse. Look for glassware, lamps, shades, mirrors, garden ornaments, rugs, and furniture. Open 10 A.M.–5 P.M. Wed.–Sat. and 1–5 P.M. Sun.

Mike's Hardware (318-253-9204), 304 East Mark St., Marksville. Walk into this old-fashioned hardware store, full of old tools, collectibles, and "gotta-have" stuff. The store carries a full line of garden seed, feed, and modern hard goods.

Paragon Casino Shops (800-946-1946, www.paragoncasinoresort.com), 711 Paragon Place, Marksville. Like most casinos, Paragon has its share of glitzy shops designed to appeal to high rollers, but there are several stores here that have extra appeal. The LA 1 Market contains Louisiana folk art, cookbooks, furniture, snacks, and items that make great "take-home" gifts. Next door, Tribal Connections sells a variety of beautiful Native American jewelry and one-of-a-kind items. If you're in the market for makeup or fragrances, pick up a take-home lotion or body scrub from Spa La Vie.

The Purple Cow (318-442-1470), 1357 Peterman Dr., Alexandria. The independently owned store features wooden toys, doll parts or accessories, yo-yos, kites, kaleidoscopes, piñatas, toy balloons, dolls, and doll houses. Fun for kids of all ages.

✳ Special Events

March: **Louisiana Nursery Festival** (318-748-8850, www.louisiananursery festival.com), Forest Hill. When the sun turns warm in early spring, Louisiana gardeners get a fever to start working in their lawns and beds. They also know it's time to head for the festival of flowers at Forest Hill. Veteran gardeners know it's *the place* to shop for all types of shrubs and trees, and most abundant blooms. Rose bushes are always popular, especially the disease-resistant Knockout. If you

don't know what to plant or where, just ask the garden experts on the site. You can visit more than 50 booths where you'll find porch swings and chairs, yard art, birdhouses, pottery, and garden tools; bigger-ticket items include golf carts, lawnmowers, tractors, and pickup trucks. Food booths sell shrimp, chicken, pork, and gator on a stick along with the expected corn dogs, funnel cakes, and snow cones. A Ferris wheel and other rides are available for the kids. Hours 8 A.M.–6 P.M. Sat. and 10 A.M.–4 P.M. Sun.

April: **Jazz on the River** (www .cenla.org), Alexandria. The annual festival at the amphitheatre downtown is a lively premier event that brings world-class jazz to the heart of Crossroads country. People gather on the banks of the Red River to hear large jazz ensembles made up of high school students as well as world-renowned musicians such as Kathy Wade, Maynard Batiste, Maurice Brown, Kent Jordan, and Nicholas Payton. The event is sponsored by the Arna Bontemps African American Museum, www.arnabontempsmuseum.org.

May: **Louisiana Dragon Boat Races** (318-442-9546, www.louisianadragon boatraces.com), Alexandria. Watch teams of paddlers race these long, colorful, canoe-like boats on the Red River from the Amphitheater downtown and enjoy live music and an expanded **Second Saturday Market at the Museum**, with locally made art, crafts, and food.

Tunica-Biloxi Indian Pow Wow (318-305-6595, www.tunica powwow.org), Chief Joseph Alcide Pierite Pow Wow Grounds on the Tunic-Biloxi Reservation, off LA 1, Marksville. Native American dancers and artisans from across the country gather for cultural festivities with authentic food, arts and crafts,

MARDI GRAS, A STATEWIDE CARNIVAL SEASON

Mardi Gras, a season devoted to parades and parties, dates from ancient times. Historians debate its origins, but some believe its roots are tribal fertility rituals that welcomed spring. The Roman poet Ovid said the rituals took place 5,000 years ago. In France, Druids sacrificed bulls to the gods in a celebration called *la fete du soleil*, and links can be traced back to the lupercalia, a Roman festival that took place in mid-February. The Catholic Church wanted to end pagan festivals, so it changed the celebration to Carnival, a time of festivity before the serious period of Lent. In the 1500s, the French added *boeuf gras*, the last meat eaten before Lent. Mardi Gras ("Fat Tuesday" in French) is the day before Ash Wednesday, the first day of Lent.

According to Arthur Hardy's *Mardi Gras in New Orleans,* the Catholic Church established the moveable dates for Mardi Gras when it developed the dates for Easter, which can occur as early as March 22 or as late as April 25. Mardi Gras is 47 days before Easter (40 days of Lent plus six Sundays), so it can be anywhere between February 3 and March 9.

Mardi Gras started in New Orleans with a carnival ball in 1743, and has grown to huge proportions. Today it is a major tourism event that draws thousands to the city. Parades are held by krewes and organizations throughout the city. Costumed and masked riders on elaborate floats toss "throws" to crowds shouting, "Throw me something, mister!" The throws are mostly shimmering plastic beads, but they can also be small stuffed animals, silly toys, or wrapped pieces of candy. Often the beads land high in tree branches and dangle there throughout the year. During the last two weeks before Mardi Gras, there are parades every day.

Mardi Gras is celebrated throughout Louisiana. Parades and Carnival parties are held in Shreveport, Morgan City, Lake Charles, Alexandria, Lafayette, Baton Rouge, and communities big and small in between. Many events in the smaller towns are family oriented, fun for children as well as adults. Some have become famous in their own right. Lake Charles is the only place is the state where the public is invited to see the ornate costumes of all the krewes at one time. The Royal Gala, held the night before Mardi Gras day, features a presen-

dancing, and sing. Special performances feature well-known Native American musicians. Prizes are awarded in dance categories including men's fancy, women's fancy shawl, and the chicken dance. Open to the public.

June: **Louisiana Corn Festival** (318-346-2575, www.bunkiechamber.net),

corner of Lake St. and 208 Pershing Ave., Bunkie. Sponsored by the Bunkie Chamber of Commerce, the festival celebrates the community's agriculture heritage. Following a city parade on Saturday, contests begin with the Corn Creature and Lizard races, corn shucking and eating contests, and pirogue

Cynthia V. Campbell

DS TOSS BEADS INTO MOUTH OF AN ANIMATED ATOR ON A MARDI GRAS FLOAT.

tation of the courts in the Convention Center. A nominal fee gets you in the door, and jeans are the dress of choice. In Baton Rouge, crowds gather in the town's oldest neighborhood near the State Capitol for the satirical Spanish Town Parade spoofing Louisiana's politicians. The small community of Mamou attracts thousands to its Courir de Mardi Gras, with costumed riders on horseback stopping at homes to sing, dance, and beg for live chickens and other makings for a gumbo. The *courir* arrives back in town in the afternoon to party until midnight.

If you want to visit Louisiana during Mardi Gras, make plans and book your hotel reservations early. In New Orleans, most hotels require a three- or four-day minimum stay during the final four days of Mardi Gras. Hotels in other cities also fill quickly since families and friends return year after year for the festivities. Wear casual, comfortable clothing for parades, and remember it can be chilly in south Louisiana in February. If you're planning to attend a formal ball or party, ask you host or hotel concierge about appropriate dress.

Because the exact dates of Mardi Gras change each year, this guide simply lists reminders of Carnival activities in the Special Events lists. To learn more about Mardi Gras history and traditions, visit www.mardigras guide.com, www.mardigrasday.com, www.neworleansonline.com, and www.library.thinkquest.org. You can also visit the convention and visitors' bureau websites of Louisiana towns and parishes for information on local Mardi Gras events.

races on the bayou. On Sunday, attend the talent contest that searches for the "Corn Idol," and the corn cooking contests. Yes, you will find plenty of food, live bands, and crafts.

September: **Jim Bowie Festival** (318-336-8223), 100 Riverview Parkway, Vidalia. This excitement-filled annual festival includes a re-enactment of the famous Sandbar Duel, the Bowie BBQ Duel, live gospel, pop, and Cajun music, food, and games.

October: ♂ ♞ **Sugar Day Festival** (318-487-5998), Alexandria. Sugar cane harvest was a special time in the 1800s. Colonial families would gather and hold parties after the fall harvest. The tradition is brought to life at Kent House with the firing up of the sugar-cane mill to make some sugar. Activities include arts and crafts, local musicians, Native American dancers, and the Bayou Rapides Vintage Dancers. The annual fund-raising *cochon de lait* (roasted suckling pig) dinner is held in the evening. Open 9 A.M.–3 P.M.

Cajun Country (Acadiana)

3

LAKE CHARLES AREA

LAFAYETTE/NEW IBERIA AREA

MORGAN CITY, HOUMA-THIBODAUX,
GRAND ISLE AREA

INTRODUCTION

Cajun Country stretches across southern Louisiana from just west of New Orleans to the Texas border on the Sabine River. The land ends with the warm waters of the Gulf of Mexico. People here are known to embrace all things with a passion for life. Many are descended from Acadians, the French-speaking people who settled eastern Canada in the 1600s. Others came seeking their fortune in a new land or looking for a better quality of life. You're also likely to meet folks who moved to the area in the last century, and are very much part of the local culture. The term Cajun also applies to someone of non-Acadian origin who became Cajun through assimilation—living and working in the region, isolated from other places. Residents are often a blend of several ethnic groups, including Spanish, French, Creole, Anglo and Native American. They love music, food, gathering with friends, and keeping their families together. They also love to share a good story with neighbors or visitors who happen to stop and enjoy life. If you can strum a guitar, dance a two-step, or stir up a mean pot of stew, so much the better.

The word *Cajun* is an adaptation of Acadian or "Cadian," and to understand the culture it helps to know something about how Cajun Country came about. The French had been working the Atlantic waters east of Canada for many years. The explorer Giovanni da Verrazzano visited the New World in 1524 and named the area Arcadia after ancient Greece. Mapmakers started labeling the Nova Scotia area as L'Arcadie, eventually leaving off the *r*. In 1603, Pierre Dugua, Sieur de Mons, first attempted a settlement in Saint Croix Island in the middle of the St. Croix River. A colony was established at Port Royal in 1605, firmly demonstrating a French presence in North America.

The French and Indian War, 1754–1756, resulted in the British expelling the Acadians from Nova Scotia, New Brunswick, and Prince Edward Island. Some were returned to British colonies or England, while others returned to France or fled to communities along the North Atlantic coast. Many died from disease or drowned on ships.

When the first Acadians arrived in Louisiana in 1764, the territory was owned by Spain. Records show that the first arrivals were 20 Acadians who had been in American colonies. They were welcomed, given land, and settled along the Mississippi River around the boundary of St. John and St. James parishes. They were soon followed by relatives and friends. At first the newcomers were offered land and assistance. As others began arriving from France and the Caribbean, they were settled according to the Spanish defense strategy along the Mississippi River at key

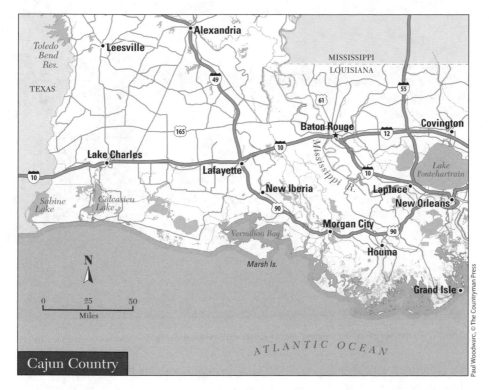

Cajun Country

points of the English/Spanish territory. The Spanish governor of Louisiana, Don Bernardo de Galvez, wanted the Acadians as a counterinfluence to the nearby British.

To sum up the Acadian arrivals in Louisiana: 20 came from New York in 1764, 311 came from Halifax in 1764–1765, 689 came from Maryland and Pennsylvania in 1766–1770, about 1,600 came from France in 1785, and 19 came from St. Pierre in 1788. Others came over the years, and documentation of their arrival is still sought by genealogists and historians.

The early Acadians were skilled farmers and trappers. They were also survivors. During the early period of resettlement in Louisiana, they had to adjust to the semi-tropical climate and deal with outbreaks of malaria and yellow fever. Those who settled in swampy lowlands became expert boaters and fishermen. In higher elevations they developed large farms and ranches. In the 1800s, they lived as their grandparents in Canada had, keeping to the old traditions. They developed cooking strategies using nature's bounty and entertained themselves with simple folk tunes and dances. Social life centered on family and the Catholic Church. In the 1900s, they continued to expand their knowledge of farming and fishing along with oil and gas exploration. In 1971, the Louisiana state legislature officially recognized 22 Louisiana parishes and "other parishes of similar cultural environment" for their strong French Acadian cultural aspects and made "The Heart of Acadiana" the official name of the region. In general, the word Acadiana is used to refer to the region. You will see it on regional maps and signs throughout Cajun Country.

FAMILIES FIND PLENTY OF PLACES TO FISH IN SOUTHWEST LOUISIANA.

Acadiana is a land of spicy people, food, and music. Don't be surprised if the folks you meet don't speak French. However, get into a conversation with locals and you'll hear a slight accent and French expressions in with the English. A few older folks still speak Acadian French, and you'll certainly hear the language when musicians break into song. The towns and cities are charming and often have street names written in English and French.

Get out into the countryside. Drive past fields of sugar cane gently swaying in the breeze and along slow-moving bayous with white, feathery egrets and herons wading beneath trees draped with Spanish moss. Ride an air boat or a shallow-draft barge to see alligators, snakes, and other critters. The semi-tropical climate allows wildlife to thrive throughout Cajun Country. Experienced guides can show you the hottest spots to lure the catch of the day in inland waters or offshore in the Gulf of Mexico. Charter a fishing boat to enjoy some of the best inland and offshore fishing in the United States. Walk along an oak-shaded *chenier* (a ridge of land) to find trees filled with warblers. Check out a festival, such as the Duck Festival in Gueydan or the French Food Festival in Larose, where locals cook more than 20 different dishes,

CATTLE REST BENEATH OAK TREES IN VERMILION PARISH

including alligator sauce piquante and white oyster soup. Tap your feet to a zydeco or Cajun band. Get to know the people of Acadiana. And keep in mind that people in these parts are great storytellers. At the same time, they are shrewd business-men and -women. After all, there's likely a tough frontier ancestor somewhere in their family trees.

Since Cajun Country stretches out across the width of Louisiana, the state's offi-cial tourism map designates main areas of interest. Travelers can easily follow major highways and roads to fascinating destinations. Look for the Lake Charles Area in the southwest, the Lafayette Area in the central portion of the region, and the combined areas of Morgan City, and Houma-Thibodaux and Grand Isle in the southeast. Major cities in each area serve as hubs and provide conveniences to small towns and villages. All of these areas encompass magnificent wetlands with distinctive features. Each time I spend time in any part of Cajun Country, I return home with my spirit renewed by colorful sunsets, sun-dappled swamps, soaring birds, and the friendly, hospitable people who find joy living with nature.

LAKE CHARLES AREA

T he southwest corner of Louisiana is perhaps the most diverse area of Cajun Country. You can relax and play in wetlands like no others in America. Visit small communities in the coastal prairies, where farmers have developed innovative agricultural techniques. Lake Charles and its environs are rich in evidence of pre-European Native American occupation, including sites where arrows and beads have been found. Attakapas Indians, hunters and gatherers, roamed the area and eventually their descendants were assimilated into the population. In the early 18th century, southwest Louisiana was not quite Spanish Texas, nor was it either French or Spanish Louisiana. Gradually, Americans and Europeans, including relocated Acadians, French and Spanish Creole privateers, started moving into the area, as did runaway slaves. Midwesterners were drawn here and developed towns like Iowa and Welsh. In the late 1800s, the principal industry was lumber. Trees were felled and milled. At one time more than 28 mills processed pine and cypress into lumber, siding, and beaded board. The southwest Louisiana area includes Lake Charles and Calcasieu Parish, Cameron Parish, Allen Parish, part of Vermilion Parish, and Jefferson Davis Parish.

In Lake Charles you'll find a vibrant community where residents cherish old traditions but relish the challenges of new enterprises. The town of Cameron, the parish seat continues to rebuild from severe damage caused by Hurricane Rita in 2005 and Hurricane Ike in 2008. Cameron Parish has a close relationship with the Gulf of Mexico. The natural beauty of the area draws people to drive the Creole Nature Trail, a network of scenic highways and walking paths through 180 miles of marsh, bayou, and shoreline. Stop to watch an alligator sunning in the middle of a walking path or a nutria swimming through thick reeds and you'll know why much of the area is called Louisiana's Outback. Allen Parish offers the excitement of the Coushatta Casino Resort as well as lakes and rivers to fish to your heart's content. Jennings, halfway between Lake Charles and Lafayette, was originally settled by wheat farmers in the Midwest. This town was incorporated in 1901 when the state's first oil field was brought in at Jennings Field.

GUIDANCE **Allen Parish Tourist Commission** (337-639-4868, www.allen parish.com), 8904 LA 165, Oberlin.

Cameron Parish Tourist Commission (337-775-5718, www.cameronparish touristcommission.org), P.O. Box 388, Cameron.

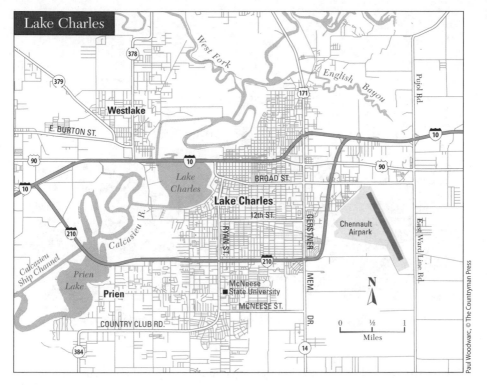

Lake Charles

Paul Woodwarc, © The Countryman Press

Jeff Davis Parish Tourist Commission (800-264-5521, www.jeffdavis.org), 100 Rue de l'Acadie, Jennings.

Lake Charles/Southwest Louisiana Convention and Visitors Bureau (800-546-7952, 337-436-9588, www.ryougame.com), 1205 North Lakeshore Dr., Lake Charles. The attractive visitors' bureau is located just off I-10, Exit 29 eastbound and Exit 30 westbound. The spacious, open center has a wall of brochures and a small cafe where people can grab a complimentary cup of coffee. Friendly travel advisors are available to answer all your questions. Visitors are invited to check their e-mail, walk out onto the patio for a grand view of the lake, or stroll to a nearby alligator pond for a photo of the King of the Marsh. Open 8 A.M.–5 P.M. weekdays and 8 A.M.–3 P.M. Sat.–Sun.

AREA CODE 337.

GETTING THERE *By car:* From In-10, take Exit 29 eastbound and Exit 30 westbound. Follow North Lakeshore Drive 0.7 mile; Lakeshore becomes Broad Street for 0.10 mile; turn right onto Ryan Street and in 0.2 mile you come to the heart of downtown.

By air: **Lake Charles Regional Airport**, 500 Airport Blvd., Lake Charles, is near Burton Coliseum. Ground transportation includes rental cars, taxis and limousine service.

Southwest Louisiana/Lake Charles Convention and Visitors Bureau

BIRDS FOLLOW A TUG AND BARGE ALONG THE CALCASIEU SHIP CHANNEL LEADING TO GULF OF MEXICO.

MEDICAL EMERGENCIES For general emergency information and inquiries call 337-491-1201 or the Calcasieu Parish Office of Emergency Preparedness, 337-721-3800. Lake Charles hospitals with emergency service include **Christus St. Patrick Hospital** (337-431-7936, www.stpatrickhospital.org), 524 Doctor Michael Debakey Dr., Lake Charles, and **Lake Charles Memorial Hospital** (337-494-3000, www.lcmh.com), 1900 West Gauthier Rd., Lake Charles.

✳ Cities, Towns, and Villages

Sulphur, named for the chemical and mining industry that helped establish Calcasieu Parish in the late 1800s, is the gateway to the Creole Nature Trail All-American Road and Audubon Society's Peveto Woods Bird & Butterfly Sanctuary in Cameron Parish. The annual Cal-Cam Fair draws visitors from throughout the country.

Cameron, the seat of Cameron Parish, is a small Gulf Coast town with some of the most resilient people in America. In 1957, the town was nearly destroyed by Hurricane Audrey. Nearly 50 years later, in late September 2005, Hurricane Rita touched down. On September 14, 2008, Hurricane Ike destroyed 90 percent of the homes in Cameron Parish. While people are returning, the community is rebuilding slowly. Cameron remains a major jumping-off spot for those who want to explore the Creole Nature Trail. The parish's long coastline, bordered by marshes and wetlands, attracts birders, photographers and outdoors enthusiasts.

Vinton has long been known for its horse racing. The Delta Downs Racetrack Casino and Hotel has been recently renovated into a multi-million dollar casino and track featuring live horse racing and other entertainment. During the Civil

War, Army regiments of the Louisiana and Texas troops were stationed near the town. Soldiers cut a road extending from an area in Vinton known as Niblett's Bluff on the Sabine River to the City of Alexandria. Defensive earthen bretworks of the Civil War were constructed at Niblett's Bluff and can still be seen today.

Jennings, midway between Lake Charles and Lafayette, is a delightful town that embraces its Cajun heritage. The Zigler Museum stuns visitors with a world-class art collection in a Colonial-era home, and the W. H. Tupper General Merchandise Museum takes you back to early 1900s country life and features an exhibit on the history of the telephone. Today's farmers and artisans bring produce, preserves, and crafts to the Main Street Farmers Market on Saturday mornings. Don't miss stopping by Chateau des Cocodries to get an up-close look at the alligator in a protected habitat just off I-10.

✳ To See

Charpentier Historic District. Not far from the Lake Charles Visitors' Bureau, this older residential section of town encompasses about 40 blocks of stunning, turn-of-the-20th-century homes and other buildings. During the 1800s, experienced lumbermen from the northern United States, known locally as "Michigan Men," arrived in Lake Charles. They brought with them the tall and angular style of construction that mirrored the Victorian tastes popular in most of America at the time. Also here is a variation of the Colonial Revival style, which became a sort of local sawmill version of the classic Southern plantation. Each house reflects the characteristics of its builder or carpenter. The very creative carpenters got their plans from pattern books and combined elements and details from various styles. This blending of features has been called Lake Charles Style architecture by Jonathan Fricker, the architectural historian for the state of Louisiana. The carpenters of that early age were recognized by naming the Historic District Charpentier, which is French for carpenter. The district was admitted to the National Historic Register in 1990. Pick up a map of the area from the Visitors' Bureau. Residences are privately owned, but private tours are conducted by the Calcasieu Preservation Society and can be arranged through the Southwest Louisiana Convention and Visitors Bureau by calling 800-456-7952.

MUSEUMS Brimstone Museum Complex (337-527-0357, www.brimstone museum.org), 900 South Huntington, Sulphur. Housed in the Old Southern Pacific Railway Depot, the museum focuses on the turn of the last century, when sulphur was mined here. Exhibits explain the development of the Frasch mining process that brought wealth to this part of Louisiana. Plan to take at least 30 minutes to view the exhibits and vintage photographs. For exhibit schedules, contact the museum.

✎ ✿ **Children's Museum** (337-433-9420, www.swlakids.org), 327 Bond St., Lake Charles. The museum has three floors and more than 45 hands-on exhibits that provide children and their parents a chance to interact, learn, and have fun in a safe atmosphere. Exhibit topics include music, visual and performing arts, folklife, storytelling, and art. The museum hosts field trips, birthday parties, and special events year round. Admission is $7 for children and adults.

DeQuincy Railroad Museum & City Park (337-786-2823, www.dequincy railroadmuseum.com), 400 Lake Charles Ave., DeQuincy. Housed in the 1923 Kansas City Southern Depot, the museum displays a large and varied collection of railroad memorabilia. You can see a 1913 steam locomotive, a 1947 passenger coach, and two vintage cabooses. Also on display are model trains and an extensive collection of Gauge 1 model steam and diesel engines. A visit takes about 2 hours.

DeQuincy Town Hall Museum (337-786-6451), 218 East Fourth St., DeQuincy. The old town hall features the Newport Industries museum. A wall of honor pays tribute to locals who have served in the U.S. military.

Imperial Calcasieu Museum (337-439-3797, www.imperialcalcasieumuseum .org), 204 West Sallier St., Lake Charles. Come here to view historical artifacts and memorabilia depicting life in the Old Imperial Calcasieu region. The museum is also home to the Gibson-Barham Gallery, featuring contemporary and traditional artists and master craftsmen as well as the 375 year-old Sallier Oak.

Mardi Gras Museum of Imperial Calcasieu (337-436-9588, www.swla mardigras.com), 809 Kirby St., Lake Charles. Lake Charles is not to be outdone by other Louisiana communities, not even including New Orleans, when it comes to Mardi Gras celebrations. Recently renovated, this museum contains one of the largest collections of Mardi Gras costumes in the world. The elaborate regalia include large headpieces and costumes for the kings, queens, princesses, dukes, and duchesses of each krewe's royal court. Especially fascinating is an exhibit on the costume design and construction process as it moves from approval of a yearly theme to pencil sketches, colored renderings, and finally the stitched, sewn, glued, and wired masterpieces. Visitors can climb aboard a float constructed in the museum to see what it's like to ride on a Mardi Gras parade.

USS *Orleck* Naval Museum Historic Naval Museum (337-433-4083, www .orleck.org), 604 North Enterprise Blvd., Lake Charles. The Naval Museum features the USS *Orleck* DD886 destroyer, which served during the close of the second World Ward, during Korea and throughout the Vietnam conflict. Overnight tours for adult and kids groups can be arranged. Open 10 A.M.–3 P.M. Mon.–Fri. and 10 A.M.–4 P.M. Sat.–Sun.

W.H. Tupper General Merchandise Museum (337- 821-5532, www.tupper museum.com), 311 North Main St., Jennings. This general store, which opened in 1910, was left completely intact when its doors were shut for the last time in 1949. The store remained shuttered, with all of its inventory undisturbed on the shelves until 1971, when the last owner died. The heir offered the building and its contents to the town as a museum. You can walk across hardwood floors and see what people shopped for in the early 1900s, from farm tools to bolts of fabric to kids' toys and medicines. Coushatta Indians once brought their pine needle baskets to the store to trade for food and merchandise. Many of these are displayed throughout the store. Open 9 A.M.–5 P.M. Mon.–Fri.

Zigler Museum (337-824-0114), 411 Clara St., Jennings. The Zigler contains a world-class art collection, including works by Anthony van Dyck, John Constable, Camille Pissaro, and Albrecht Durer. Housed in a Colonial-era home, it also features special exhibitions. The museum was created in 1963 by Ruth B. Zigler, widow of the industrialist and philanthropist Fred B. Zigler.

There's no lack of green spaces in coastal Louisiana. When trees give way to coastal marshes, you'll still find animal refuges filled with marsh grasses and cheniers topped with oak trees. Visitors can look for city and parish parks designed to give adults and children a chance to stretch their muscles in safe, clean environments. Below you'll find special places you'll never forget and want to visit often.

BEACHES Louisiana's Gulf Coast does not have any large, white-sand beaches because of the many coastal marshes and wetlands. The few beaches that exist in southwest Louisiana are best for shelling and fishing. There are no public facilities such as restrooms or showers.

Holly Beach (800-456-7952, www.visitlakecharles.org), LA 82, Lake Charles. The community of Holly Beach was completely leveled by Hurricane Rita in 2005. Some owners of beachside properties have rebuilt their homes on elevated piers, following strict new building codes. While the area has no beach amenities, it's still fun on a pretty day to look for shells and put your feet in the Gulf waters.

NATURE AND WETLANDS The **Cameron Prairie National Wildlife Refuge** (337-598-2216, www.fws.gov/swlarefugecomplex), 1428 LA 27, Bell City. The refuge opens more than 9,600 acres of marsh and prairie to the public. The Cameron Prairie Visitors' Center features state-of-the-art talking dioramas as well as over-water boardwalks and viewing areas. Open 7 A.M.–4 P.M. Mon.–Thurs., 7:30 A.M.–3 P.M. Fri., 10 A.M.–4 P.M. Sat., and noon–4 P.M. Sun.

Creole Nature Trail All-American Road. This network of scenic highways and walking paths winds through 180 miles of marsh, bayou, and shoreline, and Cameron Parish has been called Louisiana's Outback for its plentiful wildlife and untamed beauty. Along these roads you'll find outstanding national wildlife refuges, scenic roads, turnouts for photographing and viewing wildlife. Pick up a free GPS video tour from the Lake Charles Visitors' Center and have a personal guide.

Lacassine National Wildlife Refuge (337-774-5923), 209 Nature Rd., Lake Arthur. A self-guided drive at Lacassine Pool, a freshwater marsh 4 miles south of Hayes on LA 14 and 4.5 miles south on Illinois Plant Road, is excellent for bird watching. Open year-round from an hour before sunrise until an hour after sunset, the area includes a roseate spoonbill rookery.

Peveto Woods Bird and Butterfly Sanctuary (800-456-7952, www.braudubon .org), Cameron. The sanctuary is 8.5 miles west of the LA 27/LA 82 intersection. Encompassing 40 acres, the sanctuary was the first *chenier* sanctuary for migratory birds established in Louisiana. An enormous number of songbirds pass over the Cameron Parish coast in the spring and fall. Bring binoculars to view warblers, tanagers, and orioles as well as the Scarlet Tanager. Butterfly viewers enjoy the beauty of Peveto Woods on Little Florida Beach during the late fall to early summer.

⅃ **Pintail Wildlife Drive** (337-598-2216). This 3-mile driving tour just south of Cameron Prairie Refuge Visitor Center on LA 27 features a half-mile handicap-accessible boardwalk with an excellent view onto the marsh and prairie areas. It's excellent for nature photography, especially during waterfowl migrations. Open daily during daylight hours.

Rockefeller Wildlife Refuge (337-491-2593), 5476 Grand Chenier Highway, Grand Chenier. A nature drive takes you through areas where you can view alligators, shorebirds, and a wading bird rookery. There's great fishing here.

🏊 ♿ ➔ **Sabine National Wildlife Refuge** (337-762-3816), 3000 Holly Beach Highway, Hackberry. Start at the Sabine Refuge Visitors' Center, about 8 miles south of Hackberry on LA 27, to see all the exhibits. Enjoy the Sabine Wetland Walkway, a 1.5-mile paved walking trail to the edge of Lake Calcasieu. Here you can see alligators, herons, egrets, wading birds, nutria, and other critters. Listen quietly for bird songs and alligator sounds. Be watchful for gators and other critters that may cross your path. About two miles south on LA 27, you can walk the 1.5-mile Marsh Trail, where you'll find cordgrass, thick stands of cane, and more abundant wildlife. The walks are open during daylight hours, as are the Hog Island Gully, Blue Crab, and West Cove recreation areas, which offer excellent fishing, crabbing, and shrimping in season.

PARKS AND RECREATION Parks in and around the towns create spaces that make it easy to spend time outdoors without venturing into the wetlands. You can jog, bike, picnic, take photos of wildlife, and just enjoy the scenery. Many are as appealing to visitors as they are to locals who take advantage of everything the parks have to offer.

🐾 **Dog Park at Enos Derbonne Sports Complex** (337-502-5214, www.ward3 recreation.com), 7903 Lake St., Lake Charles. This is a place for dogs and their masters to have fun. Equipment in the park includes an A-frame agility walk, crawl tunnel, dog teeter-totter, dog walk ramp, fire hydrant jump, hound hoops, hurdles, a tire jump, wall jump, and weave poles. Pet owners are responsible for their animals, including curbing any aggressive behavior and cleaning up after them. The park is equipped with Mutt Mitt stations for waste pickup and disposal as well as a dog-friendly water fountain.

Herman Frasch Park (337-527-2526, www.sulphurparks.com), 400 Picard Rd., Sulphur. Situated next to the Frasch Park Golf Course, the park offers a playful setting with gyms, picnic tables, tennis courts, basketball hoops, and lots of trees.

Lakefront Promenade (800-456-7952 or 337-491-1280), 1111 Bord du Lac Dr., Lake Charles. Found along the northern and eastern shores of Lake Charles just off I-10, the promenade is a beautiful walk. It boasts a cobblestone path along the lake complete with custom lighting and seating. At the entrance, enjoy the Louisiana Landing Fountain featuring a bronze geese sculpture. Located behind the Lake Charles Civic Center, it is walking distance from Millennium Park, Bord du Lac Marina, and PPG Sprayground. A domestic alligator pond is nearby.

Niblett's Bluff Park (337-589-7117, www.niblettsbluffpark.com), 3409 Nibletts Bluff Rd., near Vinton. Niblett's Bluff Park overlooks scenic Sabine River. Operated by local citizens, the park seeks to preserve the land's natural beauty and history. During the Civil War, a fort stood where the current park exists. Features include a children's playground area, boat launch, RV sites with water and electricity hookups, and mini-cabins with air conditioning and heat for rent.

North Beach (337-491-1280), North Lakeshore Drive directly off I-10, Lake Charles. Eastbound travelers take at Exit 29; westbound travelers take Exit 30A. North Beach is the only white sand inland beach from Texas to Florida. It's a lovely area, just minutes from downtown Lake Charles. Open from 10 A.M.–8 P.M., the beach is easily accessible, and admission is $1 per car.

♪ (◦) **Prien Lake Park**, 3700 West Prien Lake Rd., Lake Charles. This 29-acre park is south of the city of Lake Charles and the lake. Overlooking Indian Bay on Prien Lake, a waterway where 19th-century schooners once sailed, you'll find trees, grass, fountains, and streams. The park features a playground and spray-ground water park, picnic areas, walking paths, an elevated boardwalk, and amphitheatre. There are canoe and boat launches as well as two pavilions and a free Wi-Fi area.

Sam Houston Jones State Park (337- 855-2665, www.lastateparks.com), 107 Sutherland Rd., off LA 378 in Moss Bluff, near Lake Charles. With 1,087 acres of lakes, trees, vistas, rivers, and streams, this is an excellent spot for bird watching in spring and fall. Camping sites are available.

✳ To Do

BIRDING **America's Wetland Birding Trail** has three loops in Cajun Country. The **Sabine Loop** begins in the mixed hardwood-pine forests and cypress-tupelo gum swamps associated with the Sabine and Calcasieu rivers. Moving south, it breaks into the isolated prairies and brush lands of Lake Charles and Sulphur, where you can spot raptors, flycatchers, sparrows, and other birds. Even further south, the loop crosses the Intracoastal Waterway into Cameron Parish and a huge

NORTH BEACH AT LAKE CHARLES, CONVENIENTLY JUST OFF INTERSTATE 10, IS MINUTES FROM DOWNTOWN.

Southwest Louisiana/Lake Charles Convention and Visitors Bureau

complex of fresh, brackish, and salt marshes rich in waterfowl and wading birds. The loop terminates along the Gulf of Mexico, harboring plovers, sandpipers, gulls, terns, and other seabirds. Offshore, you can view pelicans and other seabirds. The **Creole Loop** begins above Lake Charles in Sam Houston State Park and winds south though grassland and forest habitats. In the community of Holmwood it detours through a series of rural roads where you can find Eastern phoebes, vireos, kinglets, warblers, and Northern cardinals during the winter. Midway through the loop the landscape opens into a freshwater-brackish area where oak-studded *cheniers* (ridges) provide rest stops for migrating birds. The trail continues to the Gulf Coast region, where you can tour the Rockefeller State Wildlife Refuge Nature Drive. The **Lacassine Loop** begins directly on I-10 at the Louisiana Oil and Gas Park in Jennings. Drive on to the Lorraine birding trail to look for the anhinga, pileated woodpecker, tufted titmouse, and swamp-dwelling species. The Lake Arthur boardwalk is great for watching gulls, terns, raptors, and woodland birds. The Thornwell area offers viewings of dragonflies, waterfowl, and raptors, and in winter you're likely to see golden eagles, caracara and maybe even small sandhill cranes. As you wind through the Lacassine National Wildlife Refuge you may spot the rare black-bellied whistling duck, crested caracara, and vermilion flycatcher during spring, fall and winter months. For details and to obtain a brochure with maps, visit www.louisianatravel.com/birding, and also visit www.americaswetland.com.

BOATING Bord du Lac Marina (337-491-1256), Lakeshore Dr., Lake Charles. Operated by the City of Lake Charles, the marina, with 38 boat slips, is conveniently located near downtown.

Bowtie Marina (337-478-0130), 1245 Giovanni St., Lake Charles. This full-service marina has boat slips and a launch, gasoline and diesel fuel pumps, a full ship store, clean restrooms, and mechanics available.

Bridgepoint Yacht Center (337-436-0803), 800 Mike Hooks Rd., Westlake. The owners, Tony and John Giaimis, provide a boat launch, boat slips, and yacht repair.

FISHING AND HUNTING Fishing is a year-round pastime in Lake Charles, as it is in most of southwest Louisiana. The fall hunting season brings thousands of waterfowl to the area. Local hunting guides will explain Louisiana fishing and hunting regulations and show you the ropes. Some even offer lodging. Check www.visitlakecharles.org for a list of expert guides, including those below.

Bayou Charter Service (337-802-0522, www.bayoucharterservice.com), LA 384, Lake Charles. Specializing in inland saltwater fishing charters, this service operates out of Hebert's Marina on Calcasieu Lake about 4 miles from Hackberry.

Capt. Scott Richey's Louisiana Outfiters (337- 302-2320, www.louisiana outfitters.net), 151 West Oak Lane, Lake Charles. Louisiana Outfitters offers guided hunting for ducks and geese in southwest Louisiana, as well as saltwater fishing for speckled trout and redfish on Calcasieu Lake. The fishing lodge accommodates nine fishermen and is located in Hebert's Settlement on Calcasieu Lake. Guests have the opportunity to hunt in productive fields for ducks and speckle-belly geese. The hunting lodge accommodates 12 hunters and is 20 miles south of Lake Charles. The staff is experienced and professional.

Gotta Go Charters (337-598-2001, www.lakecalcasieu.com), P.O. Box 4973, Lake Charles. Captain Sammie Faulk offers inland and offshore fishing, with departures from Hebert's Marina or from Pecan Island, as well as hunting. The website contains links to Cameron weather, tides, sunrise and sunset times, and phases of the moon. Lodging is available at the Big Lake Guest Houses.

Hackberry Rod and Gun (337-762 3391, www.hackberryrodandgun.com), 585 Lake Breeze Dr., Hackberry. Offering experienced guides, this company has been cited in *Salt Water Sportsman Magazine* and *Outdoor Guide Magazine.* The company offers guided duck hunts with retrievers during season (usually mid-August) in sunken fiberglass blinds. Lodging is in condominium-style rooms with a separate living room and bedroom.

GAMING Coushatta Casino Resort (337-738-7300, www.coushattacasino resort.com), 777 Coushatta Dr., Kinder. Operated by the Coushatta tribe, the casino resort has thousands of slot machines, 70 tables including roulette, blackjack, craps, and mini-Baccarat, as well as live poker rooms and high-stakes gaming. The resort has six restaurants, luxury hotel rooms, and an RV resort.

Delta Downs Racetrack, Casino and Hotel (337-589-7441 or 800-589-7441, www.deltadowns.com), 2717 Delta Downs Dr., Vinton. The racetrack features a six-furlong oval with two chutes that allow for a range of races. There's a year-round schedule of regular races. Visitors will find ample seating and video screens in the grandstands. Places to eat include the Vista, with panoramic views of the racetrack; Triple Crown Buffet; Lookout Bar & Grill; and a food court. The hotel features deluxe rooms and suites and a freestyle swimming pool.

Isle of Capri Casino Hotel (337-430-2400, www.isleofcapricasinos.com), 100 Westlake Ave., Lake Charles. On the west side of the city, Isle of Capri features more than 1,800 slots including the classics, video poker, and 50 table games with the largest poker room in the mid-South, with 28 live poker tables. Four restaurants feature a wide array of choices. Stay over in the all-suite Tower or choose the newly remodeled Inn at the Isle for relaxed comfort. Live music and headline entertainment are part of the mix.

L'Auberge du Lac Casino Resort (337-395-7777, www.ldlcasino.com), 777 Avenue L'Auberge, Lake Charles. This 26-story casino resort entices visitors with 1,000 casually elegant rooms, 147 luxury suites, and 30,000 square feet of nonstop Vegas style gaming including 62 table games and 1,600-plus slot machines. The Contraband Bayou Golf Club is an 18-hole championship Tom Fazio course. Eight innovative restaurants include Ember, a fine dining steak house, and Le Beaucoup Buffet, serving American, Cajun/Creole, Chinese, and more. Guests can relax at the world-class spa and pools with a lazy river. Expect top-name entertainment.

GOLF Bayou Oaks Golf Course (337-583-7129), 2300 Bon Vie, Sulphur. Located on Choupique Bayou, Bayou Oaks opened to the public in 2005. A best-kept secret for affordable, relaxing golf with undulating greens that make rounds enjoyable and challenging. The clubhouse's lounge and grill serves great Angus hamburgers. There is a pro on duty.

The Contraband Bayou Golf Club (337- 395-7220, www.ldlcasino.com), 777 Avenue L'Auberge, Lake Charles. The world-renowned golf architect Tom Fazio emphasized the marsh and lowland features of the natural environment to enhance this unique 7,000-yard, par-71 championship golf course.

Frasch Park Golf Course (337-527-2515, www.sulphurparks.com), 400 Picard Rd., Sulphur. The 6,267-yard public course is 18 holes with a 71 par, and was ranked in the Top 75 of the United States, the Top 15 of the Southeastern United States, and number one in Louisiana in 1996.

Gray Plantation Golf Club (337-562-1663, www.graywoodllc.com), 6150 Graywood Parkway, Lake Charles. One of 12 courses on Louisiana's Audubon Golf Trail, Gray Plantation's 18-hole, 7,200-yard, semi-private championship course includes 60 acres of lakes, 94 bunkers, four par 3s, a media area, and a scoreboard. The club offers daily fees to provide public access.

Mallard Cove Golf Course (337-491-1204), I-210 exit 10B, Lake Charles. Situated on the old Chennault Airbase, the course is on 200 acres. It features a championship layout design with women's, senior, medium and championship tees. The course has 25 large bunkers and water hazards on 12 of the 18 holes. The course rating is 73.0 and the slope is 128.

National Golf Club of Louisiana (337-433-2255, www.nationalgcla.com), 1400 National Dr., Westlake. The 18-hole, par-72 course, designed by David Bennett, is set in a mature-growth pine forest, features an abundance of water hazards in preserved wetlands, has roughly 90 bunkers, and is part of a new high-end, residential community. There are five sets of tees with yardage from 6,065–7,025 yards.

TREES LADEN WITH MOSS PROVIDE A RICH HABITAT FOR HUNDREDS OF SPECIES OF BIRDS AND ANIMALS IN SOUTH LOUISIANA.

Cynthia V. Campbell

Pine Shadows Golf Course (337-433-8601), 750 Goodman Rd., Lake Charles. Just off Opelousas Street, the 214-acre, 18-hole course is only minutes from downtown Lake Charles. Features include target grounds on the driving range, a pro shop, and a snack bar. This player-friendly course has both a scoreboard and a media area located on-site.

SPECIAL TOURS Crawfish field tours offered by the **Jeff Davis Parish Tourist Commission** (337-821-5534, www.jeffdavis.org) run from January to May, the crawfish harvest season. The tours begins at the **Tietje Crawfish Farm**, where guides explain the crawfish's habitat and how they are harvested, and continues at the I-10 Crawfish Cooperative, where guests are given a cleaning demonstrating and an explanation of how they are distributed and marketed.

❋ Lodging

A number of hotels are located in the Lake Charles area. Several of the larger ones are associated with the local casino resorts. Others can be found throughout the area with easy access to Interstate 110 or the Lake Charles Loop. Boaters can look at the Marina listing for lodgings designed for fisherman. Old-fashioned bed & breakfast accommodations are limited, but a number of chain hotels offer breakfast.

L'Auberge du Lac Casino Resort (866-580-7440, www.ldlcasino.com), 777 Avenue L'Auberge, Lake Charles. Rising 26 stories, this hotel includes deluxe rooms, suites and villas. The contemporary rustic décor follows a soft gold, beige, and brown theme. You'll have plenty of amenities and room to spread out. Families can enjoy either the adult pool or the large Contraband Bayou. There's easy access to restaurants, spa, and casino. Moderate.

Comfort Inn (337-478-4650, www.comfortinn.com), 607 East Prien Lake Rd., Lake Charles. Located near McNeese State University and Lake Charles Regional Airport, this hotel offers free breakfast with hot waffles and coffee. Make use of the exercise room and outdoor pool. Moderate.

(ᵥ) **Coushatta Casino Resort** (337-738-7300, www.coushattacasinoresort.com), 777 Coushatta Dr., Kinder. The Coushatta Grand Hotel, just steps from the gaming floor, features 208 spacious rooms. The décor is in soft southwestern colors. Spacious two-room suites include marbled-lined baths, raised Jacuzzi tubs, and large-screen televisions. An original sculpture in the Promenade represents the seven clans of the Coushatta tribe: bear, beaver, bobcat, daddy long legs, deer, panther, and turkey. The Koasati Pines Lodge features 92 comfortable rooms situated on the resort's golf course. Enjoy the pool, patio, and free Wi-Fi. The Red Shoes RV Park, adjacent to the casino, has full hook-up pads and courts for tennis, basketball, volleyball, and shuffleboard. There are also two bathhouses and a swimming pool complex. Inexpensive–moderate.

Delta Downs (337-589-441, www.deltadowns.com), 2717 Deltadowns Dr., Vinton. Stylish rooms feature contemporary décor, a sitting area, and spacious bathrooms with a stand-alone glass shower. The deluxe suites include a king bed, living room, and widescreen flat-panel television. You can unwind at the swimming pool with tropical landscaping. Inexpensive–moderate.

🖉 ⅋ (ᵥ) **Holiday Inn and Suites** (337-310-7700 or 800-HOLIDAY, www.holidayinn.com), 2940 Lake St., Lake Charles. Near the center of town, this facility has a business center, health and fitness center, indoor pool, Wi-Fi, restaurant, and cocktail lounge. Kids eat free. Moderate.

Isle of Capri Casino Hotel (337-430-2400, www.isleofcapricasinos.com), 100 Westlake Ave., Westlake. Situated on the west side of Lake Charles, the resort has two hotels. The Tower has junior suites with a choice of one king bed or two queens. Amenities include cable television, business desk, and coffee. A limited number of parlor suites offer a separate bedroom and living room area with a wet bar. A fitness center and sauna is located in the Tower. The Inn at the Isle features newly remodeled rooms with pillow-top mattresses, flat-screen television and coffee. Both hotels have a seasonal pool and hot tub. The resort also features an RV park with electric hookups. Moderate.

🖉 (ᵥ) **La Quinta Inn and Suites** (337-478-9889, www.lq.com), 1201

West Prien Lake Rd., Lake Charles. With easy access to the 210 Loop off I-10, the hotel is convenient to restaurants, shops, businesses, and casinos. Amenities include Wi-Fi, indoor and outdoor pools, a fitness center, restaurant and lounge. Free breakfast and parking. Moderate.

B&BS (ᵞ) **Aunt Ruby's Bed & Breakfast** (337-430-0603, www.aunt rubys.com), 504 Pujo St., Lake Charles. Situated in the heart of downtown, this B&B was the city's first boarding house. Five luxurious guest rooms feature period furnishings and private bathrooms. Amenities include Wi-Fi access and private phone lines. A full gourmet breakfast is served. No children under age 12. Moderate.

✆ (ᵞ) **CA's House** (337-439-6672), 624 Ford St., Lake Charles. Built around 1900, the Colonial house has a lovely mahogany staircase leading up to guest quarters on the second and third floors. Outside, within a landscaped hideaway, a private hot tub waits. Rooms range from large luxury suites to single-occupancy rooms. Gourmet meals and breakfast are served in a large dining room, the King's Kitchen. The B&B caters to couples, businesspersons, and travelers. Guests have access to Wi-Fi and kayaks and bikes anytime. Moderate.

✳ Where to Eat

Certainly you can expect outstanding seafood in Louisiana, and the southwest corner of the state is no exception. There are many Cajun restaurants offering flavorful favorites, including crawfish etouffee, jambalaya, and grilled catch of the day. The area also offers an interesting variety of foods, including Asian, Mexican, Italian, and popular American dishes.

EATING OUT ✆ **Boudin King's Cajun Way restaurant** (337-824-6593, www.boudinlink.com), 906 West Division St., Jennings. This casual restaurant in an old barn is a good stop for spicy Cajun specialties, including boudin, gumbo, fried seafood, and po-boys. Open 8 A.M.–9 P.M. Mon.–Sat. Moderate.

✆ **Darrell's** (337 474-3651), 119 College St., Lake Charles. A great place for sandwiches and po-boys. Customers return here time and again. Try a sandwich of spicy Cajun shrimp sautéed in butter sauce with your choice of cheese and mustard mayo or the jalapeno mayonnaise and lettuce. Another popular choice is the tender sliced smoked brisket cooked in Darrell's BBQ sauce and topped with the same ingredients. Inexpensive.

✆ **DeAngelo's Casual Italian Restaurant** (337-478-5781), 2740 Country Club Rd., Lake Charles. The restaurant's varied menu makes it easy to join your family or a crowd of friends. Popular items include a delicious tomato basil soup and create-your-own pizzas and calzones. You can dress up an Italian sub with veggies or order lasagna served with salad and garlic bread. Open 11 A.M.–2 P.M. and 4–9 P.M. Tues.–Sun. Moderate.

Granger's Restaurant and Lounge (337-433-9130), 2636 Old Town Rd. (LA 3059), Lake Charles. Known for its excellent boiled seafood and crawfish in season, the hamburgers at Granger's are considered outstanding. Hours are 11–2 A.M. Moderate.

✆ **Luna Bar and Grill** (337-494-5862, www.lunaarocks.net/joomla), 719 Ryan St., Lake Charles. It's a kid-friendly place, but if you hang out late you can enjoy live music. The most popular appetizer is a south Louisiana favorite, a creamy spinach and artichoke dip. Popular entrees include grilled yellow fin tuna and shrimp scampi in a house sauce. There's a large sandwich selection as well as a children's menu. Live music every Thursday, Friday and Saturday night at an outdoor stage. Hours are 11 A.M.–10 P.M. Mon.–Fri., noon–10 P.M. Sat. Moderate.

Pujo Street Cafe (337- 439-2054, www.pujostreet.com), 901 Ryan St., Lake Charles. The restaurant is in the former Gordon's Drugstore. Drop in for lunch and order a vegetable burger made with a blend of mushrooms, onions, brown rice, and low-fat cheeses, or a Thai chicken satay salad. For dinner, try the andouille-stuffed grilled chicken breasts. It's a classy place with a casual atmosphere. Open 11 A.M.–9:30 P.M. Mon.–Fri. and noon–9:30 P.M. Sat. Moderate.

❃ **Richard's Boudin and Seafood Restaurant** (337-625-8474), 2250 East Napoleon St. (LA 90), Sulphur. Definitely a local hangout for friends and travelers looking for *real* Cajun food. The sausage and boudin is tasty and so are the boiled crawfish in season. Open 10 A.M.–8:30 P.M. Mon.–Thurs. and 10 A.M.–9:30 P.M. Fri.–Sat. Moderate.

❃ **Steamboat Bill's on the Lake** (337 494-1070, www.steamboatbills.com), 1004 North Lakeshore Dr., Lake Charles. Drop by this casual restaurant for its delicious shrimp and crawfish pistolettes (little rolls). Cajun dishes include piquant shrimp etouffee, and you can eat your fill with the fried seafood dinners that come with coleslaw, crispy French fries, and a roll. Kids' meal options include chicken fingers and popcorn shrimp. Hours are 10:30 A.M.–9 P.M. Mon.–Thurs., 10:30 A.M.–9:30 P.M. Fri.–Sat., and 10:30 A.M.–9 P.M. Sun. Moderate.

(800-584-7263, www.coushattacasino resort.com/dining), 777 Coushatta Dr., Kinder. Inside the Coushatta Casino Resort, this restaurant serves USDA choice and prime steaks perfectly grilled to your specifications. If you're not in the mood for boneless rib eye or prime rib, try the lemon pepper grilled salmon or the tequila grilled shrimp. A healthy option is the wild greens with fruit salad topped with roasted pecans. Open 4:30–10 P.M. Sun.–Mon., 4:30–10 P.M. Thurs., and 4:30–11 P.M. Fri.–Sat. Expensive.

Ember Grille and Wine Bar (337 395-7565, www.ldlcasino.com), 777 Avenue L'Auberge, Lake Charles. The fine dining restaurant is in the L'Auberge du Lac Casino. Select a fine wine from an extensive cellar to pair with your meal. Start with seared Hudson Valley foie gras on a toasted brioche with poached pear in port sauce, and follow with a steak or perhaps a smoked pepper crusted ahi tuna with wasabi mashed potatoes and baby bok choy. Elegant yet comfortable, the restaurant appeals to those who like a touch of luxury at the end of the day. The bar and piano lounge is open nightly 5:30 P.M.–midnight. Hours 6 P.M.–10 P.M. Sun.–Thurs. and 5:30–11 P.M. Fri.–Sat. Expensive.

Mazen's Restaurant (337-477-8207, www.mazens.com), 217 West College St., Lake Charles. Although the restaurant claims to be Mediterranean, many dishes are more French. The casual dressy atmosphere is perfect for a romantic night out. Oysters Bienville, topped with shrimp and cheese sauce, are exquisite. Try the crab cake filled with jumbo crabmeat in a mornay sauce or the roasted duck breast in a raspberry reduction. For a perfect ending to your meal, order a perfect cup of Turkish coffee. Open for lunch

11:30–2 P.M. Tues.–Fri., and dinner 5:30–10 P.M. Mon.–Sat. Expensive.

La Truffe Sauvage (337-439-8364, www.thewildtruffle.com), 815 West Bayou Pines Dr., Lake Charles. This delightful restaurant nestled in the heart of the city features delicious homemade soups, sauces, and desserts prepared by a French-trained chef. Lunch and dinner selections include Angus beef, seafood, and fresh vegetables. Lobster bisque, duck confit, and veal osso bucco with saffron risotto are delicious. Expensive.

✳ Entertainment

Artists Civic Theatre (337-433-2287, www.actstheatre.com), 1 Reid St., Lake Charles. The Artists Civil Theatre and Studio (ACTS) offers a variety of productions, including dramas, comedies and musicals. Recent productions have included Rodgers and Hammerstein's *Cinderella* and *Lilies of the Field*.

Central School Arts & Humanities Center (337-491-1292, www.artsand humanitiesswla.org), 809 Kirby St., Lake Charles. The city's old Central School is now home to the Art Associate's Gallery, Black Heritage Gallery, Mardi Gras Museum, Children's Theatre and numerous studios and leisure learning classes. Hours are 8:30 A.M.– 5 P.M. Mon.–Fri.

Historic City Hall & Cultural Center (337-491-9147, www.cityoflake charles.com), 1001 Ryan St., Lake Charles. After an extensive restoration, the historic 1911 City Hall reopened in 2004 as the city's new public art gallery and cultural facility. The center showcases numerous traveling exhibitions from all over the world as well as work by regional and local artists. Solo exhibitions have included the works of Pablo Picasso, Ansel Adams, Norman Rockwell, and Tasha Tudor. The build-

ing has three floors of gallery space, a clock tower, and a landscaped brick courtyard. You should also check for upcoming presentations and festivals.

Lake Charles Little Theatre (337-433-7988, www.thelclt.com), 813 Enterprise Blvd., Lake Charles. Founded in 1926, the community theater group has survived good times and bad. Performances are held in the New Stable Playhouse in the former U.S. Postal Service vehicle maintenance building. Performance dates and times are posted on the website.

Lake Charles Symphony (337-433-1611, www.lcsymphony.org), 809 Kirby St., Suite 210, Lake Charles. For more than 50 years, the Lake Charles Symphony has brought classical music to southwest Louisiana. Working with other community organizations, the orchestra presents free youth concerts and a free family concert in the spring featuring the winners of the annual Concerto Competition for high school students. Seasonal concerts are held in the Lake Charles Civil Concert. Visit the website for dates and times.

McNeese State University, Department of Performing Arts (800-622-3352, www.mcneese.edu/performing arts), 4205 Ryan St., Lake Charles. The department offers a variety of programs featuring performances by music and theater students, as well as faculty members. The McNeese Bayou Players began staging theatrical productions on the campus beginning in the 1950s. Information on upcoming recitals, concerts, dramas, and musicals are posted on the website's calendar.

NIGHTLIFE Big Kahuna (337-474-1311), 3426 Ryan St., Lake Charles. It's a long way from Hawaii, but here's where tropical casual meet Cajun cool. The tropical-themed bar includes a DJ, dance floor, pool tables, darts, and pin-ball. Hours are 3 P.M.–2 A.M., Mon.–Sat.

Casinos Needless to say the party doesn't stop in the casinos' gaming areas. So start by checking out the entertainment schedules at **Globar** and **Jack Daniels Bar & Grill** at **L'Auberge du Lac Casino** (777 Avenue L'Auberge,, Lake Charles, www.ldlcasino.com); the **Caribbean Cove** at Isle of Capri Casino (100 Westlake Ave., Westlake, www.isleof capricasinos.com); and **Club 1Sixty5** At **Coushatta Casino Resort** (777 Coushatta Dr., Kinder, www.coushatta casinoresort.com). The casino resorts also feature national touring acts and international headliners throughout the year.

Cigar Club (337-562-8889), 1700 East Prien Lake Rd., Suite 5, Lake Charles. The club has the largest walk-in humidor in southwest Louisiana. The elegant lounge specializes in martinis and live music on Wednesday and Friday. Hours are 10 A.M.–10 P.M. Mon.–Fri. and noon–2 A.M., Sat.

Luna Bar and Grill (337-494-5862, www.myspace.com/lunabarandgrill), 719 Ryan St., Lake Charles. This restaurant is also a top spot for listening to local music. Rub shoulders with locals and practice your Cajun lilt.

MacFarlane's Celtic Club (337-433-5992), 417 Ann St., Lake Charles. Along with people of French and Spanish heritage you'll find quite a few folks of Celtic descent in south Louisiana. MacFarlane's is a grand spot for traditional Irish-Scottish pub meals and drink. The friendly staff can help you choose from more than 120 brands of beer. Bring a buddy and you may end the evening singing a Scottish ballad.

OB's Bar & Grill (337-494-7336), 1301 Ryan St., Lake Charles. This for-mer bar is now a popular hangout for hamburgers and a variety of live music, including vintage pop, rock and alternative music. Hours are 10 A.M.–11 P.M. Mon., Tues., and Thur., 10 A.M.–4 A.M. Wed. and Fri., and 6 P.M.–2 A.M. Sat.

✴ Selective Shopping

505 Imports (337-480-6505, www .505imports.com), 1776 West Prien Lake Rd., Suite G, Lake Charles. Look here for hand-crafted imported furniture, accessories from all over the world, and home accents such as unusual cabinets, tables, rugs, benches, pottery, and pillows. Open 10 A.M.–6 P.M. Mon.–Sat. and 1–5 P.M. Sun.

Artistic Crosses by Frank Thompson (337-855-9582, www.artistic crosses.com), 5635D Welcome Rd., Moss Bluff. The crosses made from inch-thick stained glass are designed to be hung in a window, and they come in 18 different color combinations. After 25 years making windows and doors for churches and homes, the artist Frank Thompson turned to selling crosses when his studio was ravaged by Hurricane Rita. Now they are being shipped across the country.

Brousse's A Child's World (337-477-0580), 542 West Prien Lake Rd., Lake Charles. Founded by R.T. Brousse in 1948, the company specialized in wooden toys for children and Radio Flyer products. Today's owners offer traditional toys, children's fine furniture, christening gowns, vintage children's clothing, and a year-round selection of school uniforms.

Cedar Chest Antiques (337-564-5646), 210 Division St., Lake Charles. Discover rustic items for home décor and vintage cookbooks. The spacious store features collectibles, art, jewelry, furniture and crafts.

Cottage Shops (337-433-9722, www
.cottageshopslc.com), 2710 Hodges St.,
Lake Charles. Hours vary. Located
between Alamo and 12th streets, these
locally owned shops in quaint wood-
frame cottages offer a little something
for everyone, from Louisiana products
to lingerie.

Expressions (337-433-6200, www
.expressionslc.com), 3204 Ryan St.,
Lake Charles. Look for fun gifts and
accessories. The store carries limited
edition jewelry, fleur de lis–themed
items, shoes, bags and purses, and
home décor. Open 10 A.M.–5 P.M.
Mon.–Fri. and 10 A.M.–4 P.M. Sat.

**French Quarter Antique Mall and
Flea Market** (337-477-1804, www
.frenchquarterantiquemall.com), 3204
Ryan St., Lake Charles. Some 50 vendors showcase a wonderful variety of
antiques, collectibles, new and used
furniture, and unusual gifts. You'll
spy costume and fine jewelry, glassware, crystal, kitchenware, and vintage
linens. Open 10 A.M.–5:30 P.M. Mon.–
Sat. and 1–5 P.M. Sun.

Jon Margeaux (877-474-9607, www
.jonmargeaux.com), 2706 Hodges St.,
Lake Charles. Located in the Cottage
Shops, Jon Margeaux carries products
from local and American artists as well
as a few imported items. What makes
the store unique is that it also manu-
factures much of its own giftware.
Check the website for hours.

Louisiana Market (337-656-2908,
www.thelouisianamarket.com), 2710
Hodges St., Lake Charles. Pick up
gourmet foods, coffee, baskets, souvenirs, and gift items. Open 10 A.M.–
5 P.M. Mon.–Fri. and 10 A.M.–4 P.M. Sat.

Prien Lake Mall (337-477-7411), 496
West Prien Lake Rd., Lake Charles.
This regional shopping center features
95 stores. Hours are 10 a.m.–9 p.m.
Mon.–Sat. and noon–6 p.m. Sun.

✴ Special Events

February: ☙ **Lake Charles Mardi
Gras** (800 456-7952, www.swlamardi
gras.com), Lake Charles. Mardi Gras
in Lake Charles area is known for its
family friendly atmosphere. The city
has more than 50 krewes and is second
only to New Orleans in the numbers of
krewes participating in Mardi Gras
activities. It's the only place in the state
where the public is invited to see the
ornate costumes of royal courts from
all the local krewes in one place at the
Twelfth Night, usually January 6, and
at the Royal Gala the evening before
Mardi Gras day. A nominal fee is
charged at the door and jeans are the
comfort clothes of choice. One day is
devoted to children and family activities and parade routes are filled with
families lining the streets.

March: **Iowa Rabbit Festival** (337-
433-8475, www.iowarabbitfestival.org),
Iowa City Park, Iowa. The farming
community of Iowa holds its Rabbit
Festival in mid-March. As many as 400
rabbits of all breeds have been shown
during the festival. Activities include a
parade, a rabbit cook-off, and entertainment by regional bands.

April: ☙ 🐾 **Louisiana Railroad Days
Festival** (337-786-3076, www.larail
roaddaysfestival.com), DeQuincy Railroad Museum Park, DeQuincy. Held
the second weekend of April, the festival began as a county fair with food
booths and games. Activities start with
the K9 Caboose Pageant followed by
the Railroad Days Pageant, and
include a children's bicycle parade, a
main parade, carnival rides, gospel
music, and arts and crafts. The event is
alcohol free, and admission is free.

May: **Contraband Days Pirate
Festival** (337-436-5508, www.contra
band
days.com), Lake Charles Civic Center

Southwest Louisiana/Lake Charles Convention and Vistors Bureau

PIRATES MAN A FLOAT FOR THE MAY CONTRABAND FESTIVAL PARADE IN LAKE CHARLES.

Grounds just off I-10, Lake Charles. According to local legend, the pirate Jean Lafitte frequented this area, docking his boat along the lake's sandy shores. Held in May, activities center around the Civic Center's seawall. On the first night of the two-week celebration, you can see and hear cannon fire as citizens try to defend the seawall, only to have the pirates capture the mayor, put him on trial, and make him walk the plank. Don't miss the food contests, marching parades, big name musicians, carnival rides, and fireworks. Gate admission is $10 for adults, and $5 for students through high school.

August: **Gueydan Duck Festival** (888-536-6456, www.duckfestival.org) Duck Festival Grounds, Gueydan. Usually held the weekend before Labor Day, the Duck Festival celebrates the hunting heritage of Acadiana. Come for the Duck and Goose Calling contest, skeet shooting, hunting dog trials, and decoy carving. There's great food, nightly bands, a grand parade, and outdoor and indoor cooking contests.

LAFAYETTE/NEW IBERIA AREA

Lafayette is the heart of Cajun County. It's the metropolitan hub of the Acadiana region, where you can start a meal with a cup of elegant duck gumbo and dance away the night to heart-thumping music by Grammy-award winning musicians. It's easy to hit the city's cultural high notes. Stop inside the Acadiana Art Center to see exhibitions of contemporary work by regional and national artists. Pop into the theater for concerts by the current generation of Cajun, zydeco, jazz, and experimental musicians. For authentic Cajun folklife, stroll through Vermilionville, a living history village where you can learn how to cook sweet dough pie or dance a two-step. On the opposite side of town at the Acadian Village, you can walk through 19th-century homes built with wooden pegs and hand-hewn timbers.

What you can't do is escape the realities of modern city living. About 4 P.M., traffic starts to pile up along the heavily developed highways and tie up this city. Like many places in south Louisiana, the winding bayous and rivers mean roads here don't follow a tidy grid. Bring a GPS or a map. Remember, after you've reached Lafayette via I-10's Louisiana exit, Johnston Street goes all the way through the city where you'll find numerous attractions and restaurants.

Located along the Vermilion River (aka Bayou Vermilion) on the western edge of the Atchafalaya Basin, Lafayette is the seat of Lafayette Parish, which has a population of 221,578. Nicknamed the Hub City, it truly is a central point with easy access to the numerous nearby towns that embody Cajun culture. And the state's major highways, I-10 and I-49, intersect nearby.

A few trappers and traders were in the area before the Spanish occupation of 1776. The first settlement in south-central Louisiana, known as Petit Manchac, was established by the English. It was a small trading post on the banks of the Vermilion River where the Spanish Trail crossed the bayou (about where today's Pinhook Bridge is located). Acadians from French Canada resettled in the region following Le Grand Derangement of 1775, and with the Louisiana Purchase in 1803, the state became the possession of the United States.

Lafayette's founding is attributed to Jean Mouton, an Acadian who in 1821 donated land for a Catholic church. In 1822, Bishop Louis-Guillaume-Valentin Dubourg created the church parish of St. John the Evangelist of Vermilion, which encompassed the area from Mouton's plantation south to the Gulf of Mexico and west to the Sabine River. The settlement grew around the church and was called Vermilionville. On January 17, 1823, the Louisiana Legislature created Louisiana Parish from a western portion of what was St. Martin Parish. Mouton donated a

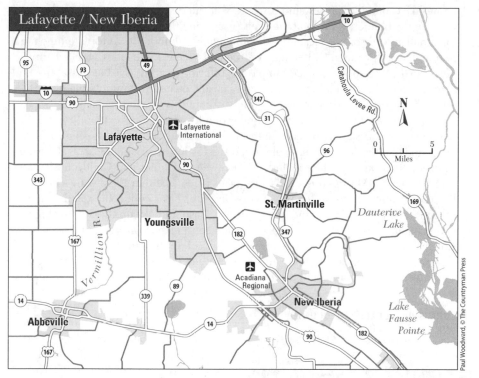

second parcel of land for a courthouse. In 1884, the town was renamed in honor of the Marquis de Lafayette. Oil was discovered in the region in the early 1900s, and by the 1950s Lafayette was an oil town. Oil-related business remains integral to the local economy today. Keep in mind that it's fewer than 50 miles to the platforms and rigs in the Gulf of Mexico. The Oil Center shopping and business district, formerly home to big-name companies, remains a go-to area.

Get a feel for historic Lafayette in the Alexandre Mouton House, once the home of the city's founding family, or the Cathedral of St. John the Evangelist on the site of the original chapel. The stately church maintains a small gift shop. Next door in the courtyard stands a magnificent live oak that is the third oldest member of the Live Oak Society, an organization dedicated to the preservation and appreciation of mature live oak trees in the United States. The nearly 500-year-old tree stands about 126 feet high with a spread of 210 feet across. Not far from downtown is the lovely University of Louisiana at Lafayette with Cypress Lake, a 2-acre, swamp-like lake that's a habitat for native irises, alligators, turtles, birds, and fish as well as a hangout for students and curious tourists. Need it be said that students and townsfolk alike are super fans of the University's football team, the Ragin' Cajuns, who play in the Cajundome.

Lafayette's collegiate atmosphere adds to its 21st-century approach to renovation and growth. Yet legendary Cajun traditions thrive. Stand shoulder-to-shoulder with music fans at the Blue Moon to hear Feufollet's version of Jolie Blonde. Works by the famed Cajun artist George Rodrigue, painter of blue dogs, adorn a namesake Cajun/Creole restaurant where you can enjoy a spicy etouffee while viewing the blue critters along the walls. Following the Cajun Boudin Trail, stop for lunch at Johnson's Boucaniere and add a link of boudin to your plate lunch (a regional term for lunch with a main entrée and two or three sides). Since eating out is an art form in Louisiana, sample the offerings during Eat Lafayette, the midsummer, monthlong celebration that gives locally owned restaurants the opportunity to show off their cuisine with a variety of mouth-watering specials.

Every winter, Lafayette offers a family friendly Mardi Gras celebration. Families stake out spots along parade routes with colorful floats and glittering royal kings and queens. The city has celebrated the festive pre-Lenten Carnival season since 1869. Popular parades include the Krewe des Chiens and Children's Parade. The Festival de Mardi Gras a Lafayette takes place at Cajun Field with a midway, live entertainment, Cajun foods, dancers, and fun, Then comes the relative quiet of Lent. Soon after Easter, the spring festival season cranks up. Lafayette's biggest gathering takes place the last week of April when Festival International de Louisiane spreads across the downtown. It is a celebration of French culture, drawing fabled Louisiana performers like Terrance Simien, Chubby Carrier and the Bayou Swamp Band, and the Lost Bayou Ramblers, as well as international musicians such as Nation Beat of Brazil, Burning Spear of Uganda, De Temps Antan of Canada, and Adowa from the Caribbean. Fall brings Festivals Acadien, celebrating food, music, and the region's colorful crafts. The calendar is filled with endless festivals, including the chic Art Walk the second Saturday of each month and the Friday musical night out called Downtown Alive! with bands playing everything from Cajun and blues to rock and salsa. Don't forget the Cajun Grammys, in August, called Le Cajun Music Awards and Festival and hosted by the Cajun French Music Association.

CORN SHUCK DOLLS AND COUNTRY BONNNETS ARE DISPLAYED IN VERMILIONVILLE'S GIFT SHOP IN LAFAYETTE.

Cynthia V. Campbell

AREA CODE 337. You do not have to dial the area code within the region.

GUIDANCE Lafayette Convention & Visitors Commission (800-346-1958 in the United States, 800-543-5340 from Canada, www.lafayette travel.com), 1400 Northwest Evangeline Thruway, Lafayette. The commission's publication, *Bon Temps*, is available at its spacious visitors' center on Evangeline Thruway south of I-10, where you can pick up tons of information about the area.

GETTING THERE *By air:* **Lafayette Regional Airport** (337-266-4400, www .lftairport.com), 200 Terminal Dr., Lafayette. Regional service is available via Delta (connecting from Atlanta); American Eagle (connecting from Dallas–Fort Worth), Continental Express through Houston, and Mesaba–The Delta Connection, available through Memphis. Car rentals, corporate aviation, and a fixed-base operator are also here.

By bus: **Greyhound Lines** (337-235-1541, www.greyhound.com) serves the city, stopping at the Lafayette Bus Center, 315 Lee Ave.

By car: Lafayette is located where I-10 and I-49 meet, a drive of about 2 hours and 20 minutes from New Orleans, an hour from Baton Rouge, and about 3½ hours from Houston, Texas, across I-10. From Lake Charles, Lafayette is about an hour and 15 minutes east.

By train: **Amtrak**'s Sunset Limited (New Orleans to Los Angeles, California, via San Antonio, Texas) stops at the Lafayette station at 100 Lee Ave. For tickets and schedules, go to www.amtrak.com or 1-800-USA-RAIL.

GETTING AROUND The city's compact downtown is eminently walkable and its restaurants, clubs, and shops will keep you busy for a day (or a few nights). When it's time to cruise outside the downtown, you'll need a car. Keep a map or GPS handy because the larger streets and highways take some unexpected turns. Local residents also use the **Lafayette Transit System**, the city bus service, which is cheap, at only $1 a ride (a day pass is $3). Catch a bus 6:30 A.M.–11:30 P.M. Mon.–Sat.; call 337-291-8570 or check www.ridelts.com. Night service operates from 6:30–11:30 p.m. Mon.–Sat.; check online for the schedule.

MEDICAL EMERGENCIES **Lafayette General Medical Center** (337-289-7991, www.lafayettegeneral.org), 1214 Coolidge St., Lafayette. Associated urgent care centers include **Family Health Plaza,** 1216 Camellia Blvd., Lafayette, 337-769-0069; and **Quick Care,** 3554 West Pinhook Rd., Lafayette, 337-837-7116.

✳ Cities, Towns, and Villages

The many villages and towns in the Lafayette area are fascinating in themselves. While you can visit them as run-out trips from Lafayette, a number of them are excellent getaways for overnight or weekend adventures. Listed here are those with special attractions and restaurants that continually draw visitors to the area.

Abbeville (www.cityofabbeville.net) means "priest's town." An enterprising Capuchin missionary, Pere Antoine Desire Megret, bought property here in 1843 and named the place after his birthplace in France. Start at the town's center, Magdalen Square. Then visit the newly renovated St. Mary Magdalen Catholic Church, which stands on a site Pere Megret selected for a chapel. Recently renovated, the historic landmark features stained-glass windows dating to 1911–1918, and restored ceiling murals. A well-kept cemetery is just behind the church. The town hosts several great festivals. Especially fun is the Giant Omelette Celebration in November, when local cooks prepare a 5,000-egg omelet in a 12-foot pan outdoors. Walk into the dirt-floored Sam Guarino & Son Blacksmith Shop Museum, where you can view original equipment and tools. The Guarinos forged and repaired everything from farm implements to ladies' scissors. "This was a meeting

Cynthia V. Campbell

ST. MARY MAGDALEN CEMETERY BEHIND THE CHURCH IN ABBEVILLE.

place for a lot of farmers," said Sam Guarino's daughter Rita. Her sister Mary Ann added, "There was a lot of fun and laughter here. It was hard work too." The shop is always open to children and school groups. It's worth the trip to eat at Shucks! The Louisiana Seafood House (337-898-3311, www.shucksrestaurant.com). Try the remarkable charbroiled oysters or the Shucks Stacker, grilled catfish topped with a grilled crab cake and grilled oyster topped with a red bell pepper and dill cream sauce. Another good spot is Dupuy's Oyster Shop (337-898-3188, www.dupuys oystershop.com), which has salty raw oysters on the half-shell along with an array of fried, grilled, or pan-broiled seafood.

Erath, a small community between Abbeville and New Iberia, is the home of the Acadian Museum, which honors the heritage of the Cajun people of Louisiana. If you're a history buff or seeking information on the Acadians, don't miss this little museum. It's packed with photos of local families and celebrities. The Acadian room contains items, paintings, and maps relating to Acadian history from 1603 to the present. The Prairie Bayou Cajun Room is filled with artifacts such as spinning wheels, blankets, and moccasin-style boots worn by Acadians. If you're in luck, Warren A. Perrin, an attorney and one of the museum's founders, will be on hand to give you a personal tour. In 1990, Perrin petitioned Queen Elizabeth II of England for an apology from the British government and the Crown for the expulsion of Acadians from Nova Scotia in 1755. His efforts resulted in a Royal Proclamation signed December 9, 2003, that decreed July 28 the annul Day of Commemoration of the Acadian Deportation. Perrin has been recognized nationally and internationally for his contributions on the behalf of the Acadians and his work on programs dealing with cultural and minority rights. Visit www.acadianmuseum.com for more information.

Breaux Bridge got its start when the Acadian pioneer Firmin Breaux built a suspension footbridge across Bayou Teche to help his family and neighbors. Giving directions, people would say, "Go to Breaux's Bridge." When Firmin's son Agricole built the first vehicular bridge, the community became the only city on Bayou Teche to evolve from both sides simultaneously. The town was officially established in 1829 when Scholastique Picou Breaux, Agicole's 33-year-old widow, drew up plans for a city and began selling property to other settlers. Today you can stroll the quaint streets and shop in boutiques and flea markets for antiques, collectibles, gifts, and yard art on Bridge and Main streets. Crawfish etouffee was invented here. Mulate's Cajun Restaurant at 325 Mills Ave. has authentic Cajun food and live Cajun music and dancing nightly, as well as Sunday lunch. Cafe Des Amis, 140 East Bridge St., an artistic eclectic cafe, is famous for its Creole/Cajun dishes and Saturday morning zydeco breakfasts. La Poussiere, a plain, old-time wooden hall on Grand Point Highway, holds Cajun dances every Saturday and Sunday 4–8 P.M. Drive to nearby Lake Martin for bird watching in spring and fall. The three-day Breaux Bridge Crawfish Festival in spring is one of the largest Cajun celebrations in the state. It features headliners such as Steve Riley and the Mamou Playboys and Corey Ledet. The heritage tent highlights Cajun traditions, including accordion making and *bourree*, a traditional card game. Information about attractions and lodgings is available at the Visitors' Center (337-332-8500, www.breauxbridge live.com) at 314 East Bridge St.

FOUNDED BY A FRENCH PRIEST, ST. MARY MAGDALEN CATHOLIC CHURCH IN ABBEVILLE IS A MAJOR LANDMARK.

Cynthia V. Campbell

Carencro, a small community near the crossroads of I-49 and I-10, is a suburb of Lafayette. The name comes from a Creole word for buzzard. The musician Marc Broussard, a native of the city, named his debut album after it. It's also the birthplace of Rockin' Dopsie. Our Lady of the Assumption Religious Complex consists of the church, rectory, school, Drexel Parish Hall (formerly the Sisters of the Blessed Sacrament Convent), the church cemetery, and the St. Katharine Drexel shrine. The complex is listed on the National Register of Historic Places. St. Peter's Catholic Church and Cemetery form an artistic centerpiece for the city.

Grand Coteau Historic District, just off I-49, stuns visitors with the beauty of its tree-lined alleys, groves, and gardens. Architecture buffs will enjoy seeing the Creole, French, Acadian, Anglo American, and Victorian houses, stores, and religious edifices. The community has deep Catholic roots. Started in 1821, the Academy of the Sacred

Heart is the second oldest institution of learning west of the Mississippi. Formal gardens and an oak alley create a lovely backdrop for one of the South's notable independent schools. It's possible to visit sections of the historic building that currently are not in use, as well as the museum, the Shrine of St. John Berchmans, where a miracle occurred: In 1866, Blessed John Berchmans (1599–1621) appeared to Mary Wilson, a novice of the Society of the Sacred Heart, and through his intercession she was miraculously cured of a debilitating disease. Berchmans was canonized by Pope Leo XIII in 1888, and the infirmary where the miracle occurred was converted to a chapel and has been preserved as a shrine. Hours are 9 A.M.–2 P.M., Monday and Tuesday by appointment only. Near the Academy of the Sacred Heart, the St. Charles College, founded in 1827 as a boarding school, now functions as a Jesuit seminary and spirituality center. The college grounds are landscaped with contemplative walks and oak alleys which visitors are welcomed to enjoy. Several intriguing gift shops

Cynthia V. Campbell

BOATS TRAVEL THROUGH A LOCK ON BAYOU TECHE, WHICH GIVES ACCESS TO THE ATCHAFALAYA RIVER.

THE HISTORIAN WARREN A. PERRIN SHOWS OFF ORIGINAL SPINNING WHEELS AND OTHER MEMORABILIA IN THE ACADIAN MUSEUM IN ERATH.

Cynthia V. Campbell

Cynthia V. Campbell

SHOPS IN RENOVATED HOMES ATTRACT VISITORS TO THE SMALL TOWN OF GRAND COTEAU NEAR LAFAYETTE.

and cafes in Grand Coteau are housed in renovated historic buildings, well worth seeing. Visit www.grandcoteau.org for more information.

Eunice, on US 190, is packed with fun and friendly people. If your time in Cajun Country is limited, spend at least one afternoon and evening here. Named for the wife of the town's founder, Eunice is the "Prairie Cajun" capital of Louisiana. Start early Saturday morning with hot coffee, boudin, and the open jam session at Savoy's Music Center. Begun by a local accordion-maker, the sessions are known to Cajun music fans worldwide. Saturday evenings, the Liberty Theater, a renovated movie house with a small dance floor just below the stage, broadcasts *Rendezvous Des Cajuns*, a live radio show. Next door, National Park rangers at the Prairie Cajun Cultural Center, a unit of Jean Lafitte National Heritage Park, join regional chefs in demonstrating Cajun cooking. The town also is home to the Cajun Music Hall of Fame and Museum, 220 South Duson Dr., where greats like Oren "Doc" Guidry, Phil Menard, and Voris "Shorty" LeBlanc are honored. Next door, the Eunice Depot Museum houses exhibits on the railroads, pioneer farming, Cajun Mardi Gras, and local life. The town, which is the home of Louisiana State University–Eunice, has a number of chain hotels and RV campgrounds. In addition to fast-food eateries, try Allison's Hickory Pitt on West Laurel and D.I.'s Restaurant on LA 97 in Basile for Cajun cuisine and truly authentic Cajun music. Visit www.eunice-la.com for more information.

Crowley, the center of Louisiana's rice industry, boasts a historic district that spans a 32-block radius with some structures dating back to the 1800s. It was here in the 1890s that the rice farmer and scientist Salmon Lusk Wright developed domestic rice seeds that revolutionized the industry. After years of testing, he produced what became known as Blue Rose rice, a medium-grain rice that's good as stuffing. Modern agricultural methods sustain rice farmers, but the community still salutes its pioneers at the International Rice Festival. Take in the festival and visit the History of Crowley Museum (425 North Parkerson, 866-4642) to see exhibits and displays on the city and the industry.

Rayne, a friendly city with a quirky personality, dates from the 1800s, when it was first called Poupeville. Most folks know the city for its frogs. It started with a trio of Parisians. Jacques Weill and his brothers began an export business shipping the area's frogs to restaurants across the country. Large murals depicting frogs of all shapes and sizes welcome visitors to the city. One of Louisiana's biggest celebrations is the Rayne Frog Festival in November, when the Lions Club Frog Derby sponsors a best-dressed frog competition. Both Crowley and Rayne are just off I-10 between Lake Charles and Lafayette.

New Iberia, 20 miles south of Lafayette via US 90, was settled in the late 1700s by colonists from Malaga, Spain. You can easily spice up a trip by visiting the town's hot spots. Tour the magnificent antebellum Shadows-on-the-Teche Plantation, a National Trust Historic Site, then meander over to shop at Konrico Company Store and Conrad Rice Mill, the oldest operating rice mill in the United States. Stop by Rosary House, manufacturer of hand-crafted religious articles, to watch rosary-making demonstrations. Walk along Main Street. Dine on savory Creole dishes at Clementine Dining and Spirits or relax with a sandwich and luscious dessert at Lagniappe Too Cafe. Rub shoulders with locals at Victor's Cafeteria, a hangout of Dave Robicheaux, the fictional detective in novels by James Lee Burke, a New Iberia native. Just a few miles away, you can tour the Rip Van Winkle Gardens and the beautiful Victorian era home of 19th-century American actor Joseph Jefferson. Here, you can view a film of the 1980 catastrophe at Lake Peigneur, where an industrial accident drained the lake into a salt mine below. Lunch at Cafe Jefferson and overnight in the Rip Van Winkle Cottages, operated as a B&B.

THE JOSEPH JEFFERSON HOME AT RIP VAN WINKLE GARDENS IN NEW IBERIA IS A VICTORIAN DELIGHT.

Cynthia V. Campbell

Cynthia V. Campbell

VISITORS LEARN HOW RED PEPPERS ARE TURNED INTO HOT SAUCE AT THE TABASCO VISITOR'S CENTER ON AVERY ISLAND.

At **Avery Island**, tour the factory where Tabasco brand pepper sauce is made. There's a short film on the hot sauce's history and a guided tour of the bottling and packaging operations. While on the island visit the Jungle Gardens, which is filled with semi-tropical plants, bamboo, wisteria, alligators, and a platform from which you can view throngs of birds at the rookery. Walk a short path to see the 800-year-old Buddha who sits on his lotus in a tiled pavilion. Spend time in the Country Store where you can get Tabasco products and myriads of colorful souvenirs. Shop at the farmers' market Saturdays 6–10 A.M. and Tuesdays 2–6 P.M. to find home-made bread, jellies, and jams, and handcrafted wooden items. Get to know locals during the Great Gator Race in March, when sponsors race small wooden alligators along Bayou Teche to raise money for charity. Activities, including food and music, center around Bouligny Plaza on the Teche. The Louisiana Sugar Cane Festival in September is a citywide event with a Midnight Fais-do-do (a dance) in Bouligny Plaza, a sugar cookery contest, sugar artistry exhibit and tasting, art show, flower show, and boat parade. New Iberia has a number of outstanding B&Bs as well as chain hotels. The town is also a hub for outdoor adventures, and the home of Lake Fausse Pointe and Cypremort Point state parks. Visit www.iberiatravel.com.

At **Opelousas**, about 20 minutes north of Lafayette, you can pack in a lot of fun in a short time. French Coureur des Bois traders were probably trading with Opelousas Indians as far back as 1690. The first courthouse was built in 1806 in the center square. During the Civil War, it became the state capital for nine months. The city loves visitors and it loves to party. The Spice and Music Festival in June has an exciting array of regional bands, workshops on everything from fiddle making to cooking, and a zydeco dance contest. A city program hosts a Zydeco Breakfast in fall. La Table Francaise, an informal group for people who want to speak French, meets regularly at a downtown cafe, and theYambilee Festival, one of the oldest in the state, is sweet indeed when folks turn out for a Yam-i-mai cooking competition and music the last full weekend in October. Visit www.city ofopelousas.com for more information.

St. Martinville, about 18 miles southeast of Lafayette in the center of Attakapas Territory, was settled by French colonists in the 1750s. The first Acadians from Nova Scotia were sent to St. Martinville in 1765 by the Spanish government. A French priest, Jean Louis Civrey, accompanied them, and eventually called his church, for which the town is named, Eglise St. Martin de Tours. The community developed around Church Square. It was accessible by steamboat, and prominent Creole families made the city a fashionable summer resort. In the early 1800s St. Martinville became known as a cultural center with good hotels and a French theater that presented operas and comedies. During that era it was called Petit Paris. The city is linked to Henry Wadsworth Longfellow's epic poem, *Evangeline: A Tale of Acadie*, a fictional tale set in the time of the expulsion of the Acadians. The beautiful Evangeline Oak, where couples come to get engaged or renew their marriage vows, stands on the banks of Bayou Teche. Next to the park, the St. Martinville Cultural Heritage Center houses the Museum of the Acadian Memorial and the African American Museum with a 32-foot mural by the local artist Dennis Williams. In the square, St. Martin de Tours Catholic Church welcomes visitors, and nearby is the Evangeline statue donated by the actress Dolores del Rio after she starred in the movie version of Longfellow's poem, filmed in the area in 1929. And you can stop by the Duchamp Opera House (open 10 A.M.–5 P.M. Tues.–Sun.), which has an antiques mall and art gallery on the first floor, and plays on the second floor. Contact the St. Martinville Tourist Information Center (337-394-2233) for more information.

Festivals include La Grande Boucherie in Magnolia Park the Saturday before Mardi Gras, featuring Cajun and zydeco music, the Squeal like a Pig Contest, a cracklin' throwing contest, food, and crafts. The Acadian Memorial Festival at Evangeline Oak Park includes a re-enactment of the arrival

COUPLES OFTEN PLEDGE OR RENEW THEIR WEDDING VOWS AT THE EVANGELINE OAK IN ST. MARTINVILLE.

Cynthia V. Campbell

Louisiana Office of Tourism

A DISPLAY AT BREAUX BRIDGE SHOWS THE SNAKE-LIKE WINDING PATH OF BAYOU TECHE.

of Acadians on Bayou Teche, storytelling, traditional Cajun food, and music. The Pepper Festival in October at Evangeline Oak Park features the World Famous Pepper Eating contest, a motorcycle race, pepper hot sauces, food, music, and fun. The St. Lucy Festival of Lights and Christmas Parade in early December features food, arts and crafts, music, and an outdoor Mass, all leading up to lighting the Church Square as evening falls. Visit www.stmartinville.org.

Located about one mile north of St. Martin Square on LA 31 is Longfellow-Evangeline State Historic Site (open daily 9–5 P.M., 800-677-2900) which explores the cultural interplay among the people of the Bayou Teche. The site includes Maison Olivier (circa 1815), an outstanding example of a raised Creole cottage, and a reproduction Acadian farmstead, typical of a single-family farm as it would have appeared in 1800. In the pasture, you'll see cattle typical of those raised by settlers of that era.

✴ To See

Acadiana Center for the Arts (337-233-7060, www.acadianacenterforthearts .org), 101 West Vermilion St., Lafayette. This impressive building and its programs are the heart of the region's considerable arts scene. An exceptional 300-seat, multi-functional theater with great acoustics, it accommodates a range of disciplines from film and media to recitals, concerts, pageants, dance, and the spoken word. Three visual art galleries are devoted to showing fine crafts and regional or national works. The programming reflects the state's lively roots via the Louisiana Crossroads concert series, the annual juried Southern Open art exhibit for artists from the Gulf states, and Film @the Center. Check the website for schedules.

♂ ♂ **Acadian Village** (337-981-2364 or 800-962-4554, www.acadianvillage.org), 200 Greenleaf Dr., Lafayette. The re-created 10-acre village captures Acadian life in the 1800s. Go to The General Store (Le Magasin General), or les maisons Bernard, Thibodeaux, LeBlanc, or St. John; or see how the doctor or the blacksmith worked. Of the 11 structures along a small waterway, four, like the New Hope Chapel, are replicas. The rest are authentic, moved here from the surrounding area. The Bernard House, built in St. Martinville, is the oldest, with a portion dating from about 1800. An eclectic array of memorabilia is organized into exhibits throughout the village. A favorite: a story entitled "Acadians, not Texans, started the cattle industry" tacked to a wall. Visitors won't want to miss the re-created Fernand Stutes Grocery Bar and Barbershop, which once stood on Ridge Road in Lafayette. There's even an old Mobil gas pump out front. Open 10 A.M.–4 P.M. Mon.–Sat. The magical Noel Acadien au Village is held Dec. 3–23, 5:30 P.M.–9 P.M. Tours cost $8 for adults, $5 for students 7–14, $7 for 65 and older. Free for kids 6 and under or military. Group rates available.

Alexandre Mouton House/Lafayette Museum (337-234-2208), 1122 Lafayette St., Lafayette. This gorgeous old place started with the small and extant "Sunday house" the plantation owner Jean Mouton used when his family came into town for Mass. The house is now named for his son, who bought the house, added on, raised a family, and became Louisiana's first democratically elected governor. Others owned the house throughout the years, and it's a showcase. In addition to period furnishings and reproduction carpets (and a beautiful original ceiling medallion), the house provides a detailed accounting of Lafayette's history. See Civil War–era swords used by yet another Mouton—Confederate General Alfred Mouton, who lost his life in the Battle of Mansfield in April 1864. You can see elaborate Mardi Gras court wear, or examine elements of the home's restoration. Open 9 A.M.–4 P.M. Tues.–Sat., 1-4 p.m., Sunday. Tour costs $2 per person; an expanded tour with light hors d'oeuvres, wine, and punch is $4.

Cathedral of St. John the Evangelist & Museum (337-232-1322, www.saint johncathedral.org), 914 St. John St., Lafayette. The museum is located in the Cathedral Center at 515 Cathedral St. The stunning brick cathedral is a city icon, and its turreted, brick Dutch Romanesque style contrasts with the region's Acadian and Creole architecture. Completed in 1916, this is the third church on the site donated by city founder Jean Mouton following the 1821 establishment of the parish of St. John du Vermilion. The first was built in 1827 and the second about the time the Civil War ended. Models of the trio stand inside the small museum devoted to the diocese of Lafayette. A flagstone plaza with a fountain joins the cathedral, the center, and St. John Cemetery, the oldest in Lafayette, which contains the tombs of Mouton, his family, and other leading citizens. Next to the cathedral stands the majestic 500-year-old St. John Oak Tree, with a circumference of 28 feet, 8 inches. Also in the museum, you'll see the Hanley-Gueno Neapolitan Presepio, an elaborate—almost stage-set—grouping of 18th-century figures in a village that includes a crèche. Museum open 9 A.M.–noon and 1–4 P.M. Mon.–Thurs. and 9 A.M.–noon Fri.

♂ ♞ **Children's Museum of Acadiana** (337-232-8500, www.childrensmuseum ofacadiana.com), 201 East Congress St., Lafayette. Numerous hands-on activities keep the little ones shopping in their own little grocery store, playing in the Bubble Factory, learning healthy eating habits, or taking a pet to the vet. A big Acadian ambulance with flashing lights has been retrofitted for children for role playing;

A RANGER AT JEAN LAFITTE NATIONAL PARK IN LAFAYETTE CONDUCTS THE ACADIAN
CULTURAL CENTER BOAT TOUR ON VERMILION BAYOU.

Cynthia V. Campbell

demystifies medical care. A toddler playhouse keeps the youngest kids safe and busy.
Open 10 A.M.–5 P.M. Tues.–Sat. Admission is $5; kids 12 months and younger free.

✦ ✦ ✪ **Jean Lafitte National Park Acadian Cultural Center** (337-232-0789,
www.nps.gov/jela), 501 Fisher Rd., Lafayette. The center tells stories of the origins, migration, settlement, and contemporary culture of the Acadians, the people
who became the Cajuns. National Park rangers give free talks daily at 2:45 P.M. on
local history and culture. Every second and fourth Saturday, enjoy a free dulcimer
jam session by the Cajun Dulcimer Society and its core group, the Lagniappe Dulcimer Society from Baton Rouge. See stunning displays of early Acadian dress,
religious artifacts, and photographs of everyday life. A timeline explains Le Grand
Derangement, the expulsion and resettlement of Canada's Acadians, and a moving
film tells the story of their exile and resettlement in Louisiana. This is also the
place to get a handle on sometimes foreign-seeming Cajun expressions and customs. Learn about *la maison, l'enfant*, the card game *bourree,* or how *l'huile* (oil)
was discovered in 1901. In spring and fall, ranger-guided boat tours on the good
ship Cocodrie cruise Bayou Vermilion, first settled by American Indians. The boat
is a shallow-draft vessel fashioned after the region's old school boats (as opposed to
school buses!). Open 8 A.M.–5 P.M. daily.

✦ **Lafayette Science Museum** (337-291-5544, www.lafayettesciencemuseum
.org), 433 Jefferson St., Lafayette. Formerly the natural history museum and planetarium, this renamed museum retains its planetarium—soon to go digital. It also
is home to more than 10,000 square feet of hands-on exhibits each year. A recent
example was Engineer It, in which kids could learn to build a boat and work with a
water tank to learn about buoyancy. A small play area for kids 5 and younger is
available. Call ahead for Saturday planetarium times, which may change. Group
tours available. Open 9 A.M.–5 P.M. Tues.–Fri., 10 A.M.–6 P.M. Sat., and 1–6 P.M.
Sun. Tickets for nonmembers: Adults $5, seniors $3, children $2. Under 3 are free.

Cynthia V. Campbell

JOYCELYN TRAHAN DEMONSTRATES THE CAJUN METHOD OF BAKING FRUIT PIES AT
VERMILIONVILLE, A LIVING HISTORY MUSEUM IN LAFAYETTE.

🔗 ⬆ **Paul and Lulu Hillard University Art Museum** (337-482-2278, www
.museum.louisiana.edu), University of Louisiana at Lafayette, 710 East Saint Mary
Blvd., Lafayette. The museum's permanent collection consists of 18th- through
21st-century European, Asian, and American art. Selections are exhibited on a
rotating basis. Artists represented include Janet Fish, Ida Kohlmeyer, Clyde
Connell, William Moreland, Cora Kelley Ward, Robert Gordy, George Rodrigue,
Elemore Morgan Jr., Clementine Hunter, and Son Ford Thomas. Look for excep-

LOUISIANA'S FRENCH LANGUAGE

In Vermilionville's one-room schoolhouse (with its 1899 desks), you may
learn about the 20th-century effort to save the French language in Acadiana. In 1916, teachers were ordered to instruct only in English. In 1968 came
the Council for the Development of French in Louisiana, or CODOFIL, whose
variety of efforts extended to importing teachers from France.

There are distinct differences between Louisianan French and the language spoken in France. Many words were developed in encounters with
the New World. For example, alligator is *un cocodril*, and mosquito is *un
maringouin* in Louisiana French. Popcorn is *du tac-tac* and a sweet potato is
une patate douce. Visit CODOFIL'S website at www.codofil.org for more
information on French and Louisianan French.

tional, well-curated shows from elsewhere. The museum has an outstanding art library and gift shop. Toddler Tuesdays (10–11 A.M.) introduce young children and their caregivers to art and to spoken and read word performances. Children can also play with a collection of toys, puzzles, and educational games. Open 9 A.M.– 5 P.M. Tues.–Thurs., 9 A.M.–noon Fri. and 10 A.M.–5 P.M. Sat. Adults $5, seniors $4, students 5–17 $3, children 5 and under free.

 **Vermilionville** (337- 233-4077 or 866-992-2968, www.bayouvermilion.org), 300 Fisher Rd., Lafayette. Located near the Jean Lafitte Acadian Cultural Center (which makes this a convenient twofer learning opportunity), Vermilionville is another re-created living history village and folk life park. It salutes the region's Cajun/Creole life between 1765 and 1890. On-site interpreters talk about such old practices as *bousillage*, the process of drying a mix of mud and the abundant Spanish moss into bricks that were then tucked into walls for insulation. The village's most historically significant home dates from 1790, and was owned by Amand (also spelled Armand) Broussard, son of the legendary Beausoleil who led the first Acadians to the area. Vermilionville also has a cooking school with demonstrations (by reservation only; full classes for up to eight). Other attractions are a barn-like building that hosts events ranging from musical performances to weddings, a beautiful "chapelle," and La Cuisine de Maman, which serves Cajun/Creole lunch every day but Monday. Cajun jam sessions take place 1–4 P.M. in the lobby on Saturdays. A brochure maps out a self-guided walking tour. The gift shop contains numerous Cajun craft items and books. Employees are bilingual. Larger groups can arrange for guides in advance. Open 10 A.M.–4 P.M. Tues.–Sun. (last tickets sold at 3 P.M.). Adults $8, seniors $6.50, and $5 for ages 6–18. Kids under 6 are free.

ON THE VERMILION RIVER NEAR ABBEVILLE, PALMETTO ISLAND STATE PARK IS DESIGNED FOR BOATING AND PICNICKING.

✳ Green Spaces

Cypress Lake (337-482-0911), 600 East St. Mary Blvd., Lafayette. This landmark on the University of Louisiana at Lafayette campus, between Hebron Boulevard and McKinley Street behind the Student Union, has been known to introduce students to alligators, who sometimes sun themselves on the nearby lawn. The large cypress trees are beautiful, and were once a grove before they were flooded under a man-made lake.

✐ **Girard Park** (337-291-8370), 500 Girard Park Dr., Lafayette. This 33-acre park is quite popular, and it has plenty to do. Here you'll find a 1.25-mile trail for walking and jogging, tennis and basketball courts, a playground, a nine-hole disc golf course, and more. The outdoor pool is open during the summer.

✐ ⊶ **Palmetto Island State Park** (337-893-3930 or 888-677-0094, www.crt.state.la.us/parks), 19501 Pleasant Rd., Abbeville. The ever-present palmetto plants, for which the park is named, along with additional native shrubbery make this a true ecological escape. The Visitors' Center, with its water playground and bathhouse, is a "must do" for the day-use visitor. Situated on the Vermilion River, the park has a boat launch for river fishing and boating. Interior lagoons allow canoeists and kayakers an up-close look at plants and animals. There are 96 campsites with water and electrical hookup, and six overnight cabins. For reservations, call 1-CAMP-N-LA.

✳ To Do

BIRDING Bird-watchers can follow sections of the America's Wetland Birding Trail through this region. In the Lafayette area, explore the Atchafalaya Loop that passes through Bayou Teche. Continue on to the Indian Bayou Natural Area, the Sherburne Wildlife Management Area Complex, and the Atchafalaya National Wildlife Refuge, all located between US 190 to the north and I-10 to the south. Then the loop travels south through St. Martinville and to Lake Fausse Pointe State Park, which has outstanding birding. Travel on to Spanish Lake in New Iberia and then on to the Jungle Gardens at Avery Island, home to a major rookery. You'll find songbirds during every season and wave after wave of migrating species in spring and fall.

CANOEING **Bayou Vermillion District** (337-237-8360) has several recreational areas that allow public access to Bayou Vermilion for boating activities. The district has 12 canoes (each can hold three people) that it lends out to groups and organizations. If you want to paddle along the bayou, launches are located at Beaver Park at University and Evangeline Thruway, North Landing at Louisiana Avenue and I-10, and several additional points.

Fausse Pointe State Park and Canoe Trail (337-229-4764). South of St. Martinville on the west guideline levee, this state park on the edge of the Atchafalaya Basin spillway has miles of waterways for canoeing and kayaking. Rental canoes are available at the park store. Entrance fee is $1 per person; free for seniors 62 and older and children age 3 and under.

Lake Martin (337-332-8500), Lake Martin Rd., Breaux Bridge. From Breaux Bridge, drive south on LA 31, take a right on Lake Martin Road and follow it to the lake. The lake is one of Louisiana's largest nesting colonies for many species of water birds. In the spring look for herons, egrets, white ibis, roseate spoonbills and wood ducks. Owned by the Nature Conservancy, Lake Martin is open year-round with free admission.

Pack & Paddle (337-232-5854, www.packpaddle.com), 601 East Pinhook Rd., Lafayette. Take a guided trip to nearby points (Lake Martin at night) or farther afield, rent canoes, or kayaks for $40 per day, and get advice about where to explore in the area. Closed Sundays.

CYCLING Cajun Cyclists Bicycle Club (cajuncyclists.bicycleracing.com). 601 East Pinhook Rd., Lafayette. This group is made up of avid cyclists who spend hours leading rides and log many miles through the year. Rides leave at 8 A.M. every Saturday morning throughout the year from Pack & Paddle on Pinhook Road. Riders of all levels enjoy a number of mapped routes to sites in neighboring towns. Most routes are about 35–40 miles, but a beginners' route is also available which is usually 10–12 miles long. Riders of all levels and ages are invited to participate. Organized rides are also held Sundays, Tuesdays, and Thursdays.

Recycled Cycles of Acadiana (337- 235-BIKE, www.facebook.com/pages /Lafayette-LA/Recycled-Cycles-of-Acadiana/85257546218), 208 East Vermilion St., Lafayette. Pick up a clunker for $5 and pedal off to explore from this shop in the renovated Tribune Press building. The staff here not only rents and sells bikes of all types, but maintains museum-worthy specimens for your viewing pleasure. Open 9 A.M.–6 P.M. Mon.–Sat.

GOLF Acadian Hills Country Club (337-232-1979, www.acadianhills.com), 500 Acadian Hills Lane, Lafayette. The semi-private course is open to the public. The par-71 course has a narrow, tree-lined layout with small greens whose tight fairways demand accurate shot making. The No. 13 hole is a 140-yard par three, with water in front; it needs a sure shot to hit the proper part of a kidney-shaped green. Call two days in advance for guests. No pull-cart rental is available. Green fees are $29.75 Tues.—Thurs. and $35 weekends. Twilight rates after 4 P.M. are $25, Tues.–Sun.

The Wetlands (337-291-7157), 2129 North University Ave., Lafayette. This is one of Louisiana's newest courses and one of the state's top municipal layouts. On the Audubon Golf Trail, the wide-open links-style layout has water coming into play on 11 holes. The course showcases the region's terrain with well-conditioned fairways and handsome landscaping. Reserve tee times two days in advance. Club rental is available through the pro shop. Green fees are $30 Mon.–Fri.; $35 weekends and holidays; $25 for seniors 65 and over and juniors 17 and under, and for all players after 3 P.M. weekdays and weekends.

SPECTATOR ACTIVITIES Movies in the Park (www.downtownlafayette.org), downtown Lafayette. Bring your blankets and chairs the third Saturday in April, May, June, September, October, and November. Enjoy movies for $2 at Park Sans Souci downtown. Free for ages 5 and younger; concessions on-site. The area is well-lighted and safe.

University of Louisiana at Lafayette (337-482-0911, www.ragincajuns.com), 600 East Saint Mary Boulevard, Lafayette. Here's the breakdown: Football is played at Cajun Field (The Swamp), basketball is at the Cajundome, baseball is at M. L. Tigue Moore Field, softball is at Lamson Park. See the website for all the details.

TOURS **The Atchafalaya Experience** (337-277-4726, 337-233-7816, www.the atchafalayaexperience.com), Lafayette. Lafayette native Coerte A. Voorhies Jr. and son Kim run this unique operation, fueled by the elder Voorhies's background as a geologist and the knowledge of the region's culture, history, and ethnicities he passed on to his son. Between them, visitors are assured an informed look at all aspects of the Atchafalaya, which Coerte Voorhies calls "Louisiana's Grand Canyon." Prices: $50 for 13 and older, $25 for 8–12. Kids 7 and under are free.

McGee's Landing (337-228-2384, www.mcgeeslanding.com), 1337 Henderson Levee Rd., Henderson. Head east to Henderson for an Atchafalaya Basin swamp tour from the region's reliable swamp tour mothership. Private airboats are available as well as large touring boats, canoes, and kayaks, and you can hire guides for birding and hunting. Check out the Allemond Point Campground and guest cabins. McGee's Cafe & Bar is a cool dining spot by the landing.

✳ Lodging

Numerous chain hotels with varying prices and amenities are located throughout Lafayette, including along the I-10 interchanges. Clever travelers will have no problem finding them. A tip: The 337-room Hilton, on the Vermilion River, is popular and full of amenities. The independents offer something unique.

Aaah T'Frere's Bed & Breakfast (337-984-9347, www.tfreres.com), 1905 Verot School Rd., Lafayette. Your hostess, Maugie Pastor, famously serves her elaborate "Oooh! La! La!" breakfasts in her red silk pajamas (purple during Mardi Gras). Forget the calorie counter and dip into the Cajun Angel eggs that may grace your plate— eggs *creme de la creme* with cheese, veggies, and spices. Or perhaps you'd prefer cheesecake-stuffed pancakes? Eight rooms offer doubles, queen-, and king-size beds, so every visitor should find something to his or her liking. Guest-friendly amenities include a fridge stocked with drinks, TVs in all the rooms, wake-up coffee, jets in many of the regular-sized tubs, and antiques in the rooms inside the main house. Out back is the *garconniere,* where young French men traditionally slept after a night dancing at the *fais do-do* or playing *bourree,* so those are

the names of these two rooms. Eight different breakfasts and the cocktail hour with T'juleps remain signatures of this well-known B&B, which has been featured in numerous publications and TV shows over the years. No pets. Moderate.

Blue Moon Saloon & Guest House (337-234-2422, www.bluemoonhostel .com), 215 East Convent St., Lafayette. More hostel than B&B, the Blue Moon nonetheless offers one heck of an amenity—its popular on-site saloon and music club. Go have yourself a great night out, then crawl upstairs to bed. Dormitory-style sleeping with shared baths is available, but so are four rooms including three with private baths (or at least toilet facilities). Funky but cool. Laundry and Internet are available. Inexpensive–moderate.

✐ ✹ **Bois des Chenes B&B** (337-233-7816; www.boisdechenes.com), 338 North Sterling St., Lafayette. This is a beautiful circa-1820 sugar plantation house built by Charles Mouton, the grandson of Lafayette's founding father, and since occupied by other local leading lights. White columns and dormers mark the French Creole house, which has three rooms in the main house for guests (including one two-bedroom suite) and three more in an adjacent carriage house. French and American antiques lend an air of authenticity, and extensive restoration has plumbed the home's history. You'll find cypress floors, and on the grounds a pretty brick patio area, gardens, and even chickens in the coop. The Voorhies family, who run the inn, also operate the Atchafalaya Experience, a well-regarded swamp tour in which visitors reap the rewards of the Voorhieses' considerable knowledgeable. Pets and kids are OK. Moderate–expensive.

Carriage House Hotel (337-769-8400; www.thecarriagehousesuites .com), 603 Silverstone Rd., Lafayette. Terrific-looking and contemporary, this 26-suite hotel is located in the recently developed River Ranch an upscale residential/town center complex. Options include 14 single-room suites, seven two-bedroom suites, and extended stays as well as unfurnished town houses. Restaurants are nearby, as is the 10,000-square foot City Club, where hotel guests have complimentary use of every recreational amenity they could want, including a pool and discounted spa services. The hotel is not near the city center, which may confound some travelers. Expensive.

Hilton Lafayette (337-235-6111, www.hilton.com), 1521 West Pinhook Rd., Lafayette. The Hilton is a full-service hotel and conference center and an excellent place to meet with business clients or friends. Guest rooms are roomy and attractive. Hotel facilities include a bar, dining room with an exceptional buffet breakfast, and an outdoor deck with a swimming pool. Moderate–expensive.

&. ❦ **La Maison de Belle** (337-235-2520), 610 Girard Park Dr., Lafayette. One of the city's Victorian homes found new life some years back when Kolleen Bowen Verlander moved it from a downtown lot threatened with demolition to a spot next to her house along Girard Park. Today it's a showcase featuring lots of deep romantic colors. Known as the Denbo-Montgomery House, this was where the grande dame Elisabeth Montgomery held court, and Verlander has placed her portrait on a mantel. The rooms include the very spacious first-floor Miss Elizabeth suite (handicapped accessible) and, appended to the back via a porch area, the very cottage where writing genius John Kennedy Toole, author of *A Confederacy of Dunces,* dwelled while studying at the University of Louisiana. It's also for rent, and quite cozy. Upstairs are two smaller but elegant rooms. No pets, no children under 12. Moderate.

The Juliet, A Boutique Hotel (337-261-2225, www.juliethotel.com), 800 Jefferson St., Lafayette. This 20-room hotel is downtown within easy walking distance of restaurants, shops, galleries, and special events like the Festival Internationale. You'll find attractive and spacious rooms with duvet-covered down comforters, a choice of pillows, and a flat-screen TV. A small buffet breakfast is provided in the comfortable second-floor sitting area, where a gas fireplace flickers beneath the mantel. No pets. Moderate–expensive.

CAMPGROUNDS Acadiana Park Campground (337-291-83881), 1201 East Alexander St., Lafayette. Located on the north side, the city-owned campground offers about 70 sites, water, electricity, showers, and a dump station in a wooded area. There's a park in the front that includes the Acadiana Nature Center, and a 26-hole disc golf course. Inexpensive.

(((ᵖ))) **KOA Lafayette** (800-562-0809, 337-235-2739, www.koa.com), 537 Apollo Rd., Scott. The campground offers concrete sites, mini-golf, cable, and Wi-Fi. Enjoy fishing in the 10-acre lake. No license is required. Greet each morning with a fresh cup of coffee or hot cappuccino served in the store. Conveniently located near I-10. Inexpensive.

✳ Where to Eat

EATING OUT ✂ **Borden's Ice Cream Store** (337-235-9291), 1103 Jefferson St., Lafayette. Built circa 1940 but recently renovated, this is the last Borden's in the country that is still scooping ice cream. Originally, this was a cooling station in the days before refrigerated trucks, a place milk trucks stopped to cool the product before moving on. Vanilla is the unquestionable favorite ice cream flavor, and you can also get lattes and coffees in the morning, protein drinks, and, in the near future, sandwiches, soups, and soft-serve ice cream. Cars vie for parking space outside when customers show up for late-night treats. Open 6:30 A.M.–10 P.M. Mon.–Fri., 8 A.M.– 10 P.M. Sat., and 10 A.M.–10 P.M. Sun. Inexpensive.

✂ ⅋ **Don's Seafood & Steakhouse** (337-235-3551, www.donsseafood online.com/lafayette), 4309 Johnston St., Lafayette. Spawned from the same family that brought you Landry's (few of which are still locally owned) and Don's Seafood Hut, this downtown flagship has grown from a single room in 1934 to the sprawling restaurant you see today. Specialties include crawfish bisque in season. If you're looking for a platter of fried seafood, this is the place. Hush puppies start the meal and, as is traditional, red beans and rice are available on Monday. There is ample parking in an adjacent lot. Open every day but Christmas and Mardi Gras for lunch and dinner.

Cynthia V. Campbell

A CRAWFISH MEAL IS GOOD ANYTIME IN BREAUX BRIDGE, THE CRAWFISH CAPITAL OF THE WORLD.

Open 11 A.M.–9 P.M. Mon.–Thurs., 11 A.M.–10 P.M. Fri.-Sat., and 11 A.M.– 9 P.M. Sun. Moderate.

✂ ⅋ **Dwyer's Cafe** (337-235-9364), 323 Jefferson St., Lafayette. Downtown's old-style diner fills up early with breakfast patrons in search of signature sweet potato pancakes. Family-owned and in operation for decades, Dwyer's moved to this corner in 1979 and for years staked its reputation on old-fashioned plate lunches with plenty of rice and gravy. You can still get those, no problem (with three sides, including rice). Choices run from country-fried steak with white gravy to calf liver with onion gravy to fried catfish to shrimp and crab etouffee on Friday. Breakfast can't be beat, from hot oatmeal to a diced smoke link omelet. Open 6 A.M.–2 P.M. Sun.–Mon. and 6 A.M.–6 P.M. Tues.–Sat. Breakfast until 11 A.M. Inexpensive.

Hawk's Restaurant (337-788-3266, www.hawkscrawfish.com/home.htm), 416 Hawks Rd., Rayne. The cafe boasts that it is truly in the middle of nowhere in Rayne, west of Lafayette. Considered some of the best boiled crawfish in Cajun Country. Avoid getting lost—use a GPS. Open in season (spring). Get directions from the website. Open 5–9 P.M. Wed., Thurs., and Sun., and 5–10 P.M. Fri. and Sat. Moderate.

✔ **Johnson's Boucanière** (337-269-8878, www.johnsonsboucaniere.com), 1111 St. John St., Lafayette. Lori Walls grew up eating *boudin* and sausage from Johnson's Grocery, her family's longtime business in nearby Eunice. When the grocery shut down in 2005, she missed the goodies for a while. Then she decided to do something about it. Today her *boucaniere*, Cajun French for smokehouse, sports an updated corrugated aluminum exterior with an outdoor side porch for dining. Inside are the original store's scale and, even better, boudin and sausage made from the original Johnson recipe along with an amazing array of goods like turkey *tasso*, beef jerky, pulled pork, pork with garlic, pure pork, and beef-pork mix. Plate lunches are served daily (cabbage rolls or smoked sausage/*tasso* sauce piquant) and there's BBQ on Saturday. Open 10 A.M.–5 P.M. Tues–Fri. and 7 A.M.–3 P.M. Sat. Brisket by the pound is $14.95. Inexpensive–moderate.

Olde Tyme Grocery (337-235-8165, www.oldetymegrocery.com), 218 West St. Mary Blvd., Lafayette. An army of young people churn out po-boys beneath a red sign that declares four seasons: winter, spring, summer, and football. This is a popular po-boy shop at the edge of the UL-Lafayette campus, with a friendly dining room papered in posters and road signs. The wide selection of po-boys includes sausage, meatball, shrimp, oyster, and crawfish in season. Shrimp is the hottest seller and the house specialty is a ham/roast beef/turkey and Swiss.

Seafood platters are available on Fridays. If it's nice out, eat in the brick patio area, and if you don't get one of a handful of parking spots in front, leave your car across the street. Open 8 A.M.–10 P.M. Mon.–Fri. and 9 A.M.–7 P.M. Sat. Inexpensive.

Paul's Pirogue (337-896-3788), 209 East St. Peter St., Carencro. Located north of Lafayette, the eatery looks like a converted old-time grocery store. Stick with the Cajun basics for a tasty meal. Open for lunch 4-9 P.M. Mon.–Sat. and for 5-10 P.M. dinner Sat.-Sun.

Prejean's Cajun Dining (337-896-3247, www.prejeans.com), 3480 I-49, Lafayette. Located on the frontage road off Exit 2, this well-known Cajun restaurant hosts nightly live music and, sometimes, dancing. While you can get a big bowl of gumbo prepared four different ways, you'll also find non-Cajun touches on the menu, like shrimp fettuccini parmesan vinaigrette salad dressing. A 14-foot alligator named Big Al, late of Grand Chenier, stretches midway through the dining room and a swamp tableau at one end centers on a large-stained glass depiction of a shrimp boat. Spanish moss hangs from the faux trees surrounding. Open 7 A.M.–9 P.M. Sun.–Thurs., and 7 A.M.–9:30 P.M. Fri.–Sat. Moderate–expensive.

Randol's (337-981-7080, www.randols.com), 2320 Kaliste Saloom Rd., Lafayette. One of the granddaddies of local Cajun restaurants, Randol's offers dancing and Cajun music every single night and a menu ranging over the full bill of Cajun fare, starting with the deep-fried alligator bites and ending with blackened catfish etouffee. In between are big broiled and fried seafood platters and sides that tell you where you are. Green beans come with tasso, and the potato hash is smoked.

You'll make a mistake if you don't plan for one of Randol's luscious desserts. Hours are 5–10 P.M. Sun-Thurs. and 5–11 P.M. Fri.–Sat. Fiddles and accordions start at 6:30 P.M., and thus the two-stepping begins. Moderate.

Whole Wheatery Eatery (337-232-7774), 326 Travis St., Lafayette. The eatery connects to Oil Center Health Foods. For a plate lunch with a healthy twist, consider the specials like green spinach pie or cabbage roll casserole on Tuesdays, along with the requisite two sides. A daily soup and sandwich menu includes items such as Nathan's hot dogs and BBQ chicken. Open 11 A.M.–2 P.M. Mon.–Fri. Inexpensive.

DINING OUT ✍ **Blue Dog Cafe** (337-237-0005, www.bluedogcafe .com), 1211 West Pinhook Rd., Lafayette. George Rodrigue's blue dog paintings have made it all the way to Capitol Hill, but here you can dine surrounded by the Cajun artist's famous subject. The comfortable dining room is home to a fabled Sunday brunch featuring popular local musicians (Corey Ledet, Vagabond Swing) and goodies ranging from crab cake Benedict to oyster cornbread stuffing. Mimosas are free. Lunch and dinner feature plenty of local dishes like crawfish etouffee, but don't be surprised to see a lil' twist on the familiar ingredients, like the popular crawfish enchilada. Open for lunch, 11 A.M.–2 P.M. Mon.–Fri.; dinner, 5–9 P.M. Mon.–Thurs. and 5–10 P.M. Fri.–Sat.; brunch Sun. is 10:30 A.M.–2 P.M. Moderate–expensive.

Bonnie Bell's Bistro (337-234-6776), 407 Brook Ave., Lafayette. This is a great little downtown spot with white tablecloths, deep red walls, and sconces that throw a romantic light at night. Add the somewhat industrial-looking cement floor and you end up with that elegant-if-distressed look that Louisianans do so well. The creative entrees include a blue corn jumbo lump crab salad that is totally awesome. This is a nice choice and a culinary change of local pace. Open 11 A.M.–2 P.M. Mon.; 11 A.M.–9 P.M. Tues.–Fri., and 5–9 P.M. Sat. Moderate.

✍ **Cafe Vermilionville** (337-237-0100, www.cafev.com), 1304 West Pinhook Rd., Lafayette. Lafayette's first inn still dishes out incredible hospitality and meals. The architecture and ambience transport diners to a more gracious era. Who built the first inn is lost to history, but businessmen traveling to the city by boat were housed here. The property came into the hands of Henry Louis Monnier, a Swiss native, around 1853. During the Civil War it was occupied by Federal soldiers. The structure has been renovated a number of times, but cypress beams, planed and beaded by hand, remain in some rooms. Start your meal with small crabmeat beignets blended with cheese and bacon and accented with spicy Creole mustard sauce, or try the tender fried alligator served with Dijon mustard aioli. Seafood and steaks are great, but we recommend the Napoleon with fresh Gulf shrimp and jumbo crab meat sautéed in butter, served between fried eggplant rounds and finished with andouille-parmesan cream sauce. Open 11 A.M.–2 P.M. and 5:30–9 P.M. Mon.–Fri.; and 5:30–9 P.M. Sat. Expensive.

Charley G's Seafood Grill (337-981-0108, www.charleygs.com), 3809 Ambassador Caffery Parkway, Lafayette. You're in for a surprise at this fine dining restaurant offering contemporary south Louisiana cuisine. The smoked duck and andouille gumbo, cooked with a rich, dark roux is amazing. The succulent Blue Point béchamel crab cakes are melt-in-your mouth perfection and come with a delightful bell pepper coulis. Tip: One crab cake is a meal in itself, especially with a cup of gumbo or a Caesar salad. Beef eaters can relax, because aged filet mignon and rib eye steaks, grilled over southern hardwoods, are cooked exactly as requested. You also won't go wrong if you select any of the daily lunch specials. Open for lunch, 11:30 A.M.–2 P.M. Mon.–Fri.; and dinner, 5:30–9 P.M. Mon.–Thurs. and 5:30–10 P.M. Fri.–Sat. Moderate–expensive.

The French Press (337-233-9449, thefrenchpresslafayette.com), 214 East Vermilion St., Lafayette. Justin Girouard, former sous chef at New Orleans's Stella!, moved home to Lafayette with his wife, Margaret, and now is serving creative fare like the Acadian breakfast sandwich of bacon, egg, cheese, and boudin on grilled Evangeline Maid Texas toast and flatout French offerings like croque monsieur. The menu includes a nice group of soups and salads, and the imaginative dinner menu changes weekly. This is a cool space in the renovated Tribune Press building, where soft morning light pours through the windows. Open for breakfast and lunch, 7 A.M.– 2 P.M. Wed.–Fri. and 9 A.M.–2 P.M. Sat.–Sun., and dinner 5:30–9:30 P.M. Fri.–Sat. Expensive.

Pamplona Tapas Bar (337-232-0070, www.pamplonatapas.com), 631 Jefferson St., Lafayette. Authentic Spanish flamenco and bullfighting posters line the walls of this intimate restaurant, which reminds us of tapas spots in Cordoba and Seville, Spain. The menu is lovely and a change from the region's heavy Cajun and Southern food. Tapas, flatbreads, salads, and entrees of meat and seafood—as well as paella—fill the bill of fare. The Catalan spinach with raisins, pine nuts, and green apples sautéed in olive oil was just what the

doctor ordered following a Mardi Gras day spent feasting on sausage and boudin. Inspired by Hemingway's favorite haunts, the cafe's dishes are delicioso. A sociable bar anchors the room. Open 11 A.M.–10 P.M. Tues.– Thurs., 11 A.M.–11 P.M. Fri., and 5– 11 P.M. Sat. Moderate.

✳ Entertainment

✐ ♿ ☂ **Acadiana Center for the Arts** (337-233-7060, www.acadiana centerforthearts.org), 101 West Vermilion St., Lafayette. This impressive new state-of-the-art building was designed for multiple use from jazz concerts to one-man shows to private receptions, and its programs are the heart of the region's considerable arts scene. Check the website for schedules.

Acadiana Symphony Orchestra and Conservatory of Music (337-232-4277, www.acadianasymphony.org), 412 Travis St., Lafayette. Founded in 1984 and incorporated in 1987, the ASO is a professional regional orchestra. Its season includes two series: one of masterworks and one of pops. Look for shows like *Chopin and Jazz* or *It's Christmas Time with Terrance Simien,* the beloved local zydeco Grammy winner. Performances are held at theaters around town (and even St. John Cathedral); call for ticket prices and calendar.

ArtWalk (337-291-5566, www.down townlafayette.org), downtown Lafayette, held the second Saturday of each month, features open galleries and studios from 6–8 P.M. Join street entertainers for music and a delightful evening stroll. For a schedule, check the website.

Bach Lunch (337-291-5544, www .lafayettesciencemuseum.org), 433 Jefferson St., Lafayette, presented by the Lafayette Science Museum foundation, gets spring and fall weekends

Cynthia V. Campbell

PEOPLE OF ALL AGES GET IN THE SWING AT FRIDAY NIGHT LIVE IN LAFAYETTE.

off to an early start with an hour of free live music at noon on Fridays in Parc Sans Souci. Local restaurants sell lunch for a nominal fee. For info check www.lafayettetravel.com.

Downtown Alive! (www.downtown lafayette), Parc Sans Souci, 201 Vermilion St., Lafayette. Live music, including Cajun, zydeco, jazz, blues, rock, and Latin, is performed in Parc Sans Souci starting at 5:30 P.M. in spring and fall. This is a very popular local gathering. For information see www.downtownlafayette.org.

NIGHTLIFE The downtown Lafayette club scene generally draws a young crowd, although Tsunami, a stylish sushi restaurant with another following at its Baton Rouge location, is recommended for the over-30 crowd; find it at 412 Jefferson St. (337-234-FISH, www.servingsushi.com). Here's where to find the music:

Blue Moon Saloon (337-234-2422, www.bluemoonpresents.com), 215

East Convent St., Lafayette. This is the place, a much-loved local institution devoted to the best in roots music complete with its own bunkhouse-ish guest house (see Lodgings) for when the night grows long.

El Sido's Zydeco & Blues Club (337-235-0647, www.facebook.com /pages/Lafayette-LA/El-Sidos-Zydeco -Blues-Club/173522632458), 1523 North St. Antoine, Lafayette. The real deal if you want to hear the region's true zydeco and blues musicians.

Grant Street Dancehall (337-237-8513, www.grantstreetdancehall.com), 113 West Grant St., Lafayette. This popular longtime local club brings in legends from near (Buckwheat Zydeco, Terrance Simien) and far (the Indigo Girls, Richie Havens). The calendar's posted on the website.

✱ Selective Shopping

712 Euphoria (337-233-2034, www.712euphoria.com), 712 West

Congress St., Lafayette. Arrested by the façade of this funky emporium—clothing racks on the front porch, its operator kibitzing on the steps with a friend—we went inside to find vintage clothing, offbeat collectibles, and the chance to get furniture upholstered or a custom scent mixed from essential oils.

Artesia (337-232-8441, www.ilove artesia.com), 2513 Johnston St., Lafayette. This stylish clothing boutique has a second store in Lake Charles.

Mall of Acadiana (337-984-8241, www.mallofacadiana.com), 5725 Johnston St., Lafayette. The region's major mall, with dozens of major outlets such as Aeropostale, Coldwater Creek, and Lady Footlocker. Chain anchors include Macy's and JC Penney.

Reflections of Olde Antique Mall (337-593-8593, www.reflectionsofolde .com), 700 West Congress St. at the corner of St. John, Lafayette. Great old jewelry, garden items (the day we visited: a wrought iron fence that once surrounded a grave in France), and a tempting warehouse full of furniture fill this 7,000-square-foot operation.

Renaissance Market (337-234-1116), 902 Harding St., Lafayette. This large and gorgeous emporium of French antiques, garden and home items, and sweet-smelling accessories like fine candles, also houses a lunchtime brasserie that serves soups, salads, sandwiches (including panini), and Middle Eastern dishes such as hummus and tabouleh.

San Souci Fine Crafts Gallery (337-266-7999, www.louisiana crafts.org), 219 East Vermilion St., Lafayette. This is headquarters to the Louisiana Craft Guild, which means top-notch jewelry, sculpture, paintings, mixed media, pottery, and other distinctive works made by the wealth of artists who call Louisiana home. It's all

housed in the city's one-time post office. Closed Mondays.

Whoojoo Stained Glass Studio (318-269-9310), 532 Jefferson St., Lafayette. The stained-glass artist Craig McCullen creates commissioned works, which have included pieces for churches and a recent collaboration featured on the Festival International poster. Works by other artists are also shown here.

✱ Special Events

February: **Mardi Gras** season, formally known as Carnival, revolves around Lafayette's traditional New Orleans–style krewes with parades for the public and a family-style carnival at the Cajun Dome. The krewes' balls are usually private, although the public can see the Southwest Louisiana Mardi Gras Association Pageant and Ball on Mardi Gras night. Festivities typically start soon after Seventh Night and swell until Fat Tuesday, the big climax. Your best source of information: www.lafayettetravel.com.

April: **Festival International de Louisiane** (337-232-8086, www.festival international.com), 735 Jefferson St., Lafayette. Six stages and three marchés help spread Francophone love throughout downtown at Festival International. This is a true multicultural jubilation. It kicks off the Wednesday evening of the last full weekend in April and runs through Sunday, with musical acts from around the world and the region. Music lovers have been known to sprint from New Orleans (where Jazz Fest starts the same weekend) to Lafayette. Festivalgoers can cherry-pick the best food and drink from fabulous regional restaurants (margaritas from one, crawfish *pistolettes* from another) and one-of-a-kind clothing, jewelry, furniture, and other pieces from artisans near and far. Book your room early.

September: **Zydeco Music Festival** (www.zydeco.org), Plaisance. Music lovers congregate Labor Day weekend in this town just north of Opelousas to celebrate zydeco, the joyous music named after a green bean. It features the best zydeco performers and bands in the state, along with dancing, traditional storytelling, and presentations about the history of the music. Activities start with an official ribbon cutting and evening street party at the Opelousas Farmer's Market. Highlights include the Zydeco Jam Session and the parade to Slim's Y-Kiki in Plaisance and the Saturday Zydeco Breakfast in Opelousas Courtyard Square. Saturday, the festival starts at 10:30 A.M. in Zydeco Park in Plaisance. Wear comfortable shoes and be prepared to dance your heart out.

October: **Festival Acadiens et Creoles** (www.festivalsacadiens.com), Girard Park, Lafayette. This is an all-out tribute to Acadiana's cultural roots, with music, food, crafts, and all other things Cajun and Creole. It has grown over the decades from its roots as part of efforts to save south Louisiana's French culture. Today, fest-goers have four days in October to gather in Girard Park to hear the best in regional music, sample awesome food (crawfish enchiladas, sweet potato bread pudding), watch cooking demonstrations, and more.

✍ **International Rice Festival** (www.ricefestival.com), Crowley. Held the third weekend of October downtown and on the Festival Grounds, the event features rice eating, a rice cook-off, a parade and a Poker Rice Run, a card game, and motorcycle race for prizes.

The three-day festival includes children's activities and live music with headliners such Tracy Lawrence, the Molly Ringwalds, and Geno Delafose and French Rockin' Boogie.

November: **Giant Omelette Celebration** (337-893-3082, www.giantomelette.org), Magdalen Square, Abbeville. The Confrerie D'Abbeville invites you to the city's 5,000-egg omelet fry. The two-day event includes a tractor "egg-cracking" competition, a juried art show, a kids' activities area and a downtown walk. On Sunday, activities open with a Mass in St. Mary Magdalen Catholic Church, then continue in Magdalen Square. In early afternoon people gather to watch the procession of chefs, eggs, and bread to the giant 12-foot skillet where participants cook a huge omelet and distribute portions to the crowd. Live music and food by local restaurants are part of the fun and folly.

✍ **The Rayne Frog Festival** (337-366-2884, www.raynefrogfestival.com), Rayne. The mid-November festival draws thousands of visitors to this hoppy—make that happy—place. Things kick off with a grand parade winding through town to the Frog Festival Fairgrounds, just off I-10. You'll love the frog racing and jumping contests offering anyone who wants to enter a chance to handle the hoppers and cheer them on. A contestant may bring his or her own frog or rent one from the Rayne Jaycees for a small fee. Some 60 booths offer food and arts and crafts, and youngsters can enjoy carnival rides presented by Miller Spectacular Shows.

MORGAN CITY, HOUMA-THIBODAUX, GRAND ISLE AREA

The southeastern section of Cajun Country is an amazing landscape of meandering bayous shaded by moss-laden oaks and native shrubs, shimmering lakes, the forceful Atchafalaya River, and finally the great Gulf of Mexico. It's no wonder most residents here are expert boaters and anglers. The Chitimacha Indians were the original inhabitants; they began settling the area around 500 A.D. and lived in permanent villages in homes constructed of cane, wood, and palmetto leaves. And they are still here. If the area's major highways and roads seemingly wander in unexpected directions, it's because they are following a waterway that was the only means of transportation for early settlers. You'll see bridges crossing the Atchafalaya River, Bayou Teche, Bayou Terrebonne, and Bayou Lafourche, and we're not counting man-made navigational channels. When driving the region, it pays to stop in small communities. Talk with locals at service stations, grocery stores, and shopping centers. They'll give you the latest news on weather and road conditions. As a lagniappe, you'll probably get tips on how to make the best alligator sauce piquant or where to buy delicious home-baked bread.

AREA CODE 985.

GUIDANCE Bayou Lafourche Area Convention and Visitors Bureau (877-537-5800, www.visitlafourche.com), 4484 LA 1, Raceland. Situated at the intersection of US 90 and LA 1, this center is a great place for information on regional events, fishing charters, and maps.

Cajun Coast Visitors' and Convention Bureau (800-256-2931, 985-305-4905, www.cajuncoast.com), 112 Main St., Patterson. The visitors' center is open 9 A.M.–5 P.M. Mon–Fri. The bureau also maintains the Franklin Visitor Center and Rest Area (337-828-2555) 15307 LA 90 West, Franklin, which is open 8:30 A.M.–4:30 P.M. Mon.–Sat.

Houma Area Convention and Visitors Bureau (800-688-2732, 985-868-2732, www.houmatravel.com), 114 Tourist Dr., Gray.

Cynthia V. Campbell

A BOAT CRUISES THE ATCHAFALAYA RIVER NEAR MORGAN CITY.

Louisiana Coastal Coalition (985-727-6774, www.visitlouisianacoast.com), 2895 US 90, Mandeville. The organization promotes coastal communities and is set up to help visitors enjoy the culture and outdoors.

GETTING THERE *By car:* Even if you have an updated GPS, listen to directions carefully unless your homing ability is better. The best way to reach Morgan City from Lafayette is to follow US 90 (I-49) through New Iberia, Franklin, and Patterson. From New Orleans, take I-10 west to I-310 crossing the Mississippi River and continue west to US 90 (I-49) West through Paradis, Raceland, and Gibson. From Baton Rouge, follow I-10 east to LA 22 at Sorrento, where you cross over the Mississippi on the Sunshine Bridge and connect with LA 70 South, which runs through Pierre Part and Belle River and on into Morgan City. If going directly to Houma and Thibodaux, follow US 90 (I-49) from New Orleans or Lafayette until you see the exits to these towns. Major routes will be LA 182 and LA 308. If you get confused, stop at the Visitors' Center at the intersection of LA 1 and US 90. If Grand Isle is your destination, take LA 1 south from the US 90 (I-49) exit until you cross the causeway to the barrier island.

MEDICAL EMERGENCIES Lady of the Sea General Hospital (985-632-6233, www.losgh.org) 200 West 134 Place, Cut Off.

Leonard J. Chabert Medical Center (985-873-2200, www.lsuhospitals.org), 1978 Industrial Blvd., Houma.

Teche Regional Medical Center in Morgan City (985-380-4434, www.teche regional.com), 1125 Marguerite St., Morgan City.

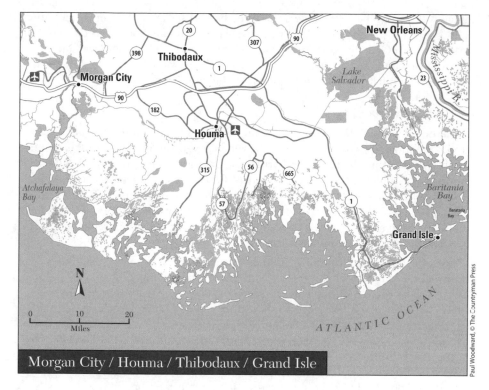

Morgan City / Houma / Thibodaux / Grand Isle

Paul Woodward, © The Countryman Press

Terrebonne General Medical Center (985-873-4141, www.tgmc.com), 8166 Main St., Houma.

MORGAN CITY AREA

Morgan City, where Bayou Teche meets the mouth of the Atchafalaya River, is in a strategic location for the marine industry and the petrochemical industry. The river has provided prosperity and challenges for the generations who have lived here. Originally called Tigre Island after a wildcat was spotted there, the area attracted the attention of the Kentucky planter and surgeon Walter Brashear. When he subdivided a portion of his sugarcane plantation in 1876, the first permanent town was called Brashear. It was later renamed Morgan City in honor of Charles Morgan, a steamship magnate who successfully dredged the Atchafalaya Bay. The city thrived as a commercial center in the late 1800s and early 1900s, as boat building, moss picking, and shell crushing broadened the economic base.

Hollywood chose the tree-laden swamps as a stand-in for Africa's jungles for the first Tarzan movie in 1917. *Tarzan of the Apes* starred Elmo Lincoln and Enid Markey. Based on Edgar Rice Burroughs's original novel, the silent film is considered one of the most faithful to the novel of all film adaptations.

You won't find any cheesy tourist attractions with posters reading ME JANE . . . YOU TARZAN around Morgan City. Instead, the town reflects its commercial heritage with one of the state's oldest chartered harvest festivals, the Louisiana Shrimp and Petroleum Festival held Labor Day weekend to honor workers in those industries. Kerr-McGee Oil Industries drilled the first successful offshore well out of sight of land and the "black gold rush" marked the new era in the city. Today, the offshore oil industry remains a major part of the area's economy.

✳ Cities, Towns, and Villages

Charenton is home to the only remaining community of Chitimacha Indians. In 1855, the tribe was seriously reduced by yellow fever. Sarah Avery McIlhenny purchased the Chitimacha land at a sheriff's sale in 1915 and ceded it to the federal government, which in turn placed it in trust for the tribe. Federal recognition followed in 1917. Today, the Chitimacha operate the lucrative Cypress Bayou Casino, which has allowed them to recover land that historically was part of the reservation. The tribe also operates a museum, fish processing plant, and school on the reservation. Visit www.chitimacha.gov.

Franklin, a singularly charming town, is surrounded by vast sugar plantations. Drive along Main Street and enjoy the distinctive street lamps. The lamps themselves can be rotated during harvest season to allow large trucks laden with cane stalks to pass through town. Take a short drive around the city to see some of the 400 structures listed on the National Register of Historic Places. Named for Benjamin Franklin, the city was incorporated in 1820, and its culture and architecture were heavily influenced by the many people who chose to settle here after the Louisiana Purchase in 1803. The town's First United Methodist Church was established in 1806, making it the first Protestant church established in the state of Louisiana. During the Civil War, the Battle of Irish Bend, also known as Neeson's Woods, was fought near here. Confederate forces commanded by General Richard Taylor cost the Union significant losses. Four hundred men were killed or wounded in the conflict. One of the city's significant landmarks is Oaklawn Manor, circa 1837, now the home of Louisiana's former Governor Mike Foster and his wife, Alice. It's open for tours on a regular basis. Each fall, downtown hosts the Harvest Moon Fest in conjunction with the Franklin Patriotic Concert, a performance on the banks of Bayou Teche. This also is the setting of the Louisiana Black Bear Festival. A public boat launch leads to the Franklin Canal and there's easy access to the Atchafalaya Basin and the wonders of the surrounding wetlands.

Patterson, a small community, is part of the Morgan City Metropolitan Statistical Area. During the early 1800s, a group of Pennsylvania Dutchmen boarded a sailing vessel in New Orleans and headed for Bayou Teche. One of them, Hans Knight, made his home in the area originally called the Dutch Settlement. In 1832, Captain John Patterson, a trader from Indiana, settled in the area that was incorporated in his name in 1907. The community's economy and history is inevitably linked to Morgan City and a number of attractions are easily reached from both towns.

✳ To See

Brownell Carillon Bell Tower (985-384-2283), 3559 LA 70, Morgan City. The 106-foot-tall tower, located in a 9.5-acre park next to Lake Palourde, appears somewhat out of place in this serene park landscaped with palmetto, elephant ear, cattail, fern, cypress, tupelo, iris, and other plants. The tower was the gift of Claire Horatio Brownell, a member of one of Louisiana's pioneer families. She conceived the idea of perpetuating the beauty of the swamp through a quiet park. It was her wish that the park be a nondenominational setting where all people could retreat to commune with God. The tower contains 61 bronze bells that were cast in Holland. A bell recital is held the first Sunday of every month at 1 P.M. and when the lilting melodies waft through this bird sanctuary, you almost think you're dreaming. Time spent here is magical.

Chitimacha Museum (337-923-4830, www.chitimacha.gov), 329 Chitimacha Trail, Charenton. The Chitimacha were the first inhabitants of this area along Bayou Teche. The tribe is widely known for its basket-weaving skills. Take a trip back in time while learning about the history of the tribe and viewing the wonderful baskets. Open 9 A.M.–4:30 P.M. Mon.–Fri. Admission free.

Downtown Main Street (985-380-1770, www.morgancitymainstreet.com), Front Street to Federal Avenue and Greenwood to Railroad, Morgan City. Tour the city's small downtown on foot and you'll get a bird's-eye view of the Atchafalaya River from the 22-foot seawall. Shop at several stores on the waterfront and enjoy lunch at Rita Mae's, Latin Corner, Atchafalaya Cafe, or Cafe Jo Jo's. Make arrangements to tour Sacred Heart Catholic Church or Trinity Episcopal Church, both with shimmering stained-glass windows.

Grevemberg House Museum (337-828-2092, www.grevemberghouse.com), 407 Sterling Rd., Franklin. The St. Mary Parish landmark, built in 1851, is an antebellum townhouse reflecting life in the mid 1800s. View period antiques and documented wallpaper. Admission is $10, adults; $8, seniors 65 and over, students under 18, and groups of 20 or more; and $5, children under age 12. Open 10 A.M.–4 P.M. Tues.–Sun.

International Petroleum Museum and Exposition (985-384-3744, www.rig museum.com), Riverfront, Morgan City. On the banks of the Atchafalaya River at the intersection of the Intracoastal Waterway in Morgan City, the museum is publicized as the only place in the world where the general public can walk aboard an authentic "working" offshore drilling rig. The Rig Museum, known as Mr. Charlie, fascinates both kids and adults. Mr. Charlie, which the museum website says "was capable of drilling wells in water depths of up to 40 feet and lasted nearly 4 decades," was built in 1952 and finished in 1953. It was put to work for Shell Oil Company in a new field in East Bay near the mouth of the Mississippi. This was the first transportable drilling ring and a springboard to current offshore rig technology. Take a tour and learn about offshore drilling techniques, the risk taken by workers, and life aboard a deepwater rig. The museum also houses the International Petroleum Training Institute, which offers educational and training to the next generation of workers. Classes include fire fighting, helicopter safety, cargo handling, rigging, seaman training, water survival, hurricane preparation, and much more. Tours last 1–1½ hours and are given at 10 A.M. and 2 P.M. Mon.–Sat. Cost is $5, adults; $4, seniors; $3.50, children under 12; and free to children under 5. Adults are expected to be with children at all times when touring the rig.

✍ ♿ ❀ **Louisiana State Museum—Patterson** (985-399-1268) 118 Cotton Rd., Patterson. This state museum combines two important collections. Though the collections are completely different and have almost nothing in common, they both

Cynthia V. Campbell

AIRPLANES DESIGNED BY AVIATION PIONEERS ARE DISPLAYED AT THE WEDELL-WILLIAMS MEMORIAL MUSEUM, IN PATTERSON.

document two fascinating eras in the rich history of coastal Louisiana. The Wedell-Williams Aviation Collection focuses on the legacy of aviation pioneers Jimmy Wedell, a daredevil flyer, and Harry Williams, a businessman. Together they formed the Wedell Williams Air Service at a landing field that was cleared on Calumet Plantation. The service expanded into Patterson, which was home base for a flight school, aerial photography service, amphibian service, and aerial transportation. At one point, Williams owned the largest privately held fleet of aircraft in the world, with 42 planes. In 1929, Wedell-Williams began construction on its initial racing design. The first plane was a racer named the We-Will. Wedell became famous for radical airplane designs that set speed records time and again. Although both Wedell and Williams perished in plane crashes, their legacy is well established in flight history. Among the planes on display are the famous *Miss Patterson 44* and the *Gilmore 121*. Also exhibited are Wedell-Williams's 1930s air-racing trophies and memorabilia. A staging area with drop-down screen features an exciting film on the 1932 Cleveland National Air Races. In the same facility, the Patterson Cypress Sawmill Collection documents the history of Louisiana's cypress lumber industry. Lumbering became the state's first significant manufacturing business, and cypress was cut and milled in Louisiana and shipped across the United States. Patterson, once home to the largest cypress sawmill in the world, was designated the cypress capitol of the state in 1997 by the Louisiana Legislature. View the photographs, machinery, and artifacts that tell the story of lumber and lumbermen. The museum also has a gallery that focuses on changing Louisiana exhibits. Open 9:30 A.M.–4 P.M. Tues.–Sat.

♂ ♞ **Oaklawn Manor** (337-828-0434, www.oaklawnmanor.com) 3296 East Oak-lawn Dr., Franklin. The private home of Louisiana's former governor Murphy J. "Mike" Foster Jr. and his wife, Alice, Oaklawn was built in 1837. The plantation is furnished with European antiques and the Foster family's personal collections, including outstanding bird carvings and an extensive Audubon collection. Open 10 A.M.–4 P.M. Tues.–Sat-and noon–4 P.M. Sun. Admission. is $15, adults and $10, students.

♞ **Young-Sanders Center** (337-413-1861, www.youngsanders.org), 104 Commer-cial St., Franklin. The center was established for the study of the War Between the States. Essentially a library, it is a repository of newspapers, records, and docu-ments covering the Civil War. Lecture series covers various topics. Open 9 A.M.–5 P.M. Mon.–Fri. Admission free.

✳ Green Spaces

Attakapas Wildlife Management Area (337-948-0255, www.wlf.louisiana.gov), headquarters located on Martin Ridge Rd., 20 miles northwest of Morgan City. The area includes 25,730 acres owned by the state of Louisiana and 2,200 acres owned by the U.S. Army Corps of Engineers. Comprised of bottomland hard-woods and cypress swamp, the area provides ample opportunity for boating, fish-ing, hunting, and birding. Access by boat only. Primitive camping available. Managed by the Louisiana Department of Wildlife and Fisheries.

Atchafalaya Delta Wildlife Management Area (337-373-0032), about 18 miles southwest of Morgan City. With 137 miles of active delta, about 45,000 of which is freshwater marsh land, this beautiful area at the mouth of the Atchafalaya River and the Wax Lake Outlet takes some getting to: It is accessible by boat only.

♂ ↬ **Cypremort Point State Park** (337-8674510 or 888-867-4510, www.crt.state .la.us/parks), 306 Beach Lane, Cypremort Point. Looking at a Louisiana state map you will see that Cypremort Point on Vermilion Bay is the only state park between Cameron and Grand Isle near the Gulf of Mexico that can be reached by car. A half-mile stretch of man-made beach is a wonderful area for enjoying the water and picnicking. It's excellent for fishing, crabbing, water skiing, windsurfing, and sailing. A boat launch outside the park's entrance is a few miles from the Gulf and fishermen can venture into the bay or the Gulf itself. With 185 acres, the park has an abundance of wildlife, including deer, black bear, rabbit, opossum, muskrat, nutria and alligator. From I-10 follow US 90 south to LA 83. Continue south and turn right onto LA 319 and follow this road to the park. Gates are open 7 A.M.–9 P.M. Sun.–Thurs. All park sites close at 10 P.M. Fri., Sat. and days preceding holi-days. Entrance fee is $1 per person. For reservations, 1-CAMP-N-LA.

Great Wall (800-256-2931, www.morgancitymainstreet.com), Front St. Riverside, Morgan City. Located along the Atchafalaya River in Morgan City and Berwick, the Great Wall stands 21 feet tall and overlooks the mighty Atchafalaya River. Visi-tors can get a spectacular bird's-eye view of water traffic from the walkway that tops the concrete floodwall.

A HERON FLIES ACROSS THE WETLANDS.

Lake Charles/Southwest Louisiana Convention and Visitors Bureau

✸ To Do

BIKING Bike through St. Mary Parish along LA 182, also known as the Old Spanish Trail, and the Bayou Teche Scenic Byway. Along the way you'll get a glimpse of sugarcane mills, plantation homes, a turn-of-the-century boulevard, Bayou Teche, and more.

BIRDING The St. Mary Birding Loop (985-385-4905). America's Wetland Birding Trail takes visitors through one swamp scene after another. The Morgan City and Berwick walking trails are perfect for power walking, or you can visit the Brownnell Memorial and Carillon Tower or travel along the Cotton Road in Paterson. Avid bird watchers and photographers may spot more than 300 species known to stay in the area. Eagles can be sighted between October and through the end of April.

FISHING Blue Dog Charters (985-384-2070), 7209 LA 182 East, Morgan City. Test your salt water fishing skills on or near the Gulf of Mexico for redfish, speckled trout, black drum, or flounder. Fish a full day or half day, all-inclusive. Ivy's Tackle Box also offers on-site rod and reel repairs.

GAMING Cypress Bayou Casino (337-923-7284, www.cypressbayou.com), 832 Martin Luther King Jr. Rd., Charenton. Louisiana's first land-based casino is 50 miles southeast of Lafayette on the Chitimacha Indian Reservation. Inside you'll find table games, slots, and a live action poker room. Restaurants include a lavish buffet and Mr. Lester's, an exceptional fine dining steak and seafood restaurant. The casino also offers an upscale nightclub featuring live entertainment every weekend. Open 11 A.M. Admission free. Must be 21 to enter.

GOLF Atachafalaya Golf Course at Idlewild (985-395-4653, www.atchafalaya golf.com), 400 Cotton Rd. at LA 90, Kemper William Park, Patterson. One of the newest additions to the Audubon Golf Trail, this championship 18-hole course was designed by internationally renowned Robert von Hagge, of von Hagge, Smelek and Baril. Public rates: $58 Mon.–Thurs., $68 Fri.–Sun.; twilight, $43 Mon.–Thurs., $48 Fri.–Sun. Seniors: $48 Mon.–Thurs. Juniors: $28 Mon.–Thurs., $33 Fri.–Sun. Rates include cart rental. Hours are 7 A.M.–6:30 P.M.; tee times start at 7:30 A.M.

St. Mary Golf & Country Club (985-384-8500), 581 Fairview Dr., Berwick. The semi-private 9-hole course has a snack bar in the clubhouse. Nonmember rates are $36 Mon.–Fri. and $24 after 2 P.M.; rates are $40 Sat.-Sun. and after 2 P.M. $27. Open 7 A.M.–dusk.

PADDLING If your passion is canoeing or kayaking, then explore the lower Atchafalaya/Bayou Teche paddling trail. Camping is available at the Two Sisters Boat Launch in Bayou Vista. Stop at the Cajun Coast Visitors and Convention Bureau for a Paddling Trails brochure with maps and a picnic lunch. Visit www.cajuncoast.com for more information.

TOURS Cajun Jack's Swamp Tours (985-395-7420, www.cajunjack.com), 118 Main St., Patterson. Sit back, relax, and let Captain Jack, a licensed boat captain, serve as your guide to the untouched natural beauty of the Atchafalaya Basin. Learn about the Cajun culture of the swamplands, fur trapping, crabbing, and crawfishing. Tours last approximately 2½ hours. Reservations recommended.

CAJUN JACK TALKS ABOUT CONSERVING THE DELICATE WETLANDS ECOSYSTEM DURING A SWAMP TOUR IN PATTERSON.

Cynthia V. Campbell

❋ Lodging

The Morgan City/Patterson area has a number of options for lodgings. Nationally recognized hotel and motel chains include **Best Western, Comfort Inn & Suites, Days Inn, Hampton Inn & Suites, Holiday Inn**, and **La Quinta Inns & Suites**. Bed & breakfasts and cabins include **Atchafalaya Oaks** (985-702-9889, www.atchafalayaoaks.biz), 501 Railroad Ave., Morgan City; and **Cypress Lake RV Resort** (985-399-5981, www.cypresslakervresort.com) between Patterson and Morgan City, which has 76 campsites and offers laundry, fishing, a swimming pool, pedal boats, canoes, and aluminum boat rentals. Pets are welcome.

CAMPGROUNDS ❧ **Cajun Houseboat & Rentals** (985-385-6621, www.cajunhouseboats.com), 10 miles north of Morgan City Located within a chain of rivers, lakes and miles of bayous, this outfit rents houseboats, day boats, canoes, and kayaks, and also offers bird and breakfast tours and evening/night swamp tours. Inexpensive.

✍ ❧ **Kemper Williams Park and Campground** (985-395-2298, www.kemperwilliamspark.com), 264 Cotton Rd. off LA 90, Patterson. The campground has a bathhouse, dump station, picnic grounds, tennis courts, nature trail, 18-hole public golf course, and 40 campsites with full hookups. Admission is $1 per car. Inexpensive.

❋ Where to Eat

EATING OUT Dixie Grill Cafe (985-385-2411), 7408 LA 182, Morgan City. This casual, friendly cafe is popular for its Sunday–Friday lunch buffet packed with Cajun favorites. Hours are 5:30 A.M.–2 P.M. and 5–9 P.M. Mon.–Fri., 6:30–8 P.M. Sat.–Sun. Inexpensive.

Jane's Steakhouse & Grill (985-385-6800, www.janessteakhousegrill.com), 1205 Clothilde St., Morgan City. Locals gather at Jane's for the steaks and crunchy fried pickles. Needless to say the grilled seafood and salad bar are equally popular. Beer and wine are available. Inexpensive.

✍ **The Original Castalano's** (985-384-6188), 1023 Sixth St., Morgan City. Popular for its sausage and Italian fare, Castalano's offers delicious chicken and pork stuffed with sausage as well as seafood, sandwiches, salads, pasta, and po-boys. Open 10:30 A.M.–2 P.M. Mon.–Sat. and 5–8 P.M. Thurs.–Fri. Moderate.

✍ **Rita Mae's Kitchen** (985 384-3550), 71 Federal Ave., Morgan City. This is down-home Southern cooking with Creole flair. Portions are large and the food is delicious. The menu includes everything from big burgers to fried seafood. Try the bread pudding or sweet potato pie.

Scully's Cajun Seafood (985-385-2388), 3141 LA 70, Morgan City. The specialty here is no surprise: the seafood is fried or boiled in season by "real" Cajuns. The casual dining room overlooks Bayou Long. Open 11 A.M.–2 P.M. and 4:30–8:15 P.M. Tues.–Fri., and 4:30–8:30 P.M. Sat.

✍ **Susie's Seafood** (985-702-0274), 6701 LA 182, Morgan City. Specializing in boiled seafood, Susie's is a simple, down-home place with excellent big crawfish and good service. Totally informal, the cafe spreads paper across tabletops before dumping steaming hot, perfectly seasoned crawfish, shrimp, and large crabs in front of hungry diners. Customers can select their favorite Cajun, swamp pop, and '70s tunes from the modified juke box on one wall. Locals drop in here to get their fill and share the latest town news with friends. Moderate.

♪ **Tampico's Mexican** (985-385-2784), 1025 Victor II Blvd., Morgan City. Stop here for Tex-Mex dishes in the heart of Cajun Country. The menu includes typical south-of-the-border fare—nachos, taco salad, carne asada, enchiladas, and delicious margaritas. Open 11 A.M.–10 P.M. Mon.–Thurs., 11 A.M.–11 P.M. Fri.–Sat., and 5–9 P.M. Sun. Moderate.

DINING OUT The Atchafalaya Restaurant Club House (985-399-3688, www.atchafalayagolf.com), 400 Cotton Rd., Patterson. The restaurant in the Atchalafalaya Golf Club is dressy casual and the back gallery offers a beautiful view of the verdant course. The menu features Cajun cuisine, fresh seafood, steaks, and more. Hours are 10:30 A.M.–2 P.M. Mon.–Sat. Moderate–expensive.

Cafe Jo Jo's (985-384-9291). 624 Front St., Morgan City. Enjoy a mix of fine Italian and Cajun cuisine from a cafe overlooking the Atchafalaya River. The menu will delight your taste buds with everything from crab cakes to tuna and filet steaks with cognac sauce. Do try the flavorful crawfish cheese bread. The décor captures the romance of a 1930s jazz club. Moderate.

Mr. Lester's Steakhouse (337-923-7408), 832 Martin Luther King Rd., Charenton. This fine-dining restaurant in Cypress Bayou Casino features delicious prime steaks as well as shrimp, lobster, and lamb entrees. Add to these side dishes such as praline sweet potatoes and marinated grilled vegetables. End your meal with white chocolate mousse praline torte or southern bread pudding a la mode. Hours are 6–11 P.M. Wed.–Thurs. and 6-11:30 P.M. Fri.–Sat. Expensive–very expensive.

✳ **Entertainment**

Bocat's Oyster Bar (337-923-7284), 823 Martin Luther King Rd., Charenton. Located in the Cypress Bayou Casino, this spot has oysters on the half shell and oyster shooters. Karaoke is offered every Thursday and bands perform on Friday and Saturday. Must be 21 to enter. Hours are 5–10 P.M. Thurs. and 5 P.M.–midnight, Fri. and Sat.

Friend's Tavern (985-384-3925), 6701 LA 182 East, Morgan City. This is a friendly tavern with excellent service. Pool tables and a jukebox add to the relaxed atmosphere. There are karaoke and disc jockey on Friday and Saturday nights. Hours are noon–2 A.M. daily.

✳ **Selective Shopping**

Bayou Chic Uniques & Antiques (985-384-2300), 612 US 90, Patterson. A good spot to browse for that roadside find you can show off to friends at home. Browse for new and old gifts. A second shop is located at 602 Brashear Ave., Morgan City. Hours are 11 A.M.–5 P.M., Mon.–Fri. and 10 A.M.–5 P.M. Sat.

Brown's Jewelers (985-385-0516), 6421 LA 182 East, Morgan City. Brown's is a traditional family-owned jewelry store offering a wide selection of rings, necklaces, pendants, and bracelets. The store's watch collection includes styles from Bulova, Fossil, and Seiko. Hours are 11 A.M.–5 P.M. Mon.–Fri. and 10 A.M.–5 P.M. Sat.

Plantation Treasures (985-384-7066), 704 Front St., Morgan City. This shop features fleur de lis jewelry, Clementine Hunter prints, decorative items for the home and ladies' accessories. Hours are 9:30 A.M.–5:30 P.M. Mon.–Fri. and 10 A.M.–3 P.M. Sat.

Shannon Design (985-702-1618), 618 Front St., Morgan City. Be prepared for the burst of joyful bright colors you'll find in this studio. Colleen Shannon showcases handcrafted tile, art glass, pottery, jewelry, and paintings. Her work is jazz for the eyes.

✳ Special Events

February: The annual **Eagle Expo** (800-256-2931, www.cajuncoast.com) has boat tours into various waterways to view American bald eagles and their nests. Wildlife professionals and photographers give presentations on the American bald eagle, wildlife, flora, fauna, and the culture of the area.

March: **Patterson Cypress Sawmill Festival** (800-256-2931, www.cypress sawmill.com), Kemper Williams Park, Patterson. Held the last weekend in March, this celebration honoring the lumber industry has been named one of the top festivals by the 20 Southeast Tourism Society. Tournaments include a *passé partout* (two-person saw) contest and a Cajun cook-off.

April: ⤷ **Bayou Teche Black Bear Festival** (337-828-2555, www.bayou techebearfest.org), Franklin. Held in historic downtown Franklin, the three-day, mid-April festival celebrates the lush environment of St. Mary Parish. Eco-friendly events raise awareness of the Louisiana black bear population and the numerous bird species that migrate through the area. Activities include boat trips into Bayou Teche Wildlife Refuge, canoe and paddling excursions in the refuge, animal and habitat conservation seminars, birding tours, a photography contest, a Teddy Bear repair clinic, a wooden boat show, music by regional bands, and a fireworks display.

Tarzan Lord of the Louisiana Jungle Festival (985-395-4905), downtown Morgan City. The first Tarzan movie filmed on location, *Tarzan of the Apes,* was filmed in Morgan City. Al Bohl, an executive film producer, spent nearly four years producing a documentary about the original movie and reworked the 1917 silent film. The mid-April festival honors this first in American film with a lively festival. Activities include a showing of the re-edited film and a Tarzan yelling contest. The festival is produced with permission from the Edgar Rice Burroughs organization.

September: ⌀ **Louisiana Shrimp and Petroleum Festival** (www.shrimp -petrofest.org), downtown and in Lawrence Park, Morgan City. The Labor Day weekend celebration started more than 70 years ago when members of the local unit of the Gulf Coast Seafood Producers and Trappers Association staged a friendly Labor Day event that became the first festival. After the oil industry planted its roots in the area economy, the name changed to celebrate both industries. The festival remains a salute to hardworking people, and there's plenty of fun for everyone. Taking place the entire Labor Day weekend, it includes a Culinary Classic, an arts and crafts show, Music in the Park, and a children's village. The highlight is the Blessing of the Fleet and the water parade with shrimp boats, pleasure craft, and the biggest "muscle boats" of the offshore oil industry.

Although they're in separate parishes, Houma and Thibodaux are close enough to be sister cities. Originally, both were part of Lafourche Interior Parish; in 1822, the western part became Terrebonne Parish. The town of Thibodaux became the seat of Lafourche Parish, and the town of Houma the seat of Terrebonne Parish. Like the rest of Cajun Country, the towns share a cultural mix of French, Spanish, French Acadian, African, German, Irish, and Italian.

Houma's name is derived from the Houma Indians, a tribe that is not recognized by the U.S. Bureau of Indian Affairs. Downtown Houma's cultural district is listed on the national Register of Historic Places. Take a downtown walking tour and visit the Bayou Terrebonne Waterlife Museum, Folklife Culture Center, and Southdown Plantation. Houma and the surrounding area served as the setting for the fictional Swamp Thing comic books, the 1994 V.C. Andrews book *Ruby*, and the 2005 film *The Skeleton Key*. The area took the brunt of Hurricane Gustav on September 1, 2008. The city and parish lost electricity for a few days, and some homes were seriously damaged.

Founded on Bayou Lafourche, Thibodaux was a trading post between New Orleans and Teche country in the 1700s. The town was named for an early settler, Henry Schuyler Thibodaux. During the Civil War, area bridges were burned during skirmishes between Confederate and Union troops. One of the least-known Louisiana events, a sugarcane workers' strike, culminated here in the Thibodaux Massacre of November 1–4, 1887. The strike for higher wages by 10,000 workers (1,000 of whom were white) alarmed the population. At the request of the planters, the governor called in the state militia. Efforts to break the strike resulted in the deaths of 30–35 African American workers. In 2008, the actor Eric Braeden produced and played the lead role in *The Man Who Came Back*, a movie based on the event.

Today, Thibodaux is a scenic community of moss-laden oaks and sugarcane fields. In addition to the cane-related industries, the town is the home of Nicholls State University. The university was named for Francis Redding Tillou Nicholls, who served as a brigadier general during the Civil War and two terms as the governor of Louisiana and chief justice of the Louisiana Supreme Court. The university opened its doors on September 23, 1948, as a junior college of LSU. In 1970, the state legislature changed its name to Nicholls State University. The 210-acre campus, about 50 miles southwest of New Orleans and 60 miles southeast of Baton Rouge, offers degrees in marine and environmental science, business administration, chemistry, culinary arts, dietetics, education, mathematics, and petroleum services.

Grand Isle, a barrier island in the Gulf of Mexico, is situated at the mouth of Barataria Bay, where it meets the Gulf of Mexico. Its only land connection to the mainland is via an auto causeway bridge. LA 1 literally ends here at the end of the island. The island has all the characteristics of an old-fashioned fishing community. European families arrived here in the 1700s, and by the early 1800s were raising a few cattle. Crops including sugarcane, cotton, and cucumbers were grown here. The island also was home to pirates and privateers.

The population of about 1,500 swells during summer when vacationers begin flocking to the island. More than 12,000 tourists take part in local activities, including the Grand Isle International Tarpon Rodeo. It's not glamorous, but there's a special beauty to its beaches and the older homes tucked beneath ancient oak groves in the center of the island. A mixture of RV homes, fishing camps, cabins, and attractive beach cottages vie for your attention, as do businesses and marinas. The Old Fishing Bridge is open 24 hours daily with lights at the top and bottom of the bridge. Stop in at the Butterfly Dome. Grand Isle State Park attracts visitors year-round. Fish on the pier and plan an overnight camping on the beach. The park is well maintained and patrolled by state park rangers. At the tip of the island is a U.S. Coast Guard station.

✳ To See

✐ �& ❀ **Bayou Terrebonne Waterlife Museum** (985-580-7200), 7910 Park Ave., Houma. Check out the interactive exhibits and displays on industrial and ecological aspects. The art gallery is delightful, and the gift shop contains an array of unusual items. Open 10 A.M.–5 P.M. Tues.–Fri. noon–5 P.M. Sat.

✐ ❀ **Butterfly Dome** (985-787-2997), 2757 LA 1, Grand Isle. The Grand Isle Butterfly Dome is a simple dome with several species of butterflies and the plants needed to sustain them. A 30-minute or hourlong tour is offered depending on the number of butterflies present at the time. Bring your sketch pad, camera, and butterfly species guide. Hours are 8 A.M.–dusk Mon.–Sun.; call ahead to schedule a tour. Donations accepted.

Chauvin Sculpture Garden (985-594-2546), 5337 Bayouside Dr., Chauvin. The garden at Nicholls State University has more than 100 concrete sculptures and is open from dusk to dawn. The NSU Folk Art Studio is open 1–3 P.M. Mon., Wed., and Fri. by appointment.

✐ ❀ **Edward Douglas White Historic Site** (800-568-6968), 2295 LA 1, Thibodaux. The birthplace of the only U.S. Supreme Court chief justice from Louisiana, this attractive home is a National Historic Landmark on the banks of Bayou Lafourche. It was the residence of two of Louisiana's foremost political figures, Edward Douglas White, who was governor from 1835-1839, and his son Edward Douglass White, who was appointed to the U.S. Supreme Court in 1894 and served as chief justice from 1910 to 1921. The original Creole-style cottage was transformed into a Greek Revival house in the mid-1800s. Put together with hand-hewn logs and fastened with wooden pegs, the structure is a study in house design for living in Louisiana's humid semitropical climate. Exhibits tell the story of early settlers and the White family.

✐ �& **Greenwood Gator Farm** (985-804-0744, www.greenwoodgatorfarm.com), 125 Gator Court, Gibson. Learn about the centuries-old techniques of alligator hunting and farming, and find out how the gators go from an egg to boots and purses and sauce piquant. Experienced guides explain how "farmers," following guidelines of Louisiana Department of Wildlife and Fisheries, obtain alligator eggs in the swamps, incubate them, and raise them for food and hides. Visitors can see gators of all sizes from hatchlings to full-grown, view large gators in special display pens, touch a baby gator, and pick up an alligator souvenir. Open year-round.

✐ �& ❀ **Jean Lafitte National Historical Park, Wetlands Acadian Cultural Center** (985-448-1375), 314 St. Mary St., LA 1, Thibodaux. Discover the story of the Cajuns who settled along the bayous and swamps of the Louisiana wetlands. The recreation, clothing, home furnishings, religion, cuisine, and fishing are explored in exhibits, artifacts, videos, and films. Kids can explore earn a badge with the Junior Ranger program. The bookstore has books for children and adults, music, and craft items. Check the website for information on wetlands walks and folk life demonstrations.

Laurel Valley Plantation (985-447-5216 or 985-446-7456), 595 LA 308, Thibodaux. The largest surviving 19th- and 20th-century sugar plantation in the United States, Laurel Valley is about one mile south of Thibodaux. Sugarcane fields, slave quarters, and a general store still exist. You'll find local arts and crafts in the store, which is open 10 A.M.–4 P.M. Tues.–Sun., and 11 A.M.–5 P.M. weekends. The Center for Traditional Boat Building has a work area where local builders demonstrate their workmanship on scheduled days. Call for pre-arranged group tours.

Madewood Plantation House (985-369-7151, www.madewood.com), 4250 LA 308, Napoleonville. The commanding Greek Revival mansion, 75 miles from New Orleans and 45 miles from Baton Rouge, was designed by the famed New Orleans architect Henry Howard to reflect East Coast architectural trends. The Civil War spared Madewood and it passed through several families until it was acquired by Naomi Marshall in 1964. For 10 years, the family hosted the acclaimed Madewood Arts Festival. In the 1980s, Keith Marshall opened the property as an elegant bed & breakfast. Guests can choose lavish rooms in the main house or well-appointed guest cottages. A full plantation breakfast is served in the elegant main dining room. Available for candlelight dinners, weddings, and receptions.

Cynthia V. Campbell

TRACY SCHEXNAYDER, THE "GATOR GIRL," SHOWS A YOUNG ANIMAL TO VISITORS AT GREENWOOD GATOR FARM IN HOUMA.

Southdowns Plantation House and Terrebonne Museum (985-851-0154, www.southdownmuseum.org), 1208 Museum Dr., Houma. Dating from the late 1700s, this property was owned by the brothers Jim and Rezin Bowie in 1821–1828 and operated as an indigo plantation. In the early 1800s, the principal crop changed to sugarcane and the first sugar mill was built in 1846. Four generations of the Minor family, along with hundreds of mill workers, fieldworkers, and their families, lived and worked at the plantation, which is now a museum focusing on the history and life of the area. The house features 12-inch-thick walls made of bricks fired on the property. The stained-glass panels, added in 1893, depict plantation surroundings with motifs of palmetto leaves, magnolia branches, and sugarcane stalks. The current pink and green scheme reproduces the 1893 colors that were discovered by paint analysis during restoration in the 1990s. The museum contains 19th-century Minor family furnishings and exhibits on the sugarcane industry, as well as Native American Indians and artifacts related to the area's history and inhabitants. Marketplace and arts and crafts festivals take place every spring and fall. Additional events include concerts and art shows. Gift shop. Open 10 A.M.–4 P.M. Tues.–Sat.

St. John's Episcopal Church (985-447-2910, www.stjohnsthibodaux.org), 718 Jackson St., Thibodaux. This church is one of the oldest Episcopal churches west of the Mississippi River. St. John's is one of the few examples of Georgian church architecture left in America, and the adjoining cemetery has many interesting graves, including the tomb of Francis Redding Tillou Nicholls, twice the governor of Louisiana.

✎ ✿ **St. Joseph Co-Cathedral** (985-446-1387, www.stjoseph-cc.org), 721 Canal Blvd., Thibodaux. The cathedral is Renaissance Romanesque in design with several features reflecting architectural common to churches in Paris and Rome. The splendid Rose Window over the main entrance is modeled after that of the Cathedral of Notre Dame in Paris. In 1977, St. Joseph was named co-cathedral for the diocese of Houma-Thibodaux. It serves the bishop and the diocesan community as well as its parishioners.

✎ ✿ **Terrebonne Folklife Culture Center** (985-873-6545, www.terrebonnefolklife.org), 317 Goode St., Houma. Dedicated to preserving Cajun culture, the folklife center was built in 1840 as a four-room gentlemen's club. Permanent exhibits include the Cajun Tool Shed showcasing wood working tools, the Louisiana decoy carving exhibit, and Native American artifacts. Cajun dancing is held the first and third Wednesday of each month. Call for hours.

✳ Green Spaces

✎ ↭ ✿ **Grand Isle State Park** (985-787-2559 or 888-787-2559), Admiral Craik Dr., Grand Isle. The state park is at the tip of the most popular barrier island off

PEOPLE CAN STAY OVERNIGHT AT NEW RV CAMPSITES AT GRAND ISLE STATE PARK ON THE GULF OF MEXICO.

Louisiana Office of State Parks

Cynthia V. Campbell

A SWAMP ROSE MALLOW BLOOMS ON A
NATURE TRAIL IN MANDALAY WILDLIFE
REFUGE IN CAJUN COUNTRY.

the coast of Louisiana. On the Gulf side, there's a long beach with sands the shade of light brown sugar. Gulf waters are enjoyed by swimmers most of the year, and the park is great for splashing in the surf. Birding enthusiasts delight in the lagoons as well as the shoreline. There's a family camping area where you can cook freshly caught seafood over a fire. Pets must be kept on a leash and are not allowed in any of the buildings. Sites with electrical and water hookup are available, as are basic bath houses. There's a ranger on site, and the area is regularly patrolled. Bring your binoculars, camera, and sunscreen. For reservations, call 877-CAMP-N-LA. Entrance station is open 8 A.M.–7 P.M. April–September and 8 A.M.–5 P.M. October–March. Fee is $1 per person; free to seniors age 62 and over and children 3 and under.

Mandalay National Wildlife Refuge (985-882-2000,www.fws.gov/mandalay), 5 miles southwest of Houma. One of eight refuges in the Southeast Louisiana Refuges Complex, the 4,619-acre refuge provides habitat for waterfowl, wading birds, and neotropical songbirds. Access is by boat. A recently created milelong-walking trail leads into a tranquil bayou. Open year-round to the public from sunrise to sunset with seasonal restrictions, it's a special space for wildlife observation, boating and fishing, and you can spot alligators and bald eagles in winter.

✳ To Do

BIRDING The Grand Isle Loop, America's Wetland Birding Trail (985-787-2229), Grand Isle. The entire island offers an almost overwhelmingly spectacular adventure for birders. Follow LA 1 to its end on the Gulf of Mexico. Before reaching the island make a detour on Fourchon Road (LA 3090). The large shallow bay on the west side of the road is often crowded with wading birds, seabirds, and shorebirds. On the isle itself, the deeply shaded oak chenier provides a safe habitat for spring and fall migration. Summer birders will find gulls, terns, pelicans, and other seabirds along the beach and near shore.

The Terrebonne Loop, America's Wetland Birding Trail (800-699-2832, www.americaswetland.com), 114 Tourist Dr., Gray. The Terrebonne Loop is made up of five distinct locations, including the Southdown Mandalay Wildlife Refuge and the Pointe-aux-Chien Wildlife Management Area. South of Houma, the loop opens up into sun-washed recesses of marshlands with herons, egrets, ibises, ospreys, and, in winter, bald eagles. Especially scenic are LA 57 and Falgout Road. The Louisiana Universities Marine Consortium Facility at Cocodrie stands alone at the southern extremity of the marsh system and offers detailed exhibits of Louisiana's wetland ecosystems.

Cynthia V. Campbell

DAWN COMES EARLY AT CHAUVIN, A FISHING VILLAGE POPULAR WITH SERIOUS ANGLERS.

FISHING Fishing—fresh, brackish and saltwater—is done year-round. There are any number of fresh and saltwater guides in the area. Most licensed charter companies, as well as marinas, are listed with regional and local tourist bureaus. Listed here are those with websites.

Apex Fishing Charters, (985-787-2419, www.apexfishingcharters.net), 1618 LA 1, Grand Isle. Apex's guides venture into the Gulf of Mexico in search of a wide variety of game fish. The company offers yellowfin tuna fishing charters, as well as deep sea fishing charters for wahoo, mahi mahi, marlin, swordfish, sailfish, red snapper, mangrove snapper, cobia, grouper, amberjack, and more. Charters leave from the Bridge Side Marina

Bayou Guide Service (985-876-4153, www.captlake.com), 208 Woodburn Dr., Houma. The company offers coastal and inland fishing, especially for speckled trout and redfish. U.S. Coast Guard and state licensed. Three boats available daily. Hours vary by season.

Captain Blaine Townsend (985-594-7772, www.redfishflyfishing.com), 6830 LA 56, Chauvin. Draw on Townsend's 38 years of experience as a charter boat captain as you fly fish for redfish in the Cocodrie area. One- or two-man charters are available. The company specializes in trout, redfish, and cobia, and offers bay, marsh offshore, and night fishing. Available daily; hours vary by season.

Grand Isle Fishcommander (225-445-1005, www.fishcommander.com), LA 1, Grand Isle. On an average offshore charter fishing trip to Grand Isle, Venice, or Port Fourchon, sportsmen find yellowfin tuna, blackfin tuna, wahoo, red snapper, mangrove snapper, marlin, mahi mahi, amberjack, and shark, all in the same day.

SWAMPS

Swamps intrigue Louisiana's visitors. They are some of the most magnificent places to view animals in their own environment. People who visit the state for the first time often ask about the difference between a swamp and a marsh. A swamp is land holding water and containing trees and woody vegetation. In Louisiana many swamps contain cypress and tupelo trees. A marsh is low-lying land holding water. It has no trees, but grassy vegetation. Louisiana has a variety of marshes ranging from freshwater to salt water, and plants in these marshes will vary accordingly. Marshes often form a transition zone between water and land. Both swamps and marshes make up Louisiana's wetlands. The best way to become familiar with this environment is to take a tour with a licensed guide who has spent years living and working in the wetlands. These guides know where to look for gators, nutria, and beaver as you glide past ancient trees draped in Spanish moss. The guides can spot an alligator or snake yards away and identify any number of birds by their calls. Once you enter a wetland, remember you are now in the animals' home; it's their environment, not yours. What you see will be determined by the season and weather. How much you learn will be determined by how well you listen to your guide's explanations and stories about the people who call south Louisiana home.

A SIGN AT JUNGLE GARDENS ON AVERY ISLANDS WARNS TOURISTS TO BEWARE OF ALIGATORS.

Cynthia V. Campbell

H&M Fishing Charter (985-787-3753, www.grand-isle.com/handm/charters .htm), 133 Pine Lane, Grand Isle. The company specializes in offshore fishing. All captains have state and coast guard licenses. You can catch speckled and white trout, red fish, flounder, mackerel, black-tip shark, and more. Services include live bait, rods and reels, fuel, and tackle. Family-built cabins are available.

TOURS ✍ ↭ 🦑 **Airboat Tours by Arthur Matherne** (985-758-5531 or 800-975-9345, www.airboattours.com), 4262 US 90 East, Des Allemands. Come to the bayou and experience the ride of your life in U.S. Coast Guard air boats. You can take a "Ride on the Wild Side" or slow it down in a kayak, canoe, or pirogue. Arthur and Katy Matherne will regale you with tales about life in the wilds.

✍ ↭ **Annie Miller's Son's Swamp and Marsh Tours** (800-341-5441, www.annie -miller.com), 4038 Bayou Black Dr., Houma. Enjoy a ride through Mandalay National Wildlife Refuge. Learn about Annie Miller, the first woman to give swamp tours in Louisiana. Tours are available year-round; hours vary by season.

↭ **Cajun Tours and Cruises** (985-872-6157, www.cajuntours.net), 709 May St., Houma. Enjoy seeing plantations, seafood factories, net making, alligators, and crab and shrimp boats on these land and swamp boat cruises.

↭ **Hammonds Cajun Air Tours** (985-876-0584), 3613 Thunderbird Rd., Houma. Take to the air and get a bird's-eye view of swamps and bayous. You'll see birds, alligators, deer, shrimp boats, oil rigs, and Indian mounds.

✍ ↭ **Munson's World Famous Swamp Tour** (985-851-3569, www.munson swamptours.com), 979 Bull Run Rd., Schriever. Adventure into pristine swamps and see large alligators handled by your tour operator. Two-hour tours are offered daily. Call for reservations.

✍ ♿ ↭ **Torres' Cajun Swamp Tours** (985-633-7739, www.torresswamptours .net), 105 Torres Rd., Kraemer. Located on LA 307 in Kraemer, Captain Torres is a professional alligator hunter, trapper, and commercial fisherman. This French-speaking, fully licensed guide has lived in the area's swamps, lakes, and bayous since boyhood. A Cajun meal, music, and dancing are available upon request. Motor coach parking, restroom facilities, handicapped-accessible. Open 9 A.M.– 5 P.M. daily. Group rates available for 15 or more people.

↭ 🦑 **Wetland Tours** (985-851-7578, www.wetlandtours.com), 2715 Bayou Dularge Rd., Theriot, south of Houma. Captain Wendy Billiot will take you on an educational tour through a cypress swamp. You can see the environment change as you cross from freshwater marsh to open saltwater. Along the way you'll see water-fowl, alligators, and aquatic plants. The tour focuses on both the beauty and plight of Louisiana's vanishing wetland.

✍ ♿ ↭ **Zam's Bayou Swamp Tours** (985-633-7881), 36 Kraemer Bayou Rd., Kraemer. The community of Kraemer is situated on LA 307 near Thibodaux. See swamps that are only accessible by boat on tours that offer educational and unique picture-taking opportunities. French-speaking guides are available. Group rates, a Cajun meal, music, and dancers are available upon request. Motor coach parking, restroom facilities, handicapped-accessible. Open 10 A.M.–4 P.M. daily.

✳ Lodging

Accommodations in this area include contemporary hotels and motels as well as bed & breakfasts. For those who plan inland and offshore fishing excursions, there are number of excellent marinas. If you're planning a sports adventure, some places offer basic overnight accommodations; others may have only primitive sites. If you're a tenderfoot, be sure to ask what to expect. The list here is a sampling. For more, check tourism websites.

((♥)) Baymont Inn and Suites (985-580-4850, www.baymontinns.com), 1254 Grand Caillou Rd., Houma. Off US 90, this hotel is convenient to local attractions, including the Intracoastal Waterway. Features include an outdoor pool, Wi-Fi, and a 24-hour business center. Moderate.

((♥)) Carmel Inn and Suites (985-446-0561, www.carmelinnofla.com), 400 East First St., Thibodaux. This unique hotel is built on the landmark site that was once a Mount Carmel convent and school, dating from before the Civil War. Elements of the original building were incorporated into the present structure. Amenities include a large outdoor swimming pool, Wi-Fi, and complimentary breakfast. Ask about Bistro Nights with dinners served by the John Folse Culinary Institute of Nicholls State University. Moderate.

Courtyard Houma (985-2213-8997, www.marriott.com/hotels/travel/msyho -courtyard-houma), 142 Library Blvd., Houma. The new hotel has attractive, clean rooms and plentiful parking. The indoor and outdoor pools are spacious and beautiful. Moderate.

Quality Hotel (985-868-5851, www .qualityinn.com), 210 South Hollywood Rd., Houma. Close to popular attractions, the hotel has spacious rooms and a large indoor pool. The restaurant serves an excellent breakfast. Service is friendly and accommodating.

La Quinta Inn & Suites (985- 985-879-1545, www.lq.com/lq), 189 Synergy Center Blvd., Houma. Rooms are attractive, spotless, comfortable, and quiet. The breakfast selection is good with a lot of variety and fresh Community Coffee. Desk for business travelers is designed with free Internet access, and the business center has a color printer. Moderate.

BED & BREAKFASTS

♪ A Chateau on the Bayou (985-879-537-6773, www.achateauonthe bayou.com), 3158 LA 308, Raceland. The four-bedroom, three-bath Victorian home on Bayou Lafouche features clean, neat guest rooms with simple furnishings, comfortable beds, and work desks. Guests can relax in rockers on the back porch and listen to the sounds of song birds, owls, crickets, and frogs. Children welcomed. Inexpensive–moderate.

♂ Dansereau House (985-227-9937, www.dansereauhouse.com), 506 Saint Philip St., Thibodaux. The National Historic Landmark is a traditional inn with elegant furnishings and large bedroom suites. Second-floor rooms all have access to a wrap-around veranda. A full gourmet breakfast is served each morning. Expensive–very expensive.

Grand Bayou Noir (985-873-5849, www.grandbayounoir.com), 1143 Bayou Black Dr., Houma. Situated on Bayou Black and surrounded by old oak trees, this B&B's rooms have queen-sized beds, oak floors, ceiling fans, and private baths. Enjoy the formal dining room with a fireplace and piano. Moderate.

Landry House (985-787-2207, www .thelandryhouse.com), 199 Hector Lane, Grand Isle. Surrounded by old oak trees, Landry House is a seaside cottage with an eclectic mix of contemporary and vintage furnishings. The B&B has a screen porch and a spacious yard with a picnic table. Enjoy a hardy Cajun breakfast. No smoking or pets in the house. Moderate.

Wildlife Gardens (985-575-3676, www.wildlifegardens.com), 5306 North Bayou Black Dr., Gibson. Try life on wild side in one of the cabins in a cypress swamp. Sit on the screen porch at night and listen to the sounds. Cabins have baths and air conditioning. Moderate.

MARINAS Bayou Black Marina (985-575-2315, www.bayoublack marina.com), 251 Marina Dr., Gibson. The full-service marina has four launches, 400 parking spaces, camper sites, swamp tours, and a weighing station for tournaments. Open 5 A.M.– 5 P.M. daily.

Coco Marina (800-648-2626, www .cocomarina.com), 106 Pier 56, Chauvin. The marina offers saltwater, off-shore, shoreline, and inland charter fishing tours specializing in speckled trout, redfish, drum, snapper, and cobia. Accommodations include a swimming pool and restaurant.

Downtown Marina (985-873-6428), P.O. Box 3797, Houma. Boaters traveling the Intracoastal Canal at mile marker 58 have safe harbor on Bayou Terrebonne in downtown Houma. Shore power, water, pump-out facilities, and transit service are all available. Open 24 hours daily.

✳ Where to Eat

For the most part, life in the Houma-Thibodaux and Grand Isle area is casual and informal. Certain occasions, such as weddings and special receptions, call for elegant dining. However, restaurants tend to be laid-back places where students like to gather and vacationers can choose casual wear even when seeking world-class dining. Many restaurants offer live music, especially on Friday and Saturday nights.

EATING OUT A-Bears Cafe (985-872-6306), 809 Bayou Black Dr., Houma. The family-owned Cajun cafe was established in 1983 in an 83-year-old building. Try the delicious etouffee and jambalaya and homemade desserts. Live Cajun music is performed every Friday night. Open for lunch 10:30 A.M.–2 P.M. Mon.–Sat. and dinner 5–9 P.M. Fri.

🍴 **Bayou Delight Restaurant** (985-876-4879), 4038 Bayou Black Dr., Houma. The cafe offers traditional fried Cajun seafood, including shrimp, crawfish, soft-shell crab, and boudin bites. Locals love the fried chicken, tender meat inside a really crispy batter. Live bands and dancing on Friday and Saturday nights.

🍴 **Big Al's Seafood Market and Restaurant** (985- 876-4030, www .bigalsseafood.net), 1377 West Tunnel Blvd., Houma. Get ready to have a delightful evening in a place where the food's great and the company's even better. There's something for everyone on the large menu, from po-boys stuffed with crispy fried shrimp or catfish to creamy pastas. Don't miss the succulent charbroiled oysters served with the restaurant's signature sauce.

Bilello's Cafe (985-872-2220, www .bilelloscafe.com), 7913 Main St., Houma. This downtown cafe is popular for its great food. Popular items are the hamburger steaks and onion rings.

Sportsman's Paradise Marina Cafe (985-594-2414, www.redfishflyfishing .com), 6830 LA 665, Chauvin. If you're out for a day of fishing in Chauvin and Cocodrie, this small land-based cafe is a grand spot. It's part of the Sports-

Cynthia V. Campbell

THE CECIL LAPERYOUSE GROCERY IN COCODRIE IS THE LAST STOP FOR SUPPLIES BEFORE THE GULF OF MEXICO.

man's Paradise marina and lodge owned by Captain Blaine Townsend and his wife, Connie. The simple menu offers big, hearty breakfast sandwiches (ham and eggs, etc.) to take out on boats. Bring in your catch of the day and get it fried to perfection, or try the simply superb shrimp gumbo. Hours are 5:30 A.M.–8 P.M. daily.

DINING OUT Cafe Milano & Aficionados (985-879-2426, www.cafe milanohouma.com), 314 Belanger St., Houma. A pleasant romantic atmosphere draws people to this downtown cafe on the former site of a livery and feed store. Popular dishes include the lasagna and bread pudding laced with coconut and Captain Morgan Spiced Rum. Lunch hours are 11 A.M.–2 P.M. Tues.–Fri.; dinner 5:30–9 P.M., Tues.–Thurs. and 5:30–10 P.M. Fri.–Sat.

Fremin's (985-449-0333, www.fremins .net), 402 West Third St., Thibodaux. Creole and Italian cooking come together in harmony at this restaurant. The menu includes signature pastas, seafood, and steaks. Start your meal with fresh-baked bread and flavored butters. The fried green tomatoes with shrimp make a great appetizer. Situated in downtown Thibodaux, the restaurant is located in the historic Roth drugstore building, built circa 1878. The first floor has a beveled glass and mahogany storefront and the original pressed tin ceiling.

✳ Entertainment

Dooley's Nightclub (985-872-0333), 1548 Barrow St., Houma. This is a friendly spot where the older and younger generations mingle as one. Later in the evening you can dance the night away. Open 10 A.M.–2 A.M. daily.

The Foundry on the Bayou (985-387-4070, www.foundryonthebayou), 715 West First St., Thibodaux. The restaurant, in a former steel foundry downtown, specializes in Cajun/Creole dishes and steaks. The Sport Bar draws crowds for special events and weekends. Local musicians perform here on weekends. Restaurant hours are 11 A.M.–2 P.M. and 5:30–9 P.M. Tues.–Thurs., 11 A.M.–2 P.M. and 5:30–10 P.M. Fri.; and 5:30–10 P.M. Sat. Sports bar hours are 6 P.M.–2 A.M.

🌀 ⇴ 🦐 **Jean Lafitte National Park Wetlands Acadian Cultural Center** (985-448-1375), 314 St. Mary St., Thibodaux. Located along the banks of Bayou LaFourche, the center features a jam session every Monday, 5–7 P.M. Musicians and dancers, professional and aspiring, are invited to the impromptu sessions. Open 9 A.M.–6 P.M. Tues.–Thurs., 9 A.M.–5 P.M. Fri.–Sun., and 9 A.M.–7 P.M. Mon.

Jolly Inn (985-872-6114, www.jolly inn.com), 1507 Barrow St., Houma. The inn serves spicy Cajun cooking in the cafe and live music in the lounge Thursday 8–11 P.M. On Friday night it hosts Cajun Night in a back hall with lively, authentic music. People young and old mix, and it's a fun, wholesome atmosphere. The band starts around 6 P.M. and ends about 11 P.M. Come back for more dancing Sunday 3–6 P.M.

Thibodaux Playhouse (985-446-1896) 314 St. Mary St. (LA 1), Thibodaux. Located in the Wetlands Acadian Cultural Center, the 200-seat theater presents various performances during the year, including comedies and children's plays.

✴ Selective Shopping

Blue Water Souvenirs (985-787-2212), 3011 LA 1, Grand Isle. Drop by this island shop to find swimsuits, beach shoes, towels, inflatables sun shades, jewelry, gifts, and novelties.

Bourgeois Meat Market (985-447-7128), 543 West Main St., Thibodaux. The meat market has been in the Bourgeois family for three generations and has a following throughout Bayou Country. It offers a variety of smoked meats, but the specialty is the chewy, spicy Cajun beef jerky.

Cajun Meat Market (985-851-1727, www.cajunmarket.net), 216 Mystic Blvd., Houma. Special meat products are handmade from the freshest ingredients. Choose from an array of turduckens, smoked turkeys, deboned stuffed chickens, steaks, and sausages. Items are vacuum packed to ensure freshness.

Cajun Pecan House and Gifts (985-872-1510, www.cajunpecanhouse.com), 5658 West Main St., Houma. The sweets include pralines, cakes, pecan pies, Queen Elizabeth cookies, and Mardi Gras specialties.

Imperial Flea Market (985-851-5982), 1437 St. Charles St., Suite 105, Houma. The largest flea market in Houma contains antiques, coins, furniture, crafts, jewelry, and pottery. Open 10:30 A.M.–6 P.M. Fri.–Sat. and 1–5 P.M. Sun.

Southdown Plantation Gift Shop (985-851-0154, www.southdown museum.org), 1208 Museum Dr., Houma. The museum shop features offers souvenirs, history books, cookbooks, and local items.

✴ Special Events

April: **Grand Isle Migratory Bird Festival** (985-447-0868 or 800-259-0869, http://grandisle.btnep.org/Grand IsleHome.aspx), Grand Isle. Usually held in mid-April throughout the island, this event draws serious bird watchers from across the globe to raise money to protect the habitat. Activities include bird walks and boat tours. Within two hours from New Orleans, you can see hundreds of species, including peregrine falcons, roseate spoonbills, black whiskered vireos, snowy and piping plovers, scissor-tailed flycatchers, yellow-headed blackbirds, brown pelicans, frigate birds, gulls, and terns.

June: **Golden Meadow Fourchon International Tarpon Rodeo** (985-860 328), Morans Marina, Fourchon. Scheduled the first week of July, this is one of the oldest fishing rodeos in Louisiana. Profits go toward scholarships for area high school students.

July: **Grand Isle International Tarpon Rodeo** (504-615-0099, www .tarponrodeo.org), Grand Isle. Established in 1928, the oldest fishing tournament in the United States is held in the last weekend of July. Live entertainment includes groups such as the Hurricane Levee Band and the Topcats. Activities include children's crab races, educational booths, and participation by the U.S. Coast Guard.

September: **Uplifting the Coast Festival** (www.upliftingthecoast.org), Bridge Side Marina, Grand Isle. Free to the public, this early September festival features food, a silent auction, a kids' zone, and crafts. Musicians include popular Cajun performers such as Steve Riley and the Mamou Playboys, Chris LeBlanc, and Waylon Thibodeaux.

October: **Louisiana Gumbo Festival** (985- 633-7789, www.lagumbofest .com), Chackbay/Choupic Fairgrounds, 346 LA 304, just north of Thibodaux. This mid-October event has outstanding Cajun food, music, dancing, carnival, and midway. There's a firemen's parade and live auction on Sunday. Free parking and no gate fee.

Bayou Music Festival (985-632-4247 or 985-696-4642), Oakridge Park, LA 3235, Golden Meadow. Held the first of October, the festival is presented by the Golden Meadow Rotary Club. Crowds thrill to at least 15 bands from throughout the south Louisiana bayou area. Music for all generations includes zydeco, country, rock, and pop. Food items include jambalaya, white beans,

burgers, hotdogs, and sweets. A kid's zone has a variety of inflatables.

French Food Festival (985-693-7355), 307 East Fifth St., Larose (off LA 308, in Larose Civic Center). An amazing gathering of cooks, the event is held the first full weekend of October. Volunteers cook more than 40 dishes, many of which originated locally. Only in Louisiana will you find such dishes as shrimp *boulettes* and *tartes a la bouille* (sweet Cajun custard tarts). Enjoy the music, gourmet food, and hospitality.

RED TRUMPET VINES ADD SPLENDOR TO A NATURE TRAIL IN THE MANDALAY WILDLIFE REFUGE NEAR HOUMA.

Cynthia V. Campbell

Greater New Orleans

4

NEW ORLEANS—THE CITY

NORTHSHORE AREA

New Orleans CVB/Jay Combe

INTRODUCTION

With a culture like no other, New Orleans is one of the world's premiere travel destinations. What makes it so appealing is its blend of Old World charm and New World brashness. Greater New Orleans is a region of many textures and colors. The people who inhabit the city come from many groups including Native American, French, Spanish, African, and Caribbean. Immigrants from Germany, Ireland, and Italy added to that early mixture. The result is a truly multicultural city where it simply isn't considered unusual to find a fusion of flavors, rhythms, and language.

To really get to know Greater New Orleans, you need to know a little of its history. Get beyond the familiar tourist corridors and visit the neighborhoods, some of which are villages in their own right. Go beyond the city limits into the surrounding parishes, where towns share a history with the Big Easy, where there are vast networks of rivers and bayous, where the Gulf of Mexico is a short boat ride away, and where people with big hearts are ready to welcome you with biscuits and gravy, crawfish stew, and pecan pie.

In 1699, the French explorers and brothers Pierre Le Moyne, Sieur d'Iberville, and Jean-Baptiste Le Moyne, Sieur de Bienville, found the mouth of the Mississippi. Directed to continue explorations, Bienville explored the area, and with the help of Native Americans he discovered a passage through Lake Borgne, Lake Pontchartrain, and Bayou Saint John to a stretch of swampy land between the Mississippi River and Lake Pontchartrain. By 1718, Bienville established a community on higher ground along the crescent of the Mississippi River.

As the area grew, French entrepreneurs acquired large land holdings around New Orleans. A number of plantations developed along the north shore of Lake Pontchartrain as well as along the east and west banks of the Mississippi. Other adventurers, including pirates, explored the bayous, rivers, and swamps, finding outlets to the Gulf of Mexico. Eventually, the territory was divided into parishes. Making up the Greater New Orleans Region are St. Bernard, Jefferson, and Plaquemines parishes and portions of St. Charles, St. John, Livingston, Tangipahoa, and St. Tammany, as well as Washington in the eastern corner of the state.

The portion of St. Tammany Parish along Lake Pontchartrain is referred to as the Northshore. Soon after New Orleans was founded, the French began to settle in the heavily wooded area. Their primary production was pitch, tar, turpentine, and resin. In the early 1800s, the area developed as a fashionable retreat for New Orleans residents escaping the summer heat. Today, the Northshore is one of the

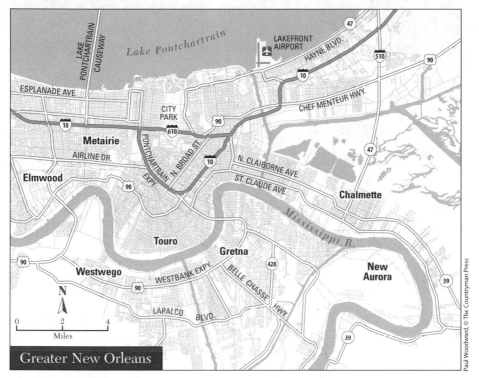

Greater New Orleans

Paul Woodward, © The Countryman Press

fastest-growing areas in Louisiana and offers numerous dining, music, art, and recreational opportunities. In neighboring Tangipahoa and Livingston parishes, people enjoy boating, fishing, and casual fun in the bayous and rivers and along Lake Maurepas.

Further north, Washington Parish is a scenic rural area with rolling hills, pine forests, and inviting back roads. It is the most northeasterly of the Florida parishes, once a part of Spanish West Florida and later under British control. Early settlers moved into the area from the Carolinas, Tennessee, Kentucky, and Virginia. When Andrew Jackson marched his soldiers across the Pearl River and improvised a road through the forests, a number of local citizens joined him at the Battle of New Orleans. Today about half the parish is used for agricultural

A START ON THE BAYOU
After the brothers Pierre and Jean-Baptiste Le Moyne found the mouth of the Mississippi in 1699, near what is now called Passe-a-Loutre, they traveled upriver to the first major bend and camped there. The site was covered with wild persimmon trees. They found a small bayou just south of the trees. They raised a large cross made of logs and held Mass there the next day, Mardi Gras day. They named the bayou Bayou Mardi Gras, the first non-Indian place name on the lower Mississippi River.

Louisiana Office of Tourism

ANCIENT OAKS LINE THE HIGHWAY PAST DOCVILLE AND PECAN GROVE FARMS IN ST.
BERNARD PARISH

purposes. Much of the remainder is timber and the paper industry. It's a great get-away for country fairs and festivals, fishing, canoeing and tubing.

St. Bernard Parish, which runs along the east bank of the Mississippi River south of New Orleans, was settled by French and Canary Islanders in the late 1700s. You can visit the site of the Battle of New Orleans in Chalmette and relax in a local cafe and enjoy foods that have evolved from the Isleno/Sicilian and African cultures. Jefferson Parish, once part of Orleans Parish, was among the first areas settled by the French. Metairie, along Lake Pontchartrain, is a bustling metropolis immediately west of New Orleans proper. The southern part of the parish offers water sports, birding, and hunting in the Barataria Basin and some of the world's best offshore fishing at Grand Isle, a barrier island on the Gulf of Mexico. Plaque-mines Parish runs along the east bank of the Mississippi through small towns where LA 23 ends at Venice, just above the major outlets to the Gulf of Mexico. Plaquemines has the largest land and water mass of any parish in Louisiana. Pro-jecting into the Gulf, it is a major seafood-producing area. Communities in the lower part of the parish serve as bases for riverboat pilots and those working on offshore rigs in the Gulf. As the entrance to America's greatest flyway, it is an excellent destination for people devoted to eco-system studies and conservation.

Embrace the diversity of people and cultures in the Greater New Orleans area. From fine dining in an award-winning restaurant to stumbling on a really good buy at a back-roads country market, the Big Easy is a roadie's dream.

NEW ORLEANS—THE CITY

Without doubt, New Orleans is a unique place. The city's reputation for exquisite cuisine and incredible music is not exaggerated. But what truly makes the city so wonderful is its blend of people. Their customs and traditions enrich every aspect of life.

Known as the Birthplace of Jazz, the city is an incubator for young musicians, who learn from parents, teachers, and friends. You'll hear music in clubs, small cafes, and large nightspots. This is also a place where chefs are as famous as actors or politicians. Respect comes from knowing exactly how to cook a perfect pot of gumbo or turn out a delicious crème brulée. People here embrace the significant moments of life—birthdays, anniversaries, weddings, and yes, even funerals. Mardi Gras, a Carnival season that lasts for weeks, may seem wicked to some, but to New Orleans residents it's a reaffirmation that life is worth living.

Stroll through romantic courtyards with big green banana plants, red hibiscus blooms and pale lavender indigo. Stand on a wrought-iron balcony, reminiscent of Seville, and watch the crowds strolling below. If you choose to party until early in the morning, you'll find plenty of others doing the same at nightspots all over the city. However, if you seek solitude in a retreat house, New Orleans has that too. Visit St. Louis Cathedral, the Presbytere, and the Cabildo. View Creole cottages in Treme and Faubourg Marigny, and Victorian mansions on St. Charles Avenue. Tour the above-ground cemeteries and playing fields in City Park and Audubon Park. Absorb the feel of this city, and you'll understand why people love it dearly.

I've often wondered if Bienville had any idea what the future would bring when he first saw this land in 1699.

AN ENTERTAINER RELAXES BY A LUCKY DOG STAND IN THE FRENCH QUARTER.

Cynthia V. Campbell

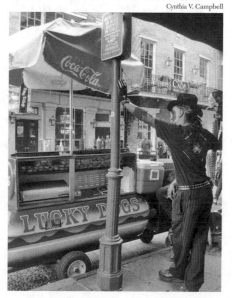

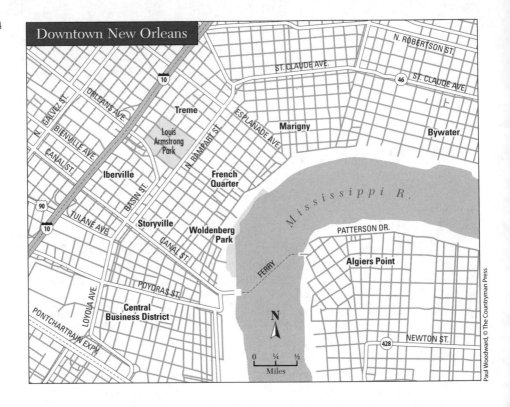

Downtown New Orleans

During his explorations, native tribesmen showed him the swampy land between Lake Pontchartrain and the Mississippi River. He established the settlement of New Orleans, named for Philip II, Duke of Orleans, in 1718, on a patch of high ground along the Mississippi River. In September of that year a hurricane blew down most of the structures. The authorities then enforced a grid pattern that remains today in the French Quarter. Most of the early inhabitants were riffraff: deported galley slaves, sailors, trappers, and ruffians. Civilized settlers came a bit later.

In 1763, following Britain's victory in the Seven Years' War, the colony west of the Mississippi was ceded to the Spanish Empire. No Spanish governor came to take control until 1766, and French and German settlers, hoping to restore New Orleans to France, forced the Spanish governor to flee home in the Rebellion of 1768. The Spanish reasserted control a year later. The great New Orleans Fire of 1788 destroyed 856 buildings, and in 1794 another fired destroyed 212 more. After that, the city was rebuilt in the Spanish style, with bricks, firewalls, and iron balconies. What people see today is Spanish Colonial architecture. By the late 1700s, the sugar industry was firmly established in the area.

The population of New Orleans suffered from epidemics of yellow fever, malaria, and smallpox. Doctors did not understand how diseases were transmitted, and primitive sanitization made conditions worse. The city first successfully suppressed a outbreak of yellow fever in 1905.

Louisiana Office of Tourism

A CANNON OVERLOOKS THE CHALMETTE BATTLEFIELD AT JEAN LAFITTE NATIONAL PARK.

In 1800, Spain and France signed a secret treaty that gave Louisiana back to France, though it had to remain under Spanish control as long as France wished to postpone the transfer of power. In 1803 Napoleon sold Louisiana to the United States in the Louisiana Purchase. During the early 1800s the sugar industry thrived in the area, and the population grew rapidly with influxes of Americans, Africans, French and Creole French, many of the latter two groups fleeing from a revolution in Haiti.

During the War of 1812, the British sent an army to conquer the city but it was defeated by regular and militia forces commanded by General Andrew Jackson at Chalmette. Privateers led by the pirate Jean Lafitte were recruited by Jackson for the battle.

The following years were marked by growth and prosperity. By 1840 New Orleans was the wealthiest and third most populous city in the nation. The introduction of natural gas, the building of the Pontchartrain Railroad, and the introduction of the first steam cotton press marked this period. The U.S. government established a mint here in 1838 and produced gold and silver coinage. On May 3, 1849, a levee breach on the Mississippi upriver created a huge flood that left thousands homeless. It was the worst flood the city experienced until the waters after Katrina in 2005.

During the Civil War, New Orleans was captured by the Union without a battle in the city. Forts Jackson and St. Philip, situated below the city, surrendered to Captain David G. Farragut's fleet after heavy bombardment. General Benjamin Butler was placed in charge of New Orleans, and his tactless administration drew great hostility from Southerners. Yet New Orleans survived unscathed.

The 19th century brought reconstruction, the struggle between political and ethnic groups for political control. In the 1870s New Orleans annexed the towns of

Louisiana Office of Tourism

A MEMORIAL AT SHELL BEACH, SOUTHEAST OF NEW ORLEANS, HONORS VICTIMS OF HURRICANE KATRINA.

Algiers and Carrollton, and in 1884 the city hosted a World's Fair called the Cotton Centennial. In the early 1900s the engineer A. Baldwin Wood designed a system of large pumps and canals to push rain water out of areas lying below sea level. During World War II, New Orleans was the manufacturing site of Higgins boats built under the direction of Andrew Higgins, who designed them. The shallow-draft landing craft was used to land troops on the beaches of Normandy during the invasion of Europe. They also were used for troop landings in North Africa, Italy and on beaches in the Pacific Theatre of war during battles against Japan. Today, the Higgins boat, along with other military equipment, films, and displays, is a major exhibit at the World War II Museum in New Orleans.

In the post–World War II era, New Orleans became a metropolis with numerous suburbs, the largest being Metairie, an unincorporated subdivision of Jefferson Parish bordering the western side of the city. Neighborhoods such as Lakeview and New Orleans East added to suburban development. Yet the Gulf weather system remained a constant. In 1947, the Fort Lauderdale Hurricane or Hurricane George hit the city in September. The levees and pumping system held, but areas of Jefferson Parish were deluged and Moisant Airport was shut down. In 1961, white business leaders publicly endorsed desegregation of the city's public schools. In 1965 the city was hit by Hurricane Betsy, and a breach in the Industrial Canal produced catastrophic flooding in the Lower 9th Ward as well as in Arabi and Chalmette. In 2005, Hurricane Karina made landfall near the city on August 29. In the aftermath, the levee and floodwall system protecting New Orleans failed. Aware of the hurricane's tracks, the city had issued a voluntary evacuation order on August 27, converting major highways to a contraflow (reverse traffic flow system) in outbound lanes in Orleans, Jefferson, and St. Charles Parishes. On August 28,

Mayor Francis Naquin issued a mandatory evacuation of the entire city. Some 20 percent of the population did not leave for various reasons. While the eye of the storm missed the city, strong winds and heavy rains created heavy damage and some flooding. Although people thought the worst was over, the situation worsened when levees on four canals were breached. A storm surge was funneled via the Mississippi River Gulf Outlet and filled the Industrial Canal, which breached from the surge or the effects of being hit by a loose barge. The London Avenue and 17th Street canals were breached by the elevated waters of Lake Pontchartrain. About 80 percent of the city flooded, and more than 1,000 people died; there may never be an exact count of the victims. While many political figures took fire for the flooding and resulting deaths, investigators eventually pinned the blame on the U.S. Army Corps of Engineers for its design of the levee and floodwall system and the contractors who failed in some places to build the system to the requirements of the Corps of Engineers contracts.

New Orleans is still rebounding from Katrina, and probably will be for years. But on any given day, the French Quarter and Canal Street are bustling with visitors. Not only are the streetcar lines are running on St. Charles, Canal Street, and the Riverfront, but a route is planned to run on Poydras Street past the Superdome. A number of new hotels are scheduled to go up in the next few years, and there are some 1,212 restaurants in the city.

New Orleans and the entire Louisiana Gulf Coast are subject to tropical storms and hurricanes. In 2010, Louisiana's lieutenant governor, Mitch Landrieu, won the mayor's race with widespread support. Along with the City Council and numerous business leaders, he has said he is dedicated to meeting the challenges the city faces.

I recently asked one New Orleans businesswoman who had returned to New Orleans after working in another state what had made her decide to come back.

"There's no place in the world like New Orleans. You can go out any day of the week and have a good time. It's the people, the food, the music. My grandfather's a jazz musician, and I now realize how much he does. As I get older I understand how much respect these musicians have for each other. We really appreciate music down here. It's really a way of life," she said. "Ultimately, my family brought me back here."

A VETERAN TELLS VISITORS TO THE WORLD WAR II MUSEUM ABOUT THE HIGGENS BOATS USED FOR BEACH LANDINGS.
Cynthia V. Campbell

GUIDANCE **Basin St. Station** (888-626-5860 or 504-293-2600, www.basin station.com), 501 Basin St., New Orleans. The station provides New Orleans information and serves as a cultural center with travel counselors, exhibits, refreshments, a gift shop, and a free movie. Open 9 A.M.–5 P.M. daily.

Gretna Visitor Center (888-447-3862, 504-368-1580, www.gretnala.com), Huey P. Long Ave. at Fourth St., Gretna. Across the Mississippi River from New Orleans, this center will direct you to attractions in National Historic District, Gretna's museums, architecture, landmarks, restaurants, and events. Open 9 A.M.–3 P.M. Mon.–Fri.

Jefferson Convention and Visitors Bureau (504-731-7083 or 877-572-747, www.experiencejefferson.com), 1221 East Elmwood Park Blvd., New Orleans. A good complement to neighboring Orleans Parish, this is a place to can get information on Jefferson Parish shopping, museums, nature trails, and restaurants.

New Orleans Metropolitan Convention and Visitors Bureau (888-672-6124, 504-566-5011, www.neworleanscvb.com), 2020 St. Charles Ave., New Orleans. This bureau is a top source for jazzing up your travels by visiting the birthplace of jazz, unique food, and good times. Bureau experts are prepared to provide information on regional accommodations, restaurants, music, neighborhoods, architecture, Mardi Gras, Jazz Fest, and other festivals and other events.

ST. LOUIS CATHEDRAL FACES JACKSON SQUARE IN HEART OF NEW ORLEANS' FRENCH QUARTER.

New Orleans CVB/Jeff Anding

New Orleans Tourism Marketing Corporation (866-380-5234 or 504-524-4784, www.neworleansonline .com), 365 Canal St., Suite 1120, New Orleans. This is the city's official visitor resource, with a calendar of information about things to see and do and information about accommodations and famous cuisine.

New Orleans Welcome Center (504-568-5661, www.crt.state.la.us), 529 St. Ann St., New Orleans. This statewide tourism information center has well-trained travel counselors who provide tourism information not only about the city but about the entire state. Brochures and maps are available. The center is located in one of the historic Pontalba apartment buildings facing Jackson Square. This is a pedestrian-only street. Open 8:30 A.M.–5 P.M. daily.

Plaquemines Parish Office of Economic Development and Tourism (504-394-0018 or 888-745-0642,

www.plaqueminestourism.com), 104 New Orleans St., Belle Chasse. Within minutes of downtown New Orleans via the New Orleans Connection bridge, the
parish is a gateway to the Gulf of Mexico.

St. Bernard Parish Tourist Commission (888-278-2054 or 504-278-4242,
www.visitstbernard.com), 8201 West Judge Perez Dr., Chalmette. The folks at this
tourist commission are excellent sources of information about the site of the Battle
of New Orleans, San Bernardo Scenic Byway, Islenos Museum, local festivals, and
world-class fishing and birding sites.

GETTING THERE New Orleans attracts visitors from all over the world for business, vacation, and education. Most long-distance travel is best accomplished by
air, although many U.S. travelers prefer to arrive by personal vehicle. There are
other options if you consider boat, motorcycle, bicycle, or foot.

By air: **Louis Armstrong New Orleans International Airport** (504-303-7500,
www.flymsy.com), 900 Airline Dr., Kenner. The airport is served by American,
Continental, Delta, United, AirTran, US Airways and Southwest airlines with connecting flights to major hubs. Facilities include advance baggage check-in, financial services, Louisiana Tax-Free Shopping for international travelers, police
station, post office, free Wi-Fi assistance, covered parking, facilities for the disabled, restaurants, and lounges. The New Orleans Musicians Assistance Foundation, Delaware North Companies, and Abita Beer provide some live musical
performances in the Jazz Alley Lounge near the entrance to Concourse C.

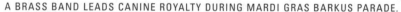

A BRASS BAND LEADS CANINE ROYALTY DURING MARDI GRAS BARKUS PARADE.

New Orleans CVB/Jay Combe

By car: I-10 runs through the center of New Orleans. People traveling from Texas take I-10 east through Baton Rouge to the northwestern tip of the city. If traveling from Florida and the Mississippi Gulf Coast, travelers stay in I-10 west into eastern New Orleans. If you're not in a rush to get to New Orleans from Lafayette on I-10, you can take a leisurely drive on I-49 (US 90) south through New Iberia, Franklin, and Morgan City. Another route is to take US 61 south from Baton Rouge to the center of New Orleans. If traveling from Jackson, Mississippi, follow I- 55 south to where it connects with I-10 in New Orleans. If you wish to bypass New Orleans proper or visit communities in the Northshore area, take I-12, which runs north of Lake Pontchartrain and connects with I-10 at both Baton Rouge and Slidell.

GETTING AROUND For detailed information on transportation in the Greater New Orleans region visit the website www.neworleansonline.com/tools /transportation. People who plan to visit the French Quarter, Central Business District, Garden District, and City Park will find that walking, buses, cabs, and trolleys are the best means of transportation. However, if you want to roam neighborhoods and towns in the surrounding area, you will need a car or van.

By cab: A cab or taxi ride in New Orleans costs about $33 from the airport to the Central Business District for one person and $14 per passenger for three or more passengers. The website has a list of cab companies and their phone numbers. Airport Shuttle Service to and from downtown New Orleans hotels, the French Quarter and the Convention Center is available daily (except from 2 A.M.–3:30 P.M.) with vans departing about every 30 minutes. Purchase tickets in person at the Airport Shuttle Ticket Desk or make a reservation at 866-596-2699. Cost is $20 one-way or $38 round-trip for adults and children age 6 and older. Children under 6 ride free.

By bus: Bus lines run by the New Orleans Regional Transit Authority are an affordable way to get around. For $1.25 one-way you can get to most areas of town. The NORTA operates some 30 bus and streetcar routes.

By streetcar: Don't leave New Orleans without taking a least one streetcar ride. The streetcars are one of the best ways to see the city and rub shoulders with locals. There are three different lines: St. Charles, Canal Street, and the Riverfront. Each line originates downtown, but takes you to a different part of the city. One-way fares are $1.25 and can be paid with exact change when you board. One, three-, and five-day unlimited ride passes are available for $5, $12, and $20. For fare and route information, visit www.norta.com.

By ferry: You'll see some of the best views of the original city of New Orleans during a Canal Street Ferry ride across the Mississippi River. The ferry traverses the river's natural crescent to Algiers Point on the West Bank. Board at the foot of Canal Street next to the Aquarium of the Americas. The ride is free for pedestrians and $1 for cars. The ferry runs 6 A.M.–12:15 P.M. daily.

By boat: The Mississippi River is far too busy as a commercial port for most private boats or yachts to navigate safely. However, many travelers choose to take a cruise to or from New Orleans. Carnival Cruise Line operates four- and five-night cruises to Playa del Carmen, Cozumel, and Costa Maya, Mexico. Royal Caribbean offers a seven-night Western Caribbean cruise from New Orleans during the winter. Ship itineraries and sailing dates are subject to change. Contact a travel agent or the cruise lines for details. American Cruise Lines will start sailing its new sternwheeler, the Queen of the Mississippi, on April 11, 2012. The boat, which will carry 150 passengers, will offer seven-, 10-, and 14-day cruises as far as St. Paul, Minnesota, on the Mississippi River and Pittsburgh, Pennsylvania, on the Ohio River. Cruise boats dock at the Port of New Orleans (Julia Street terminal or Erato Street Terminal) on the East Bank of the River behind the Moral Convention Center downtown, just minutes from the French Quarter.

By bicycle: For those who want to leave the car behind, there are several places to rent bikes in New Orleans. Here are several companies to contact; ask for types of bikes available and current rates. The **American Bicycle Rental Company** (866-293-4037, www.amebrc.com), 317 Burgundy St., Suite 24, New Orleans, is in the French Quarter. **Ride This Bike** (504-324-2492, www.ridethisbike.com), 325 Burgundy St., Suite 23, New Orleans, is also in the French Quarter. **Bicycle Michael's** (504-945-9505, www.bicyclemichaels.com), 622 Frenchmen St., New Orleans, is in the Faubourg Marigny/Bywater neighborhood near the French Quarter. **City Park Boat & Bike Rentals** (504 -224-2601, www.neworleanscitypark.com), Big Lake Trail, New Orleans, is located in the Lakefront and Lakeview area.

MEDICAL EMERGENCIES New Orleans Urgent Care (504-349-5525, www.neworleansurgentcare.com), 900 Magazine St., New Orleans. The center on the Magazine bus route serves people with minor emergencies and accepts all major insurance plans and credit cards. Walk-ins welcome. It is open 10 A.M.–7 P.M. Mon.–Sat. and 9–11 A.M. Sun.

Tulane Medical Center (504-988-5800 or 800-588-5800, www.tulanehealthcare.com), 1415 Tulane Ave., New Orleans. Located near the French Quarter, the center offers adult and pediatric emergency services.

✳ Cities, Towns, and Villages

Algiers is situated on the west bank of the Mississippi River. In its early years it served as a holding area for slaves brought by ship from Africa and later for Cajuns who survived the Grand Derangement from Nova Scotia. The oldest part of the town is Algiers Point, across the river from the French quarter, on the National Register of Historic Places. Ride the free Canal Street/Algiers Point Ferry and take a self-guided "Over Da River" walking tour of sites linked to famous jazz musicians. Stop by the Old Point Bar, one of the oldest jazz bars in the area.

Kenner, once a wilderness of cane reeds, is a suburb of New Orleans and the largest incorporated city in Jefferson Parish. As home to the Louis Armstrong International Airport, the city has a number of hotels and restaurants that are about 20-30 minutes away from downtown New Orleans via I-10. Attractions include the attractive Esplanade Mall, the Treasure Chest Casino, and the Rivertown, a 16-block historic district containing a family oriented museum and attractions that delight youngsters. Visit LaSalle's Landing for a great view of the Mississippi River.

Metairie, while a major part of the New Orleans metropolitan area, is an unincorporated section of Jefferson Parish. Veterans Boulevard is a major commercial thoroughfare. The central business district is located on Causeway Boulevard leading to the Lake Pontchartrain Causeway. Metairie has several malls, including Lakeside Shopping Center, the highest-grossing mall in the New Orleans area, and Clearview Mall. The area is home to numerous neighborhoods, churches, schools, hospitals, subdivisions, restaurants, and hotels.

It's somewhat confusing, but **Grand Isle**, Louisiana's major barrier island on the Gulf of Mexico, is officially a part of the New Orleans–Metairie–Kenner Metropolitan Statistical Area in Jefferson Parish. The island's only land connection is via an automobile causeway bridge that connects it to southern Lafourche Parish. To reach it from New Orleans takes about 95 miles. The community, with its simple lodges, cafes, sandy beaches, fishing, and birding, recalls old-time Gulf fishing villages.

Gretna, founded in 1836 on the west bank of the Mississippi River, is a small town with Creole cottages and shotgun houses. In the 1800s, a marrying judge made the area a destination for couples seeking quickie weddings. Museums and restaurants salute the city's original settlers, including many German immigrants. A Saturday morning farmers' market is held in the historic train depot, and the Gretna Art Walk is held the second Saturday of the month. A free pedestrian ferry takes visitors from New Orleans to the town center.

Westwego, according to local lore, was so named because it was a major crossing point during the westward movement in the late 1800s. Many families resettled here when their homes were destroyed in 1893 by an unnamed storm that hit Cheniere Caminada. The captivating historic district, including Sala Avenue, is a trip back in time. The Westwego Historical Museum houses a wonderful early 20th-century hardware store. The Westwego Farmers and Fisheries Market is a great spot early in the morning, when vendors bring in fish, crabs and shrimp fresh from the Gulf and area waterways. Teatro Wego Dinner Theater is a fun spot for dinner and performances by the Jefferson Performing Arts Society. Just beyond

LOOK FOR THE PAINTED LADIES

New Orleans's tiny shotgun houses have been referred to as painted ladies, since many are painted in ice-cream colors of soft blue, green, yellow, and pink. However, innovative owners sometimes turn the houses into knockout, dazzling, bright showplaces. A shotgun is a narrow, rectangular dwelling, often no more than 12 feet wide, with a door at each end. It was the most popular style of house in the southern United States following the Civil War. The term *shotgun house* became more popular about 1940. It is often said to come from the observation that one could fire a shotgun through the front door, and the pellets would fly cleanly through the house and out the back. In New Orleans, you'll see variations throughout the city. It's not unusual to see a shotgun turned into an appealing gift shop, candy store, or cozy cafe. A "double-barrel" shotgun house is built with two houses sharing a central wall. The "camelback" shotgun house has a second floor at the rear of the house.

town, Bayou Segnette State Park offers camping, boating, and a wave pool in summer.

Two distinctive parishes south of New Orleans have ties to the city's history. **St. Bernard Parish**, situated on the east side of the Mississippi River, is a paradise for fishing, hunting, and bird watching. Here you can visit the spot at the National Historical Park Chalmette Battlefield where the nation was defended against the British during the Battle of New Orleans. The San Bernardo Scenic Byway (LA 46) follows a bayou where you can see historic homes and where Canary Islanders settled in the area.

Plaquemines Parish runs along the west side of the Mississippi to the river's mouth where it flows into the Gulf of Mexico. Spread out over hundreds of miles of coastline with more than 78 fresh and saltwater lakes, the parish's economy is tied to the seafood and oil industries. Because of the warm, semi-tropical climate, the parish also is the center of a thriving citrus industry. Louisiana residents welcome late fall, when bags of sweet satsuma oranges begin to appear in the markets. A visit to towns in St. Bernard and Plaquemines will introduce you to openhearted, friendly people and special festivals. See the special events listing.

✳ To See

There are so many fascinating attractions in New Orleans, there's really no way to see them all in one trip unless you stay in the city several months. Your best bet is to make a list of must-see places based on your interests. You may choose history, architecture, music, food, or gardening, or you may go for quirky shops or offbeat art. You will get the most out of your visit if you allow plenty of time to investigate each attraction thoroughly. Absorb what you learn and turn the trip into a memory

TOURISTS GET CLOSE TO NATURE ON HONEY ISLAND SWAMP, NEAR SLIDELL.

Louisiana Northshore CVB

that won't slip away. If this is a family trip, let the kids and grandparents help with the decision-making. Make lists of rainy-day and sunny-day attractions. Indoor sights, such as museums, home tours, and shopping centers, work well for days when the weather is foul or the sun is too hot. Outdoor sights, such as gardens, zoos, and swamp tours, are better for clement, sunny days. If you are unfamiliar with New Orleans, then sign up for a guided tour that suits your interests and budget. To learn more, visit the Preservation Resource Center at www.prcno.org.

ARCHITECTURE New Orleans boasts a myriad of architectural styles ranging from the 1700s to the present. The best time of day to go on a leisurely walking tour through one of the city's neighborhoods is 8–10 A.M., when it's cooler and streets are less congested. To really learn more about the architecture, join an organized tour with an experienced guide. You will see Creole cottages in the French Quarter, American townhouses in the Central Business and Lower Garden districts, and Creole townhouses in the Quarter and surrounding neighborhoods. Look for raised center-hall cottages or villas in the Garden District, Uptown, Carrollton and elsewhere. Double-gallery houses are found in the Lower Garden District, Garden District, Uptown, and Esplanade Ridge.

Historic Home Tour Once a year (usually in March or April) during the annual Spring Fiesta, and Historic Home Tour, many elegant private homes are opened to the public. For that week, the Spring Fiesta Association, dedicated to historic preservation, offers tours of some 20 homes in the French Quarter, Uptown, and Garden District. The festival includes a parade of horse-drawn carriages through the French Quarter. For information, contact the association's headquarters at 826 St. Ann St., 504-581-1367, or www.springfiesta.com.

Historic New Orleans Collection (504-523-4662, www.hnoc.org), 533 Royal St., New Orleans. The Historic New Orleans Collection gives a docent-guided tour of its buildings and courtyards in the French Quarter. The tour explores the history of the architecture, how courtyards developed, the architectural styles represented, and the history of some of the people who lived in the buildings. Tours are given on the hour 10 A.M.–3 P.M. Tues.–Sat. and 11 A.M., 2 P.M., and 3 P.M. Sun.

Loyola University (504-865-3240, 800-456-9652, www.loyno.edu), 6363 St. Charles Ave., New Orleans. Established as a college in 1904 and as a university in 1912, Loyola offers numerous undergraduate and graduate degrees. A Jesuit and Catholic institution, the school has been named among the top 10 Southern regional schools by *U.S. News & World Report*. Student life includes fraternities and sororities, an international student association, and volunteer projects in the New Orleans community. Loyola is across from Audubon Park and can be easily reached by the St. Charles Avenue streetcar.

St. Charles Avenue. A ride on the St. Charles Avenue Streetcar is a pleasant way to view residential splendor. The Avenue is the site of Audubon Park, Loyola, and Tulane universities, and a score of churches and synagogues. Along the way at 2265 St. Charles you'll see the Diocesan House designed by James Gallier Jr. and completed in 1857. At 2524 see The Marigny, a center-hall Greek Revival home built in 1857 by John Vittie for Sophronie Claiborne Marigny, daughter of Louisiana's first governor. At 3029 sits the Elms Manson, built in 1869. The building later served as the German Consulate General from 1931-1941. Tours are

Cynthia V. Campbell

THE ST. CHARLES AVENUE TROLLEY HAS BEEN ROLLING ALONG THE NEUTRAL GROUND FOR MORE THAN 150 YEARS.

given weekdays 10 A.M.–2:30 P.M. A must-see is the Latter Library at 5120. The neo-Italianate mansion was built in 1907 for Mark Issacs, a wealthy merchant. After Issacs's death, Frank B. Williams purchased the home. His son, Harry Palmerston Williams, became vice president of the Wedell-Williams Air Service Corporation and married the silent-screen star Marguerite Clark on Aug. 5, 1918; the couple were part of the New Orleans social scene. After Williams's death in 1936, Clark left Louisiana. Eventually, a later owner, Harry Latter, transformed the house into a public library in memory of his son Milton, who died in Okinawa in World War II. It is open to the public and includes many beautiful features.

Tulane University (504-865-5000, www.tulane.edu), 6823 St. Charles Ave., New Orleans. Established in 1864 in New Orleans, Tulane is a private independent research university. It's one of the oldest law schools in the country, and its School of Public Health and Tropical Medicine is the oldest school of public health and the only school of tropical medicine in America. Tulane's School of Medicine also offers a preventive medicine residency program. Among more than 4,300 universities in the United States ranked by the Carnegie Foundation for the advancement of teaching, Tulane is placed in the prestigious category. The main campus on St. Charles Avenue is next to Loyola University. It also faces Audubon Park.

CITY SIGHTS There are numerous famous attractions throughout the Crescent City. The French Quarter, the oldest section of the city on the Mississippi River, is one of the world's major tourist destinations. Other major attractions are found in neighborhoods along Canal Street, St. Charles Avenue, Magazine Street, and Esplanade Avenue. Simple tourist maps are available at welcome centers and in most hotel lobbies.

Bourbon Street The street extends 13 blocks from Canal Street to Esplanade Avenue. While this French Quarter stretch has a bawdy reputation because of its burlesque clubs and all-night partying, it's worth taking the time to experience its historical side. Bourbon Street was named for the House of Bourbon, the ruling French royal family at the time of the city's founding. If you're a people watcher, then Bourbon Street is probably the best spot to watch crowds from mid-afternoon until the wee hours of the morning. Favorite stopping points include Jean Lafitte's Blacksmith Shop, a bar and restaurant in a Creole cottage built before 1772; Old Absinthe House, erected in 1806 as a family importing firm and now a landmark saloon; and Galatoire's Restaurant, founded in 1905 and still the hot spot for lunch on Fridays. The intersection with St. Ann Street begins the section of Bourbon Street that caters to the gay community. Lafittes in Exile here is the oldest gay bar in the country.

Canal Street A major thoroughfare, Canal Street runs from the Mississippi to its terminus at a collection of mid-city cemeteries. When developed, Canal Street acted as a dividing line between the old Colonial-era city (the French Quarter) and the newer American sector. It was referred to by early inhabitants as the "neutral ground" between early Colonial inhabitants and newly arrived "Americans" following the Louisiana Purchase. It has three lanes of traffic in both directions and a pair of streetcar tracks in the center. A number of major hotels, including the New Orleans Marriott, Sheraton New Orleans, JW Marriott, and Ritz Carlton New Orleans are located on Canal Street. Near the river you'll find the Canal Place shopping center, the Audubon Insectarium, Harrah's Casino, and the Aquarium of the Americas.

French Market (504-522-2621, www.frenchmarket.org), 2 French Market Place, New Orleans. Founded in 1791, the New Orleans French Market is the oldest public market in the country. Walk through the produce area to view stalls filled with colorful fresh vegetables and fruits. The covered, open-air mall includes a flea market, shops, music, and casual dining.

✔ **Jackson Square**. The square between the Mississippi River waterfront and St. Louis Cathedral receives its name from the three bronze statues of Andrew Jackson in its center. People from all corners of the world stop to get their photos taken by the landmark statue or simply to meet with friends. On any given day, people gather to watch mimes, street musicians, and artists busy painting. Morning hours are a good time to bring children to see the fun and a get a taste of the Quarter.

Royal Street One block over from Bourbon Street, Royal Street is an elegant stretch through the French Quarter. Visitor find upscale, classic antiques shops, fine jewelry stores, art galleries, world-class restaurants, and hotels. This is a good place to find an exquisite chandelier or delicate porcelain punch bowl. Perhaps you're looking for a painting to accent your foyer. As you stroll along, study the buildings with iron lace balconies, many of which date from the 1700s and 1800s. A number of restaurants with courtyards and colorful gardens provide shade and refreshment from long, sunny-day walks. Among the internationally known restaurants here are Brennan's, Mr. B's, and Court of Two Sisters. As you near Esplanade Street, you'll come to a more tranquil area where you begin to see the neighborhood aspect of the Quarter. Residents may be out walking their dogs or visiting beneath balconies as they welcome dusk.

Cynthia V. Campbell

STREET ENTERTAINERS GIVE AN IMPROMPTU JAZZ CONCERT ON ROYAL STREET.

FAMILY FUN ✐ ⅄ **Audubon Aquarium of the Americas** (504- 581-4629 or 800- 774-7394, www.auduboninstitute.org), 1 Canal St., New Orleans. Situated at the end of Canal Street on the Mississippi River, the Aquarium contains magical exhibits with 15,000 aquatic animals representing about 600 species. The Caribbean Reef tunnel delights visitors as they view sea creatures swimming above their heads. See fish from the Mississippi estuary and rare white alligators that are not albinos. The Gulf of Mexico exhibit teems with fully grown sharks and undersea life. The Amazon rain forest exhibit features exotic birds and poisonous frogs. The Aquarium has a small cafe and the gift shop has quality items. While here, you also can view films in the Imax theater. Check the website for individual and combination ticket prices.

✐ ⅄ **Audubon Insectarium** (504-410-2847, www.auduboninstitute.org), 423 Canal St., New Orleans. Located in the old U.S. Custom House, the Insectarium is North America's largest facility devoted to insects and their relatives. Be amazed at what the largest group of the smallest animals on the planet can do. Join an active audience at an awards show for bugs, by bugs. See butterflies in flight in the Asian garden. Plan your visit to catch insect cooking demonstrations and tastings, usually at 10 A.M. daily. Open 10 A.M.–5 P.M. Tues.–Sun.

✐ ⅄ **Audubon Zoo** (504-581-4629 or 800-774-7394; www.auduboninstitute.org), 6500 Magazine St., New Orleans. Ranked one of the top zoos in America, the Audubon features some 1,500 animals in their natural habitats. Favorites include the white tiger brothers from California, the Komodo dragon, and the elephants. Monkey Hill was built as a Works Progress Administration project in the 1930s to show New Orleans children what a hill looked like. Visitors can stroll through a swamp area and see a lagoon full of 14-foot alligators and other swamp animals. Nearby is the special exhibit of world-famous white alligators. The zoo also features cafes and an attractive gift shop. Open at 10 A.M. Tues.–Sun. Closing times vary by season. Closed major holidays, Mardi Gas, and the first Friday in May. Story time is 11 A.M. and 1 P.M. Mon.–Sat. Admission $14.95 adults; $11.95, seniors; $9.95, children ages 2–12.

✐ **Blaine Kern's Mardi Gras World** (504-361-7821 or 800-362-8213, www .mardigrasworld.com), 1380 Port of New Orleans Place, New Orleans. The city's Mardi Gras parades, which take place the weeks before Ash Wednesday, are world-famous. To get the feeling of Mardi Gras year-round, visit the largest float-designing and -building facility in the world. More than 80 percent of the floats that travel New Orleans's streets during Carnival are created here. View authentic glittering and feathered Mardi Gras costumes and tour enormous warehouses filled with floats. See the short film and hear a guide talk about the history and customs of Mardi Gras. Learn about parades, balls, and music. For an authentic taste of the festival, sample a king cake and hot New Orleans coffee. Open 9:30 A.M.–5 P.M. daily. Admission is $19.95, adults; $15.95, seniors 65 and over; and $12.95, children 1–11. Discounts available for groups of 10 or more.

✐ **Louisiana Children's Museum** (504-523-1357, www.lcm.org), 420 Julia St., New Orleans. The laughter of children here is captivating. More than 30,000 square feet of hands-on, interactive exhibits invite youngsters to explore art, music, science, math, and health. You'll find the Little Port of New Orleans where kids can pilot a towboat down the Mississippi River. Step into giant eyeballs and peer through their lenses to understand the eye's anatomy. Youngsters can role play in the Kids' Cafe and pretend to be a restaurant waitress, chef, or guest. The gift shop is filled with puzzles, games, and more. Open 9:30 A.M.–4:30 P.M. Wed.–Sat., noon–4:30 P.M. Sun. Summer months the hours are 9:30 A.M.–4:30 P.M. Mon.,

A WOMAN FEEDS SWANS AND DUCKS IN NEW ORLEANS CITY PARK.

New Orleans CVB/Jay Combe

9:30 A.M.–5 P.M. Tues.–Sat., and noon to 5 P.M. Sunday. Admission is $8 adults and children. Toddlers under age 1 are admitted free.

🖊 🐚 **New Orleans City Park** (504-483-9357, www.neworleanscitypark.com), 1 Collins Diboll Circle, City Park, New Orleans. Designed as a grand park for the entire community, City Park has many components with drives traversing beautiful green spaces. One of the top activities that appeal to children is the Carousel Gardens Amusement Park. Since 1906, little ones and kids at heart have enjoyed the "flying horses" of the park's antique carousel, at 1 Palm Terrace. This is one of only about 100 antique wooden carousels left in the country and the last one in Louisiana. Elsewhere there are other rides to keep your kids twisting, turning, whirling, and twirling, including the Rockin' Tug, bumper cars, Red Baron Miniplane, Scrambler, Tilt-A-Whirl, a 40-foot fun slide, Umbrella Cars, Ferris wheel, a children's construction zone, the Live Oak Lady Bug roller coaster, and a miniature train ride that tours the park. Open seasonally. Storyland, 1 Palm Dr., is a kids' play area where favorite animals, cartoon characters, and fairy tale legends are themes of various gentle rides and climb-about attractions. Train Garden near Storyland features buildings made entirely of botanical materials in a replica of New Orleans. As visitors walk on a pathway, they overlook 1,300 feet of track carrying trains and streetcars like those that traveled in New Orleans in the late 1800s to early 1900s, at 1/22 of their actual size. Spring hours, March 12–May 29, 11 A.M.– 6 P.M. Sat.–Sun. Summer hours, June 2–Aug. 7, 10 A.M.–3 P.M. Thurs., 10 A.M.– 10 P.M. Fri., 11 A.M.–10 P.M. Sat., and 11 A.M.–6 P.M. Sun. Fall hours, Aug. 13–Nov. 13, are 11 A.M.–6 P.M. Sat. and Sun. Storyland only (no rides) 10 A.M.–4 P.M. Mon.– Fri., 11 A.M.–6 P.M. Sat.–Sun. Amusement Park admission is $3 per person (36 inches tall and up). Children under 36 inches and Friends of City Park, free.

MUSEUMS Amistad Research Center (504-862-3222, www.amistadresearch center.org), 6823 St. Charles Ave., Tilton Memorial Hall, Tulane University, New Orleans. The Amistad Research Center houses the country's largest collection of manuscripts about African Americans, race relations, and civil rights. This center is a focal point of research for historians, nonfiction authors, and novelists. It's also an important resource for people pursuing information about their family's history.

🖊 **Backstreet Cultural Museum** (504-522-4806, www.backstreetmuseum.org), 1116 St. Claude Ave., New Orleans. Filled with delightful collections of memorabilia from Mardi Gras, jazz funerals, and other events important to African American culture, the museum is thoroughly entertaining. It houses the city's largest collection of brilliant and intricately designed Mardi Gras Indian costumes handmade by local artisans. Situated in the Treme neighborhood, the museum also has an enormous collection of still photos and video footage of Mardi Gras Indians, jazz funerals, and second lines. New Orleans's second line parades started with mourners following bands at a jazz funeral. Today, the parades are put on throughout the year for various occasions. They include a brass band and spontaneous dancing in the street with participants dressed in colorful attire, carrying umbrellas, and often waving handkerchiefs or scarves. Open 10 A.M.–5 P.M. Tues.–Sat. Admission $8.

Beauregard-Keyes House (504-523-7257, www.bkhouse.org), 1113 Chartres St., New Orleans. This historic French Quarter home is a raised-center hall house. It is named for two of its former residents, the Confederate General Pierre Gustave Toutant Beauregard and the author Frances Parkinson Keyes. The furnishings reflect the lifestyles of both these celebrities. The Beauregard Chamber is furnished with original furnishings used by the general and his family. Also displayed are Mrs. Keyes's collections of more than 200 antique dolls, delicate fans, and folk costumes. Tours are given on the hour 10 A.M.–3 P.M. Mon.–Sat. Admission is $10 adults; $9, students and seniors; $4, children ages 6–12.

Confederate Memorial Hall Museum (504-523-4522, www.confederate museum.com), 929 Camp St., New Orleans. The oldest museum in Louisiana, Confederate Memorial Hall opened its doors on January 8, 1891. It was built through the generosity of Frank Howard, a wealthy philanthropist, and operated by the Louisiana Historical Society. Confederate veterans and their families donated numerous historical objects, including battle flags, uniforms, swords, sabers, rare photographs, and personal relics. It is one of the largest repositories of Civil War artifacts and history in the country. Open 10 a.m.–4 p.m. Tues.–Sat.

Gallier House (504-525-5661, www.hgghh.org), 1132 Royal St., New Orleans. Designed and built in 1857 by the prominent New Orleans architect James Gallier Jr., the elegant Victorian home reflects the lifestyle of a successful man in post-Civil War New Orleans. Experience the impressive furnishings, detailed garden, carriageway, and restored slave quarters. Open 10 A.M.–3 P.M. Mon.–Fri., with tours on the hour 10 A.M.–2 P.M. weekdays and noon–3 P.M. Sat. Tours last about 45 minutes. Admission $15.

Hermann-Grima House (504-525-5661, www.hgghh.org), 820 St. Louis St., New Orleans. Built in 831, this house in the French Quarter is thought to be the best example of American architecture in the area. The Federal mansion boasts a lovely courtyard garden, a stable, and a functional outdoor kitchen. Carefully restored through research and archaeological studies, it depicts the lifestyle of a wealthy Creole family from 1830–1860. Open for tours, on the hour 10 A.M.–2 P.M. Mon.–Tues and Thurs.–Fri. and noon–3 P.M. Sat. Admission is $10, adults; $8, AAA members, seniors 65 and over, students 18 and over, and children ages 8–12; free to children younger than 8.

Historic New Orleans Collection (504-523-4662, www.hnoc.org), 533 Royal St., New Orleans. Visit the Royal Street complex, where the Merieult House serves as the entrance to a web of buildings and courtyards that has been in continuous use since the 1720s. Touring the property, you'll see historical paintings, furnishings, and objets d'art seldom on view elsewhere in New Orleans. For a short time in the 1930s, a young playwright—Tennessee Williams—lived in a garret room in the Louis Adams House. Changing exhibits in the ground level galleries focus on numerous aspects of New Orleans and Louisiana history. Open 9:30 A.M.–4:30 P.M. Tues.–Sat. and 10:30 A.M.–4:30 P.M. Sun.

Longue Vue (504-488-5488, www.longuevue.com), 7 Bamboo Rd., New Orleans. This remarkable house museum and its exceptional gardens had been an 8-acre estate built by New Orleans civic activists and philanthropists. One of the last great houses to be custom-built in America, it took three years (1939–1942) to create. Touring the house, you'll see rooms with the original English and American furnishings, intricate European and Eastern carpets, collections of needlework, chintz, Chinese and European porcelain, and Wedgwood pearlware. The home was a social center, whose notable guests included Eleanor Roosevelt, John and Robert Kennedy, and Pablo Casals. The ever-changing gardens include the Azalea Walk, the Pan Garden (named after the Greek god of nature), and the Wild Garden, which features flowers native to Louisiana, including iris and camellia. The Discovery Garden is a learning space for children with a bamboo tunnel, worm dig, and herb maze. Open 10 A.M.–4:30 P.M. Mon.–Sat., 1–5 P.M. Sun. Last tour at 4 P.M. Admission is $10, house and garden, $7, gardens only.

Louisiana State Museum The Louisiana State Museum has numerous components in New Orleans that are true treasures. The Cabildo (701 Chartres St., 504-568-6968) is the site of the 1803 Louisiana Purchase. The Presbytere (751 Chartres St., 504-568-6968) was built on the side of the residence of the Capuchin monks. It was designed in 1791 to match the Cabildo on the other side of St. Louis Cathedral. The Presbytere's second floor contains fascinating exhibits and interactive displays on Mardi Gras, and encourages visitors to explore the fantasy and all aspects of Carnival through rare artifacts and imaginative technology. Madame John's Legacy (632 Dumaine St.) took its name from a story by George Washington Cable. The house, which escaped fires in 1788 and 1795, is one of the finest 18th-century building complexes in Louisiana. The French West Indies style is the type of dwelling that colonists built in the French Quarter after progressing from their first rude cabin. The 1850 House (523 St. Ann St., Lower Pontalba Building, Jackson Square) is one of the townhouses built in 1850 by Baroness Micaela Almonester de Pontalba, daughter of Don Andres Almonester y Roxas, the Spanish Colonial landowner and businessman. The residence is decorated with artifacts and mid-19th-century furnishings that exemplify the life of a middle-class family during New Orleans's most prosperous era. The U.S. Mint (400 Esplanade Ave.) is a National Historic Landmark. It is the only mint to have produced both Federal and Confederate coinage. The building was erected in 1835 during the presidency of Andrew Jackson. Visitors will find the New Orleans Jazz exhibit here absolutely outstanding. Exhibits feature instruments played by significant jazz musicians, sheet music, and memorabilia associated with the history of jazz music from its beginnings on the streets of New Orleans. Another permanent exhibit features Newcomb Pottery and crafts. A third, The Mississippi and the Making of a Nation, is based on National Geographic's 2002 book of the same name by the historians Douglas Brinkley and the late Stephen Ambrose. In addition, the Old U.S. Mint presents rotating exhibits and houses a Historical Center with an archive of maps and documents. Hours at the Cabildo, Presbytere, Old U.S. Mint, and the 1850 House are 10 a.m.–4:30 p.m. Tues.–Sun. Closed Monday and state holidays. To schedule research, call 504-568-3660. For information on admission prices and to confirm hours, call 504-568-6968 or 800-568-6968. From time to time, these buildings may be closed for renovations or special events. Hours of operation and admission prices are subject to change.

Musee Conti Wax Museum (504 947-7673, www.neworleanswaxmuseum .com), 917 Conti St., New Orleans. A guided tour of more than 150 life-size wax figures tells the story of New Orleans from city's founding to Battle of New Orleans, to the mysterious world of voodoo. It's informative, entertaining, and not spooky. Open 10 A.M.–4 P.M. Mon., Fri., Sat. Admission is $7, adults; $6.25, seniors; and $6, children ages 4–17. Ask about a group rate for 25 persons or more.

🖉 ♿ **National World War II Museum** (504-528-1944, www.nationalww2 museum.org), 945 Magazine St., New Orleans. Situated in the Arts/Warehouse District, the museum is a must-see for history lovers and patriots. Powerful exhibits feature oral histories from veterans worldwide, artifacts, documents, photographs, and film footage. From the 1930s prelude to war to the Normandy Invasion and the battles of the Pacific islands, visitors can trace America's role in World War II and on the home front. The Louisiana Memorial Pavilion showcases military vehicles, planes, and the famous Higgins landing craft that was built in New Orleans. The Stage Door Canteen presents a weekly series of evenings and matinees showcasing 1940s entertainment. The American Sector Restaurant offers a menu of traditional favorites. The Soda Shop is open daily. Before 3 P.M., bring your parking stub inside to receive credit when you purchase $20 in food and beverages. Open 9 A.M.–5 P.M. daily. General admission tickets are $19, adults; $15, seniors; $9, children age K–12, college students, and military with ID. In the Solomon Victory Theater, the "4-D" cinema presentation engages all senses including sight, hearing, and touch. It gives viewers an armchair seat to history as snow falls from the ceiling and seats rumbling when the tank comes through. Tickets for the *Beyond All Boundaries* cinema experience cost $11, adults; $9, seniors and military with ID; $8, children K–12; $5, children under 5; and $8, college students and military in uniform, Combo tickets available.

🖉 **New Orleans African American Museum** (504-566-1136, www.thenoaam .org), 1418 Governor Nicholls St., New Orleans. The museum is located in Treme, the oldest surviving black community in the United States, in the lovely Treme villa, one of the finest examples of a Creole villa in the city. Built in 1828–1829, it has many of its original features. Its grounds cover one city block and include additional buildings and beautiful courtyards with original handmade bricks. The museum is dedicated to protecting, preserving, and promoting through education the history, art, and communities of African Americans in New Orleans. Exhibits change regularly. Open 11 a.m.–4 p.m. Wed.–Sat. and by special appointment on off days. Admission is $7, adults; $5, seniors and students; $3, children 2–12.

🖉 ♿ **New Orleans Museum of Art** (504-658-4100, www.noma.org), 1 Collins Diboll Circle, City Park, New Orleans. New Orleans's oldest fine arts institution, NOMA has a magnificent permanent collection of more than 40,000 objects. Among these are noted works in French and American art, glass, and photography, and Japanese and African art. The five-acre Sydney and Walda Besthoff Sculpture Garden features more than 60 sculptures in a handsome landscaped site with footpaths and reflecting lagoons, live oak, magnolias, and camellias. The museum continues to exhibit and interpret works from ancient to modern times. Among its treasures is a group of works by the French Impressionist Edgar Degas, who visited maternal relatives in New Orleans in 1871 and 1872 and painted in a home 20 blocks from the museum site. The museum is known for its creative special events, including varied Friday evening programs of music, children's activities, exhibition walkthroughs, food, and art. All programs are free with admission. Open 10 a.m.– 5 p.m. Tues.–Sun. and Fri. for Where Y'Art until 9 p.m. Regular admission is $10 adults; $8 seniors, students, and active military; $6 children 7–17; and free to children age 6 and under.

🖉 **Ogden Museum of Southern Art** (504-539-9600, www.ogdenmuseum.org), 925 Camp St., New Orleans. Affiliated with the Smithsonian Institution, the Ogden

Museum contains one of the most comprehensive collections of Southern art in the world. The museum is dedicated to telling the story of art in the American South through visual art from the Colonial period to the present. Collections include paintings, sculpture, photography, works on paper, self-taught art, ceramics and mixed media. Museum programs include special exhibitions and other programs. Open 10 A.M.–5 P.M. Wed.–Mon. Closed major holidays.

✔ **Old Ursuline Convent** (504-529-3040), 1100 Chartres St., New Orleans. The Ursuline convent is the oldest building in the Mississippi River Valley. Completed in 1752, it also is the oldest surviving example of the French Colonial period in the United States. Also known as the Archbishop Antoine Blanc Memorial Complex, the Old Ursuline Convent houses the Archdiocesan archives and is often referred to as the "treasure of the archdiocese." Open 10 A.M.–4 P.M. Mon.–Sat. Admission $5, adults; $4, seniors; $3, students with a valid ID; and free for children under age 6. Group discounts available.

Pharmacy Museum (504-565-8027, www.pharmacymuseum.org), 514 Chartres St., New Orleans. Louis Joseph Dufilho Jr. of New Orleans became America's first licensed pharmacist. Today, Dufilho's 1823 apothecary shop on Chartres Street in the French Quarter houses what is widely believed to be the largest and most diverse pharmaceutical collection in a single location in the United States, containing old patent medicines, books, and pharmaceutical equipment dating from the early 1800s. Be sure to climb the stairs to the second floor, where you will learn more about health care and medical treatments in the era. It also is a great opportunity to study the architecture of an early French Quarter building. Open 10 A.M.–2 P.M. Tues.–Fri. and 10 A.M.–5 P.M. Sat. Admission is $5, adults, and $4, students and seniors; free to children younger than 6.

Southern Food and Beverage Museum (504-569-0405, www.southernfood .org), 500 Port of New Orleans Place, Suite 169, Riverwalk, New Orleans. Take the Julia Street entrance at the Riverwalk Mall. You'll delight in this museum dedicated to the discovery, understanding, and celebration of the food and beverages of the South. See cooking utensils, meat cleavers, pots, pans, old stoves, pie-safes, graters, crockery, uniforms and aprons. There are exhibits on bar items, photographs documenting food history, recipe scrapbooks, a collection of menus, and historic cookbooks. Open 10 a.m.–7 p.m. Mon.–Sat. and noon–6 p.m. Sun. Admission is $10, adults; $5, students, seniors, and military; and $8, AAA members.

Voodoo Museum (504-680-0128, www.voodoomuseum.com), 724 Dumaine St., New Orleans. This small museum has been a French Quarter curiosity since 1972. Voodoo came to America with the African salve trade. It is a spiritual system based on God, spirits, and ancestors that developed in three historical phases: African, Creole, and American. The museum highlights includes displays on various beliefs and rituals, and it arranges for psychic readings and cemetery walking tours. Open 10 A.M.–6 P.M. daily.

✳ Green Spaces

Audubon Park (504-581-4629, www.auduboninstitute.org), 6500 Magazine St., New Orleans. Located in an uptown neighborhood, the park is about 6 miles from downtown, and was once Plantation de Bore. It's bordered on one side by the Mississippi River and on the other by St. Charles Avenue, and across from Tulane and

Loyola universities. During the Civil War, the land was used by both Confederate and Union soldiers, and it was a staging grounds for the Buffalo Soldiers. The amazingly beautiful park follows a design drafted by John Charles Olmsted, of the famed Olmsted Brothers landscape architecture firm. Join locals jogging or playing soccer in the fields. There's a biking route, and Ochsner Island bird sanctuary. It's also home to the Audubon Zoo and a Riverview park area known locally as the Fly.

Barataria Preserve (504-689-3690), 6588 Barataria Blvd., Marraro. This 23,000-acre preserve is a unit of the Jean Lafitte National Historical Park. It's a wild, wetland wilderness within 30 minutes of downtown New Orleans. It's a living laboratory of Louisiana's wildlife, including alligators, armadillos, otters, and some 300 species of birds. Boardwalks and dirt trails wind through the preserve. Pick up a trail map at the visitors' center and enjoy a self-guided tour or get some guidance with a cellphone tour. You can explore the waterways by canoe or kayak. Exhibits at the center explain how the Mississippi River built Louisiana's wetlands and the importance of the river. Kids can earn a badge with the Junior Ranger Program. The attractive, well-designed education center is used for special programs and the bookstore has books, music, and field guides on sale. Open 9 A.M.–5 P.M. daily. Closed Christmas Day and Mardi Gras.

Bayou Segnette State Park (504-736-7140 or 888-677-2296), 7777 Westbank Expressway, Westwego. About a 30-minute drive across the Mississippi River from New Orleans, the state park is planned for family getaways. Both salt- and freshwater fishing are available because of the park's location. From the boat launch you can explore many areas not accessible by road. Catches of bass, catfish, bream, perch, redfish, and trout are common. The park has campsites and cabins overlooking the bayou. A special summer feature is the large wave pool that's carefully supervised. Gates open 6 A.M.–9 P.M. Sun.–Thurs., April–September. The entrance station is open 8 A.M.–5 P.M. October–March. All park gates close at 10 P.M. Fri.–Sat. and days preceding holidays. Fee is $1 per person; free for seniors 62 and over and children age 3 and under. Call for wave pool fee.

✔ ✹ **City Park** (504-483-9357, www.neworleanscitypark.com), 1 Collins Diboll Circle, City Park, New Orleans. As noted in the To Do listing, this is one of American's outstanding urban parks, as well as one of its oldest (the first parcel was acquired in 1854). Once the site of Allard Plantation facing Bayou St. John, City Park has 1,300 acres devoted to the community. Attractions include a botanical garden, Storyland, the Carousel Gardens Amusement Park, a dog park, and hundreds of acres for walking, jogging, biking, fishing, horseback riding, softball, soccer, football, and tennis. It is the home of the New Orleans Museum of Art and one of the largest collections of live oaks in the world. It's the site of numerous special events, including the Celebration Under the Oaks during the Christmas season. New Orleanians cherish this park. After the Katrina disaster, hundreds of residents came out with their own equipment to shovel mud and put the gardens back in shape for a fund-raiser and mini-version of Celebration Under the Oaks.

Woldenberg Park (504-565-3033, www.auduboninstitute.org), 1 Canal St., New Orleans. At any time of day you will see people relaxing at this park next to the mighty Mississippi. Watch ships floating past on the river or study the interesting sculptures that enhance the landscape. There's plenty of grass for picnicking or letting toddlers run. The benches along the wide, bricked walkways are perfect after a tour of the French Quarter. The docking area is where you can catch a steamboat for a dinner cruise. Visitors are sometimes serenaded by local musicians and street performers. For a special quiet stroll or jog, visit early in the morning. You can catch a cool breeze, listen to the ship's horns, and watch the city awaken to a new day.

✴ To Do

BOWLING While every city has bowling alleys, New Orleans has a unique touch with its Rock 'n' Bowl night, which adds music, food, and dancing to the fun. Other bowling alleys in various neighborhoods appeal to those who prefer to enjoy it in traditional venues.

✐ **AWF All Star Lanes** (504-443-5353, www.amf.com), 3640 Williams Blvd., Kenner. This is a local spot for great bowling. The fun includes group events, birthday parties, and bowling leagues. There's bumper bowling for kids, Xtreme bowling, and a Grip and Sip menu from a full service bar with signature drinks. Open 9– 1 A.M. Sun.–Thurs. and 9–2 A.M. Fri.–Sat.

Colonial Bowling Lanes (504-737-2400, www.colonialbowling.net), 6601 Jefferson Hwy., Harahan. Locally owned and operated, this is a family bowling center in Jefferson Parish with 24 wood lanes. The nonsmoking facility features Twelve Strike Automatic Scoring with 32-inch flat-screen TVs, a game room, pro shop, and lounge. Open 8 A.M.–midnight Mon.–Thurs., 8–1 A.M. Fri.–Sat., and 10 A.M.– midnight Sun.

Mid-City Lanes Rock 'n' Bowl (504-861-1700, www.rockandbowl.com), 3000 South Carrollton Ave., New Orleans. Rock 'n' Bowl is a New Orleans institution that lets you rock 'n' roll while you bowl! Locals and tourists go to the 18-hole lane center to dance until 2 or 3 in the morning. Every night brings new live entertainment. You might start with the two-step or jitterbug and move onto zydeco before the evening is through. Performers include local and national musicians, including Kermit Ruffins, The Iguanas, The Topcats, Swingaroux, Vince Vance and the Valiants, and Chris Ardoin. Open Mon.–Fri. 4 P.M.–midnight , and 2 P.M.–2 A.M. Sat.–Sun.

FISHING AND BOATING Surrounded by lakes and bayous, it's little wonder that New Orleans is a major gateway to spectacular fishing and boating. About 24 miles from the French Quarter, Barataria Bay, once the "kingdom" of the pirate Jean Lafitte and his brother Pierre, is a vast area of area of bayous, swamps, and marshes. The waters contain abundant catches of fish and shrimp. Most fishermen have no trouble taking their legal limit of speckled trout, redfish, or flounder. Follow the West Bank Expressway to the Lafitte Barataria exit and head south. Equally challenging adventures await where the Mississippi River meets the Gulf of Mexico. About 70 miles south of New Orleans down LA 23 is Venice, where anglers can launch from the Venice or Cypress Cove marinas. A number of outstanding fishing charter companies operate from these marinas, where you can find excellent ramps, tackle, fuel, beverages and snacks. Restaurants and lodgings are available for those who want to overnight in the area. Before choosing a charter company, talk to one of the licensed captains. Experienced guides can tell you the best seasons and hot spots for fishing inland and in the Gulf of Mexico. Non-Louisiana resident fishing licenses can be purchased for $5 online from the Louisiana Department of Wildlife and Fisheries at www.lawildlifelicense.com.

Bourgeois Fishing Charters (504-341-5614, www.neworleansfishing.com), Privateer Boulevard, Barataria. You pronounce his name Toe-Feel, and Capt. Theophile Bourgeois is one of Louisiana's top fishing charter operators. Fish for redfish and speckled trout in Gosier islands and Chandeleur islands, or try fly-fishing in the bayous with boats designed to float in five inches of water. The company also offers a crabbing excursion, a fishing and duck hunting adventure, bow fishing excursions in the bayous, and a sea plane adventure. Trips include gear, bait, ice fuel, drinks, sandwiches, and fish cleaning and packing. Accommodations for groups are available at Cajun Vista on the Bayou or Cajun Chalet.

Crescent City Fishing Charters (504-915-0392, www.lafittefishing.com), 2828 Laurie Lane, Marrero. Captain Scott Poche has owned and operated Crescent City Fishing Charters, about 35 minutes from downtown New Orleans, since 1996. He has been featured on several television shows on Louisiana Sportsman TV and The Outdoors Network, and featured in *Outdoor Life Magazine, Louisiana Sportsman Magazine*, and *Field and Stream.* Poche and his partner, Captain Todd Dufour, won the Inshore Fishing Association Redfish Tournament in April 2011. Inland fishing trips give you a chance to catch redfish, speckled trout, flounder, black drum, and bass.

A SHRINE, TOMB OF THE UNKNOWN SLAVE, AT ST. AUGUSTINE CHURCH IN TREME, HONORS ALL AFRICAN AMERICANS WHO SUFFERED INGLORIOUS DEATHS.
Louisiana Office of Tourism

Go Long Charters (225-252-5315, www.golongcharters.com), Captain Gray Long and his licensed guides operate out of Venice Marina and offer exciting offshore fishing adventures with 10–15 hours of fishing. On a day or night trip you will encounter different fishing techniques that could include trolling blue water grass rips for yellow-fin tuna, mahi mahi, wahoo, and marlin at floating offshore installations. Boats include top-of-the-line radar to get fishermen out to the fishing grounds and safely back to port. Bring ice chests, cameras, hats, sunglasses, food, and drinks. Lodging is available in the Venice area.

Jean Lafitte Fishing Charters (504-689-4120 or 877-689-4120, www.jean lafittecharters.com), 4915 Joan Marie Dr., Barataria. Captain E. J. Plaisance and his fishing guides have been fishing the bayous, marshes, and swamps of Barataria for more than 30 years. Guides are certified by the U.S. Coast Guard , and trained in first aid. The bay boats are in top condition and equipped with VHF radios, cellphones, and navigational devices. The charter includes ice, bait, tackle, rods, reels, and refreshments. Fish are cleaned and bagged at no additional charge. The company accommodates groups at its lodge and provides transportation to and from the airport or the French Quarter. Swamp tours are also offered. Call for seasonal prices.

L.A. Charters Guide Service (225-268-9616, www.lacharters.com), 11420 Mill Creek Lane, Slaughter. Captain Larry Averitt, who is U.S. Coast Guard licensed, has been fishing in the lower Mississippi River Delta for more than 20 years. On a typical day, the charter leaves the Venice Marina at safe light and returns between 1:30 and 2 P.M. Starting in October, fishing for redfish, and big trout is great, and it stays that way through December. Spring and summer, you'll find opportunities to catch the fish of a lifetime. The close-in oil rigs and wellheads in the Gulf of Mexico are teeming with fish. Charters include rods and reels, artificial lures, fuel, and ice for drinks.

MLC Fishing Charters (225-262-1082 or 225-939-3525, www.mlccharters.com), 7415 Frontier Dr., Greenwell Springs. Fish with Captain Dan Dix out of the Cypress Cove Marina at Venice and expect a memorable experience. You never know what you'll catch—redfish, speckled trout, drum, flounder, angel fish, Spanish mackerel, sail catfish, hardhead catfish, or king mackerel. Fishing starts before delight and the boat returns to the dock around 1 P.M. Make arrangements to overnight at the MLC Lodge, a nonsmoking place with a family feel, individual bedrooms, and a large great room. If you wish to prepare your own meals, a full kitchen is available.

Reel Peace Charters (504-858-8862, www.reelpeace.com), Venice Marina, Venice. With seven boats on the water, Reel Peace gets daily feedback from captains about fish patterns. Fishing out of Venice has the advantage of being close to the mouth of the Mississippi River and the Gulf of Mexico. Nutrients carried by the river attract every type of baitfish, which in turn attract every type of game fish. Expect to find tuna, wahoo, and swordfish. Trips start at safe light (around 6 A.M.) and the boats arrive back at Venice Marina in late afternoon. Lodging is available at Cajun Adventure Lodge in Lower Plaquemines Parish. Amenities include a restaurant, swimming pool, and hot tub.

GOLF Audubon Golf Course (504-212-5290, www.auduboninstitute.org), 6500 Magazine St., New Orleans. The beautiful 18-hole course has lush landscapes and four lagoons brimming with geese and ducks. Over 81 acres and 4,189 yards, the par-62 course has 12 par 3s, four par 4s, and two par 5s. Located in the Uptown-Garden District, across from the Audubon Zoo, the course is on the Audubon Golf Trail, and it's considered one of the top public courses in Louisiana. Call the pro shop at the number above to set up tee times. Open 11 A.M.–dusk Mon. and 7 A.M.–dusk Tues.–Sun.

Brechtel Memorial Park Municipal Golf Course (504-362-4761, www.thegolf courses.net), 3700 Behrman Place, New Orleans. Brechtel is an 18-hole municipal course across the Mississippi River in Algiers. The short layout has three sets of tee boxes. The course features 6,030 yards of golf from the longest tees for a par of 70. The course rating is 67.2 and it has a slope rating of 97. It's good practice for beginners and high-handicap golfers interested in working on their game. The greens are in poor condition and there are no carts. Open sunrise–sunset. Cost is $8, weekdays and $12, weekends. Rental carts cost $10.

✏ 🏌 **City Park Golf Course** (504-482-4888, www.cityparkgolf.com), 1040 Filmore Ave., New Orleans. With four sets of tees ranging from almost 5,740 yards at the tips to about 4,300 yards from the gold tees, City Park offers challenges for every levels of golfer. Water comes into play on eight of the holes, making club and shot selection important. The Practice offers a full-service driving range with 74 range stalls and two grass hitting areas. U.S. Golf Association rules govern all play. The park welcomes golfers with disabilities. The park accepts advance reservations 24 hours a day, seven days a week, for tee times up to eight days in advance via the Internet or seven days in advance by telephone. Rates are $20, Mon.–Thurs.; $22.50, Fri.; and $25, weekends and holidays. Twilight rates (starting at 2 P.M.) are $14 Mon.–Thurs.; $16.50, Fri.; and $19, weekends and holidays. Senior rates are $12, Mon.–Thurs.; $13, Fri.; and $15, weekends and holidays. Hours are 11 A.M.–dusk Mon. and 7 A.M.–dusk Tues.–Sun.

English Turn (504-391-8018, www.englishturn.com), 1 Clubhouse Dr., New Orleans. The Jack Nicklaus–designed par 72 championship course is a challenge to golfers of any skill level. Water comes into play on every hole. Giant sand and waste bunkers guard many holes, and the huge tiered greens are notoriously undulating. This course is the home of the 2006 Zurich Classic PGA Tournament. For tee times call the Golf Shop at the above number. Hours are 8 A.M.–dusk Mon. and 7 A.M.–dusk Fri.–Sun. Weekend green fees are $150.

Tournament Players Club of Louisiana (504-436-8721, 866-665-2872, www .tpc.com), 11001 Lapalco Blvd., Avondale. Located about 15 minutes from the French Quarter, TPC Louisiana is the home of Louisiana's only PGA event, the Zurich Classic. Working with the Australian pro Steve Elkington and the American golfer Kelly Gibson, a Louisiana native, the architect Pete Dye created this 7,600-yard, par-72 championship course. Open to the public, TPC Louisiana is on the state's Audubon Golf Trail. The TPC Grill features New Orleans cuisine at breakfast, lunch, and twilight. Call for tee times. Hours are 7 A.M.–6 P.M. daily. Fees are $119 daily.

HORSEBACK RIDING **Cascade Stables** (504-891-2246, www.cascadestables .net), 700 East Dr., New Orleans. Cascade's state-of-the-art riding facility opened in 2006 in Audubon Park. It stables its horses in 12-by-12 rubber-matted stalls, each equipped with cross ties, hay rack, automatic water, corner feed, and an automatic spray system. Boarding price is $700 a month. Amenities for riders include restroom, laundry service with washer and dryer, drink vending machine, and air-conditioned office with television. The stables offer a 2-mile guided ride around Audubon Park. The rides are held on the hour 1 P.M.–4 P.M. Fri.–Sun. Call for reservations age 8 and up. Cost is $40 for an hourlong ride.

Equest Stables (504-483-9398, www.equestfarm.com), 1001 Filmore Ave., New Orleans. Located in the north section of New Orleans City Park, Equest Farm provides a wholesome experience for the public to enjoy horses in the middle of a city. Options range from visiting horses at the stables to boarding a horse and competing in Hunters and Jumpers contests. The farm operates a riding school for ages 6 and up, with lessons Tues.–Sun. Field trips for groups include a short ride during which participants learn how to mount and dismount; how to stop, go forward, and steer; proper riding posture; and riding safety. Price is $50 base plus $15 if you ride a horse.

JOGGING AND WALKING Joggers and walkers will find a number of trails, parks, and neighborhoods where they can enjoy stretching their legs. It doesn't matter if you're staying in a downtown cityscape hotel or a bed & breakfast in a tree-shaded neighborhood, the Crescent City is a lovely place for a morning run or jog. You'll find the best spots listed under Green Spaces.

TENNIS You can play tennis in New Orleans year-round. The city has variety of courts: clay, hard, grass, indoors and outdoors. Seek out places where you can practice your best strokes or just enjoy the day.

Atkinson-Stern Tennis Center (504-658-3060, www.tennismetro.com), 4025 South Saratoga St., New Orleans. The historic Uptown complex was restored for $2.2 million four years after the devastation of Hurricane Katrina. The public tennis center, managed by the New Orleans Recreation Department, has nine clay courts, lights, and a pro shop. The facility includes high-mast lighting, chain-link fencing, main clubhouse, annex building, bathrooms, court benches, and siding. The site first opened in 1897 as a private club. It was named for the philanthropist Edgar Stern, and the name was expanded to honor Nehemiah Atkinson, a talented player and coach who mentored countless New Orleanians. Hours are 8 A.M.–3 P.M. Sat.–Sun. and 8 A.M.–8 P.M. Mon.–Thurs. Closed Friday.

Audubon Park Tennis Courts (504-895-1042, www.auduboninstitute.org/visit /audubon-park), 6320 Tchoupitoulas St., New Orleans. The tennis courts are a clay court facility located on the riverside of Magazine Street, off Henry Clay Avenue, with 10 courts for public play. Open 8 A.M.–7 P.M. Mon.–Thurs., 8 A.M.–6 P.M. Fri., and 8 A.M.–5 P.M. Sat.–Sun. Court cost is $10 per hour. Private lessons group lessons and clinics are available for juniors and adults.

City Park Tennis Courts (504-483-9383, www.neworleanscitypark.com), 951 Marconi Meadows, New Orleans. The City Park/Pepsi Tennis Center has 16 hard clay courts, a clubhouse, pro shop, restrooms, showers, and a meeting room. The facility is located off Marconi Boulevard between I-610 and Harrison Avenue. Open 7 A.M.–10 P.M. Mon.–Thurs. and 7 A.M.–8 P.M. Fri.–Sun. Cost is $10 per hour for hard courts and $13 per hour for clay courts; ball machine rental is $20.

Hilton Indoor Tennis Courts (504-556-3742, 504-584-3941, www.thehealth club.us), at the Health Club by Hilton, 2 Poydras St., New Orleans. These are the only indoor, air-conditioned courts in New Orleans with a professional Plexipave hard court surface. Court time can be scheduled up to three days in advance. Tennis instruction is available. Call for guest court fees or to schedule a court. Open 5:30 A.M.–7 P.M. Mon.–Fri. and 6 A.M.–9 P.M. Sat.–Sun.

TOURS New Orleans has numerous tours on just about every topic linked to the city. Visitors can take swamp tours, riverboat tours, cemetery tours, historical tours, garden tours, voodoo tours, plantation tours, and Mardi Gras tours. To find one to suit your tastes, contact the New Orleans Convention and Visitors Bureau (504-566-5011, www.neworleanscvb.com) or New Orleans Tourism Marketing (504-524-4784, www.neworleansonline.com) and request an Official New Orleans Visitors Guide. Once in the city, you will find information on tours at every major hotel. Listed here are just a few to give you an idea of what's available.

Bloody Mary Tours (504-523-7684, www.bloodymarystours.com), New Orleans. Take a walk around the city's cemetery with the folk historian and storyteller Mary

Millan, whose pen name is Bloody Mary, for an in-depth tour of the paranormal, voodoo, and New Orleans's haunted places. Tours are 5:30 P.M. Fri.–Sat. Cost is $20. Reservations suggested.

French Quarter AIA New Orleans Center for Design (504-526-8320, www .aianeworleans.org), 1000 St. Charles Ave., New Orleans. The American Institute of Architects offers walking tours, bus and van tours, bicycle tours, and history/ heritage tours of the French Quarter as well as city/neighborhood tours. Call for times and fees.

✆ 🎗 **Friends of the Cabildo** (504-523-3939, www.friendsofthecabildo.org), 523 St. Ann St., New Orleans. The volunteer group that supports the Louisiana State Museum system gives walking tours of the Quarter and the 1850 House Museum. Their Ghostly Galavant Weekend is a perfect way to observe Halloween in New Orleans. Tours at 10 A.M. and 1:30 P.M. Tues.–Sun. Cost is $15, adults; $10, students age 13–20. No tours on Monday or state holidays.

✆ **Gray Line Tours** (504-569-1401 or 800-233-2628, www.graylineneworleans .com), 400 Toulouse St., New Orleans. One of the city's major touring companies, Gray Line offers not only French Quarter and haunted tours, but history/heritage tours, swamp tours, night tours, city/neighborhood tours, culinary tours, cocktail tours, cemetery tours, multilingual tours, plantation tours, and personalized or specialized tours. The well-trained guides are friendly and informative and, when relevant, tastings are included. Call for times and prices.

Haunted History Tours (504-861-2727 or 888-644-6787, www.hauntedhistory tours.com), 723 St. Peter St., New Orleans. One of the more popular tours in the French Quarter and Garden District, the guides are mildly theatrical, historical

A PADDLEWHEELER AT NEW ORLEANS DOCK WAITS FOR PASSENGERS FOR A CRUISE ON THE MISSISSIPPI RIVER.

Cynthia V. Campbell

St. Bernard CVB

TOURISTS ON THE CREOLE QUEEN VISIT
CHALMETTE BATTLEFIELD, THE SITE OF THE
BATTLE OF NEW ORLEANS.

informative, and entertaining. See the tomb of the Voodoo Queen Marie Laveau, or choose a tour of the elegant antebellum homes in the Garden District. Tours offered daily and nightly.

Historic New Orleans Walking Tours (504-947-2120, www.tournew orleans.com), 2727 Prytania St., Suite 8, New Orleans. Explore New Orleans's oldest cemetery, St. Louis No. 1, with the author and preservationist Robert Florence and other top guides. Visit a functioning voodoo temple and other historic sites. A portion of the tour cost is dedicated to tomb restoration. Tours are at 10 A.M. and 1 P.M., Mon.–Sat., 10 A.M. only Sun., and begin at 334-B Royal St. in the courtyard of Royal Cafe Beignet. Arrive 15 minutes before tour time. Cost is $20, adults; $15, seniors and students; $7, children age 6–12; free for children younger than 6.

New Orleans Culinary History Tour (504-427-9595, www.noculinary tours.com), 4648 Lafayette St., New Orleans. Stroll through the French Quarter with a knowledgeable tour guide and learn the social history of food.

Old New Orleans Rum Distillery (504945-9400, www.neworleansrum .com), 2815 Frenchmen St., New Orleans. Visit the oldest premium rum distillery in the United States, where award-winning rums are made with Louisiana sugarcane molasses. An employee will show you the inner workings of the distillery and production process, and you can enjoy a complimentary rum cocktail. Tours offered noon, 2 and 4 P.M. Mon.–Fri., and 2 and 4 P.M. Sat.

Riverboat Tours: During the 1800s, steam-driven paddleboats were a major means of transportation on the Mississippi River, and you can still experience the river aboard a paddlewheeler today. Tours leave from the New Orleans riverfront area next to Woldenberg Park on a regular basis. Choose a tour that's best for your time and budget. Keep in mind that the licensed riverboat captains who operate the vessels follow strict river traffic regulations.

Creole Queen (504-529-4567 or 800-445-4109, www.creolequeen.com), 1 Poydras St. at Riverwalk Marketplace, New Orleans. The 1,000-passenger paddlewheeler offers daily excursions on the Mississippi River, evening dinner cruises, and private charters.

Friends of the Ferry (504-363-9090, www.friendsoftheferry.org), 525 Pelican St., New Orleans. The best free ride in New Orleans. Take the ferry at the foot of

Canal Street, and when it lands on the west bank of the Mississippi take a walk along the picturesque streets of Algiers Point. Ferry runs daily.

Steamboat Natchez (504-586-8777 or 800-233-2628, www.steamboatnatchez .com). The last authentic steamboat cruising the Mississippi River daily. Departing from the French Quarter, the boat offers two-hour Harbor Jazz Day Cruises and dinner cruises with the Dukes of Dixieland. Take advantage of the optional buffet, a steam calliope, and a visit to the engine room.

Swamp Tours: While swamp tours are given throughout the year, opportunities to see animals and birds vary with weather and season. Spring is wonderful, with flowers blooming and nesting period for waterfowl begins. Summer brings out the alligators and big birds like the white egret and great blue heron.

Cajun Critters Swamp Tours (504- 347-0962, or 800-575-5578, www.cajun swamptour.com), 363 Louisiana St., Westwego. Situated just off the Westbank Expressway, this company provides exciting tours in Jefferson Parish.

Cajun Pride Tours (504-467-0758, 800-467-0758, www.cajunpridetours.com), 110 Frenier Rd., LaPlace. A ride through Manchac Swamp in a privately owned wildlife refuge gives you an opportunity to view swamps with an informed guide.

Jean Lafitte Swamp and Airboat Tours (504-587-1719, 800-445-4109, www .jeanlafitteswamptour.com), 6601 Leo Kerner Parkway, Marrero. Located about 25 minutes from downtown New Orleans, this company explores back country along meandering bayous in the Barataria-Terrebonne Estuary. The 1 hour and 45 minute boat tour introduces you to alligators, snakes, egrets, and other critters. Bring a camera. The airboat tour takes about two hours. Tours are at 10 A.M. and 2 P.M. Children younger than age 8 are not allowed.

✳ Lodging

New Orleans is a major U.S tourist destination. Accommodations, including luxury and budget hotels, are comparable to those in Washington, D.C., Miami, or Houston. During special events, such as Mardi Gras, Jazz Fest, and major sports weekends, most hotels require a two- or three-night minimum. Rates vary by season, and they are highest during major event weekends. Low season is late summer, when south Louisiana's climate is hot and muggy. Make reservations early. Ask about special rates for organizations such as AAA, and look for specials on the Internet. Most accommodations are located in the city's tourist and business areas, including the French Quarter, Central Business District, Warehouse/Arts district near the Convention Center, and along St.

Charles Avenue. Some are found near the Louis Armstrong International Airport, Metairie suburbs, and across the Mississippi River in Gretna and Westwego. It's always wise to choose your lodging in the area where you plan to spend the most time. The hotels listed here were selected for their ambience, convenient location, and reputation for outstanding service.

Astor Crowne Plaza (504-962-0500, 888-696-4806, www.astorneworleans .com), Bourbon St., New Orleans. The Crown Plaza is at one of the main gateways into the French Quarter as well as Canal Street. Guest rooms feature traditional furnishings and plenty of amenities like flat-screen TV. Executive guests receive a daily complimentary continental breakfast and complimentary hors d'oeuvres in the evening. The hotel is home to Dickie Brennan's Bourbon House, which has gained a local following for its seafood and steak menu. The bourbon bar is a good place to gather and rub shoulders with fellow travelers as well as locals. Football packages are available for Saints home games. Moderate–expensive.

Columns Hotel (504-899-9308 or 800-445-9308, www.thecolumns.com), 3811 St. Charles Ave., New Orleans. Built in 1883 and listed in the National Register of Historic Places, the Columns is in the beautiful Garden District. It is the only remaining example of a large group of Italianate houses designed by the architect Thomas Sully in the late 1880s. Restored to its late Victorian elegance, the Columns features rooms with Victorian furnishings and a complimentary Southern breakfast and daily newspaper. Moderate.

(ꜛ) **Cornstalk Hotel** (504-523-1515, 800-759-6112, www.cornstalkhotel .com), 915 Royal St., New Orleans. The French Quarter hotel sits behind the often photographed "cornstalk" cast iron fence commissioned and erected in 1856. People stop to study its ornate design and the ripe ears of corn on flourishing stalks. Fourteen guest rooms are filled with antiques and period furniture. Complimentary high-speed Wi-Fi and local phone calls. Expensive.

Dauphine Orleans (504-586-1800, 800-521-7111, www.dauphineorleans .com), 415 Dauphine St., New Orleans. This site of this French Quarter hotel has been in use since 1775. The property contains the Audubon Cottage, where John James Audubon painted some of his *Birds of America* series and which now serves as a main meeting room. One corner, May Baily's Place, was once one of the better-known bordellos in the red-light district. Fourteen rooms, some of them

suites, across Dauphine Street were built in 1834 as a town home, and renovations revealed original brick walls and wooden posts. The continental breakfast includes fresh fruit and baked goodies. There's a palm-filled courtyard with a saltwater pool and an on-site garage. Moderate.

Embassy Suites-Arts District (504-525-1993 or 800-362-2779, www.new orleans.embassysuites.com), 315 Julia St., New Orleans. Featuring contemporary furnishings, a complimentary breakfast, and a restaurant on-site, the hotel is conveniently located near the Ernest N. Morial Convention Center, the Riverwalk Shopping Center, Contemporary Arts Center, and National World War II Museum. Guest room amenities include a small kitchen with a microwave and a refrigerator. Mulate's and Emeril's restaurants are within walking distance. Moderate.

Hampton Inn Garden District (504-899-9990 or 800-426-7866, www.new orleanshamptoninns.com), 3626 St. Charles Ave., New Orleans. The inn on the St. Charles streetcar line is only minutes from Tulane University, Loyola University, and the Audubon Zoo. In nonsuites, rooms feature a mini-fridge, microwave, and coffee maker. Guests receive complimentary hot breakfast buffet, high-speed Internet access, and free parking Moderate–expensive.

Harrah's New Orleans Hotel (504-533-6000, or 800- 847-5299, www .harrahsneworleans.com), 228 Poydras St., New Orleans. Just blocks from the French Quarter, the hotel has 450 oversized, luxurious guest rooms and suites, many with great views of the Mississippi River and the New Orleans skyline. A side entrance opens to Fulton Street, often the setting for outdoor concerts, fan sports events, and Mardi Gras and Christmas celebrations. Take the tunnel to enter Harrah's Casino for gaming and an array of excellent restaurants. Expensive.

Hilton New Orleans Riverside (504-556-3712 or 800-445-8667, www.new orleans.hilton.com), 2 Poydras St., New Orleans. One of New Orleans's grandest hotels, the Hilton Riverside offers full-service luxury. Start the day with coffee and breakfast in the lobby. Later, relax in the Spirits Bar, followed by dinner in Dragon's Seafood Restaurant. All newly renovated rooms feature flat-screen TVs, Hilton Sweet Dreams bedding, and efficient work stations. Enjoy the huge Health Club by Hilton, with indoor tennis, racquetball, full weight training equipment, and more. Best of all, the Riverwalk Marketplace, with some 100 stores, is within steps of the lobby. Harrah's Casino, the Aquarium of the Americas, the Insectarium, Imax theater, and the French Quarter are all a short walk from the front door. Moderate–expensive.

Hotel Monteleone (504-523-3341 or 800 or 535-9595, www.hotel monteleone.com), 214 Royal St., New Orleans. This grande dame of a hotel is a city landmark. Step outside for a walk along Royal Street, known for its fabulous antiques shops, estate jewelry, Oriental rugs, chandeliers, and antiquities. A member of Historic Hotels of America, the Monteleone is famous for, among other things, its Carousel Bar, where you can sit and enjoy a martini or sazerac (the city's official cocktail) while the bar slowly circles. The hotel is rich in stories, including tales of ghosts and celebrity guests. There are two excellent restaurants. You never know who you're going to

MIXOLOGISTS SHOW OFF THEIR INNOVATIONS AT TALES OF THE COCKTAIL IN THE MONTELEONE HOTEL IN NEW ORLEANS.

Cynthia V. Campbell

Louisiana Northshore

CHEF JOHN BESH SELECTS HERBS FROM HIS GARDEN AT LA PROVENCE RESTAURANT IN LACOMBE.

bump into coming in and out of the Monteleone. Expensive.

Hyatt Regency (504-561-1234, www .neworleanshyatt.com), 601 Loyola St., New Orleans. Experience the rebirth of one of the city's popular hotels. Very much a part of the city scene for more than 30 years, the hotel was badly damaged by Hurricane Katrina. Following a dramatic renovation, it is once again accepting reservations and welcoming guests who want to relax and play in the heart of the city. Adjacent to the newly named Mercedes-Benz Superdome and New Orleans Arena, the hotel is prepared to greet visitors to championship games including the 2013 Super Bowl. Facilities include Vitascope Hall, a media and sports bar,

and Borgne, John Besh's newest restaurant. Moderate–expensive.

International House (504-553-9550 or 800-633-5770, www.ihhotel.com), 221 Camp St., New Orleans. The boutique hotel is in the Central Business District, two blocks from Canal Street, in a Beaux-Arts building renovated in 2007 by L. M. Pagano, designer for Nicholas Cage and Johnny Depp. You'll see work by local artists in the hotel's mix of objects—old, new, bought, and found. Guest rooms have a contemporary feel with an elegant and subtle décor. Services include a complimentary morning newspaper and continental breakfast. Enjoy the glow of candlelight in the Loa bar and the Basque-influenced cuisine in Rambla restaurant. Moderate–expensive.

New Orleans Marriott (504-581-1000, www.marriott.com), 555 Canal St., New Orleans. Within easy walk of the French Quarter and other downtown attractions, the Marriott is a 41-story hotel with panoramic views of the Mississippi River and the city skyline. Guest rooms feature plush bedding and high-speed Internet access. Premiere suites are on the concierge level. There are two heated pools (one for children), a large gym, a Starbucks, a gift shop, and bar. Check out the high-tech, user-friendly elevators.

Omni Royal Orleans (504-527-0006 or 800-843-6664, www.omnihotels .com), 621 St Louis St., New Orleans. Designed after the historic, fashionable St. Louis Hotel, the Royal Orleans is one of the favorites of locals. Guest rooms feature 19th-century New Orleans décor and some have private balconies overlooking Royal and St. Louis streets. There's a rooftop pool, observation deck and fitness center. The hotel's graceful lobby is a popular meeting place for locals as well as guests. The Rib Room restaurant is known for exceptional cuisine and service. Moderate–expensive.

Le Pavillon Hotel (504-581-3111 or 800-535-9095, www.lepavillon.com), 833 Poydras St., New Orleans. The historic hotel in the Central Business District features a grand lobby with crystal chandeliers and marble railings from the lobby of the Grand Hotel in Paris. Amenities include in-room, high-speed Internet, a fitness center, swimming pool, and nightly peanut butter and jelly sandwiches served with cold beverages in the lobby. Moderate–expensive.

Place d'Armes Hotel (504-524-4531 or 800-366-2743, www.placedarmes .com), 625 St. Ann St., New Orleans. You can enjoy delightful courtyard settings at this boutique French Quarter hotel. Guest rooms, furnished with antiques reproductions, are set in eight historic restored townhouses and equipped with the latest amenities, including high-speed Internet. Enjoy the tropical courtyards with fountains and pool. A complimentary continental breakfast is served daily.

Le Richelieu (504-529-2492 or 800-535-9653, www.lerichelieuhotel.com), 234 Chartres St., New Orleans. Situated in a quiet section of the French Quarter, this European-style hotel is made up of two historic buildings built 1845–1902. All rooms are decorated with fine furnishings and brass ceiling fans. Breakfast is served all day in the Terrace Cafe and the lounge is open 7 A.M.–midnight. Moderate.

Ritz-Carlton, New Orleans (504-524-1331 or 800-241-3333, www.ritz carlton.com), 921 Canal St., New Orleans. This luxury hotel pampers its guests. Rooms are plush and immaculate. The club level is a hotel within a hotel, and the Davenport Lounge has great jazz and food. Expensive–very expensive.

Roosevelt Hotel (504-648-1200 or 800-925-3673, www.therooseveltnew orleans.com), 123 Baronne St., New Orleans. Enter the block-long canopied lobby of columns and crystal chandeliers, and you know this is a *grand* hotel. A $145 million restoration returned the historic Roosevelt to its premier position. Now on par with the Waldorf Astoria Collection, the hotel features luxurious guest rooms and Dine in Domenica, created by award-winning chef John Besh. The Sazerac Bar, flanked by 1930s murals, is the place to linger over well-crafted drinks. Just steps away are the Sazerac Restaurant and Teddy's Cafe, a coffee and sweets shop offering cafe au lait and more. Plan for the champagne Jazz Sunday Brunch in the Blue Room, where Louis Armstrong, Ray Charles, and Frank Sinatra once performed. Expensive–very expensive.

Royal Sonesta Hotel (504-586-0300 or 800-766-3782, www.royalsonesta no.com), 300 Bourbon St., New Orleans. While the Royal Sonesta fronts the bustling Bourbon Street and the lobby is abuzz at all hours, you'll find the guest rooms spacious, comfortable, and quiet. Many overlook the large tropical courtyard; others feature cast-iron balconies. Pop into the Desire Seafood and Oyster Bar bistro overlooking Bourbon Street, especially for a New Orleans–style breakfast. For some of the best entertainment in town, plan an evening in Irvin Mayfield's Jazz Playhouse. Friday is Burlesque night.

Soniat House (504-522-0570 or 800-544-8808, www.soniathouse.com), 1133 Chartres St., New Orleans. This small luxury hotel is in the quiet residential section of the French Quarter. It is comprised of three elegant, historic guesthouses with secluded courtyards. Guest rooms are filled with period antiques and luxury fabrics. Wake up to homemade biscuits, Louisiana strawberry preserves, and hot, French roast coffee. A member of the Small Luxury Hotels of the World. Expensive–very expensive.

Windsor Court (504-523-6000 or 800-403-4945, www.windsorcourthotel.com), 300 Gravier St., New Orleans. Consistently ranked one of the top hotels in the United States, the Windsor Court treats every guest as royalty. More than 80 percent of the guest rooms are spacious suites. The luxury hotel boasts stunning views of the Mississippi and the city skyline. Situated in the Central Business District, it's within walking distance of the French Quarter and the Mississippi River. The Grill Room, a four-star restaurant, serves breakfast, lunch, and dinner, and tea is served in Le Salon in the afternoon. Relax in the Polo Club Lounge with champagne, cognac, and choice tidbits like crab cakes and truffle fries. Also take time to view the hotel's world-class art collection. Expensive–very expensive.

BED & BREAKFASTS Many New Orleans bed & breakfasts are found in the French Quarter and neighborhoods accessible by streetcar. Most serve breakfast, but a few have found that guests prefer to explore the city's many restaurants instead. Rates will vary according to seasons and special events. Ask if children and/or pets are welcomed. Also check on parking availability.

1896 O'Malley House (866-226-1896 or 504-488-58-96, www.1896omalley house.com), 120 South Pierce St., New Orleans. Every room in this Colonial Revival house one block from Canal Street features a private bath, and most have Jacuzzi tubs. Amenities include free wireless DSL, free snacks,

and free wine and beer. A generous New Orleans breakfast is served daily. Moderate.

Ashtons New Orleans Bed and Breakfast (800-725-4131, 504-942-7048, www.ashtonsbb.com), 2023 Esplanade Ave., New Orleans. Restored after Hurricane Katrina, the charming guesthouse has eight guestrooms decorated with attractive furnishings and chandeliers. Rooms have wooden floors. Guests are served full breakfasts, with goodies such as bananas Foster waffles and sweet-potato stuffed French toast. Free, secure parking. Moderate.

Avenue Inn Bed and Breakfast (504-269-2640 or 800-490-8542, www.avenueinnbb.com), 4125 St. Charles Ave., New Orleans. A wonderful 1891 Queen Anne mansion, the inn features rooms with high ceilings and a mix of period and eclectic furniture. Amenities include private baths, irons, hair dryers, data ports, and cable TV. A delicious breakfast is served in the dining room or on the Creole-style veranda (weather permitting). Avenue Inn was named one of the Best of the South in the 2010-2011 Best of BedandBreakfast.com awards. Moderate.

Chimes (504-899-2621 or 504-453-2183, www.chimesneworleans.com), 1146 Constantinople St., New Orleans. Situated in the Uptown/Garden District neighborhood, the Chimes is a delightful inn with five rooms, all with private entrances, private baths, and French doors opening on a tropical courtyard. Each room has a drip coffeemaker and ceramic cups. A laundry room is available and there is a laptop computer for your use. Guests are served a lavish breakfast with French breads and pastries baked daily, along with Louisiana's Community Coffee and assorted loose teas. The hosts are knowledgeable about the city. They offer guests a laminated local map to use during their stay, and a local restaurant guide with printed directions. Moderate.

Dive Inn (504-895-6555 or 888-788-3483, www.thediveinn.com), 4417 Dryades St., New Orleans. This is a truly unusual B&B, with a laid-back, funky atmosphere. In 1908, the Mexican consul to New Orleans bought the property with two homes on Napoleon Avenue. He tore down the Victorian double to make way for a gymnasium for his family. In 1927, a ceramic tile pool was constructed within a domed structure. The current owner has turned this unusual structure into a zany work of art. Enjoy the heated indoor pool or two hot tubs. Breakfast is not served. There are no telephones and no televisions in the rooms, though there is a TV at the bar. This is a clothing-optional guest house for mature, sensible adults. Inexpensive–moderate

Edgar Degas House (504-821-5009 or 800-755-6730, www.degashouse.com), 2306 Esplanade Ave., New Orleans. Dating from the 1850s, this house was home to French impressionist Edgar Degas during his visit with New Orleans's relatives 1872–1873. The artist kept every portrait of his family that he painted in this house until the day he died. Guests experience the legendary lifestyle of French Creole families. Rooms and suites are named for members of the Musson-Degas family. A Creole breakfast is served daily. Separate guided tours are conducted by Degas' great-grand-niece by appointment only. Moderate–expensive.

& **Elysian Fields Inn** (504-948-9420 or 866- 948-9420, www.elysianfieldsinn.com), 930 Elysian Fields Ave., New Orleans. Located in the Fau-

bourg Marigny district, the restored 1860s Greek Revival Mansion has eight guestrooms, each featuring Italian marble private bathrooms, most with Jacuzzi tubs. Rooms are handicapped accessible. There's an elevator and free, off-street parking. Breakfast is served daily. Moderate.

Grand Victorian Bed & Breakfast (504-895-1104 or 800 or 977-0008, www.gvbb.com), 2727 St. Charles Ave., New Orleans. Built in the 1890s by the architect Thomas Sully, this dramatic mansion has been lovingly restored to its former glory. The Garden District/Uptown inn was selected as a 2011 Fodor's Choice property. Each room features a full bath, computer port, and charming period furnishings. Sit in the glamorous living room with a cup of coffee and gaze out the windows as the St. Charles streetcar passes by. Moderate–expensive.

Hubbard Mansion (504- 897-3535, www.hubbardmansion.com), 3535 St. Charles Ave., New Orleans. The elegant Greek Revival home has five guest rooms with suite combinations. All rooms are furnished with period antiques and family heirlooms. The décor reflects the deep ruby shades favored by Victorians. The deluxe continental breakfast includes an assortment of delicious muffins, croissants, bagels, pastries, and yogurt along with a fresh fruit medley. Hosts offer tips on New Orleans and gladly assist in making your New Orleans visit special. Moderate.

Marigny Manor House (504-943-7826, www.marignymanorhouse.com), 2125 North Rampart St., New Orleans. The Greek Revival–style cottage was built in 1848 by William Daniel as a gift to his bride. Situated in the Faubourg Marigny neighborhood, it is five blocks from the French Quarter. Enjoy architectural details, classic furnishings, and a rear courtyard with fountains. An expanded continental breakfast is served weekdays. Friday, Saturday and Sunday, guests receive a full deluxe Southern breakfast, including upside-down pancakes and buttermilk biscuits. Moderate.

CAMPGROUNDS Since New Orleans is a major urban center, most campgrounds are situated in shaded areas around the perimeter of the city. We recommend checking the Louisiana Campground Owners booklet available at welcome centers and parks or the website www.camping louisiana.com.

✐ ↭ **Bayou Segnette State Park** (504-736-7140 or 888-677-2296). Situated on the west side of the Mississippi River, the park is accessible from I-10 via the Huey P. Long Bridge. It offers a swimming pool and wave pool in summer, a boat launch, and fishing. The campground area has 98 premium campsites with water and electrical hookup. For reservations, 866-226-7652. Inexpensive.

French Quarter RV Resort (504-586-3000, www.fqrv.com/location .html), 565 Crozat St., New Orleans. Situated off I-10 within blocks of the French Quarter, the urban campground maintains 24-hour, on-site management and security. Each of 52 paved sites offers electric, hardwire, and wireless Internet access, live telephone line, satellite TV, city water and sewer. The clubhouse features fitness and laundry rooms, four private baths with shower, and a business office. The courtyard has a saltwater pool, a gazebo with a bar, and a gas BBQ. Rates vary according to season and special events may require a three- or four-night minimum stay. Inexpensive.

🦅 **New Orleans East Kampground** (800-562-2128), 56009 LA 433 (Old Spanish Trail), Slidell. The quiet, safe campground has 130 sites with full hook-up and level pull through sites. Amenities include a pool, laundry, gas, store, and dog run. Rental cars are available and there's a free shuttle to the French Quarter. Inexpensive.

✐ **New Orleans West KOA** (800-562-5110 or 504-467-1792), 1129 Jefferson Hwy., River Ridge. This is the Kampgrounds of America (KOA) affiliate site closest to the French Quarter. It's situated off Williams Boulevard and near the Louis Armstrong International Airport. There are 130 full hookup sites. Amenities include a pool, laundry, gas, and a shuttle to the French Quarter. Pets are allowed, but they must be kept on a leash no longer than 6 feet when outside your vehicle. Dogs are not allowed in the tent sites. Inexpensive.

((ᵠ)) **Pontchartrain Landing** (877-376-7850, www.pontchartrainlanding.com), 6001 France Rd., New Orleans. New Orleans's premier waterfront park, the campground is located just off I-10 on the navigational canal to Lake Pontchartrain. There are picnic tables at every site, free cable and Wi-Fi, waterfall Jacuzzi, pool, showers, laundry, camp store, dog run, and 24-hour security. Inexpensive.

✐ 🐾 **St. Bernard State Park** (1-877-376-7850), 501 St. Bernard Parkway, Braithwaite. Camp near the Mississippi River in a semi-tropical park with picnic tables, grills, and a swimming pool in summer. There are 51 improved campsites with full hookup. Prices vary. Day-use entrance is $1 per person, free to age 62 and older and children 12 and under. Inexpensive.

✳ Where to Eat

With more than 1,200 restaurants and an entire community of award-winning chefs, the question in New Orleans is not so much where to eat, but what you want to eat. Keep in mind, there are almost no bad restaurants in the city. If a new cafe or restaurant isn't up to the locals' very high standards of well-prepared, savory food, it rarely survives more than three or four months. You'll find amazingly great restaurants not only along the tourist corridors, but everywhere in the city. Selecting a restaurant depends on personal taste. The food writer Tom Fitzmorris writes that deliciousness plays the most important role. In this city, you can dine in some of the world's most glamorous restaurants or eat very well indeed in tiny neighborhood cafes. Of all cities in the world, this is one where you should "Dine Out" at least once to experience the incredible food and service. The lists here are a selection of long-established and new favorites patronized by expert cooks and foodies. When in doubt, just follow your nose. Good resources: www.nomenu.com, www.nola.com, and www.neworleansonline.com.

EATING OUT Acme Oyster House (504-522-5973, www.acmeoyster.com), 724 Iberville, New Orleans. The cafe opened at this address in 1924, and it's

A BOX OF BLUE CRABS FROM VIOLET AWAIT THE CHEF'S POT.

Louisiana Office of Tourism

been shucking oysters ever since. People crowd into the small spot for fresh raw oysters, big seafood po-boys on fresh French bread, gumbo, red beans and rice, coleslaw, and potato salad. Eat under neon lights at tables with red-checkered cloths and soak up the atmosphere. Inexpensive–moderate.

Blue Plate Cafe (504-309-9500), 1330 Prytania St, New Orleans. Not far from Lee Circle in the Lower Garden District, the cafe serves freshly made Southern cooking. Breakfasts are especially great, including crawfish cakes and eggs, omelets, and blueberry *pain perdu*. The mostly Creole lunch menu includes some Mexican and Asian dishes, hamburgers, and sandwiches. This is an old corner cafe in a small hotel. It's a good place for families traveling with children. Inexpensive.

Cafe Degas (504-945-5635, www.cafedegas.com), 3127 Esplanade, New Orleans. This French bistro near the New Orleans Museum of Art was named after Edgar Degas, who visited New Orleans in 1872 and stayed for a short time down the street at 2306 Esplanade. The tiny cafe, basically an open-air patio that's enclosed in winter, has a reputation for excellent cuisine made with fresh ingredients. You may have to wait in the petite bar or on the front steps for a table, but it's worth it. Moderate–expensive.

Cafe Nino (504-865-9200), 1519 South Carrollton Ave., New Orleans. This Italian cafe in the Riverbend District has a New Orleans dive atmosphere, but it's a good place for a quick Italian meal. The thin-crust pizza is some of the best in town and the Philly cheese steak sandwich is tops. The menu includes basic pasta dishes and daily specials. Order at the counter, take a tray with a plastic plate and utensils and enjoy. You may get a chance to chat a bit with the owner,

Nino Bongiorno, a native of Sicily. Inexpensive–moderate.

✍ **Central Grocery** (504-523-1620), 923 Decatur St., New Orleans. This is not really a cafe, but a small old-fashioned Italian-American grocery store with a sandwich counter. It's near Jackson Square in the French Quarter. It's famous as the home of the *muffaletta* sandwich invented by Salvatore Lupo to feed Sicilian farmers who trucked into the city to sell their produce at the Farmer's Market. The round loaf of seeded bread is filled with layers of ham, salami, provolone, and Swiss cheese, with a marinated olive salad mixture. You can buy one to eat in or take out, or you can take home containers of the olive salad that gives the huge sandwich its distinctive flavor. Inexpensive.

✍ ❦ **Courtyard Cafe at NOMA** (504-488-2631, www.noma.org), 317 City Park Ave., New Orleans. A delightful spot for breakfast or lunch is this Ralph Brennan restaurant in the New Orleans Museum of Art. Nestled inside the museum, where windows overlook winding lagoons, the cafe tempts you with crisp salads, warm paninis, and flatbread pizzas. The menu includes dishes borrowed from Brennan's restaurants, including Ralph's on the Park, and seafood gumbo from Red Fish Grill. Moderate.

Irish House (504-595-6755, www.the irishhouseneworleans.com), 1432 St. Charles Ave., New Orleans. Matt Murphy, previously executive chef at the Ritz-Carlton, designed his new restaurant to mimic the feel of places in his native Dublin. You'll find hearty pub grub like shepherd's pie and fish and chips on the lunch and bar menu, but dinner features more sophisticated fare, such as braised lamb shanks with apple brandy and shrimp and artichoke risotto with wild mushrooms. Break-

fast, served all day, includes a traditional Irish breakfast of eggs, Irish bacon sausage, black and white puddings (blood and oatmeal sausages), beans, and tomatoes. Murphy's soda bread is delicious. Sure, and if it's oatmeal you like, then try the Irish steel-cut to start your day. Moderate–expensive.

DINING OUT Antoine's (504-581-4422, www.antoines.com), 713 St. Louis St., New Orleans. The historic restaurant opened in 1840 and is still managed by descendants of its founder, Antoine Alciatore. Hurricane Katrina severely damaged the oldest part of the restaurant, but it has returned with new culinary treats. This is an Old New Orleans place with its own customs. Regular patrons establish a rapport here, and usually they have a regular waiter. Start by recognizing your server's knowledge of the menu. The light lunch special is a good place to begin. If you're planning on getting the famed Baked Alaska for dessert, order it at the beginning of your meal. Suggestions include oysters Rockefeller or Bienville and chicken Rochambeau. Ask about a tour of the 14 famous dining rooms. The Hermes Bar offers live music Friday and Saturday, 9:30 P.M.–midnight. Expensive–very expensive.

Arnaud's (504-523-5433, www.arnauds restaurant.com), 813 Bienville, New Orleans. French-Creole style of cooking remains the strong suit at Arnaud's, which was founded in 1918 by "Count" Arnaud Cazenave. The family stays active in the management. You *must* dine in the room with tiled floors, tin ceiling, ancient overhead fans, and beveled glass windows. Seafood dishes are the best, including shrimp Arnaud, oysters Bienville, and speckled trout amandine. Be sure to see the exhibit of elaborate Mardi Gras costumes upstairs. Expensive–very expensive.

Brennan's (504-525-9711, www.brennansneworleans.com), 417 Royal St., New Orleans. Established in 1946, Brennan's remains a New Orleans landmark restaurant. For dinner, try Gulf shrimp in a traditional Creole sauce over rice. The restaurant is famous for its elaborate breakfast menu, including eggs Hussarde (poached eggs with rusks, bacon, and wine sauce, topped with Hollandaise) and bananas Foster, cooked at your table, set aflame, and served with a flourish. Expensive–very expensive.

Cafe Adelaide (504-595-3305, www.cafeadelaide.com), 300 Poydras St., New Orleans. Situated in Loews New Orleans Hotel, this has become a local favorite. The cafe and its Swizzle Stick Bar were inspired the Brennan family's Aunt Adelaide and her pursuit of the good life.

✐ **Camellia Grill** (504-309-2679, www.camelliagrill.net), 626 South Carrollton Ave., New Orleans. The diner is a beloved landmark to hundreds who went to college or spent their dating years in the Big Easy. The university crowd (Loyola, Tulane, etc.) still hangs out here. You can order breakfast all day. Go for the big hamburgers and sandwiches loaded with meats and cheeses. A new owner brought the cafe back to life after Hurricane Katrina, and it's as popular as ever. The waiters are famous for their personalities and the way they hand out cloth napkins with a grand flourish. Open all afternoon and after midnight. Open Sunday and Monday for lunch and dinner. Bring the kids and grandparents. A second location is now in the French Quarter at 540 Chartres St.

Ciro's Cote Sud (504-866-9551, www.cotesudrestaurant.com), 7918 Maple St., New Orleans. The casual French bistro attracts a mix of college students and Riverbend District residents. The menu includes mussels, steak, pasta with seafood, and charcuterie and cheese plates. The surprise is the delicious thin-crust pizza with a sturdy garlic and herb sauce and excellent toppings. Try the tarte tatin a la mode for dessert. Inexpensive–moderate.

Cochon (504-588-2123, www.cochonrestaurant.com), 930 Tchoupitoulas St., New Orleans. Couchon in the Warehouse District features a menu built around a Cajun butcher shop. The restaurant cures and smokes its own meats and sausages, including andouille and boudin. The menu includes dishes inspired by Acadian farm life, such as chicken and andouille gumbo, oyster and meat pie, rabbit and dumplings, and fried pig ears with cane syrup mustard. The dining room is a former factory with a brick wall, tall ceilings, and an open kitchen. Next door, Cochon Butcher (www.coochonbutcher.com) specializes in sandwiches, including pastrami on rye and a Carolina-style classic Cuban. Choose from an eclectic list of wines that pair well with sausages and small plates. The sandwich shop is popular with the business lunch crowd. Moderate.

Commander's Palace (504-899-8221, www.commanderspalace.com), 1403 Washington Ave., New Orleans. One of the city's icons, Commander's is a big restaurant in a Victorian mansion with a variety of rooms. The upstairs Garden Room is the most popular among locals. The menu, under the direction of chef Tory McPhail, is superb. Start with crawfish and dumplings or the gumbo du jour, then perhaps the grilled-seared Gulf fish. Lunch is always a bargain at Commander's. Expensive–very expensive.

Emeril's (504-528-9393, www.emerils
.com), 800 Tchoupitoulas St., New
Orleans. Emeril Lagasse's flagship
restaurant in a renovated pharmacy
warehouse reflects the feel of the Arts
District. Entrees are huge and the
introduction of small plates is a pleasure for those who believe that less is
more. However, check out the maple-
rosemary glazed chicken breast and
saffron-chili dusted jumbo shrimp
entrees. Don't pass up desserts, including Emeril's banana crème pie and the
chocolate chip–blackberry crumble tart
with coffee. Expensive–very expensive.

Galatoire's Restaurant (504-525-
2021, www.galatoires.com), 209 Bourbon St., New Orleans. Located in the
French Quarter, the restaurant dishes
up excellent French Creole dishes with
a true New Orleans attitude. Run by
fourth-generation proprietors, it's popular with locals, especially on Fridays
when they gather to relax and catch up
on the day's gossip. Jackets are
required nightly and all day Sunday.
An absolute must: the yummy soufflé
potatoes and Louisiana seafood eggplant cake. Expensive–very expensive.

Gott Gourmet Cafe (504-373-6579,
www.gottgourmetcafe.com), 3100
Magazine, New Orleans. This Uptown
dining spot appeals to food lovers who
want something beyond the typical
restaurant fare. David Gotter, the
owner and chef, has created a menu
featuring special salads and sandwiches, soups, and gourmet burgers.
The curry chicken salad is loaded with
celery, cashews, and fresh greens.
Seafood lovers can try the fried oyster
and baby spinach salad. The Loaded
Gumbo, a complete meal, is topped
with a scoop of potato salad. A small
bar is tucked into the corner of this
colorful, artistic cafe. Drop by on Saturday or Sunday for a hearty breakfast.
Moderate.

Meson 923 (504-523-9200, www
.meson923.com), 923 South Peters St.,
New Orleans. Near the World War II
Museum in the Warehouse/Arts District, the contemporary restaurant
opened in 2010 and is already getting
accolades. It's become popular with
fashionable 20-somethings. Sophisticated diners will enjoy the grilled quail
appetizer and the slow-roasted duck
breast entrée. Expensive.

Mother's (504-523-9656, www
.mothersrestaurant.net), 401 Poydras,
New Orleans. The Mother's crowd is
made up of just about everyone who's
really hungry. The cafe opened in 1938
on Restaurant Row to serve po-boys to
longshoremen and laborers, newspaper
reporters, and attorneys. During World
War II, it was a U.S. Marine Corps
hangout. Today, you find locals rubbing
elbows with visitors, politicians, and
celebrities. The huge menu runs from
traditional New Orleans Creole and
Cajun dishes, seafood platters, and red
beans and rice, to daily specials. Breakfast is served all day. Longshoremen
and everyone else still line up for the
po-boys. Inexpensive.

Palace Cafe (504-523-1661, www
.palacecafe.com), 605 Canal St., New
Orleans. Owned and operated by
Dickie Brennan, this delightful restaurant is housed in the Werlein Building,
formerly the nation's oldest family-
owned retail music chain. Ask the
server for the special cocktail of the
day, and pair it with a small plate of
BLT wraps or the crabmeat cheese-
cake. For dinner, try the andouille-
crusted fish or fried softshell crab in
season. Ask to be seated upstairs at a
table by tall windows overlooking
Canal Street. Expensive.

Redemption (504-309-3570, www
.redemption-nola.com), 3835 Iberville
St., New Orleans The Mid-City restaurant (formerly Christians) is housed in

an 1914 historic church "redeemed" after Hurricane Katrina. The pink structure, complete with steeple, features high ceilings and stained glass to add to the romantic setting. The culinary preservation hall serves Cajun/Creole dishes. Moderate.

Restaurant August (504-299-9777, www.restaurantaugust.com), 301 Tchoupitoulas St., New Orleans. Chef-owner John Besh's flagship restaurant in the Central Business District is memorable for its unforgettable gourmet cookery. The menu changes frequently according to the freshest available ingredients. You may try gnocchi tossed with blue crab and black truffle or a salad of heirloom beets and crabmeat with black-eyed pea croutons. We like the sugar and spice duckling with stone-ground grits for lunch or dinner. You'll love the 1800s building with soaring ceilings, mahogany paneling, and antique mirrors. Ultra-romantic. Very expensive.

⚘ **Ruby Slipper Cafe** (504-309-5531, www.therubyslippercafe.net), 139 South Cortez, New Orleans; there's a second location at 200 Magazine St. This Mid-City neighborhood restaurant serves breakfast all day. Choose a basic breakfast or try pancakes or the bananas Foster pain perdu. Lunch includes a daily special and a variety of sandwiches. A kids' menu will appeal to most youngsters. The owners are committed to using New Orleans and regional products. They also participate in two ecologically sound recycling programs. Inexpensive.

Stella! (504-587-0091, www.restaurant stella.com), 1032 Chartres, New Orleans. One of New Orleans's leading new chefs, Scott Boswell, who owns the restaurant, presents innovative meals with ingredients inspired by world cuisine. Try the risotto of the day or the tandoori-roasted king salmon. How about a trio of crèmes brulée? The restaurant is enclosed by the Provincial Hotel in the French Quarter. Two rooms flank the carriageway of an old mansion. The name is taken from *A Streetcar Named Desire* by Tennessee Williams, who once lived in the Quarter. Expensive.

Sylvain (504-265-8123, www.sylvain nola.com), 625 Chartres St., New Orleans. This French Quarter oasis of style is one of the new places to see and be seen. In 1796, when construction began on the building at 625 Chartres, New Orleans was captivated by Jean-Francois Marmontel and Andre Getry's one-act comic opera *Sylvain*. Since then the building has been owned by numerous people, including the 6-foot-tall French Quarter madam Aunt Rose Arnold, a friend to neighborhood bohemians and authors. It is thought that William Faulkner patterned his character Miss Reba in *Sanctuary* and *The Reivers* her. In keeping with the past, an offering of a sazerac is left on the bar every night for Miss Reba. The restaurant's creative and varied menu includes everything from a roasted pork po-boy to seared coriander tuna. For dessert, try the Sylvain Float (Abita root beer, caramel ice cream, and ginger crisps). Moderate.

✴ Entertainment

There's no end to entertainment possibilities in New Orleans. This is America's premier city for live music—jazz, Cajun, zydeco, rock 'n' roll, blues, country, funk, contemporary, and classical. Musicians perform in clubs, restaurants, churches, major concert venues, and at festivals. New Orleans has no closing laws. Most clubs and jazz spots stay open until the last customer leaves in the morning. The city's love for the classics, including opera, ballet, and symphonic music, dates from the early 1800s. Schedules of weekly events are listed in calendars in the entertainment sections of the newspapers and local magazines. Visit www.nola.com for an up-to-date guide to what's on in arts, music, movies, and events. Also check out www .neworleanswebsites.com and www .wwoz.org and click on the music calendar. Listed here are some of the popular places that attract both tourists and locals. Hours and cover prices may vary. Call ahead for current programs.

Ⴟ **Blue Nile** (504-948-2583, www .bluenilelive.com), 532 Frenchman St., New Orleans. The club features an array of international acts and up-and-coming musicians. Housed in an 1832 building, it was the first musical venue on Frenchmen Street, known as the Dream Palace. Featured artists have included Kermit Ruffins, Troy "Trombone Shorty" Andrews, Cyril Neville, Bonerama, and the Soul Rebels. Live music begins nightly at 10. Cover charges vary.

Ⴟ **Davenport Lounge** (504-524-1331, www.ritzcarlton.com), 921 Canal St., New Orleans. On the third floor of the Ritz-Carlton Hotel, this is a classy club featuring the headlining trumpeter Jeremy Davenport. During the day, the lounge is a perfect setting for afternoon tea. At night you can order cocktails or champagne by the glass and enjoy fantastic music. Open 5:30–9 P.M. Thurs., 9 P.M.–1 A.M. Fri.–Sat.

Ⴟ **d.b.a.** (504- 942-3731, www.drink goodstuff.com), 618 Frenchman St., New Orleans. This is a hip, trendy spot geared toward local music lovers. The building dates from the 1880s, and musicians play in a room paneled in cypress. Perfect for those who like off-the-cuff music. The club opens 5 P.M. Mon.–Thurs. and 4 P.M. Fri.–Sun. It closes after the last patron leaves.

Ⴟ ✦ ♿ **House of Blues** (504-529-2583, www.hob.com), 225 Decatur St., New Orleans. The outstanding restaurant and live music club in the French Quarter is a classy and comfortable. The club has hosted world-class musicians from Fats Domino to Eric Clapton. A good place to head on Sunday morning, when there's a lavish gospel brunch and joyous music. Hours are 11:30 A.M.–10 P.M. Mon.–Sun.

Ⴟ **Howlin' Wolf** (504-522-9653, www .howlin-wolf.com), 907 St. Peters. St., New Orleans. The club is a high-velocity outlet for rock bands and occasional blues and jazz groups. Have a great time in air-conditioned comfort.

A MIXOLOGIST SERVES CUSTOMERS AT TUJAGUE'S, WHICH STILL HAS ITS ORIGINAL 1800S CYPRESS BAR AND IMPORTED FRENCH MIRROR.

Cynthia V. Campbell

Located in the Warehouse District near Convention Center Boulevard. Hours are 11–1 A.M. Mon.–Thurs. and 11–3 A.M. Fri.–Sat.

Ψ **Irvin Mayfield's Jazz Playhouse** (504-553-2331, www.sonesta.com), 300 Bourbon St., New Orleans. The Royal Sonesta Hotel presents Grammy and Billboard award–winning jazz trumpeter Irvin Mayfield in one of America's coolest jazz clubs. Enjoy cocktails and appetizers in the luxurious club on the hotel's lobby level. The show is Wednesday, 8–11 P.M.

Ψ **The Maison** (504-371 5543, www .maisonfrenchmen.com), 508 Frenchman St., New Orleans. This is a party spot for dancing. Swing dances are held several nights a week, and there are classes on Monday and Tuesday. The club has frequent Cajun *fais dodoes*, dance parties, and brass band throwdowns. Live music nightly. Hours are 5 P.M. until all the customers leave.

Ψ ⅙ **Maple Leaf Bar** (504- 866-9359, www.mapleleafbar.com), 8316 Oak St., New Orleans. Originally a chess and music club in the Uptown/Garden District, the bar became famed for James Booker's fiery piano recitals. It's the place to go any night of the week for brass bands, blues, and funk that sometimes continues until sunrise.

Ψ **Palm Court Jazz Cafe** (504-525-0200, www.palmcourtjazzcafe.com), 1204 Decatur St., New Orleans. Located in the refurbished French Market warehouse, the dinner club features traditional jazz. Many of the musicians also perform at Preservation Hall. The menu features a mix of British and Creole food. Open 7–11 P.M. Wed.–Sun.

Preservation Hall (504-523-8939 or 888-946-5299, www.preservationhall .com), 726 St. Peter St., New Orleans. In the days when traditional jazz seemed to be disappearing from the popular music scene, Preservation Hall was the place to find it. Many of the Preservation Hall Jazz Band's founding members performed with the people who invented jazz, including Buddy Bolden, Jelly Roll Morton, Bunk Johnson, and Louis Armstrong. To this day, the hall has no drinks or air conditioning, and only a few benches. But people of all ages who want a pure jazz experience line up outside about a half-hour before the music starts. Jazz is played nightly 8–11 P.M.

Ψ **Snug Harbor** (504- 949-0696, www .snugjazz.com), 626 Frenchmen St., New Orleans. Currently, the city's top jazz club, Snug Harbor offers live music nightly. Ellis Marsalis, pianist and music educator, is on stage most Fridays and Charmaine Neville sings most Mondays. There are two shows nightly at 9 and 11 P.M. The restaurant menu includes hamburgers and steaks.

Ψ **The Spotted Cat** (504-943-3887), 623 Frenchmen St., New Orleans. Music here runs from blues to traditional jazz to Latin. There's also a lot of funky roots music. At least two bands perform nightly. Hours are 6 P.M.–2 A.M.

Ψ **Sweet Lorraine's Jazz Club** (504-945-9654, www.sweetlorrainesjazz club.com), 1931 St. Claude Ave., New Orleans. Located in the Faubourg Marigny District, the cafe features live jazz on weekends with such performers as Clarence Johnson III, Michael Ward, Nicholas Payton, Deacon John, Angela Bofill, Roy Ayers, Kurt Brunus, and Gina Brown. The dinner menu features a blend of Creole and Southern cuisine. Open Tues.–Sat. and Jazz Brunch on Sun.

Ψ **Tipitina's** (504-895-8477, www .tipitinas.com), 501 Napoleon Ave., New Orleans. The club was started in 1977 by music fans to provide a place for Henry Roeland Byrd (a.k.a. Professor Longhair) to perform in his final years. This historic music spot is one of the city's funkiest joints. Tips: Tipitina's hosts music workshops where students have a chance to play with and learn from the best musicians in the city. Featured artists have included Stanton Moore, Johnny Vidacovich, Kirk Joseph, and Theresa Andersson. Live music most nights. Hours are 5 P.M.– 2 A.M. Thurs.–Sun. On Sunday, the club presents its youth music workshop 1–3 P.M. and a Cajun *fais do-do* with Bruce Daigrepoint 5:30–9 P.M.

CULTURE New Orleans has a long history of outstanding performance groups. Visitors will find a number of professional and nonprofessional groups, many supporting youth involvement, offering a variety of programs. Visit www.neworleanswebsites .com for more listings.

Louisiana Philharmonic Orchestra (504-523-6530, www.lpomusic.com) 2120 Common St., New Orleans. From Mozart to Marsallis, the Louisiana Philharmonic Orchestra, the first symphony orchestra totally self-owned in the United States, presents diverse music programs. Led by music director Carlos Miguel Prieto, the LPO has great mobility and offers two to three dozen concerts a year. Performances take place in the city's acoustically ideal old theaters as well as small, more intimate venues.

New Orleans Ballet Association (504-522-0996 or 800-745-3000, www .nobadance.com), 226 Carondelet St., 3rd Floor, New Orleans. Incorporated in 1969, the association's Main Stage season features a diverse array of world-class companies and artists. Its award-winning education programs give students access to 2,500 free dance classes and workshops each year. Presentations, mainly held in the Mahalia Jackson Theater near the French Quarter, have included the Joffrey Ballet, Shen Wei Dance Arts, and Complexions Contemporary Ballet.

New Orleans Opera Association (504-529-2278, www.neworleans online.com), 1010 Common St., New Orleans. The opera association continues a tradition that began with the city's first opera staged on May 22, 1796 and flourished with the opening of the French Opera House in 1859. The tradition continues today with 19th- and 20th-century classics as well as a few contemporary works. The lead singers are internationally known performers, and regional singers are featured in lesser roles. Each season includes two major operas in the fall and two in early spring. The Opera Association's educational program presents live performances in New Orleans's schools.

The NOLA Project (www.nola project), 2716 Magazine St., New Orleans. The company is dedicated to renewing and strengthening theater in the city. Productions held in a various sites have included *A Midsummer Night's Dream, The Misanthrope,* and *Wind in the Willows.*

Le Petit Theatre (504 523-6530, www.lepetittheatre.com), 616 St. Peter St., New Orleans. The regional theater in the French Quarter is more than 80 years old. It is one of the nation's leading community theaters offering both traditional and innovative shows.

Southern Repertory Theater (504-522-6545, www.southernrep.com), 365 Canal St., third floor, New Orleans. Located in the Shops at Canal Place on the edge of the French Quarter, this is the city's premier professional theater company. It is dedicated to producing plays by American playwrights.

✳ Selective Shopping

Fashionable or quirky, antique or avant-garde—name it and you'll find in the Big Easy, even if you have to meander off the beaten path. Keep in mind, a seemingly dull façade may be deceptive. Walk in to find the world beyond the front door. Shops listed here are just a sampling of the variety you will find. When you find something you cannot live without, get it. As an artist friend once told me, always get what you truly love because beauty is always in the eye of the beholder.

French Quarter

French Quarter Shopping centers include: **Canal Place**, 333 Canal St., an upscale center with a beautiful atrium, whose shops include the designer boutiques Saks Fifth Avenue, Mignon Faget, Adrienne Vittadini, Ann Taylor, L'Occitane en Provence, and Lee Michaels Fine Jewelry. Located in the center is The Westin New Orleans Canal Place, with a food court on the third floor for quick meals. The **Jax Brewery** shopping center, 600 Decatur St., a brewery from 1891 to the mid-1970s, is a French Quarter mall with dozens of shops selling New Orleans art and apparel, Louisiana food products, and team sports wear. The **1791 French Market**, 2 French Market Place, is the oldest open-air public market in the country. Browse for Louisiana gift baskets, fleur de lis decorative items, pralines, fruits and vegetables. The famous Cafe du Monde coffee shop anchors one end. On weekends, the open-air Gazebo Restaurant and Market Cafe feature live music.

A BOON TO FOREIGN GUESTS: TAX-FREE SHOPPING

Visitors from other countries are eligible to participate in Louisiana's Tax-Free Shopping plan, which provides refunds of Louisiana state sales tax, and in some cases local sales taxes. International visitors with a valid foreign passport and roundtrip ticket of less than 90 days duration find this an incredible bargain. At time of purchase, international visitors are charged full price, including taxes. The international visitor must show his/her passport and travel ticket when making a purchase and ask for a tax-fee refund voucher. To redeem the vouchers, visitors must present them, with their national IDs and international ticket at designated sites for sales tax refunds.

Two places to get sales tax refunds in New Orleans are the Louis Armstrong International Airport and the Riverwalk Shopping Center on Poydras Street at the Mississippi River. Visitors can also receive sales tax refunds via U.S. mail to Louisiana Tax Free Shopping Commission, P.O. Box 20125, New Orleans, LA 70141.

In the case of Canadians only, a driver's license or birth certificate may be substituted for a passport. For sailors, a shore pass, which contains their passport number, may be substituted for a foreign passport. Contact 504-467-0721 or www.louisianataxfree.com.

Angela King Gallery (504-524-8211, www.angelakinggallery.com), 523 Royal St., New Orleans. On the corner of Royal and Bienville, the studio has 2,000 square feet of exhibition space for stimulating art shows and events. It's a welcoming place to learn about art and meet artists. Among the artists represented here are Andrew Baird, Michelle Gagliano, Frederick Hart, Peter Max, Leroy Neiman, Margarita Sikorskaia, and Christian Vey. Open 10 A.M.–5 P.M. Mon.–Sat. and 11 A.M.–5 P.M. Sun.

✆ **Aunt Sally's Praline Shops** (504-944-6090, 800-642-7257, www.aunt sallys.com), 810 Decatur St., New Orleans. Witness talented cooks stirring copper pots full of sweet Creole praline mixtures at this shop operated by the Bagur family. The company is famous for its hand-poured pralines, New Orleans spices, cookbooks, music, and more. It's always good for take-home gifts. Open 9 A.M.–7 P.M. Sun.–Mon., 9 A.M.–6 P.M. Tues.–Thurs., 9 A.M.–8 P.M. Fri.–Sat.

Beads by the Dozen (504-734-9966 or 877-734-9966, www.beadsbythe dozen.com), 333 Edwards Ave., New Orleans. While this store in Jefferson Parish will take you beyond the main shopping areas, it's only 15 minutes from downtown. This is the largest Mardi Gras store in the area, with more than 6,000 items. You can find beads to throw, wrap around your neck, or use for holiday decorations. There are masks, feather boas, souvenirs, and gifts. A must-stop for the serious reveler. Open 9 A.M.–5:30 P.M. Mon.–Fri. and 10 A.M.–4 P.M. Sat.

The Crabnet (504-522-3478, www .thecrabnet.com), 925 Decatur, New Orleans. The shop features native wildlife artists, including several who have received national recognition. Look for John Perry sculptures,

GOOD TO THE LAST MORSEL: CAFÉ AU LAIT AND SUGARY BEIGNETS AT CAFÉ DU MONDE IN THE FRENCH QUARTER

Cynthia V. Campbell

Wilderness Woods boxes, fleur-de-lis jewelry, and fishing shirts and shorts. Open 10 A.M.–6 P.M. Mon.–Sat. and 10 A.M.–5 P.M. Sun.

&. **The Cigar Factory New Orleans** (504-568-1003 or 800-550-0775, www.cigarfactoryneworleans.com), 415 Decatur St., New Orleans. Aficionados will love their choices—panatela, Robusto, Churchill, double corona, Big Easy Natural. The city's oldest cigar factory is rolling fine cigars daily. Select your special cigar or pick up a sampler pack. Open daily 10 A.M.–10 P.M.

Elliott Gallery (504-523-3554, www.elliottgallery.com), 540 Royal St., New Orleans. The gallery sells only original art; there are no reproductions and no giclees (copies of originals printed on canvas or paper). This is fine art at affordable prices by artists who have works in museums. Open daily 10 A.M.–5 P.M.

Faulkner House Books (504-524-2940, www.faulknerhouse.net), 624 Pirate's Alley, New Orleans. William Faulkner lived here for six months in 1925 and wrote his novel *Soldier's Pay* here. The shop sells first editions of his works, as well as collections of his letters and contemporary works by local and national authors. Open 10 A.M.–5:30 P.M. daily.

The French Antique Shop (504-524-9861 or 866-524-9861, www.gofrenchantiques.com), 225 Royal St., New Orleans. The family-owned business specializes in 18th- and 19th-century French furnishings and antique lighting. The ceilings are ablaze with exquisite chandeliers. The shop also sells gold-leaf mirrors and lovely home accessories. Open 9:30 A.M.–4:30 P.M. Mon.–Fri. and 9:30 A.M.–4:30 P.M. Sat.

A Gallery for Fine Photography (504-568-1313, www.agallery.com), 241 Chartres St., New Orleans. Established in 1973, the gallery exhibits and sells original works from master photographers including Ansel Adams, Alfred Stieglitz, Peter Beard, Herman Leonard, Richard Sexton, and Annie Leibovitz. There's also a selection of photography books. Open 10:30 A.M.–5:30 P.M. Thurs.–Mon.; by appointment only Tues.–Wed.

M.S. Rau Antiques (504- 523-5660 or 800 -544-9440, www.rauantiques.com), 630 Royal St., New Orleans. One of the premiere antiques galleries in the country, the store has some of the most stunning collections of rare antiques, including porcelains, cut glass, fine paintings, and stunning jewelry. It's perfect for serious collectors or those looking for that one special item to set off a room. Open 9 A.M.–5:15 P.M. Mon.–Sat.

Mystic Tea Leaves (504-523-1063, www.frenchquartervoodoo.com), 638 Royal St., New Orleans. This is an authentic establishment for the psychic arts. Obtain a reading you're comfortable with. Hear about past lives, present relationships, and what awaits you in the future. You can also tour the Tea Cup Galleria, with more than 800 cups from around the world. Open daily, but hours vary. Call for a guaranteed appointment.

New Orleans Party and Costume (504-525-4744, www.partyandcostume), 705 Camp St., New Orleans. Visit the second floor to find costumes arranged by themes. Complete your look with accessories, hats, shoes, weapons, wigs, and masks. Open 10 A.M.–6 P.M. Mon.–Sat.

New Orleans Silversmiths (504-522-8333 or 800-219-8333, www.neworleanssilversmiths.com), 600 Chartres, New Orleans. The lovely shop specializes in antique English silver and fine estate and contemporary jewelry. The inventory of silverware and hollowware includes wine and cocktail accoutrements. The jewelry is often unique and of excellent quality. Open 10 A.M.–5 P.M. Mon.–Sat. and 11 A.M.–4 P.M. Sun.

Vintage 329/429 (504-529-2286, www.vintage329.com), 429 Royal St., New Orleans. The gallery is about following your passions. The shop attracts collectors looking for antique weaponry, rare books, maps, authentic memorabilia, autographed music albums, and instruments, as well as signed items from the world of sports. Open 10 A.M.–6 P.M. daily.

Violet's (504-569-0088), 800 Chartres St., New Orleans. Shop for one-of-a-kind clothing and jewelry with Edwardian and '20s flair. Colorful, playful clothing will inspire you to stretch your fashion sense. You'll find hats and scarves too. Open 11 A.M.–7 P.M. Sun.–Thurs. and 10 A.M.–8 P.M. Fri.–Sat.

Magazine Street Area

As You Like It Silver Shop (504-897-6915 or 800- 828-2311, www.asyoulikeitsilvershop.com) 3033 Magazine St., New Orleans. The shop contains silver flatware and hollowware, including active, inactive, and obsolete patterns. Open 11 A.M.–5 P.M. Mon.–Fri. and 10 A.M.–5 P.M. Sat.

Blue Frog Chocolates (504-269-570, www.bluefrogchocolates.com), 5707 Magazine St., New Orleans. Don't pass up a luscious treat in a quaint old cottage, especially if you're a chocolate lover. Specialties include fantastic Blue Frog Chocolates and Joseph Schmidt confections, yummy toffee, truffles, bon-bons, hot chocolate, and cooking chocolate. Louisiana favorites include chocolate voodoo queens, chocolate alligators and Cajun chocolate bites, made with cayenne pepper. Open 10 A.M.–6 P.M. Mon.–Fri., 10 A.M.–5 P.M. Sat., and noon–5 P.M. Sun.

Bush Antiques (504-581-3518, www.bushantiques.com), 2109 Magazine St., New Orleans. A fascinating establishment. Look for a variety of beds, continental furniture, ironwork, mirrors, lighting, and religious artifacts in 12 showrooms around a lush courtyard. Open 11 A.M.–5 P.M. Mon.–Sat.

Fleurty Girl (504-301-2557, www.fleurtygirl.net), 3117 Magazine St., New Orleans. A perfect place to find that offbeat but still chic T-shirt or funky Saints jewelry. Check out items to perk up your condo or newly acquired apartment. Popular with the Magazine Street regulars. Open 11 A.M.–6 P.M. Mon.–Thurs., 10 A.M.–5 P.M. Fri.–Sat, and noon–4 P.M. Sun.

Funky Monkey (504-899-5587), 3127 Magazine St., New Orleans. This is just the place for locally designed clothes and costumes or vintage T-shirts, jackets, and dresses. Really funky accessories will demand attention. Open 11 A.M.–6 P.M. Mon.–Wed.,

FLEURTY GIRL SHOP ON MAGAZINE STREET DISPLAYS ORIGINAL "WHO DAT" T-SHIRT WITH A FLUFFY TUTU.

Cynthia V. Campbell

11 A.M.–7 P.M. Thurs.–Sat., and noon.– 6 P.M. Sun.

Martin Wine Cellar (504- 894-7420, www.martinwine.com), 3500 Magazine St., New Orleans. Everyone in the city knows about Martin's incredible selection of both fine wines and basic table wines. Consultants are on hand at all times to help customers choose the best vintages and even the best glassware to use. You can also pick up gourmet food items like Sicilian olives, Chilean extra virgin olive oil, and caper berries from Spain. Open 10 A.M.– 7 P.M. Tues.–Sat.

Mignon Faget (504- 891-2005 or 800-375-7557, www.mignonfaget.com), 3801 Magazine St., New Orleans. Discover the incredible beauty of jewelry and specialty items created by this famed local artist. Many of her designs are inspired by New Orleans architecture and nature. Her silver, gold, precious, and semi-precious gemstones are handcrafted in the city. Open 10 A.M.–6 P.M. Mon.–Sat.

Neal Auction Company (504-899-5329, or 800-467-5329, www.neal auction.com), 4038 Magazine St., New Orleans. The city's oldest auction house continually sets record prices for paintings, furniture, art, pottery, porcelain, and decorative arts. Fully catalogued auctions are scheduled six times a year. This is not a retail business. However, the house opens to viewers two weeks prior to every auction. Visit in advance and learn about consignments accepted for future auctions. Also find out about online bidding. Open 9 A.M.–5 P.M. Mon.–Fri.

✳ Special Events

New Orleans and the neighboring communities have dozens of special events and festivals, not counting Mardi Gras. There's a wide diversity of events. Many are free and open to the public. If you're not a late-night party person, attend a daytime event; if you get there by 10 A.M. the crowds won't be too big yet. Parking is at a premium during Carnival and major sporting events. It's safest to park in a paid lot, and leave a little early so you can reach your car safely and avoid traffic jams. During highly advertized big events, such as Jazz Fest and Mardi Gras, hotels often require a two-, three-, or four-night minimum stay. Call far in advance for information and reservations. However, it always pays to call and see if any guests have canceled reservations at the last minute.

January: **Battle of New Orleans Commemoration** (504-589-3882, www.nps.gov/jela/chalmette-battle field.htm), 8606 West St. Bernard Highway, Chalmette. Each January, Chalmette Battlefield of Jean Lafitte National Park hosts a wreath-laying ceremony to honor the troops who fought at the Battle of New Orleans on January 8, 1815. Return to the 19th century with troops and civilian in authentic period dress, cannon and musket firings, military drills, American and British camps, and a "night before the battle" tour by lantern.

February: **Mardi Gras.** The carnival seasons in New Orleans runs from January 6 through Mardi Gras (Fat Tuesday, the day before Ash Wednesday). Parties and parades are heavily concentrated about two weeks before the final day. See the sidebar on Mardi Gras.

Valentine's Day (888-447-3862, www.gretnala.com), 205 Lafayette St., Gretna. The Blacksmith Shop in downtown Gretna hosts this romantic event. Following a tradition that started in Gretna Green, Scotland, a marrying judge made the same-named town in Louisiana a destination for couples

New Orleans CVB/Pat Guerin

JESTERS OF EVERY SIZE FILL A FLOAT
DURING A DAYTIME MARDI GRAS PARADE
IN NEW ORLEANS.

seeking quickie weddings in the 1800s. That legacy is celebrated each Valentine's Day when the local Justice of the Peace conducts ceremonies and renewals of vows over the anvil inside the historic Gretna Green Blacksmith Shop. Special certificates and proclamations are part of the ceremony. Legal details are available at the Clerk of Court, Marriage License Division, Jefferson Parish, 200 Derbigney St., Gretna, 504-364-2922.

March: **Los Islenos Festival** (504-874-0635, www.losislenos.org), 1345-47 Bayou Rd., Chalmette. This two-day event is a salute to the Canary Islanders who settled the area. Learn about their journey while sipping cool sangria and eating paella and enjoy Islenos music, dancing, and folk arts demonstrations.

St. Patrick's Day (www.irishchannel no.org). New Orleans history is rich with Irish influence, and when March 17 rolls around many put on a "bit o' green" to announce their loyalty. The best place to be is Parasol's Bar in the Irish Channel, a neighborhood near the Garden District that was originally named for its heavy concentration of Irish families. The entire block is

---

HAVE AN EPIPHANY: KING CAKE IS WORTH IT!

Twelfth Night, also called the Feast of the Epiphany or King's Day, is January 6, the twelfth night after Christmas. In New Orleans it marks the official end of the Christmas season and the official start of Carnival. One tradition is to gather with friends for a quiet dinner or party and cut the first King Cake of the year. Whoever gets the slice containing the plastic baby Jesus is obliged to buy the cake for the next gathering. For almost a century, the Twelfth Night Revelers have held a private ball on January 6 to recognize the season. On the same night, a group called the Phunny Phorty Phellows takes to a streetcar and with banners tied to the side that announce to the world that "IT'S CARNIVAL TIME."

packed with people and there's always plenty of green beer. The annual St. Patrick's Day Parade rolls down lower Magazine Street and St. Charles Avenue. You might catch a coveted potato or a head of cabbage tossed by parade participants to crowds. A block party at Annunciation Square, near Chippewa and Race streets, features Irish music and dancers, food, and arts and crafts. Proceeds benefit St. Michael's Special School and other charities. Visit the Irish Chanel St. Patrick's Day Club website for more information and dates for the parade and block party.

Tennessee Williams/New Orleans Literary Festival (504-581-1144, www.tennesseewilliams.net), 938 Lafayette St., Suite 514, New Orleans. The festival is named for the playwright who lived in New Orleans during one of his most creative periods.

Top playwrights, authors, actors, and speakers sit on literary panels and provided master classes. There are tours to take part in, but the festival highlight is the "Stella!" shouting contest, where participants, usually attired in Stanley Kowalski–style sleeveless undershirts, compete to make the most plaintive appeal to the judges on the balcony of the Pontalba Apartment on Jackson Square.

April: 🏵 **French Quarter Festival** (504-522-5730 or 800-673-5725, www .fqfi.org). A joyous spring event when French Quarter residents and their friends invite the world to share their love of the city's music, food, and fun. The three-day free event features more than a dozen stages throughout the Quarter with more than 100 of the city's favorite performers entertaining the crowds. The signature event is the "world's largest jazz brunch" in Wol-

DANCERS FROM THE CANARY ISLANDS PERFORM TRADITIONAL DANCES DURING THE ISLENOS FIESTA IN ST. BERNARD PARISH.

St. Bernard CVB /Karen Turni Bazile

New Orleans CVB/ Pat Garin

THE FREE FRENCH QUARTER FESTIVAL IS A
LIVELY SPING EVENT WITH MUSIC STAGES
AND FOOD BOOTHS.

denberg Riverfront Park, with beverages and delicious food items on offer from world-famed bars and restaurants. All dishes (served on paper plates) are priced in the $3–5 range. Other activities include free tours of hidden patios and gardens, the world's largest praline, and a fireworks display.

✎ ↬ **Grand Isle Migratory Bird Celebration** (985-787-2559 or 888-787-2559, www.grand-isle.com). Louisiana's major barrier island, part of Jefferson Parish, is an essential stop for migratory birds during their spring and fall migrations across the Gulf of Mexico. The Grand Isle Sanctuary Group's spring celebration includes bird watch-

ing tours, bird banding, bird art and crafts, fun for children, colorful bird publications, T-shirts, posters, and hats. Bring binoculars, cameras, and sunscreen.

Jazz and Heritage Festival (www .nojazzfest.com), New Orleans Fair Grounds Race Course, 1751 Gentilly Blvd., New Orleans. Thousands flock to the Fair Grounds for this incredible event that locals call the Jazz Fest. It celebrates the creativity and excitement of essential American music styles. It has showcased most of New Orleans and Louisiana's great artists, including Ellis Marsalis, Wynton Marsalis, Branford Marsalis, Professor Longhair, Fats Domino, Dr. John, Allen Toussaint, Irma Thomas, the Dirty Dozen Brass Band, and many others. International artists who have appeared include Aretha Franklin, Miles Davis, Sarah Vaughan, Paul Simon, Patti LaBelle, Stevie Ray Vaughan, Bonnie Raitt, Willie Nelson, Dave Brubeck, and many, many more. Check the website for performance schedule, ticket information, and more. Activities include food booths, handmade arts and crafts, and a music heritage tent. Special event buses transport people from convenient downtown sites to the Fair Grounds.

May: **New Orleans Wine & Food Experience** (504-529-9463, www .nowfe.com). Spotlighting the city's legendary restaurants and fine wines from around the globe, this is a foodie's dream experience. Events include two days of tastings from more than 100 restaurants, wine seminars, vintner dinners at restaurants throughout the city, and the Royal Street Experience, a wine stroll amid fine antiques stores and nifty shops.

June: **Vieux to Do** (www.french market.org, www.jazzandheritage.org), French Quarter, New Orleans. This is three festivals in one: **The French Market Creole Tomato Festival** (504-522-2621), with a tomato parade; **Cajun-Zydeco Festival** (504-558-6100), at the Old U.S. Mint with free music; and the **Louisiana Seafood Festival** (504-293-2657), also at the Mint, celebrating the Louisiana harvest with celebrity chefs, cooking demonstrations, and behind-the-scenes cooking tours.

July: **Tales of the Cocktail** (888-299-0404, www.talesofthecocktail.com). Legend has it that the first true cocktail, the sazerac, was mixed with stomach bitters in the early 19th century by New Orleans pharmacist Antoine Amadee Peychaud. Held in various locations, the four-day event spotlights the city's best-known mixologists and bartenders from around the world at lectures, book signings, and mixing demonstrations. Thousands of guests enjoy events, attend dinner pairings, and take history tours of New Orleans sites connected to the invention of various cocktails.

Essence Festival (www.essencemusic festival.com and www.nola.com /essencefest), Louisiana Superdome and other New Orleans venues. Held over the Fourth of July weekend, the festival, sponsored by *Essence Magazine*, is a gathering of the nation's top African American writers, artists, craftsmen, culinary artists, musicians, and business people. It's an opportunity for African Americans to display their arts, present their opinions, and give inspirational lectures in pleasant venues. Some activities take place in the Ernest N. Morial Convention Center. Entertainers who have made the scene in the past include Beyonce, Prince, Mary J. Blige, and Lionel Richie.

August: **COOLinary New Orleans** (800-672-6124, www.neworleans online.com). City restaurants participate in money-saving lunch and dinner specials, offering three-course lunches at $20 or less and three-course dinners at $34. Check the website for details.

Satchmo Summer Fest (504-522-5730, www.fqfi.org). The Old U.S. Mint at Barracks and Esplanade Avenue is the setting for this event. Sponsored by French Quarter Festivals, the festival honors the legendary trumpeter and music ambassador Louis "Satchmo" Armstrong. This is a mini–Jazz Fest with three days of concerts, music seminars, a jazz Mass, a second-line parade, and a "Satchmo Strut" down Frenchman Street.

Whitney White Linen Night (504-528-38-05, www.cacno.org), Contemporary Arts Center, 900 Camp St., New Orleans. The arts center is the headquarters for this gathering along Julia Street and adjacent side streets. It's a summer must. When New Orleans gets hot and steamy, people turn out in cool white linens and gauzy attire to take a leisurely stroll, hop from art gallery to gallery, and sip chilled wine. The official after party at the Contemporary Arts Center features some of the city's most eclectic musicians. In response, Royal Street shops in the French Quarter host **Dirty Linen Night** the second Saturday of the month. Shops give away dirty martinis and dirty rice (white rice studded with Cajun-style chopped chicken livers).

September: **Southern Decadence** (www.southerndecadence.com). Nicknamed the Gay Mardi Gras, the annual Labor Day weekend event attracts some 100,000 participants from around the world. It's considered the largest gay event in New Orleans. A highlight is the parade that rolls the Sunday before Labor Day with costumed marchers and floats. Purchase weekend passes to special events in advance. Securing hotel recommendations early is strongly recommended.

New Orleans Seafood Festival, Lafayette Square across from historic Gallier Hall, New Orleans. The free three-day festival features live entertainment and seafood delicacies from such restaurants as the Acme Oyster House, Arnaud's, Red Fish Grill, and Saltwater Grill. Proceeds benefit the Louisiana Hospitality Foundation, which supports the health and social welfare of children across the state.

October: **Gretna Heritage Festival** (www.gretnafest.com), Huey P. Long Avenue, Historic District, Gretna. Encompassing some 25 city blocks, the festival features more than 75 local and international acts with such headliners as Lynyrd Skynyrd, Brian Howe, and Tracy Lawrence. Food court specialties include corn crab bisque in a bread bowl and Cajun crawfish pasta. The German Beer Garden kicks off the opening of Oktoberfest, and the Italian Village offers music by Louis Prima Jr., Bobby Lonero, and others.

New Orleans Film Festival (www.neworleansfilmfest.com). The film industry is booming in Louisiana, and in recent years this festival has been getting bigger and better. Held under the auspices of the New Orleans Film Society, the mid-October event attracts thousands of producers, directors, writers, actors, and actresses. Films are shown at venues throughout the city, including the Theaters at Canal Place, Prytania Theatre, and the new Solomon Victory Theatre at the World War II Museum. Admissions are charged and the public is invited.

Voodoo Music Experience (www.thevoodooexperience.com), New Orleans City Park. The action-packed,

BRILLIANT FLAMINGOS ENJOY THE SUNLIGHT IN NEW ORLEANS' AUDUBON ZOO.

Cynthia V. Campbell

multi-day music and arts event is held the last weekend in October. Participants get an explosion of musical talent on two main stages and several small stages. Headliners have included the Original Meters, Snoop Dogg, Nine Inch Nails, Eminem, Kiss, and the Soul Rebels Brass Band. Expect wonderful food beverages, and arts.

November: ✍ ❦ **Louisiana Swamp Festival** (www.auduboninstitute.org), Audubon Zoo, 6500 Magazine St., New Orleans. Held over two days in early November, this wonderful celebration of Cajun culture is free with general zoo admission. Bring the family for special animal feedings and hands-on encounters with critters as well as Cajun storytelling, pirogue-building, and wild fowl carving in the Louisiana Swamp Exhibit. Bands perform live throughout both days on stages throughout the zoo.

December: ❦ **Christmas New Orleans Style** (www.neworleansonline.com). New Orleans is truly magical at Christmastime, with French Quarter balconies, Canal Street lamps, and even streetcars decorated for the season. Nearly two million lights illuminate gardens and structures at City Park's Celebration in the Oaks. You can attend a free holiday concert in St. Louis Cathedral and join the crowd for caroling in Jackson Square. Hanukkah at the Riverwalk lights the largest menorah in Louisiana and features contemporary Jewish music and free latkes, the traditional potato pancakes. Restaurants offer a modern version of Reveillon dinners, which derive from an old Creole custom that saw families gathering at home after Christmas Eve Midnight Mass for a feast that could last for hours. Check the website to order a brochure and obtain a schedule of activities.

Orange Festival (504-398-4434), Fort Jackson, Boothville. Join the citrus growers of Plaquemines Parish at their annual harvest festival. Taste a slice of Louisiana with locally grown satsuma oranges and grapefruits. Activities include a 5K Run for the Oranges, a citrus dessert contest, and live music.

NORTHSHORE AREA

Louisiana's Northshore encompasses a large section of the eastern part of the state. The name was coined by New Orleans residents who referred to the plantations and towns on the north side of Lake Pontchartrain as "the North Shore." For more than 200 years, the area's serene beauty and rich lands have enchanted visitors. The Northshore encompasses three parishes, St. Tammany, Tangipahoa, and Washington, each with distinct features.

The lake area retains the atmosphere of the old South, with Spanish moss on ancient oak trees and mansions that evoke romance and mystery. The distinct architecture of Creole cottages adds to the area's charm. There are towns with quaint shops and remarkable restaurants. Tranquil bed & breakfasts landscaped with palms, azaleas, and roses attract people seeking relaxing getaways. The area is a sailor's heaven. Sailboats and pleasure boats skim across lakes and dock in well-run marinas. The bayous and rivers that feed the lake provides a safe haven when weather gets rough. A number of fun cafes and bars can be reached by either boat or car. During the early 1800s, the Northshore was a playground for New Orleanians seeking escape from the summer heat and waves of yellow fever. Today, it's a booming area where residents and visitors alike avoid the complexities of metropolitan life.

French explorers were drawn to the area from the beginning. Lake Pontchartrain is named for Louis Phelypeaux, Comte de Pontchartrain, Minister of the Marine, Chancellor of France, and Controller-General of Finances for Louis XIV, the Sun King. Pontchartrain is not a true lake, but an estuary connected to the Gulf of Mexico by way of the Rigolets into Lake Borgne, a large lagoon. These bodies of water experience small tidal changes. The lake receives fresh water from the Tangipahoa, Tchefuncte, Tickfaw, Amite, and Bogue Falaya rivers as well as from Bayou Lacombe and Bayou Chinchuba. The waterways provide numerous recreational opportunities.

Pontchatrain is brackish, the second-largest inland saltwater body of water in the United States after Great Salt Lake in Utah. It's about 40 miles from east to west and 24 from north to south. On the west side, it connects to Lake Maurepas, a freshwater lake, via Pass Manchac. Also on the west, the Bonnet Carre Spillway diverts water from the Mississippi into the lake during times of flooding. In spring 2011, spillway gates were opened here and at the Morganza Spillway further north to avoid flooding in the Greater New Orleans area.

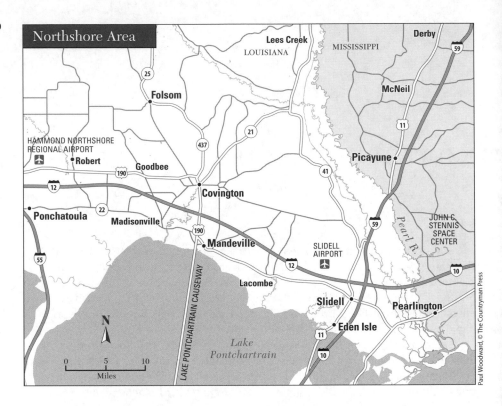

Northshore Area

Paul Woodward, © The Countryman Press

If you look at a map of south Louisiana, you'll see that Lake Pontchartrain forms a rather large oval above New Orleans. Neighborhoods along Pontchartrain are most often referred to as being located on the East Bank or West Bank. The towns that ring the lake are tied to boating, fishing, and recreational activities. Further inland the communities reflect their beginnings in agriculture and lumber.

In 1699, Pierre Le Moyne d'Iberville explored lakes Pontchartrain and Maurepas and wrote in his journal, "This place where I am is one of the prettiest I have seen . . ." It didn't take long for the French to start establishing plantations in the area. In 1810, President James Madison sent William C. C. Claiborne to claim the territory. Madison named St. Tammany Parish after the Delaware Indian Chief Tamanend, who had made peace with William Penn and was known for his goodness. Among nine Louisiana parishes named for saints, St. Tammany is the only one not recognized as a saint by the Roman Catholic Church. In the early 1830s, there were two towns in St. Tammany: Covington, a retreat with summer homes, and Madisonville, a shipbuilding and sawmill town.

GUIDANCE Louisiana State Welcome Centers. Louisiana maintains three welcome centers on highways that are main entry points into the state. They are the **Kentwood, I-55 Welcome Center** (985-229-8338), 77479 I-55 South; the **Pearl River Welcome Center** (985-6466450), 614411 I-59 South; and the **Slidell Welcome Center** (985-229-8338), I-10 West at the State Line, 41300 Crawford Landing Rd. The centers are open daily 8:30 A.M.-5 P.M. They are staffed by well-trained travel counselors who can answer your questions and provide maps, brochures, and information about the entire state. They welcome visits from schools and group tours. For more details, visit www.crt.state.la.us/tourism /itwelcome.aspx.

Louisiana's Northshore/St. Tammany Parish Tourist and Convention Commission (800-634-9443 or 985-892-0520, www.louisiananorthshore.com), 68099 LA 59, Mandeville. Situated conveniently off I-12, this is an excellent visitor center with plenty of information on the entire area, including accommodations, restaurants, attractions, recreational activities, and off-the-beaten-path surprises.

Ponchatoula Chamber of Commerce (985-386-2536, www.ponchatoula chamber.com), 109 West Pine St., Ponchatoula. If you have any questions about this small town, which offers antiques, homemade items, strawberries, and fun, then drop by this office to chat with locals for updated information.

Tangipahoa Parish Convention and Visitors Bureau (800-617-4506 or 985-542-7520, www.tangitourism.com), 13143 Wardine Rd., Hammond. The full-service center provides visitor information and assistance, a community calendar, and information about local hotspots.

Washington Parish Tourism Commission (888-827-7118 or 985-839-5228, www.washingtonparishtourism.com), 908 Mill St., Franklinton. The tourist center helps with information on fishing, hunting, canoeing, and tubing in rural areas from Franklinton to Bogalusa and through forested areas.

GETTING THERE *By car:* To reach the Northshore from New Orleans, take the Pontchartrain Causeway across the lake to I-12 and US 190, and follow the signs to Covington. To reach Slidell and the lower section of the Northshore, take I-10 East until it connects to I-12 West. If you are entering Louisiana from the Mississippi Gulf Coast, follow I-10 West until it connects with I-12 West. From the Jackson, Mississippi, area, take I-55 South to I-12 East and then follow signs to your destination. Travelers from south-central Mississippi can follow I-59 into Louisiana across the Pearl River, then follow signs to I-12 West. From Baton Rouge, the quickest way to the Northshore area is I-12 east.

By air: **Louis Armstrong New Orleans International Airport** (504-303-7500, www.flymsy.com), 900 Airline Dr., Kenner, is the major airport in the Greater New Orleans area, and it is served by major airlines and rental car companies. It is a short distance via I-10 to the Pontchartrain Causeway, which connects with I-12 and the Northshore Area. **New Orleans Lakefront Airport** (504-248-5240, www.lakefrontairport.com), 6401 Stars and Stripes Blvd., New Orleans, is a general aviation center private, corporate, military and commercial aircraft; occasional military operations take place here. There's a pilot lounge, and on-site car rental is available. The terminal building and other facilities were damaged by Hurricane Katrina and are still slowly being repaired. The exterior of the classic art deco terminal has been fully restored and was used as the headquarters of the fictional Ferris Aircraft in the 2011 movie *Green Lantern,* starring Ryan Reynolds and Blake Lively. **St. Tammany Regional Airport** (985-8982362, www.airnav.com /airport/L31), Airport Rd., Abita Springs, about six miles southeast of Covington, is a general aviation and public-use airport with one runway. Self-service fueling is available 24 hours with credit card. **Hammond Northshore Regional Airport** (985-277-5667, www.hammond.org/departments/airport), 600 Judge Leon Ford

Dr., Hammond. This is a city-owned, general-aviation, reliever airport with two runways with concrete surfaces. Services include 24-hour self-service fueling with credit card on the west ramp, and full service on the southeast ramp, hangars, and tiedowns. The Louisiana Army National Guard maintains a 56-acre site at the airport.

AREA CODE 985.

MEDICAL EMERGENCIES **Fairway Medical Urgent Care** (985-809-8989), 70340 LA 21, Suite A, Covington. Services include treatment for cold and flu symptoms, cuts and stitches, minor eye problems, sprains, sports injuries, and simple fractures. Open 9 A.M.–8 P.M. Mon.–Fri; 10 A.M.–5 P.M. Sat.–Sun.

St. Tammany Parish Hospital (985-898-4438, www.stph.org), 1202 South Tyler St., Covington. The hospital offers emergency medicine care 24 hours daily.

North Oaks Health System (985-345-2700, www.northoaks.org), 15790 Paul Vega Dr., Hammond. The emergency department has 21 rooms, including four trauma rooms and one room with a specialized EMT and eye equipment.

Ochsner Medical Center-Northshore (985-649-7070, www.ochsner.org), 100 Medical Center Dr., Slidell. The acute-care center has a 24-hour emergency room.

✳ Cities, Towns, and Villages

Slidell, where I-10 enters the state from the east, was founded around 1882 as a major railroad center connecting New Orleans to Meridian, Mississippi, and eventually New York. It was named by Baron Frederic Erlanger, head of a banking syndicate, for his deceased father-in-law, John Slidell, a prominent national and Confederate figure. Slidell is proud of its historic Olde Towne and its restaurants, antiques shops, and early 20th-century ambience. Visitors will find fall and spring street fairs and concerts in Heritage Park. Since it's surrounded by waterways, the city is a hub for outdoors activities, including tours of the Honey Island Swamp, Cajun Encounters, and Big Branch Marsh National Wildlife Refuge. The Louisiana State Welcome Center on I-10, designed for westbound traffic, is one of the busiest in the state. It's open daily year-round, 9 A.M.–5 P.M., and closed major holidays. The center is an ideal place to pick up information from knowledgeable travel counselors as well as maps, printed guides, and brochures.

Covington, on the Bogue Falaya River, is a lovely city founded on July 4, 1813, by John Wharton Collins as the town of Wharton. Collins laid out the town on a pattern of squares within squares that were accessed by alleyways, and named the center the Division of St. John, It is now the Historic District. Wharton was incorporated in 1816 by the state legislature and renamed Covington. In the 1800s, it became a tourist destination. People believed the ozone waters of the Northshore were healthy and they visited hotels in Covington to bathe and partake of "the cure." In 1891 Covington was named the Most Healthy Place in the United States. Today, people love the city for its chic boutiques and top-drawer art galleries. Its fine restaurants vie with New Orleans for exquisite cuisine. The calendar is filled with gallery openings, main street happenings, and the annual Three Rivers Arts Festival. It's also a choice place for launching outdoor adventures. You can enter the Tammany Trace, one of America's successful rails-to-trails nature trails.

Louisiana Office of Tourism

SUNSHINE BRINGS OUT THE ALLIGATORS IN THE HONEY ISLAND SWAMP.

Abita Springs has always been a popular destination. Originally a Choctaw village, the community took its name from its fresh spring water. The Indians traded with early settlers and showed the newcomers how to convert local timbers into cured planks, how to tar and pitch log cabins, and how to use the native herbs and plants for medicine. In the 1800s, New Orleans residents traveled by steamboat to Mandeville and then by carriage or streetcar to Abita Springs to enjoy its spring-fed creeks, tall pines, and proximity to Lake Pontchartrain. A new rail line in 1887 brought more people, and a number of guest houses and hotels were added to the mix. Much of Abita Springs' charm is that it remains little changed. Enjoy the Tammany Trace Trailhead and Park on the Abita River, where bird watchers, hikers, bikers, roller bladers, and horseback riders love spending hours. A lovely pavilion designed by Thomas K. Sully for the New Orleans Cotton Centennial Exposition of 1884 was later moved to the city to cover the then-famous free-flowing spring. Other attractions include guest houses, restaurants, a folk art museum, and the Abita Springs Brewery, which gives free tours on weekends.

Mandeville, situated directly on Lake Pontchartrain, was laid out in 1834 by Bernard Xavier Phillipe de Marigny de Mandeville. By 1840, it was a popular summer destination for wealthy New Orleanians, and by the end of the Victorian era its popularity had spread to middle-class families as well. Bands would play music on boats crossing the lake and at pavilions and dance halls in the city. It was one of the first places outside New Orleans where the new jazz music was heard. Bunk Johnson, Papa Celestin, Kid Ory, George Lewis, and other artists played regularly in Mandeville, and two buildings from jazz's early days still stand here. Ruby's Roadhouse has been in continuous operation since the 1920s, and is still popular. The Dew Drop Social and Benevolent Hall, closed for decades, was reopened in

2000 as the Dew Drop Jazz & Social Hall, a live jazz spot. The Mandeville Trailhead on the Tammany Trace has a delightful cultural center where people gather for lakeside concerts, art shows and a Community Market every Saturday morning, rain or shine. Children delight in being sprinkled at the center's water park.

Madisonville, a nearby small town on the banks of the Tchefuncte River, is a great place for cameras and smiles. It was founded in 1800s on the site of a Native American village, and named Cocquille or Cokie because of the abundance of shells in the area. In 1810, it was renamed in honor of President James Madison. Stop by the Lake Pontchartrain Basin Maritime Museum and Research Center to learn about the area's maritime history. Every year, thousands of people fill the town for the Wooden Boat Festival at celebration of beautiful boats, great food, and music.

Louisiana Northshore Tourism

KIDS PLAY IN THE MANDEVILLE TRAILHEAD INTERACTIVE FOUNTAIN.

Ponchatoula, on LA 22, in the lower end of Tangipahoa Parish, makes its claim to fame with strawberries and antiques. The small city's name comes from the Choctaw Indian word for "hair to hang" because of the abundance of Spanish moss dripping from the trees in the area. You'll see visitors strolling along Main Street, popping in and out of the art and antiques shops housed in restored buildings. The

BANDS STILL PERFORM IN RUBY'S ROADHOUSE IN MANDEVILLE, ONE OF AMERICA'S OLDEST JAZZ VENUES.

Louisiana Northshore CVB

old train depot has been turned into a country market where local craftspersons and artists show their wares. It's a good place to search for knitted and hand-stitched items, baby clothes, nifty bags, hairpieces, handmade soaps, and preserves. Outside by the railroad tracks, a large exhibit honors Ole Hardhide, an alligator that's almost the community mascot. The current Hardhide is not the first, nor likely the last gator to bear the name. Also near the tracks is the Strawberry Train, a steam engine and single car roped off in a way that allows children to safely climb them. Visitors come for miles to enjoy the Ponchatoula Strawberry Festival celebrating the area's commercial strawberry industry with a grand parade, music, and, of course, fruit.

Hammond, near the bustling intersection of I-10 and I-55, is the busy commercial hub of Tangipahoa Parish, about an hour's drive from New Orleans and Baton Rouge. Amtrak's City of New Orleans train makes daily stops in Hammond en route to Chicago and New Orleans. The depot in the center of downtown is a city landmark and a good place to start a tour. The city is named for Peter Hammond, a Swedish immigrant who settled the area around 1818. A former sailor, he started a plantation to grow trees, which he turned into masts, charcoal, and other products for New Orleans's maritime industry. During the Civil War the city was a Confederate shoemaking center. Later, it became a major railroad shipping point for strawberries. Visitors will find several modern shopping centers, fine restaurants, and the home of Southeastern Louisiana University, offering more than 60 undergraduate degrees and a number of additional programs. Area attractions include the Tangipahoa Parish African American Heritage Museum, Global Wildlife Center, Camp Moore Confederate Museum and Cemetery, Kliebert's Turtle and Alligator Farm, and the Louisiana Renaissance Fest.

As you travel north of Hammond, you'll find **Independence**, known for its lively Italian Festival and Amato's Winery, and **Amite**, the seat of Tangipahoa Parish and home of the Amite Oyster Festival. Near the Mississippi border is **Kentwood**, famed for its clear water and as the hometown of entertainer Britney Spears. Drive across Louisiana scenic byways of LA 10 and 21 to see one of the most scenic and rural parishes in the state. The countryside is dotted with rolling hills, pine forests, farms, and back roads. Waterways here attract those who enjoy fishing, hunting, and canoeing in remote spots.

In **Franklinton**, the parish seat, you'll find the D.A. Varnado Store Museum, a century-old general store, with displays on local history, art, and more. Mile Branch Historical Settlement, on the Parish Fairgrounds, features an outstanding collection of well-preserved pioneer cabins built of hand-hewn logs in the mid- to late 1800s. In mid-October, the town is home to the Washington Parish Free Fair, one of the largest and oldest county fairs in the state. Near town is Bogue Chitto State Park with streams, forests, and equestrian trails, made for days of recreational fun.

✳ To See

🐊 🌿 **Abita Mystery House/UCM Museum** (985-892-2624, www.ucmmuseum .com), 22275 LA 36, Abita Springs. Founded by the artist John Preble, the mystery house was inspired by roadside attractions of the mid-20th-century. A vintage gas station serves as the entrance to this gift shop and labyrinth of buildings filled with more than 50,000 found and recycled objects. View everything from Preble's clever vignettes of Southern life to the fascinating House of Shards. It's wild, wacky, and fun. Open 10 a.m.–5 p.m. daily. Admission $3.

🔖 🌿 **Abita Trailhead Museum** (985-892-3597, www.townofabitasprings.com), 22049 Main St., Abita Springs. The Tammany Trace passes through the center of town, and the Trailhead Museum features photographs and displays on the history and culture of the area. It also serves as a gathering place for art shows and special events. Open 10 a.m.–5 p.m. Fri.-Sat. and noon–5 p.m. Sun.

Camp Moore Confederate Cemetery and Museum (985-229-2438), 70640 Camp Moore Rd., Tangipahoa. This site served as the largest Confederate training camp in Louisiana. During the Civil War, people traveled by train from New Orleans to visit their sons and husbands. A burial ground was established at the camp to bury the soldiers who died there of disease or their wounds. Displays include original battle flags, uniforms, soldiers' letters, and other artifacts. A re-enactment is held here the weekend before Thanksgiving. Open 10 a.m.–3 p.m. Wed.–Sat. Admission $3, adults; $2, children; free to age 6 and under.

D.A. Varnado Store Museum (985-795-0680, www.varnadostoremuseum.org), 936 Pearl St., Franklinton. This century-old general store was a hub of activity in the early days of Washington Parish. Permanent and changing exhibits focus on early 19-century life in the community.

🔖 **Global Wildlife Center** (986-796-3585, www.globalwildlife.com), 26389 LA 40, Folsom. Pick up a big plastic cup full of special food to feed giraffes on a safari wagon tour. At this free-roaming 900-acre nature preserve, children, adults, students, and teachers embrace the values of conservation and wildlife preservation. Wiggle a camel's hump on a safari with 3,000 animals. There's a relaxing picnic area and a large gift shop with quality animal-themed items. Open 8 a.m.–5 p.m. daily. Safari Tour costs $17, adults; $15, seniors; $11, children ages 2–11. Feed for animals costs $2 for a 32-ounce cup. Group rates available.

🔖 🐊 **Insta-Gator Ranch and Hatchery** (888-448-1560, www.insta-gatorranch .com), 23440 Lowe Davis Rd., Covington. Visit this working alligator ranch and hatchery to see the animals in crystal-clear water in a climate-controlled environment. An entertaining guided tour gives visitors a first-hand account of the state's alligator industry, from hatchling to handbag. You'll get to feed the critters and learn through touch. Open year-round, rain or shine. Closed major holidays. Call ahead for hours and tour times. Reservations strongly recommended. Tours cost $16, adults; $14, seniors and military; and $10 children ages 12 and under. No fee for infants.

Kentwood Historical and Cultural Arts Museum (504-229-4656), 204 Ave. East, Kentwood. The small museum has displays on the local lifestyles and industry from the 1800s. The history of the famous Kentwood Spring Water from its beginnings as a deep artesian well is on display, as is as an exhibit of memorabilia from native daughter Britney Spears, including a re-creation of her childhood bedroom. Open 10 A.M.–4 P.M. Tues.–Sat.

🔖 **Kliebert's Turtle and Alligator Farm** (985-345-36171, www.kliebertgator tours.com), 41083 West Yellow Water Rd., Hammond. An hourlong tour takes you on a guided path through the world's first and largest alligator farm. You'll see massive gators in their swampy natural environment and watch them feed. Open March 1–Nov. 1, noon–dark. Admission is $10 adults; $5, ages 3–12.

⚓ ↝ Lake Pontchartrain Basin Maritime Museum and Research Center

(985-845-9200, www.lpbmaritimemuseum.com), 133 Mabel Dr., Madisonville. Once the site of the Jahncke Shipyard, the museum features exhibits related to the lake, the New Orleans area, and the lower Mississippi Valley. Topics include the canals of New Orleans, the lighthouses of Louisiana, the Steamboat Era, and Louisiana boatbuilding. Open 10 a.m.–4 p.m. Tues.–Sat. and noon–4 p.m. Sun. Admission $5, adults; $3, children and seniors.

Louisiana Furniture and Art Gallery (985-386-0471, www.hemmerlingart.com), 495 Southwest Railroad Ave., Ponchatoula. The Louisiana Furniture Industry Association spotlights Louisiana's outstanding builders of signature furniture, accessories, and fine art. Open 11 A.M.–5 P.M. Wed.–Sat.

Louisiana Treasures Museum and Educational Center (225-294-8325), 10290 LA 22 West at Pumpkin Center Rd., Ponchatoula. Stop by this rustic museum for a visual and hands-on exploration of Louisiana country life in days gone by. Open 10–4 P.M. Sat., noon–4 Sun., and by appointment weekdays. Admission $3.

Otis House Museum (985-792-4652, www.crt.state.la.us/parks), 119 Fairview Dr., Madisonville. Inside Fairview-Riverside State Park, this museum was built in the 1880s as the family home of sawmill owner William Theodore Jay. The house features furnishings and artifacts from the late Victorian period, and programs are themed to Victorian social life and traditions. The state park is open from 8 A.M.– dusk. The museum is open for tours 9 A.M.–5 P.M. Wed.–Sun. Park admission is $1 for adults, free to seniors 62 and over and children 12 and under. Museum admission is $4 for adults, free to seniors 62 and over and children 12 and under.

St. Joseph Abbey (985-892-1800), 76376 River Rd., Saint Benedict. Established in 1889, the Benedictine monastery and seminary welcomes day visitors who can tour the abbey, church, and rectory and see the murals created by the artist Dom Gregory de Wit. Visitors may join the monks at dawn for vigils and lauds or chant vespers at sunset. The Abbey Gift Shop and Book Store features devotional items, icons from Russia and Greece, bronze works from Germany, and Spanish Colonial–style paintings from Peru. Also available are handcrafted artisanal soap bars made at the abbey. Call for group tours. Gift shop is open 9–11 A.M. and noon–4 P.M.

Tangipahoa African American Heritage Museum (985-542-4259), 1600 Phoenix Square, Hammond. The museum features eight exhibition rooms and 26 permanent murals, a restaurant and dinner theater, a recording studio, and a heritage garden. Open 10 A.M.–4 P.M. Mon.–Fri., Saturday by appointment for groups of 10 or more. Admission is $10, adults 18 and over; $7, seniors over 65; $5, ages 5–17 and college students with IDs; and $2, children 2–4.

✳ Green Spaces

🐾 ↝ **Big Branch Marsh National Wildlife Refuge** (985-882-2000, www.fws.gov/bigbranchmarsh), 61389 LA 434, Lacombe. The largest undeveloped natural area along Lake Pontchartrain's northern shore, the refuge covers thousands of acres. It contains sandy beaches, marshes, hardwood hammocks, and pine flatwoods. Among the wildlife visitors may encounter are red-cockaded woodpeckers, brown pelicans, bald eagles, neo-tropical birds, deer, squirrels, rabbits, and ospreys. A major public use area is the Boy Scout Road boardwalk. The southeast Louisiana refuges' headquarters, the Bayou Lacombe Center, is LA 434, 2 miles south of I-12, Exit 74, and just north of the intersection of LA 434 and US 190. Look for the Big Branch Marsh Refuge sign. A visitors' center is staffed by volunteers 9 A.M.–4 P.M. Thurs.–Sat. It includes wildlife dioramas, displays, and a bookstore. The gardens, grounds, and trails are open for self-guided exploration, 7 A.M.–4 P.M. Mon.–Fri. and 9 A.M.–4 P.M. Sat.

✐ ✧ ✿ **Bogue Chitto State Park** (985-839-5707 or 888-677-7312, www.crt.state .la.us/parks), 17049 State Park Blvd., Franklinton. This lovely park near the border with Mississippi offers a rolling landscape, hardwood and upland forests, cypress tupelo swamps, and small streams. It's an excellent day trip for families, with 11 lakes stocked with freshwater fish, a water playground, and picnic pavilions. There are 14 miles of equestrian trails. Frickes Cave, actually more of a gorge, possesses sandstone spires. Boardwalks have been built so visitors can see the spires from afar; they are too delicate to allow people to walk among them. The park has more than 81 premium campsites, four deluxe cabins and a deluxe lodge, and a group camp.

✐ ✿ **Bogue Falaya Park** (985-892-1873), 213 Park Dr., Covington. This city park is a beautiful spot with large shady trees. It's a great spot for a midday walk or to meet friends. Children love the large playground with plenty of safe equipment. There are lots of benches and tables to sit and relax.

✐ ✿ **Cate Square Park** (985, 542-3471, www.dddhammond.com), 200 West Charles St., Hammond. This attractive park, a project of the Hammond Downtown Development District, is a good spot for a green break on a busy day. It has a

AIR-CONDITIONED CABINS AWAIT VISITORS AT BOGUE CHITTO STATE PARK ON THE PEARL RIVER IN ST. TAMMANY PARISH.

Louisiana Office of State Parks

walking path, benches, and a gazebo. Children can enjoy the play area with mon-key bars, a jungle gym, swings, and a slide.

✐ ↬ 🐾 **Fairview-Riverview State Park** (985-845-3318 or 888-677-3247, www .crt.state.la.us/parks), 119 Fairview Dr., Madisonville. Situated on the Tchefuncte River, the park offers a canopy of huge oaks shading numerous picnic tables and a large playground. A nature trail takes you to the river, where you can enjoy the view. Freshwater fishing from the banks delights both the experienced and casual fisherman. Two miles away by road and a few minutes by water is the Madisonville public boat launch. Visitors can use the launch to access the calm waters of the river or Lake Pontchartrain.

✐ ↬ 🐾 **Fontainebleau State Park** 985-624-4443 or 888-677-3668, www.crt.state .la.us/parks), LA 1089, Mandeville. View the crumbling brick ruins of a sugar mill built in 1829 by Bernard Xavier Philippe de Marigny de Mandeville, who founded the city and owned a large plantation here. He named his estate Fontainebleau after the forest near Paris. Located on Lake Pontchartrain, the park features a sandy beach and a shady nature trail perfect for walks or hiking. Bordered on three sides by Pontchartrain, Bayou Cane, and Bayou Castine, the park has numerous habitats for birds. The old railroad track runs through the park, in what is now part of the Tammany Trace. The park has 10 deluxe cabins, 23 premium campsites, 103 improved campsites, 37 campsites with no hookup, and a primitive group camping area. The park hosts the annual Mandeville Seafood Festival during the Fourth of July holiday weekend. Adult visitors to the festival area, including those staying at Fontainebleau State Park, are assessed a $15 admission fee. Free to children 10 and younger, seniors 65 and older, and active-duty military.

Pearl River Wildlife Management Area (985-543-4777), Slidell. About 6 miles east of Slidell, this is a massive area of mixed hardwoods with numerous streams and bayous that provide opportunities for fishing and canoeing. Access is available via car from old LA 11 and by boat. Several ramps are located along US 90; concrete ramps have been built at Davis and Crawford Landings, and there's a commercial ramp at Old Indian Village. The ramps along US 90 and those at Davis and Crawford Landings have ample parking space. Several ponds are located on the northern end of the area along I-59. Camping is available only at Crawford Landing.

Zemurray Gardens (504-878-2284), 23115 Zemurray Gardens Dr. (LA 40), Loranger, near Hammond and about 9 miles west of the Global Wildlife Center at Folsom. This private 150-acre azalea garden also features blooming trees and flowering shrubs. The nature trail winds around the gardens' scenic 20-acre lake. Take a self-guided walking tour. Open March through mid-April. Call about admission fees.

✱ To Do

FAMILY FRIENDLY ✐ 🐾 **Hammond Dreamland Skatepark** (985-277-5900), 601 West Coleman Ave., Hammond. A wonderful facility at the corner of South Oak Street and West Coleman Avenue, the skatepark is constantly busy. Professional and novice skaters work out and swap trade tricks all year long. Open from dawn to dusk. No admission fee, and all ages are welcomed.

✎ **Louisiana's Children's Discovery Center** (985-340-9150), 113 North Cypress, Hammond. This is a good spot for families with toddlers and children up to age 12 to learn and explore together in a safe, fun, hands-on environment. Open 10 A.M.–6 P.M. Tue–Sat. and 1–5 P.M. Sun.

Louisiana Office of State Parks

FISHING, BOATING, AND CANOEING Lakes Pontchartrain, Maurepas, and Borgne, along with the many rivers and bayous in the area, provide major recreational outlets for locals and visitors alike. You can see numerous boats tied up at marinas, and any number of charter companies offer daylong fishing adventures. If traveling by boat, you will find parks with boat launches for easy access to waterways. If you have your own canoe or kayak, slip into any of the Northshore's swamps, rivers, lakes or bayous. Among the best easily accessible put-in points are Mandeville Harbor, Bayou Cane off LA 190, and the Tchefuncte River at Madisonville near the LA 22 bridge. The list here is just a start, visit www.louisiananorthshore.com for more information.

LOUISIANA'S TRANQUIL BAYOUS AND RIVERS PROMISE SCENIC CANOEING ADVENTURES

Angling Adventures of Louisiana (985-781-7811, www.aaofla.com), 53105 LA 433, Slidell. The company has year-round fishing adventures with a fully insured and licensed guide.

Bayou Sailing Adventures (504-606-9029, http://bayousailing.com), Lake Pontchartrain, Madisonville. The company operates ComPac yachts and other vessels. It will arrange for sailing adventures as well as on-the-water instructions. It specializes in speckled trout, redfish and flounder in Louisiana's Biloxi Marsh, Lake Pontchartrain, and surrounding areas.

Bogue Chitto State Park (985-839-5707 or 888-677-7312). This state park near Franklinton features a river just perfect for canoeing or kayaking. There are 11 lakes stocked with a variety of freshwater fish. See Green Spaces for additional information.

Charter Boat Charlie (985-886-3728, www.charterboatcharlie.com), Rigolets Marina, Slidell. Fish for reds, specks, white trout, flounder, black drum, croaker, and occasionally shark. The company operates the 22-foot Nautic Star, rigged out with VHF radio and HDS GPS with live satellite.

GOLF Abita Springs Golf and Country Club (504-893-2463, www.abitagolf .com), 73433 Oliver St., Abita Springs. Enjoy 18 holes of golf on a 72-par course with water elements amid strands of towering pine and hardwood trees. There's a clubhouse and pro shop. Members can bring a guest for $20. Weekday rate is $11; weekend and holiday rates are $30 until 11 A.M. and $25 after 11 A.M.

Covington Country Club (985-892-1900, www.covingtoncountryclub.com), 200 Country Club Dr., Covington. Located on the Tchefuncte River, the 18-hole course offers a relaxing day of golf on a course with a clubhouse and pro shop.

Open 7 A.M.–dusk. Rates are $41 and $25 after 3 P.M. Mon.–Thurs.; Mon. senior special age 55 and over, $25; and Fri.–Sun. $58 before noon, $48 after noon and $36 after 3 P.M.

Franklinton Country Club (985-839-4195), 46402 Poplarhead Rd., Franklinton. The 18-hole, semi-private course features 6,470 yards of golf from the longest tees for a par of 72. Weekend fees are $35.

Gemstone Plantation Country Club (985-795-8900), 266 Gemstone Dr., Franklinton. The 18-hole course features immaculate greens. There are 6,657 yards of golf from the longest tees for a par of 72. The course rating is 72.5. Designed by James Ray Carpenter, the golf course opened in 1998. Open daily 6:30 A.M.–5 P.M. Green fees are $35 weekdays and $43, weekends. Ask about discounts for seniors age 60 and over.

Ironwood Golf Center (985-542-7908, www.ironwoodgolfcenter.net), 15592 West Club Deluxe Rd., Hammond. The center, featuring nine fine holes, is owned by the golf professional Larry Milosh. Facilities include a driving range with 40 tees, five of which are covered and heated. There's a short-game practice area with chipping and putting greens. There's also a pro shop, and lessons are available. Open daily 8 A.M. until 30 minutes after dark. Fees to play nine holes are $7 to walk and $12 to ride a cart. Fees for the 18-hole course are $18.95, Mon.–Fri. and $20.95 Sat.–Sun.

Oak Harbor Golf Club (985-646-0110, www.oakharborgolf.com), 201 Oak Harbor Blvd., Slidell. The 18-hole championship layout is a semi-private course known for its well-manicured conditions, undulating greens, and water elements. Begin and end your visit at the clubhouse with a snack bar, restaurant, and well-stocked golf shop. Open 7 A.M.–5:30 P.M. Fees are $40 and $30 after 1 P.M. Mon.–Thurs.; $45 all day Fri.; and $50, $40 after 1 P.M., Sat.–Sun.

Springwood Country Club (985-748-9760), 17233 Country Club Rd., Amite. The par-72 golf club offers 18 holes of rolling hills. Amenities include a club house, snack bar, and pool. Golf lessons are available. Open daily 8 A.M.–dusk Mon.–Fri. and 7 A.M.–dusk Sat.–Sun. Fees are $10, Mon.–Tues., $20, Wed.–Fri., and $25 Sat.–Sun.

TOURS Canoe and Trail Adventures (504-834-5257, www.canoeandtrail.com), 1049 Hesper Ave., Metairie. Operating out of the New Orleans suburb of Metairie, the company offers canoe adventures in the waterways of Lake Pontchartrain and the Pearl River area. River skills weekends are held on the Bogue Chitto River near Tylertown, Mississippi. Popular with avid canoers are Moonlight Paddles in the Manchac Wetlands and Big Branch Wildlife Refuge. With a launch at sunset, experience the sounds of the wetlands at night with just the moon to light your way. Check the website for trip schedules and costs.

Honey Island Swamp Tour (985-641-1769, www.honeyislandswamp.com), tours depart from Crawford Landing on West Pearl River, Slidell. Two-hour tours are offered year-round. Professional guides in small boats (both covered and uncovered) take visitors deep into the Honey Island cypress swamp. Learn about the abundant wildlife here, including alligators, herons, egrets, ibises, deer, feral hogs, nutrias, turtles, and frogs. Boat tour is $23, adults, and $15, children.

Joyce Wildlife Management Area (985-543-4777, www.lf.louisiana.gov), about 5 miles south of Hammond. The area consists of 12,809 acres owned by the

Department of Wildlife and Fisheries. Access to the property is very limited. Old logging runs are narrow and during high-water periods, travel is allowed only by pirogue and canoe. Access by outboard motor is limited to the upper reaches of Middle Bayou and Black Bayou. Public boat launches are available at the North Pass Bridge along LA 51.

✳ Lodging

Berry Creek Cabins (985-730-4395, www.berrycreekcabins.com), 12101 George Jenkins Rd., Bogalusa. The cabins, set in the wooded countryside, are perfect for people on a tubing trip. The grounds are charming and the air-conditioned cabins are well outfitted with a full kitchen. A hot tub and party deck add to the fun. Moderate.

Country Inns & Suites (985-809-0467, www.countryinns.com), 130 Holiday Blvd., Covington. Rooms and suites feature warm, relaxing décor. Amenities include high-speed Internet, microwave, coffee maker, and free chocolate-chip cookies. Children age 18 and under stay free in the same room with an adult. Handicapped-accessible rooms are available. Moderate.

Courtyard Covington Mandeville (985-871-0244, www.marriott.com), 101 Northpark Blvd., Covington. Situated on a shining pond surrounded by lush foliage and stately trees, the hotel has a calming atmosphere. Features include a 24-hour food market, breakfast buffet, heated pool, hot tub, indoor pool, laundry, and valet service. Weekdays, the lounge invites casual relaxation. Shopping and restaurants are nearby. Moderate.

Hampton Inn (985-419-2188, www.hamptoninn.com), 401 Weston Oak Dr., Hammond. The 81-room hotel has clean, comfortable rooms with plush beds. Amenities include free high-speed Internet and a laptop desk. There's a complimentary breakfast and laundry and valet service are available. Moderate.

Holiday Inn and Suites (985-639-0890, www.holidayinn.com), 372 Voters Rd., Slidell. Situated at the intersection of I-10, I-12 and I-59, the hotel is convenient to both the Greater New Orleans area and the Mississippi Gulf Coast. Rooms feature pillowtop mattresses and high-speed Internet, and the hotel has a cafe, an indoor pool, and a 24-hour fitness center. Moderate.

La Quinta Covington (985-871-0356, www.lq.com), 200 Pinnacle Pkwy., Covington. The hotel features free high-speed Internet, an outdoor pool, free breakfast, guest laundry facilities, and a fitness center. Pets are welcomed. Moderate.

BED & BREAKFASTS

Annadele's Plantation (985-809-7669, www.annadeles.com), 71495 Chestnut St., Covington. This West Indies–style plantation includes four spacious rooms and baths. A gourmet breakfast is included. The restaurant specializes in Creole and French dishes. Expensive.

Blue Willow (985-892-0011, www.bluewillowbandb.com), 505 East Rutland St., Covington. This cozy, blissful retreat features comfortable suites and screened porches. Suites have private entrances through a gated courtyard. The courtyard screens a large outdoor Jacuzzi where you can soak up the atmosphere. The "Continental Plus" breakfast includes fresh pastries, fresh fruit in season, coffee, teas, and hot and cold cereals. Moderate–expensive.

Camilla House Bed & Breakfast (985-264-4973, www.camelliahouse

.net), 426 East Rutland St., Covington. The B&B, a raised Creole Cottage, offers great bedding and breakfasts. Other amenities include fresh flowers in room, bikes for guest use, a front porch swing, fountains and a hammock, and the biggest little extras— movies, magazines, and foot scrub. Moderate–expensive.

Hughes House (985-542-0148, www .hughesbb.com), 300 North Holly St., Hammond. Built at the turn of the century by Jefferson Davis Hughes, the grandson of Peter Hammond, the Queen Anne–style mansion was built by area craftsmen. Three-quarter-inch tongue-and-groove boards are used throughout the building. Rooms are filled with elegant antique furnishings. Breakfast is served in the spacious Pearl room, which has multidirectional windows. Moderate–expensive.

Maison Reve Farm (985-796-8103, www.maisonrevefarm.com), 76251 LA 1077, Folsom. Six miles north of I-12, this French-style inn is on a 30-acre estate. The furnishings reflect the owner's own casual elegance. The property is a bird sanctuary, and walks will reveal deer, wild turkey, ducks, and a variety of other wildlife. And you can take a cooking class from the owner. There's a two-night weekend minimum. Moderate–expensive.

MarVilla Guesthouse (985-626-5975, www.marvilla.com), 2013 Claiborne St., Mandeville. This is an 1870s boarding house where palms and elephant ears grace the garden. One block off Lake Pontchartrain, the guest house is within walking distance of fine restaurants and antiques shops. Moderate.

♂ **Michabelle Inn** (985-419-0550, www.michabelle.com), 1106 South Holly St., Hammond. The roses, camellias, and azaleas that surround the historic McGehee house make it a romantic setting for an inn and restaurant. Rooms and suites are named after three famous women of history, Marie Antoinette, Empress Josephine, and Madame Pompadour, and one of fiction, Evangeline. The furnishings reflect the lifestyles of these women. Michel Marcais, the chef and owner, who formerly worked at the Pebble Beach Country Club and the Royal Sonesta in New Orleans, has earned the title of Louisiana Chef of the Year. His wife, Isabel, a native of Portugal, is responsible for Michabelle's elegant furnishings. Moderate.

CAMPGROUNDS ✔ 🐾 **Hidden Oaks Family Campground** (800-359-0940, www.hiddenoaksfamily campground.com), 21544 LA 190 East, Hammond. With 200 primitive sites and hook-ups, this campground is truly designed for families. Facilities include cabins, a laundry, store, snack bar, bath houses, fishing boats, canoes, tube rentals, playgrounds, ball fields, pool, lake, beach, and picnic areas. Pets are allowed on a leash. Inexpensive.

✔ 🐾 **Indian Creek Campground and RV Park** (888-716-4687, www .indiancreek55.com), 53013 West Fontana Rd., Independence. Situated north of Hammond, the campground offers 152 sites with water and electricity and 32 full-hook-ups. Amenities include a bath house, pool, paddle boats, canoes, camp store, cabins, a playground, fishing, a game room, and hiking. Pets are allowed on a leash. Inexpensive.

Indian Hills Nudist Park (985-641-9998, www.indianhillspark.com), 2484 Gause Blvd. West, Slidell. The camp has 15 full hookups and 10 with electricity and water. Amenities include a pool, hot tub, board games, volleyball, horseshoes, darts, Indian room club-house, laundromat, fishing, showers, and a dump station. Inexpensive–moderate.

𝄢 ((•)) **Land-o-Pines Family Camp-ground** (985-892-6023 or 800-443-469, 17145 Million Dollar Rd., Covington. The campground features 276 sites, full-hookups or water/electric only. Padded and pull-through sites are available. The campground includes cabin rentals, laundry, bath houses, a country store, WiFi, cable, a pool, waterslide, a river with white sand beaches, a game room, fishing, mini-golf, volleyball, basketball, a base-ball diamond, and a horseshoe pit. Inexpensive.

𝄢 **Silvercreek Campground** (985-877-4256), 37567 LA 1055, Mount Hermon. The campground features a bathhouse, laundromat, and swimming pool. A pavilion is available for com-pany picnics, birthday parties, and family gatherings. Inexpensive.

𝄢 **Tchefuncte Family Camp-ground** (985-796-3654, www .tchefunctecampground.com), 54492 Campground Rd., Folsom. The camp has 90 sites. Amenities include rental cabins and campers, a large recreation building, access to a river, a swimming pool, a fishing pond, a horseshoe pit, a baseball diamond, basketball, a play-ground, and hayrides. Inexpensive.

𝄢 ❀ **Yogi Bear's Jellystone Park** (985-542-1507 or 800-349-YOGI), 46049 LA 445N, Robert. This large campground has 316 rentable sites: 44 with water and electricity; 171 with water, electricity and sewage; and 101 with 50 amp and full hookup. There are 88 cabins. Amenities include a swimming pool, mini-golf, boat rentals, playgrounds, and an activities sched-ule. Pets are allowed on a leash, but are not allowed in cabins. Inexpensive.

HOW TO EAT A CRAWFISH
First-time visitors often sit and stare at steaming piles of boiled crawfish and ask "How do you eat these things?" It's simple. Holding the tail, peel away the first couple of rings of the shell, then pinch the tail at the bottom. Slide the meat out and pop it into your mouth. Feeling feisty? Suck the head for spicy juices before setting it aside. It takes no time to be a specialist. And don't call them crayfish!

✳ **Where to Eat**

A number of leading chefs have opened restaurants throughout the Northshore. Locals and visitors enjoy the exciting mix of fine dining estab-lishments and small casual eateries specializing in regional dishes.

EATING OUT Abita Brew Pub (985-892-5837, www.abitabrewpub .com), 72011 Holly St., Abita Springs. The 10-ounce brew burgers are awe-some. So are the fried quail stuffed with *boudin* and the blackened chicken. Housed in a renovated build-ing where Abita Brewery produced its beers until 1994, the pub features attractive cypress window frames and a cypress and slate bar. Beers on tap include Turbodog, a dark brown ale; Andygator, a Helles Dopplebock; and Abita Golden, a crisp, clean continen-tal lager. Be sure to try the sweet, creamy, old-fashioned root beer. Hours are 11 A.M.–9 P.M. Tues.–Thurs., 11 A.M.–10 P.M. Sat.–Sun., and 11 A.M.–9 P.M. Sun. Moderate.

Beck-n-Call Cafe (985-875-9390, www.beckncallcafe.com), 534 North New Hampshire St., Covington. This small cafe across from the St. Tammany Courthouse serves Southern comfort food, including red beans and rice, fried chicken, and meatloaf. Daily specials are based on family recipes. Open for breakfast 6 A.M.–11 A.M. Mon.–Fri. and 7 A.M.–noon Sat.; and lunch 11 A.M.–3 P.M. Mon.–Fri. Inexpensive–moderate.

Buster's Place Restaurant and Oyster Bar (985-809-3880, www.bustersplaceonline.com), 519 East Boston St., Covington. One of the best Northshore spots for enjoying oysters on the half shell, char-grilled, or fried to perfection. The bar is a gathering spot for watching LSU and Saints football games. Hours 11 A.M.–9 P.M. Mon.–Thurs., 11 A.M.–10 P.M. Fri.–Sat., and 11 A.M.–8 P.M. Sun. Inexpensive–moderate.

Coffee's Boilin' Pot (985-845-2348, www.coffeesboilinpot.com), 305 Covington St., Madisonville. This well-known seafood cafe is popular with locals. The cafe, which survived Hurricane Katrina, has been featured in *Coastal Living* magazine. Try the fried or grilled catfish, shrimp, crab, and oysters, the crabmeat au gratin, or the frog legs. Kid's meals every Wednesday and Thursday are $2.50. Open 4–9 P.M. Tues.–Wed.; 11 A.M.–9 P.M. Thursday; and 11–10 P.M. Fri.–Sat. Inexpensive–moderate.

Coffee Rani (985-893-6158, www.coffeerani.com), 234 Lee Lane, Suite A, Covington. This cafe serves healthy entrée-sized salads, grilled sandwiches, seafood, and pasta. Start the day with fresh pastries, assorted coffees, and teas. Open 7 A.M.–3 P.M. Mon.–Sat. and 8 A.M.–3 P.M. Sun. Moderate.

Middendorf's (985-386-6666, www.middendorfsrestaurant.com), 30160 US 51 South, Akers. People will drive for miles to eat at this seafood restaurant situated at Pass Manchac between Lake Maurepas and Lake Pontchartrain. The restaurant, which opened in 1934, is famous for its thin fried catfish and lavish seafood platters. Barbecued

THE ABITA BREW PUB IS THE HOME OF ABITA BEERS.

Louisiana Northshore CVB

oysters, with house-made sauce, and oysters on the half shell are great with cold beer or iced tea. In fall or spring, sit on the patio and enjoy the lake breeze. If you're boating, tie up at Middendorf's dock for a memorable experience. Open 10:30 A.M.–9 P.M. Wed.–Sun. Moderate.

N'Tini's (985-626-5566, www.ntinis .com), 2891 LA 190, Mandeville. A casual atmosphere and really good steaks make this a relaxing spot for lunch and dinner. There's a large martini menu and $1 martinis on Friday are a big attraction. Hours are 11 A.M.– 9 P.M. Mon.–Wed. and 11 A.M.–10 P.M. Thurs.–Sat. Moderate.

Taste of Bavaria Restaurant and Bakery (985-386-3634, www.tasteof bavariarestaurant.com), 14476 LA 22, Ponchatoula. Situated on a country byway, this cafe brings a touch of Germany to south Louisiana. Pop in for a delicious apple pancake for breakfast. For lunch or dinner, try German sausage and sauerkraut or hearty potato soup. Open 8 A.M.–3 P.M. Wed.– Sun. Moderate.

DINING OUT Dakota Restaurant (985-892-3712, www.restaurantcuvee .com/dakota/index.htm), 629 North US 190, Covington. Exceptional cooking draws patrons who are particular about well-seasoned contemporary and continental cuisine. The restaurant's signature dish is crabmeat and brie soup. Entrees include duck and dumplings with pecan–sweet potato gnocchi and soft-shell crab. Mahogany millwork and earth-tone colors set the stage for an elegant, yet casual, dining experience. Lunch hours are 11 A.M.– 2:30 P.M. Mon.–Fri.; dinner hours are 5–10 P.M. Mon.–Thurs.; dinner is 5– 11 P.M. Fri.–Sat. Expensive.

Del Porto Restaurant (985-875- 1006, www.delportoristorante.com), 501 East Boston St., Covington. Situated in a renovated building downtown, Del Porto's contemporary Italian menu includes dishes made in-house from locally grown items. Fruits and vegetables are mainstays, as are breads, pastas, cheeses, and sausages. The lunch menu includes a variety of panini on homemade focaccia and ciabatta as well as Roman-styled pizzas. The menu changes daily with the seasons and the availability of produce. Hours are 11:30 A.M.–2 P.M. and 5:30- 10 P.M., Tues.–Fri and 5:30-10 P.M. Sat. Moderate–expensive.

Jacmel Inn (985-542-0043, www .jacmelinn.com), 903 East Morris Avenue, Hammond. Set in a 100-year-old home, the inn is named for Jaque de Melo, an Italian pirate who sailed the Caribbean. The restaurant's Caribbean, Creole, and French atmosphere carries over on the menu with items such as Creole turtle soup or pan-seared scallops and oysters wrapped in smoked bacon with sweet anise. The setting is casual and romantic. Open for lunch 11:30 A.M.–2 P.M. Wed.–Fri.; dinner 5–10 P.M. Tues.– Sun.; and Sunday brunch 11 A.M.– 3 P.M. Moderate–expensive.

La Provence (985-626-7662, www .laprovencerestaurant.com), 25020 LA 190, Lacombe. One of the leading restaurants in Louisiana, La Provence is a warm, comfortable place with gleaming hardwood floors and oak ceiling beams. Chef John Besh's menu includes country-style pate on toasted brioche, ravioli of slow cooked rabbit, and local soft-shell crab. A specialty on the brunch menu is a bouillabaisse with redfish, Gulf shrimp, oysters, mussels, clams, fennel, and saffron broth. Open 5–9 P.M. Wed.–Sat. and 11 A.M.–9 P.M. Sun. Expensive–very expensive.

Trey Yuen (985-345-6789, www.trey yuen.com), 2100 North Morrison Blvd., Hammond. The Chinese restaurant features imported rosewood ceilings, carved wall panels, and antique furnishings. Lush gardens, waterfalls, and koi ponds surround it. Dishes include alligator stir-fry and crawfish in a spicy lobster sauce. Lunch hours are 11 A.M.–2 P.M. Mon.–Fri. and dinner hours are 5–10 P.M. Mon.–Thurs., 5– 11 P.M. Fri.-Sat., and 11:30 A.M.– 9:30 P.M. Sun. Moderate.

✱ Entertainment

Columbia Street Tap Room & Grill (985-898-0899, www.columbiastreet taproom.com), 434 North Columbia St., Covington. Block parties are featured the last Friday of the month, March through April. The popular spot serves up 30 beers on tap and excellent sandwiches, burgers, and salads. Live music is featured Thursday, Friday, and Saturday nights. Regional rock acts include Bag of Donuts, Soul Revival, and Rick Samson and Friends. There's room to dance and a great patio. Open 11 A.M.–10 P.M. Mon.; 11 A.M.–midnight Tues.–Thurs.; 11 A.M.– 1:30 A.M. Fri.; and noon–1:30 A.M. Sat.

Dew Drop Jazz & Social Hall (985-624-9604, www.dewdropjazzhall.com), 400 Lamarque St., Mandeville. Surrounded by ancient live oaks, this small, unpainted, wood-frame building built in 1895 is considered the world's oldest, unaltered rural jazz dance hall. Pioneer young musicians, like Kid Ory, Bunk Johnson, Buddy Petit, Louis Armstrong, and others came by steamboat across Lake Pontchartrain to play their new and exciting music here. The hall presents a spring and fall series each year. Times vary. The website posts events.

Green Room (985-892-2225, www .greenroomlive.net), 521 East Boston St., Covington. Bring your instruments or just enjoy the show. There's plenty of room to dance to the sounds of regional acts like the Zydepunks,

PEOPLE PICNIC AT JAZZ IN THE VINES AT PONTCHARTRAIN VINEYARDS NEAR COVINGTON.

Northshore Tourism

Eggyolk Jubilee, Bonerama, Johnny Sketch and the Dirty Notes and more. Patrons jive well into the night. Open 2 P.M.–2 A.M. daily.

Pontchartrain Vineyards (985-892-9742, www.pontchartrainvineyards .com), 812 LA 1082, Bush. This winery, about 20 minutes outside downtown Covington, hosts an outdoor concert series, Jazz 'n the Vines, twice monthly in May, June, September, October, and November. Pack a picnic, bring blankets or lawn chairs, and relax on a grassy slope while listening to regional musicians perform on a small outdoor stage. You can buy light meals here, but guests can't take their own beverages onto the property. Bring a flashlight to find your way back to the car after dark. Concerts run 6:30–9 P.M.

Ruby's Roadhouse (985-892-2225, www.rubysroadhouse.com), 840 Lamarque St., Mandeville. Northshore and New Orleans acts rock in this one-time juke joint with a bouncy wood floor, long bar, and friendly regulars. Rockin' Dopsie plays here; so do the Iguanas, Tab Benoit, and Four Unplugged. Show off your talent on the dance floor, then head outside for a drink and fresh air on the patio. Open 10–2 A.M. Mon.–Fri. and 9–2 A.M. Sat.–Sun.

Sunset at the Landing (985-898-4722,www.cityofcovingtonla.com), Covington. Free concerts take place every third Friday March-October on the Columbia Street Landing to the Bogue Falaya River. Regional musical groups play jazz, fusion, pop, and more. The City Council encourages people to bring their own chairs, blankets, and refreshments. Hours are 6–8 P.M.

MOVIES AMC Palace Theater 10 (888-262-4386, www.amctheatres.com /HammondPalace), 801 CM Fagan Dr., Hammond. Convenient to downtown, the theater has 13 auditoriums and carries first-run movies as well as independent films.

Hollywood Theaters (800-FAN-DANGO, www.gohollywood.com), 69348 LA 21, Covington. Situated in the Stirling Covington Shopping Center near I-12, the theater has state-of-the-art digital projection in all its auditoriums, as well as Dolby digital sound and Dolby digital RealD 3-D movies. It also boasts massive wall-to-wall screens, stadium seating, and arcade games. The box office offers military, senior and children discounts with proper ID. Children age 16 and under must be accompanied by a legal guardian or parent for all shows starting after 8 P.M. on Friday and Saturday.

THEATER The Columbia Theater (985-543-4366, www.columbiatheatre .org), 220 East Thomas St., Hammond. The vintage theater, which once presented vaudeville acts, was restored to its original glory through the efforts of Southeastern Louisiana University, the City of Hammond, and the Hammond Downtown Development District. It serves as the centerpiece for the town's major performing arts events. The theater presents drama, music, dance performances, and other events throughout the year.

✱ Selective Shopping

Bayou Country Village (985-649-3264, www.bayoucountry.com), 1101 East Howze Beach Rd., Slidell. This lively country store is a handy stop for people traveling between the Northshore and New Orleans. Handmade pralines are cooked daily and make great take-home gifts. Look for Swamp Cabin art and cards by Louisiana artist Craig Routh. Open 9 A.M.–5:30 P.M. Mon.–Sat.

Cottage Antiques (985-892-7995), 205 Lee St., Covington. This is a browser's delight, filled with heirlooms linens, silver books, mirrors, furniture, and more. Open 10 A.M.–5 P.M. Mon.–Sat. and noon–4 P.M. Sun.

Meme's Beads & Things (985-643-5700, www.memesbeadsandthings.com), 106 Gause Blvd., Suite A5, Slidell. Just the place for crafters who work beads into magical designs. New beads and buttons are constantly arriving at this delightful shop. Also shop for watches, link bracelets, and inspirational jewelry. Open 10 a.m.–6 p.m. Mon.–Thurs. and 10 a.m.–6 p.m. Fri.–Sat.

Purple Armadillo Again (985-641-6316, www.purplearmadillo.net), 124 Erlanger St., Olde Towne, Slidell. The shop carries a variety of accessories to accent your home with the latest in home décor. Check out the Trapp candles, fleur de lis items, and baby gifts. Open 10 a.m.–5:30 p.m. Tues.–Fri. and 10 p.m.–4 p.m. Sat.

Slidell Historic Antique District (985-641-6316, www.slidellantiques.com), Second and Erlanger streets, Slidell. Browse in Olde Town Slidell for antique furniture, art, jewelry, home décor, and gift items. Street fairs

THE NORTHLAKE NATURE CENTER AT BAYOU CASTINE NEAR MANDEVILLE IS A PEACEFUL RETREAT.

St. Tamany Tourism

are held the last full weekend of October and the third weekend in April.

✳ Special Events

February: **Mardi Gras Parades** (985-892-0520), St. Tammany Parish. In Covington, the Krewe of Covington Lions Club starts its family oriented parade downtown at 10 A.M. It's followed by the Mystic Krewe of Covington at 11 A.M. Not far away in the village of Lacombe, the Krewe of Skunks begins its parade at 1 P.M., followed by the Krewe of Chahta-Ima. The Sunday before Mardi Gras, the Krewe of Tchefuncte navigates boats down the Tchefuncte River at 2 P.M. and boaters toss beads to crowds on both sides of the LA 22 Bridge. They tie up at Madisonville, where the celebration continues along Water Street. Check www.louisiananorthshore.com for a schedule.

April: **Great Louisiana Bird Fest** (985-626-1238), 23135 US 190 East, Mandeville. With the Northlake Nature Center as a focal point, the event features birding field trips and photography workshops. Local experts guide birders to locations throughout St. Tammany Parish.

The Italian Festival (985-878-6081, www.theitalianfestivalorg.com), 52012 Redhill Rd., Independence. The people of Independence honor their Italian heritage with a three-day festival in April. Is there a better way to celebrate than to host an annual Spaghetti Cook-off? The three-day festival includes live musical entertainment, carnival rides, and a motorcycle run.

June: **Lacombe Crab Festival** (985-882-5528, www.lacombecrab.com), John Davis Park, Lacombe. Held in late June under a stand of oaks, the event serves crabs prepared in dozens of ways. Try the soft-shell crabs. The fun includes live entertainment and carnival rides. Admission is $5. Free to children age 10 and under.

Louisiana Bicycle Festival (985-892-2624), Abita Springs. A June treat for bicycle enthusiasts, the event includes antique bicycle exhibits and a bicycle flea market. Other activities include a St. Tammany Trace bike cruise, a log pull bike contest, and high-wheeler demonstration. Hours are 10 a.m.–4 p.m.

October: **Washington Parish Free Fair** (985-848-5937, www.freefair.com), Main St. Fairgrounds, Bogalusa. Since its beginning in 1911, this parish fair has grown bigger each successive year. Based upon attendance records, it is believed to be the largest county fair in the United States. It's a family fair with exhibits of cut flowers, home-making, livestock, and agricultural products. There's a large midway, rodeo, food court, and Old McDonald's Farm. At Mile Branch Settlement, stroll through a historical pioneer village with historic log cabins and watch volunteers demonstrate crafts of yesteryear.

Madisonville Wooden Boat Festival (985-845-9200, www.woodenboatfest.org), Madisonville. Hundreds of wooden boats line the shore of the Tchefuncte River in mid-October for the largest gathering of watercraft on the Gulf Coast. The biggest event is the Quick and Dirty Boat Building Contest and Race. Other activities include a large food court with seafood specialties and live music.

November: **Arts Evening** (985-646-4375, www.slidell.la.us/artsevening), Slidell. Held in Olde Towne Slidell, this event celebrates the visual and performing arts, dance, and music. It showcases more than 100 local artists. Enjoy browsing for antiques. Free.

Three Rivers Art Festival (985-327-9797, www.threeriversartfestival.com), Covington. The two-day festival spreads out along downtown. Visitors meander through tents displaying fine art and crafts. You'll find some exceptional artwork at this festival during south Louisiana's best time of year. Activities include a children's discovery area, a food court, and the Arts Alive! Stage. Grab some kettle corn and lemonade and settle down to hear a mix of pop music, blues, and jazz.

Louisiana Renaissance Festival (985-429-9992, www.larf.net), 46468 River Rd., Hammond. The festival runs the six weekends following Halloween. Organized like a mini–theme park, it features jousting and falconry displays. Meet historical characters like peasants, merchants, knights, and Queen Elizabeth I. Wear walking shoes and dress comfortably. Children can wear their Halloween costumes, or you can rent a costume for a day. Open 9:45 A.M.–5 P.M. Ticket sales start in September. Prices vary.

December: **Winter on the Water** (9885-626-3147, www.cityofmandeville.com), Mandeville. Throughout December, you can enjoy a laser light show set to holiday tunes along the shore of Lake Pontchartrain. Activities include horse-and buggy rides at the Mandeville Trailhead and a Christmas tour of homes on Lakeshore Drive.

Christmas Under the Stars (985-646-4375, www.slidell.la.us), Griffith Park, Slidell. This is a spectacular 10-night event with holiday lights, decorated trees, gingerbread houses, a miniature train village, and Christmas cottages with animated figures and a life-size nativity scene with live animals.

Plantation Country

5

BATON ROUGE AREA

INTRODUCTION

Gigantic oaks with Spanish moss gracing broad green lawns and slower-paced conversations lend a timelessness to Louisiana's Plantation Country. The area is defined by the Mississippi River flowing past stately antebellum homes, many still intact and restored to mid-1800 grandeur. Dozens are found along the Great River Road corridor and in the countryside. The area offers abundant opportunities to step back in time. Romantic B&Bs with four-poster beds and gardens with sweet magnolias and brilliant azaleas are part of the scene. Evening dinners can be enjoyed on courtyards softly lit by candles or lanterns.

At the same time, the Mississippi River, which served as the main commercial highway for plantation owners, remains a major route of commercial transportation. It's one of the catalysts that adds to the area's current economic and cultural

A GUN EMPLACEMENT OVERLOOKS THE PORT HUDSON BATTLEFIELD.

Louisiana Office of Tourism

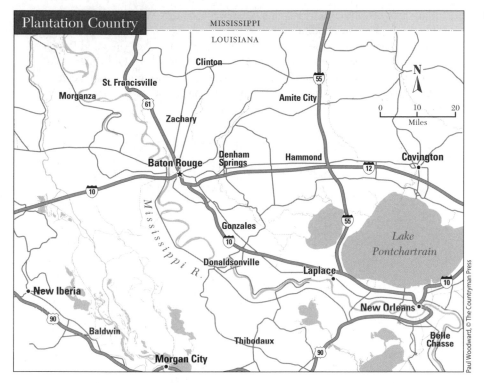

Plantation Country

MISSISSIPPI
LOUISIANA

Clinton

St. Francisville

Morganza

61

Amite City

Zachary

N

0   10   20
Miles

Denham
Springs

Hammond

Covington

Baton Rouge

Mississippi R.

55

Lake
Pontchartrain

Gonzales

10

Donaldsonville

Laplace

New Iberia

90

New Orleans

Baldwin

Belle
Chasse

Thibodaux

90

Morgan City

Paul Woodward, © The Countryman Press

growth. Agricultural and other industries flourish here. You can feel the energy. Communities such as Gonzales and Denham Springs are booming. In the area's northern section, East and West Feliciana parishes capitalize on outdoor fun in rolling hills and pre-Civil War heritage. On the west side of the Mississippi the landscape is more pastoral. People enjoy fishing on False River and shopping in New Roads, a quaint lakeside community. Old-time family festivals and values are celebrated in West Baton Rouge. Sugarcane fields, golfing, and the grand Nottoway Plantation attract people further down river.

History comes to life in Plantation Country. The Port Hudson State National Historic Site hosts a re-enactment of the Civil War Battle of Port Hudson, the site of the U.S. military's longest land siege in American history. Downtown Baton Rouge has a number of historical sites. In nearby Jackson, you can attend a re-enactment of the Battle of Jackson Crossroads or stop by Centenary Historic Site, which focuses on early education in Louisiana. In St. Francisville, the Rosedown Plantation State Historic Site interprets life at one of the most elegant antebellum homes and gardens in the American South.

Spring is a wonderful time in Plantation Country. From late February until late May, blooming shrubbery dresses up lawns as well as public parks and building landscapes. The weather is sunny and cool. Fall, late September through November, is equally pleasant. Trees don't turn the brilliant colors you find in New England. Instead you will find subtle hint of yellow and brown mixed with bits of red from swamp maples. It's perfect football and golf weather. Locals admit that it's just plain hot in summer. During this season, guests are welcomed with house parties, icy drinks, and air-conditioning.

In Plantation Country, people definitely take time to savor the good things of life. Great food, great music, and great friends are cherished. Old-timers take pride in their skills dishing out Southern hospitality. Newcomers soon realize that the hospitality is genuine and helps to build lasting friendships. Visitors are welcomed with smiles and good will.

BATON ROUGE AREA

Baton Rouge is the hub of Plantation Country. The pace is seemingly slower here than in many cities, but don't be fooled. This Mississippi River community long ago learned to shift with the times. Things speed up when business calls for swift action or when people drive in for a Mardi Gras Parade or a championship football or baseball game.

There's a tendency to compare Baton Rouge to New Orleans, but there's a distinct difference. Certainly the topography is different. Baton Rouge, west by northwest of New Orleans, lies on high land on the east side of the Mississippi River. It's far enough inland from the Gulf of Mexico to escape severe damage from most of the Gulf storms. The city is a thriving commercial, agricultural, educational, and transportation center. However, many neighborhoods retain a small-town feel. In many ways residents enjoy the quality of life found in rural America while having the conveniences of a major city.

As the capital of Louisiana, Baton Rouge is famous for its intriguing politics. People come to Baton Rouge to lobby legislators for changing laws. Others meet here to discuss new directions in high-tech businesses. Academic research thrives at Louisiana State University and Southern University, major centers of learning. Young adults come here to study everything from music composition to chemical engineering. Many breeze into town just for collegiate sports. Families travel to the city to watch their kids compete in junior high and high school sports meets. Some visit just for pleasure. No matter what is brewing here, Old Man River, wider than a mile, just keeps rolling along.

As the political and cultural center of Louisiana, Baton Rouge is packed with historical places. Visit museums

AN ILLUMINATED MAP IN THE LOUISIANA STATE MUSEUM IN BATON ROUGE SHOWS THE TERRITORY BOUGHT IN THE LOUISIANA PURCHASE.

Cynthia V. Campbell

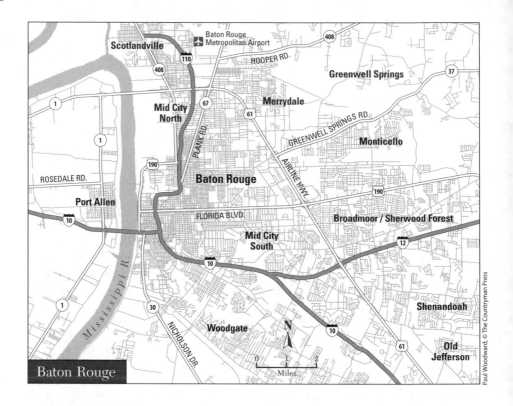

Paul Woodward, © The Countryman Press

and sites to learn about the state's dramatic history, which began in the 1700s. This is also a sports center, with the universities drawing thousands of fans on game days. Tailgating is an art form here, with families and friends setting up colorful tents and BBQ gear often for an entire weekend of fun. Make the city a hub for run-out trips to plantation homes, the Atchafalaya Heritage Area, and small Main Street towns that preserve their 19th- and early 20th-century charm.

Baton Rouge should not be compared to New Orleans, famous for its historic French Quarter and all-night party scene. It has its own distinct music performed by local musicians and celebrated during the annual Baton Rouge Blues Festival. If you're a night person, the downtown entertainment district, centered on Third Street, offers wine bars and clubs with live bands performing everything from zydeco and blues to traditional jazz and new music. More nightlife is found near the LSU campus and along major corridors in all areas of the city, including Perkins Road, Florida Boulevard, Coursey Boulevard, and Airline Highway. On Memorial Day weekend in 2010, the city inaugurated its first Bayou Country Superfest in LSU's Tiger Stadium, bringing together many of America's top country music entertainers. In addition, Baton Rouge nightspots serve as incubators for young musicians trying to break into the big time. Friday and Saturday nights things are buzzing all over the city. Closing time is 2 A.M.

The performing and visual arts here reflect Baton Rouge's diverse cultural heritage. Visitors can enjoy seeing outstanding actors and musicians in dramas, comedies, and musicals at by the Baton Rouge Little Theater, one of the country's

Louisiana Office of Tourism

A PELICAN SCULPTURE ON THE SOUTHERN UNIVERSITY CAMPUS SITS ON THE BLUFF OVERLOOKING THE MISSISSIPPI RIVER.

oldest regional theater groups; Playmakers; Swine Palace; and LSU Theater. The River Center Performing Arts Theatre is home to the Baton Rouge Symphony, and is the main venue for traveling shows. Nearby the River Center Arena serves as the venue for rock concerts, circuses, and special exhibitions.

Visual artists long ago discovered the untold wealth of Louisiana's beautiful landscapes and sunlit skies. People will find paintings and drawings by local artists in outstanding galleries, art walks, the LSU Museum of Art, and the Southern University Museum of Art. The annual FestForAll sponsored by Baton Rouge Arts Council draws artists and art lovers from throughout the region.

When it comes to outstanding Louisiana cuisine, Baton Rouge stands proud. The city has some 600 restaurants. From boiled crawfish to shrimp *etouffee*, bread pudding topped with whiskey sauce to sweet potato pie, local cuisine tends to be traditional Southern, Cajun, and Creole. Yet international restaurants, including Japanese and Nepalese, are staking their gustatory claims. Fresh seafood from the Gulf of Mexico is found on almost every menu. Shrimp and oysters (baked, broiled, and raw) are common fare. People think nothing of driving across the city to try a new restaurant or eat a simple bowl of gumbo at their favorite eatery. Ask a resident where to go for seafood, steaks, hamburgers, and dessert. You will likely be given the name of a different restaurant for each dish, and you're not likely to be steered wrong. Dining out is a form of entertainment here. People take their time and socialize before, during, and after meals. If you're looking for a quick bite, then head for one of the fast-food spots found throughout town. Restaurants range from the elegant and distinctive to the small and cozy. People in Baton Rouge have discerning, sophisticated palates. They expect the food to be exceptionally good and the wait staff to be friendly and professional. Anything less is an insult.

Baton Rougeans are so accustomed to towering trees—stately oaks, glorious magnolias, willowy cypresses—that they sometimes take the region's beauty for granted. Visitors find it especially lovely. This is a naturally green city. After Hurricane Gustav swept through Baton Rouge in 2008, as soon as the roofs were repaired folks were talking about replacing lost trees. In spring, dogwoods, camellias, azaleas, Indian hawthorn, swamp maple, and Bradford pear trees work their colorful magic. Waterfowl and warblers sweep through the area on their annual migratory paths.

Around Easter you can expect oak trees to rain green pollen and blooming shrubs to set your nose twitching. With an annual 60-inch rainfall, you can feel a bit ducky at times. But watering the lawn isn't much of a problem. Don't worry if you forget your umbrella. You can pick up an inexpensive bumbershoot at shops and grocery stores all over town.

In fall, with temperatures in the 60s, trees develop just a subtle hint of color. It's no wonder that most people enjoy outdoor activities yearlong. The city boasts walking and hiking trails, bike paths, and public and private golf courses. The Baton Rouge Recreation Commission (BREC) operates 184 neighborhood and community parks across the parish.

THE LSU MEMORIAL TOWER STANDS AT THE HEART OF LOUISIANA STATE UNIVERSITY IN BATON ROUGE.

Cynthia V. Campbell

Like most of the Deep South, Baton Rouge has long, hot, humid summers. The secret to survival is to enjoy sightseeing, shopping, and inside entertainment during the hot midday hours. Plan outdoor activities, such as biking, hiking, and tennis, for early morning or twilight. Bring sunglasses and a hat if you intend to spend much time outdoors. Winter is short, and the coldest months are January and February. While snow is rare, you can run into cold, rainy weather that cuts through to the bone. It's the perfect time for lingering over steaming-hot seafood gumbo and dessert served with French roast coffee.

If food is a major topic of conversation in Baton Rouge, so are sports and politics. You never know when you'll run into a legendary athlete icon as Shaquille O'Neal or a high-profile political figure such as James Carville. This is, after all, the state capital.

Keeping track of visitors and new residents since Hurricane Katrina in 2005 has been tricky. Thousands of displaced New Orleans residents sought refuge in Baton Rouge in the days following the hurricane. More than 250,000 moved into the city overnight, while thousands of first responders and repair crews came through the capital en route to providing badly needed aid. In the months that followed, local residents took in friends, relatives, and even perfect strangers. Most moved on, but many remained. Prior to the 2010 U.S. Census, the city parish government estimated a population of 774,000 in the greater Baton Rouge region.

Through the years people have arrived in Baton Rouge for business or study and decided to make it their home. The social climate and economic possibilities make it an easy place to live. Since the city thrives as a political center, governmental dealings often serve as the topic du jour when people gather for lunch or evening cocktails. The city's history is riddled with both scoundrels and saints.

Prehistoric Indian mounds are evidence of human habitation in the area eons ago. Two mounds on the LSU campus indicate that mound builders were in the area more than 5,000 years ago. In 1698, the French-Canadian Pierre Le Moyne, Sieur d'Iberville, was commissioned by the king of France to found a colony in Louisiana. Traveling up the Mississippi River, Iberville and his crew first saw the bluffs of Baton Rouge on March 17, 1699. There are several versions of how the area was named. One states the explorers found a tall reddened tree or pole with animal hides attached. Rose Meyers writes in *A History of Baton Rouge 1699–1812* that the ship's daily log reported the explorers landed near a small stream at 3 P.M. They found several cabins covered with palmetto leaves and a tall reddened pole on which there were fish heads. Members of the Houma tribe lived to the north of the red stick and Bayagoulas to the south. The explorers designated the site Baton Rouge—Red Stick.

During the early 1700s the area belonged to France. It's thought that the French constructed a fort to protect river travelers in 1719, but there's some doubt that it ever existed. The area was transferred to England by the Treaty of Paris in 1763, and the settlement was renamed New Richmond. Most of the settlers during this period were British. In 1779, the Spanish defeated the English at Fort Butte on Bayou Manchac, captured Baton Rouge, and named the fort here San Carlos. Thus by 1781 West Florida, including East Baton Rouge, was under Spanish rule. In 1810, when the Spanish were overthrown by local settlers, people declared themselves independent and renamed the area the West Florida Republic. Through all these political changes, the locals here continued to call the community Baton Rouge. In a few months, the territory was annexed by Louisiana and East Baton Rouge Parish was created. Louisiana was admitted to the United States on April 8, 1812, and Baton Rouge was incorporated in 1817. It became the state capital in 1849. Baton Rouge remained under Union control during the Civil War. During the war the capital was relocated several times. In 1882, the center of government was returned to Baton Rouge.

As Baton Rouge moved into the 20th century, the city began to develop as an industrial center because of its strategic location on the Mississippi River. Coca-Cola Bottling Company of Atlanta opened a branch here in1896. Standard Oil established Standard Oil of Louisiana in 1909. Today, ExxonMobil employs some 4,000 people. The oil-based economy saved Baton Rouge from the worst of the Great Depression. However, the era did give rise to Huey Pierce Long, who dominated the state's politics between 1918 and 1935. Long served as governor from 1928 to 1932 and as U.S. senator from 1932 to 1935, when he was assassinated in the Capitol he built. His radical populist policies and aggressive nature often disturbed Baton Rouge businessmen. While governor, Long doubled the size of

Louisiana's road system, expanded the public school system, and doubled funding for the public Charity Hospital system. Long's flamboyant personality and controversial style has been the subject of numerous books and movies.

Corrupt and scandalous or innovative and progressive, politics dominates Baton Rouge. In recent years, voters have chosen the state's first female governor, Kathleen Blanco, and its first governor of Indian descent, Bobby Jindal. Visitors are encouraged to learn more by touring the Old State Capitol and the State Capitol. You also can tour the Old Governor's Mansion and the current Governor's Mansion (by appointment).

Stroll along the lighted levee downtown. Pay homage to the early settlers at the Red Stick sculpture created by Frank Hayden and watch the sunset across the Mississippi River. Visit Mike the Tiger at LSU. Jog around University Lake. If you run out of things to do, just ask a local. After all, this is a friendly, welcoming city.

THE LOUISIANA STATE CAPITOL IS THE TALLEST CAPITOL BUILDING IN THE UNITED STATES.

Larry B. Campbell

AREA CODE 225.

GUIDANCE The Baton Rouge Convention and Visitors' Bureau (225-383-1825 or 800-LA-ROUGE, www.visitbatonrouge.com), 359 Third St., Baton Rouge. This is an excellent source for information on the city, towns within East Baton Rouge Parish, and surrounding parishes. The bureau's official visitors' guide, *Welcome*, is packed with information, including lists of accommodations, restaurants, museums, plantations, attractions, outdoor activities, parks, nightlife, and shopping. Especially helpful is the section on culture trails, which has small maps that pinpoint special areas with numerous things to see and do. The bureau also distributes maps and separate brochures on area attractions, walking tours, B&Bs, and special activities. Open 8 A.M.–5 P.M. Mon.–Fri.

There are several other excellent downtown sites for getting tourist information. The **State Capitol Welcome Center** (225-342-7317), 900 North Third St., is just inside the main entrance of the Capitol. It's open daily 8 A.M.–4:30 P.M. The recently renovated **Observation Tower and Shop at the Top** in the Capitol are open 8 A.M.–4 P.M. In addition to providing information, travel counselors conduct free 20-minute tours of the capitol building. Parking is available in front of the building, but it's at a premium when the legislature is in session. State-operated parking garages are within easy walking distance. The **Capitol Park Center** (225-219-1200), 702 River Rd., is situated in a handsome new building facing the Mississippi River and has a complete array of brochures and tourism guides for the entire state. The center also features changing exhibits on Louisiana and its culture. Open daily 8 A.M.–4:30 P.M. Closed Christmas Day, Thanksgiving Day, New Year's Day, and Easter Sunday. Parking is impossible by this center, but it is available across the road on the Mississippi River levee parking lot.

When touring on the west side of the Mississippi River, make your first stop the **Visitors' Welcome Center** operated by the West Baton Rouge Convention and Visitors Bureau (225-344-2920), 2750 N. Westport Dr. The center is open daily 8:30 A.M.–4:30 P.M. It's located just off I-10 west at Exit 151, and offers complete information on the west side and the entire state.

Additional Plantation Country tourism sources: **Ascension Parish Tourist Commission** (225-675-6550, www.ascensiontourism.com), 6967 LA 22, Sorrento; **East Feliciana Parish Tourist Commission** (225-634-7155, www.felicianatourism.org), 1752 High St., Jackson; **Greater Pointe Coupee Chamber of Commerce** (225-638-3500, www.pcchamber.org), 2506 False River Dr., New Roads; **Iberville Parish Tourist Commission** (225-687-5198, www.visitiberville.com), 17525 LA 77, Grosse Tete; **Livingston Parish Convention and Visitors Bureau** (888-317-7899, www.visitlivingstonparish.com), 30340 Catholic Hill Rd., Albany; and **West Feliciana Parish Tourist Commission** (225-635-4224, www.stfrancisville.us), 11757 Ferdinand St., St. Francisville.

GETTING THERE *By car:* I-10, which runs from Florida to southern California, cuts through the heart of Plantation Country. In Baton Rouge, I-10 connects the city on the east side of the Mississippi River with West Baton Rouge Parish on the west bank. New Orleans is approximately 80 miles east by southeast and Houston, Texas, is about 260 miles west. Interstate 12 (the Republic of West Florida Parkway) starts in Baton Rouge and runs east to Denham Springs and along the north shore of Lake Pontchatrain before merging with I-10 and I-59 near Slidell. For many drivers it serves as a bypass around New Orleans. US 61 starts in New Orleans, runs through Baton Rouge and continues north about 1,400 miles to the town of Wyoming, Minnesota. Both interstates become extremely congested during rush hours on weekdays. When there is a wreck or construction work on I-10 or on the Mississippi River Bridge, traffic can come to a halt for miles on either side of the river. The best traveling hours on weekdays are from about 10 A.M.–3:30 P.M. and again from 7 P.M.–6:30 A.M.

By air: **Baton Rouge Metro Airport** (225-355-0333, www.flybtr.com) is located north of the city at 9430 Jackie Cochran Dr., just off I-110. The airport serves travelers not only to the Plantation Country region, but to the Natchez, Mississippi, area as well. It's served by Delta, American, Continental, United, and U.S. Airways. Nonstop flights are available to Atlanta, Memphis, Dallas, Houston, and Charlotte. The airport's attractive terminal features a central atrium landscaped with semi-tropical plants. Facilities include a small food court and a gift shop, and services include an ATM, business center, courtesy phones, hotel phone board, kids' room, nondenominational chapel, nursing room, reading room, and pay phones. Other services include rental cars, parking, taxis, and van pickup. About 70 miles southeast of Baton Rouge is **Louis Armstrong New Orleans International Airport** (504-464-0831), 900 Airline Dr., Kenner. It is serviced by most major airlines. There is no direct bus service to Baton Rouge. Car rentals, taxis, and limousines are available.

By bus: **Greyhound Bus Lines'** station is at 1253 Florida Blvd. (225- 383-3811, www.greyhound.com). The station is clean and well-maintained and open 24 hours; the ticket office is open 7–1 A.M. daily. There's a small snack shop in the station, but no cafes or accommodations nearby. Downtown is 12 blocks away.

GETTING AROUND *By car:* Once you arrive in Baton Rouge and settle in your lodgings, check with your hotel's desk for the latest information on street and highway construction. As of early 2012, the city has several street improvement programs underway, and the state is widening sections of I-10 and I-12. Driving downtown can be confusing because most streets are one-way. A good map and a GPS system will help you get around and save time. Many major streets start downtown and lead away from the Mississippi River, in a semi-circular wagon wheel pattern. Most attractions, shopping areas, and services are situated on or near these major streets. From time to time, you will find that a street stops at a bayou or creek where there is no bridge. It will more than likely continue on the other side of the waterway in a different neighborhood. Check before heading out.

By bus: The **Capitol Area Transit System** (225-389-8282), has bus routes going through the city. Fares are $1.75 for adults; free for children under 5; and 35 cents for seniors age 62 and over, people with disabilities that show a CATS card, anyone with a Medicaid card, and students through high school with an ID card. In addition, the Capitol Park Trolley Service serving downtown area operates for free 10:30 A.M.–2:30 P.M. Mon.–Fri.

By foot: East Baton Rouge Parish has more than 75 buildings and sites listed on the National Register of Historic Places. Fortunately, many of these can be viewed on walks downtown. The Foundation for Historic Louisiana has published an excellent walking tour brochure and map, *Baton Rouge, City of Landmarks,* which pinpoints important landmarks. Pick up a brochure at one of the Welcome Centers and explore at your leisure. We recommend you limit your walking to one section at a time. They include the Capitol Park and Complex, Spanish Town, Third Street/Business Area, River Center/Municipal Buildings and Beauregard Town. If you visit the Louisiana State University campus, start at the visitors' center on the corner of Highland Road and Dalrymple. Ask for a campus map detailing buildings and sports facilities. Also, there's an excellent path for walking or jogging around University Lake on the east side of the campus. If you come in spring or fall, you will see a variety of waterfowl and songbirds. At times, flocks of pelicans land here to the delight of youngsters. The shallow lake is popular with university students and local residents alike.

MEDICAL EMERGENCIES The Baton Rouge area is recognized as a primary health care center in the Gulf South. The following hospitals operate 24-hour emergency rooms.

Baton Rouge General Medical Center/Mid City (225-387-7000, www.br general.org), 3600 Florida Blvd., and **Baton Rouge General Bluebonnet** (225-

763-4000), 8585 Picardy Ave., Baton Rouge. The General is a full-service hospital and the only hospital in the region with a burn unit. Special units include the Pennington Cancer Center and the Womack Heart Center.

Ochsner Medical Center Baton Rouge (225-752-2470, www.ochsner.org/br), 16777 Medical Center Dr., Baton Rouge. This 200-bed hospital offers a complete array of inpatient and outpatient services, including cardiopulmonary, oncology, radiology, and imaging surgery.

Our Lady of the Lake Regional Medical Center (225-765-6565, www.ololrmc .com), 5000 Hennessy Blvd., Baton Rouge. Operated by the Franciscan Missionaries of Our Lady, the hospital provides services in more than 60 specialties, including, cardiology, surgery, oncology, and pediatrics. Lake After Hours, satellite clinics in the city's neighborhoods, provide walk-in care for minor injuries and illness (sport injuries, flu, fevers). Visit www.lakeafterhours.com for a listing and hours.

St. Elizabeth Hospital (225-647-5000, www.steh.com), 1125 West LA 30, Gonzales. The physicians and nurses here are trained in advanced cardiac life support, pediatric advanced life support, and trauma care.

✷ Cities, Towns, and Villages

St. Francisville, about 30 minutes north of Baton Rouge via US 61, St., enchants visitors with its 19th-century atmosphere. The oldest town in the Florida Parishes has been called the town that is two miles long and two miles wide since it lies on a loess-soil ridge, a narrow strip of land that runs from Baton Rouge into Tennessee. Spanish Capuchins established a cemetery and monastery here in the early 1700s. Below St. Francisville, another early settlement named, Bayou Sara, was established in the 1790s and before the Civil War was the largest shipping port on the Mississippi River between New Orleans and Memphis. Destroyed by floods, Bayou Sara doesn't exist anymore, but a number of its structures were hauled up the bluff into St. Francisville in the 1920s. Today, the community proudly showcases numerous historic antebellum town houses and plantations, including the Rosedown Plantation State Historic Site, Audubon State Historic Site, The Myrtles, the Cottage Plantation, Butler-Greenwood Plantation, and Greenwood Plantation (they're different places). A number of these are among the town's many delightful B&Bs. Architecture, gardens, gift shops, and exceptional restaurants make St. Francisville a great tourist destination. The surrounding countryside attracts bikers, birders, and hikers. Stop at the West Feliciana Historical Society headquarters on Ferdinand Street to pick up a map and chat with locals about the latest happenings in town. Shop for Audubon prints, silver, crystal, and special gifts at Shanty Too, and books and specialized coffees at Birdman Books. Another shop, Grandmother's Buttons, housed in a 19th-century bank building, is headquarters for the firm known nationwide for its unique antique button jewelry. Visitors can pick up designer sandwiches and salads at Magnolia Cafe. The Carriage House restaurant at the Myrtles serves regional favorites in a dreamy plantation setting, and Oxbow Restaurant is known for its crawfish etouffee and crabmeat au gratin. Outdoor enthusiasts can spend hours wandering the area's back roads. Birders, bikers, and hikers seek out the Clark Creek Nature Area near Pond, Mississippi, where there are primitive and improved trails as well as waterfalls. Locals also enjoy the beauty of Mary Ann Brown Preserve, seven miles east of town. Contact www.stfrancisville.us or 800-789-4221.

Gonzales/Donaldsonville are two towns south of Baton Rouge are in Ascension Parish, which is divided by the Mississippi River yet linked by the Sunshine Bridge. **Gonzales** is about 28 minutes from Baton Rouge by way of I-10 and US 61 (Airline Highway). Early settlers were Spanish and Canary Islanders, but today's population is similar to the multicultural mix found throughout south Louisiana. The commercial hub of the parish, Gonzales is the home of the world-famous Jambalaya Festival. You'll find more than 50 shops at Tanger Outlet Center at I-10 and LA 30 and everything you could possibly use for a sporting vacation at Cabela's just across the road. Nearby are several of Louisiana's most elegant plantation homes. Houmas House Plantation and Gardens is incredibly beautiful. A short drive upriver is Bocage Plantation, which is filled with a magnificent collection of antique furniture, and has reopened to the public as a B&B.

Donaldsonville, which briefly served as the Louisiana state capital (1830–1831), boasts a historic district with about 640 buildings on the National Register. You'll see shotgun houses, cottages, bungalows, and commercial buildings that look much as they did more than 100 years ago. Don't miss the Romanesque Revival courthouse on Houmas Street. Needing a facelift but fun to see is the Lemann Store on Mississippi Street, once one of the finest commercial buildings on the river and now a museum displaying local memorabilia. It's a good spot to pick up local tourism brochures. Spend time on Railroad Avenue, where you'll find The Grapevine Cafe and Gallery, which serves great meals in an artsy setting, and several B&Bs. Learn more about the community's rich African American culture at the River Road African American Museum. If you're lucky, Kathe Hambrick Jackson, the founder, will regale you with information about African American educators, doctors, lawyers, and other leaders who contributed so much to this parish.

PIONEER CABIN IS ONE OF THE AUTHENTIC EARLY SOUTHERN STRUCTURES AT LSU RURAL LIFE MUSEUM.

Cynthia V. Campbell

Included in this list are famous jazzman Joe King Oliver, who was born in nearby Abend, and Plas Johnson, who played the familiar intro to Henry Mancini's theme to *The Pink Panther*. More information is available from the Ascension Parish Tourism office, www.ascensiontourism.com or 888-775-7990.

Denham Springs is located about 18 miles east of Baton Rouge at the intersection of US 190, I-12 and LA 16. Browsing for collectibles and antiques is one of the town's main attractions. The community's school system and growing suburbs attract young families. Visitors spend casual, relaxing outings at Antique Village, where more than 100 dealers display items in nifty shops offering glassware, porcelain, jewelry, and toys as well as furniture from Federal and Victorian to '50s and modern styles. The village includes several restaurants, including A Taste of Louisiana, popular for its Louisiana dishes, and Sweethearts, an ice cream and coffee shop. For an experience taking you back to yesteryear stop by the Whistle Stop Coffee for coffee and a luscious dessert. There's a visitor's center in the Old City Hall. The city is the setting of family oriented festivals including Spring Antique, Jazz Fest, and Independence Day Festival. With more than 600 waterway miles, the area attracts anglers and boaters, and the city also boasts one of the country's largest Bass Pro shops. Denham Springs is named for William Denham, who settled here in 1827. You can still visit the site of the original groundwater spring and walk the trail leading to the Amite River. The Old City Hall on Mattie Street is now a visitors' center where you'll find a museum and public restrooms. The center is open 8 A.M.–5 P.M., Mon.–Fri. Call 225-667-7512 or visit www.livingstonparish.com.

New Roads is west of the Mississippi River on False River, a lovely oxbow lake. The city is one of the oldest communities in the Mississippi Valley. The Poste de Pointe Coupee was founded in the 1720s by settlers from France. In 1776, a new road was built connecting the Mississippi with False River, and the community became New Roads. Today, it can easily be reached from St. Francisville by taking the new John James Audubon Bridge off US 61. Hugging the lake, the city has inviting shops and cafes. Launch your boat or bait a hook and cast a line from the public dock. Keep in mind that there are no boat rentals here; you'll have to bring your own. Restaurants, including Ma Mama's Kitchen and Satterfield's, specialize in local cuisine. Browse for antiques and pick up a bag of Bergeron's pecans to bring home. You can find more information at www.newroads.net.

West Baton Rouge Parish, situated on the west side of the Mississippi River, is the smallest of Louisiana's 64 parishes. While part of the Baton Rouge Metropolitan Statistical Area, it contains a number of interesting communities. In Port Allen, the parish seat, drop by the West Baton Rouge Museum to learn about life on a sugar plantation and see five historic

THE MARYLAND CONNECTION WITH THE DEEP SOUTH

James Ryder Randall, an English professor, wrote the poem "Maryland, My Maryland" in April 1861 at Poydras College on False River. The poem was later put to music. Though the school was destroyed by fire in 1881, the site where it stood is still known as Randall Oak. The poem is now Maryland's official state song.

West Baton Rouge CVB

RIVERFRONT PARK IN PORT ALLEN OFFERS A GREAT VIEW OF THE STATE CAPITOL.

dwellings and furnishings from the 1800s. Scott's Cemetery is a historic African American burial ground dating from the 1850s. Don't miss the visitors' center at the Port Allen Locks, where you can see tugboats, or the Plaquemine Lock State Historic Site in Plaquemine, where you'll learn about the development of Intracoastal Waterways. In Port Allen, you'll find new chain hotels convenient to I-10, minutes from downtown Baton Rouge. Go to www.westbatonrouge.net for more information.

✴ To See

✿ **Beauregard Town,** bordered by Government Street on the north, South Boulevard on the south, the Mississippi River on the west, and East Boulevard on the east. The beautiful old neighborhood was created in 1806 by Elias Beauregard as a planned town. His design followed the European manner, with tree-lined boulevards, fountains, squares, and formal gardens. Although Beauregard's blueprint was never completed, the area became fashionable following the Civil War. Drive or walk through the area to see classic and romantic structures still used as residences or offices. Look for old-fashioned heritage plants and flowers on a number of the properties.

✐ ✿ **Louisiana's Governor's Mansion** (225-342-5855, www.lamansionfoundation .org), 1001 Capitol Access Rd., Baton Rouge. The stately mansion was built in 1963 during the administration of Jimmie Davis. Inspired by the Greek Revival Oak Alley Plantation in Vacherie, it incorporates several Georgian features including dormers and a fanlight above the front entrance. By law, the Louisiana Governor's Mansion Foundation serves as the steward and fund-raiser of its fine arts and furnishings, including Louisiana antiques. Of special interest is the mural of Louisiana scenes painted by Auseklis Ozols. As of this writing, the mansion's residents are Governor Bobby Jindal, the first lady, Supriya Jindal, and their family. Tours can be scheduled by appointment 9:30 A.M. to 3:30 P.M. (with the exception of the lunch hour, noon–1 P.M.), Tues.–Thurs. Free.

✒ 🏛 **Louisiana State Capitol** (225-342-7317), State Capitol Dr., Baton Rouge. Completed in 1932 by Governor Huey P. Long at a cost of $5 million, the Capitol is an art deco masterpiece with more than $1 million worth of art. Visitors delight in finding their own state's name carved into the 49 granite steps leading to the entrance. The 34-story building is the tallest state Capitol in the United States. The 13 original colonies make up the first group; the rest follow with their dates of entrance into the Union. The U.S. motto, *E Pluribus Unum,* along with the last two states admitted, Alaska and Hawaii, are on the top step. Stop at the information desk just inside the entrance and ask about free tours. The recently renovated observation deck, with a gift shop, affords magnificent views of the Mississippi River and the city. Elevators to the observation deck close at 4 P.M. The Capitol is open daily 8:30 A.M.– 4:30 P.M. Closed Christmas Day, Thanksgiving Day, Easter Day, and New Year's Day. Free.

THE FORMAL DINING ROOM OF THE LOUISIANA GOVERNOR'S MANSION SERVES AS SETTING FOR IMPORTANT RECEPTIONS.
Cynthia V. Campbell

✒ 🏛 **Louisiana State Capitol Grounds and Grave,** State Capitol Dr., Baton Rouge. Stretching out in front of the capitol are 27 acres of gardens landscaped with more than 300 plants. Stately oaks and dark-green magnolias provide ample shade from the sun. On clear, sunny days, you'll find downtown workers, tourists with kids, and seniors enjoying the beauty of the park. Huey P. Long, one of Louisiana's most flamboyant and controversial political figures, is buried in the garden. His statue at the gravesite faces the capitol where he was fatally wounded by an assassin's bullet in 1935.

✒ 🐾 🏛 **Old Governor's Mansion** (225-387-2464, www.fhl.org), 502 North Blvd., Baton Rouge. Called "Louisiana's White House," this Georgian Mansion is a major landmark and it's the headquarters of the Foundation for Historical Louisiana. It served as the official residence for nine governors and their families. Docents give tours with interesting information on the personal lives of the governors and their families. Memorabilia on display includes Jimmie Davis's gold records and Huey Long's straw boater hat and walking stick. The tour includes the elegant east wing ballroom, state dining room, governor's home office, as well as bedrooms on the second floor. Designated a historic house museum, the building also serves as a venue for receptions, weddings, and special events. There's an exceptional gift shop. Open 9 A.M.–4 P.M. Tues.–Fri. Tours are given on the hour. Last tour starts at 3 P.M. Admission is $7, adults, $6 seniors over 62, $5 students kindergarten–12th grade; and free to children under 5.

Louisiana's Secetrary of State

THE INTRICATE IRON STAIRCASE AND LAVISH DÉCOR ARE THE FOCAL POINT OF THE ENTRANCE HALL OF THE ANTEBELLUM OLD STATE CAPITOL.

🏛 **Pentagon Barracks,** River Rd. North and North Third, across from Capitol grounds, Baton Rouge. Comprised of four brick buildings with an open courtyard, formerly a parade ground, the barracks were built 1819–22 in the Classical Revival style with Doric columns. The barracks originally housed U.S. troops garrisoned in Baton Rouge, and before his election as president, Zachary Taylor was the barracks commander. The buildings and grounds were the site of Louisiana State University from 1886–1925. Today the buildings are used as offices of the lieutenant governor and private apartments for legislators. The Pentagon Barracks apartments are not open to the public, but visitors are welcomed to walk into the courtyard, examine how the structures were built, and take in the view of the Mississippi.

✏ ♿ **Shaw Center for the Arts** (225-346-5001, www.shawcenter.org), 100 Lafayette St., Baton Rouge. This is a $55 million contemporary center housing theatrical spaces, art museums, and more. A cornerstone of the downtown entertainment district, it incorporates the 1922 Auto Hotel and old Stroube's Drug Store (now a restaurant), the 325-seat Manship Theatre, two black-box theaters, LSU School of Art Gallery, LSU Museum Street, Capital City Grill, PJ's Coffee House, and the rooftop Tsunami restaurant. Families gather here at the Lafayette Street entrance to cool off by the fountains. Periodic mini-concerts are held beneath the Standpipe water tower in Lafayette Park across the street.

🏛 **Spanish Town Historic District,** north of downtown bound by North Street and Spanish Town Rd. This area was commissioned in 1805 by Don Carlos de Grandpre, the governor of West Florida, as a formal planned community. The area was settled by early Spanish and Canary Islanders. Just east of the state capitol, this is still a residential neighborhood. Stroll through the streets and view a variety of architectural styles, from antebellum to American bungalow. When walking, watch your step; ancient tree roots sometimes crack the old sidewalks in the neighborhood. The area is famous for the Spanish Town Mardi Gras Parade that satirizes national and state politics. Pink flamingos, symbols of the parade, can be seen everywhere. An alcohol-free zone is popular with families.

 ⛫ **St. James Episcopal Church** (225-387-5141, www.stjamesbr.org), 205 North Fourth St., Baton Rouge. This historic church was founded in 1819 and received its charter in 1844. One of the original founders was Margaret Taylor, the wife of President Zachary Taylor. The Gothic Revival church, built in 1895, has a beautiful interior with spectacular Tiffany windows behind the altar.

 ⛫ **St. Joseph Cathedral** (225-387-5928, www.cathedralofstjoseph.org), 412 North St., Baton Rouge. With a dramatic spire, this Gothic Revival church is the third to stand on land donated by Don Antonio Gras, a Spanish resident. It was designed by a Jesuit architect, the Rev. John Cambiasco, and constructed 1853–1856. The structure was extensively remodeled in 1921 and again in 1966. Two Ivan Mestrovic sculptures can be viewed at the church.

 ⛫ **Third Street Downtown,** Third St. east of the Mississippi River, runs from North Boulevard to State Capitol Drive. This historic street is fun to walk during the daytime. The street retains the look of an early 1900s town with an interesting mix of commercial architectural styles. Many of the buildings have been restored to preserve their original facades. For example, the Fuqua Hardware building, 358 Third St., was built in 1905 by Henry L. Fuqua, who later became manager of the state prison system and governor of Louisiana. There's little shopping, however, a number of restaurants are available. Don't be surprised to see politicians, lobbyists, state police, and office workers all rubbing shoulders during the lunch hours. The street, which suffered from urban blight in 1970s, '80s, and '90s, is booming now as an entertainment district at night, especially on weekends. Handicapped-accessible curbs are designed at every corner.

 ⛵ ⛫ **USS** *Kidd* **and Veterans Memorial** (225-342-1942, www .usskidd.com), 305 South River Rd., Baton Rouge. This is a World War II Fletcher–class destroyer restored to its 1945 configuration. One of America's famous fighting ships, it was named for Admiral Isaac C. Kidd, who was killed aboard his flagship, the USS *Arizona,* during the surprise attack on Pearl Harbor. The ship is situated in its own

MUSIC, THEATER, AND ART ARE SHOWCASED AT THE SHAW CENTER FOR THE ARTS DOWNTOWN.

Larry B. Campbell

Cynthia V. Campbell

A RESTORED WORLD WAR II DESTROYER, MILITARY EXHIBITS, AND EVENTS ARE AMONG WHAT'S ON OFFER AT THE USS KIDD VETERANS MEMORIAL AND MUSEUM.

special dock on the Mississippi River. Children and families can tour the decks and see the inner workings of the ship. The adjacent museum features intricate ship models, artifacts, aircraft, and a gift shop with plenty of nautical-themed items. The Kidd is the top vessel in America for hosting military reunions. Open 9 A.M.– 5 P.M. daily. Admission $4–$8.

ACADEMIC REALMS ✍ ↬ ⚘ **Louisiana State University and Agricultural and Mechanical College** (225-578-3202, www.lsu.edu) is situated on 2,000 acres of land south of downtown Baton Rouge and bordered by the Mississippi River on the west. Many of the historic buildings on the main campus were built between 1925 and 1940. The Italian Renaissance architectural style is recognizable by the red tile roofs and honey-colored stucco. Among buildings to see are Foster Hall, the School of Landscape Design, College of Music and Dramatic Arts, Student Union, Middleton Library, and the Law School. The grounds are beautifully land-scaped with native plants, oaks, azaleas, and magnolias. In addition to academic awards, LSU is nationally recognized for its championships in various sports. Its outstanding athletic facilities include Tiger Stadium, Maravich Center, Alex Box Stadium, Bernie Moore Track and Field, Carl Maddox Field House, the Natato-rium, W. T. "Dub" Robinson Tennis Stadium, soccer complex, and the new softball field, Tiger Park. Visit www.lsusports.net for more details. University Lake is a popular area for jogging and nature walks, enjoyed by students and townspeople alike. Stop by the visitors' center at the corner of Highland Road and Dalrymple to obtain information, a campus map, and details on campus parking. The center is open 7 A.M.–7 P.M. Mon.–Fri.

✍ ↬ ⚘ **Southern University and Agricultural and Mechanical College** (225-359-9328, www.web.subr.edu), US 61 and Harding Boulevard, is now recognized as the only historically black university system in the United States. Organized in New Orleans in 1880, SU was relocated to Baton Rouge in 1914. In addition to undergraduate degree programs, the university system offers a comprehensive graduate degree program. The Southern University Law Center graduates the majority of Louisiana's African American lawyers. Southern's sports teams' devoted fans proudly call themselves the Jaguar Nation. Visit the campus for exciting football games where you can also watch the dynamic Jaguar Band, nicknamed the Human Jukebox, and join a lavish tailgating party. The F. G. Clark Activity Center is a multi-purpose facility where students, alumni, and guests can attend a basketball game or cultural event.

MUSEUMS & ⛵ 🐾 **Bogan Fire Station** (225-344-8558), 427 Laurel St., Baton Rouge. Although small, this museum appeals to children and adults interested in seeing antique fire equipment. The 1914 Gothic Revival brick firehouse was named the Bogan Fire Station in honor of Robert A. Bogan, the city's first paid fire chief, who served from 1918 to 1959. The museum contains two antique fire trucks, fire-fighting equipment, and wonderful old photographs of early firefighters. The building also serves as headquarters for the Baton Rouge Arts Council and Community Fund for the Arts. Hours are 9 A.M.–4 P.M., Mon.–Fri.

✐ & ⛵ 🐾 **Enchanted Museum: A Doll Museum** (225-765-2437, www.lsumoa .com), 190 Lee Dr., Baton Rouge. The museum delights not only children but adults. It's a fantasy come true for doll lovers and collectors, a place to walk through a life-sized Victorian dollhouse. In this land of angels, fairies, antiques, and one-of-a-kind dolls, you can forget the bustling world outside. Tour the Enchanted Mansion on Thursday and enjoy complimentary tea. The gift shop is exceptional and a great place to buy a special present for that special little person in your life. The sole purpose of this museum is to benefit the handicapped, and

THE ALEX BOX STADIUM WELCOMES BASEBALL FANS TO LSU, WHILE TIGER STADIUM IN THE BACKGROUND IS AN ICONIC FOOTBALL HAVEN.

Cynthia V. Campbell

there is no fee for handicapped visitors. Hours are 10 A.M.–5 P.M. Thurs.–Sat. General admission is $4.50, adults; $3.50, seniors; and $2, children. Children under 2 admitted free.

✂ ☥ ⬆ **Louisiana Art and Science Museum and Planetarium** (225-344-5272, www.lasm.org), 100 River Rd. South, Baton Rouge. Housed in the historic Yazoo and Mississippi Valley Railway Station on the banks of the Mississippi River, this museum offers inspirational entertainment for all ages. Visitors will find art galleries displaying works from the museum's private collection as well as special exhibitions. The art and science galleries are especially appealing to youngsters, as is the Ancient Egypt Gallery (kids always ask to see the mummy exhibit). The museum also features the Irene W. Pennington Planetarium, with large-format films and galleries devoted to astronomy. Open 10 A.M.–3 P.M. Tues.–Fri., 10 A.M.–5 P.M. Sat., 10 A.M.–4 P.M. Sun. Closed major holidays. Admission is $7, adults; $6, children 2–12 and seniors 65 and over.

✂ ☥ ⬆ ✿ **Louisiana Old State Capitol** (225-342-0500, www.louisianaoldstate capitol.org/museum), 100 North Blvd., Baton Rouge. Louisiana's Old State Capitol stands high on a bluff overlooking the Mississippi River. A Gothic Revival treasure, the statehouse has withstood war, fire, scandal, abandonment, and the occasional fistfight. In 1990, the Louisiana Legislature placed the former state house under the jurisdiction of the Secretary of State and funded a major restoration. Now a museum of political history, the Old State Capitol has received awards for its architectural exhibits and preservation. Walk up the spiral staircase and admire the magnificent stained-glass windows. Displays on Louisiana history include the gun used to assassinate Huey P. Long. Open 9 A.M.–4 P.M. Tues.–Sat. Handicapped entrance is available through ground-level entrance at rear parking lot.

✂ ☥ ⬆ ✿ **Louisiana State Museum—Baton Rouge** (225-342-5428), Fourth St. and Spanish Town Rd., Baton Rouge. Filled with dynamic and colorful exhibits,

LOUISIANA ARTS AND SCIENCE MUSEUM'S PLANETARIUM AND THE BATON ROUGE DOCK ARE TOP LOUISIANA ATTRACTIONS.

Larry B. Campbell

Larry B. Campbell

A MAGNIFICENT STAINED-GLASS SKYLIGHT DOMINATES LOUISIANA'S OLD STATE CAPITOL.

the museum tells the story of the state's cultural heritage and historical milestones, including explorers, wars, the 1927 flood, jazz, blues, country and pop music, cuisine, agriculture, Mardi Gras, civil rights, folk art, and legendary characters. Enjoy relaxing by the fountain at the canopied front entrance and take in one of the museum's special programs. Hours are 9 A.M.–5 P.M., Tues.–Sat. and noon–5 P.M. Sun.

🕯 ♿ ⛲ 🎨 **Louisiana State University Museum of Art** (225-389-7200, www.lsumoa.com), 100 Lafayette St., Baton Rouge. Located in the Shaw Center for the Arts downtown, the museum's permanent collection includes 17th- to 20th-century portraiture, including works by Sir Joshua Reynolds, Thomas Gainsborough, and William Hogarth. Other displays include rare New Orleans silver, Newcomb pottery, and crafts. Also shown are works by former and current LSU faculty and students, as well as modern and contemporary Southern paintings, drawings, and sculpture. Open 10 A.M.–4 P.M. Tues.–Sat. with late hours until 8 P.M. Thurs., and 1–5 P.M. Sun. Admission $5, adults and teens; free, children 12 and younger and university students with ID.

A CONFEDERATE SUBMARINE INTRIGUES VISITORS AT THE LOUISIANA STATE MUSEUM IN BATON ROUGE.

Cynthia V. Campbell

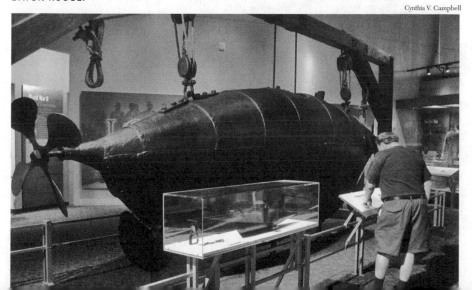

⚪ ♿ ↩ ⚙ ℘ **Louisiana State University Rural Life Museum and Windrush Gardens** (225-765-2437, http://rurallife.lsu.edu), 4560 Essen Lane, Baton Rouge. An outstanding living history museum, Rural Life is a country retreat surrounded by a city. Visitors quickly feel like they are miles away from urban life and years away from traffic and cellphones. Focusing on life in preindustrial Louisiana, the museum has completed a major expansion. Visitors see more than 25 buildings from the 19th century, including an overseer's house, Acadian house, dogtrot house, and outhouses. Take a gander at the collection of tools, household utensils, vehicles, and farm implements. Walk through Windrush Gardens and view heritage plants and flowers cherished by previous generations. It's great place for kids to romp and learn about history, too. The museum staff claims that pet mules, oxen, and chickens are admitted free. Open 8:30 A.M.–5 P.M. daily. Admission is $7, adults; $6, children 5–11, seniors 62 and older, LSU faculty, staff, and students with ID; children under 5, free.

Cynthia V. Campbell

YOU CAN SEE FILMS OF HUEY P. LONG IN ACTION AT THE LOUISIANA STATE MUSEUM IN BATON ROUGE.

AN AUTHENTIC BUGGY AND MID-1800S COSTUME ARE AMONG MANY DISPLAYS AT LSU RURAL LIFE MUSEUM IN BATON ROUGE.

Cynthia V. Campbell

℘ **National Hansen's Disease Museum** (225-642-1950, www.hrsa.gov /hansens/museum), 5445 Point Clair Rd., Carville. Visitors learn the history of Hansen's disease, also known as leprosy, on the site of the only national leprosarium. Photographs, medical artifacts, and personal memorabilia left behind by patients and the Daughters of Charity of St. Vincent de Paul, a Catholic religious order of women that cared for the patients, are on display. Walking tours are conducted the last Saturday of each month, 2–4 P.M. Before the walk visitors will see *Exiles in Our Own Country,* an hourlong film outlining the history of leprosy in the United States. The tour includes stairways that may be difficult for some visitors to climb. It's advisable to call to verify museum accessibility because the Louisiana Army National Guard operates a program for at-risk youth on the property and observes Homeland Security regulations at the gatehouse. Open 10 A.M.–4 P.M. Tues.–Sat. Closed federal holidays.

Odell S. Williams Now and Then Museum of African American History (225-343-4431), 538 South Blvd., Baton Rouge. The museum, located on the southern perimeter of Beauregard Town, focuses on African American contributions in medicine, science, and politics. Other displays cover minority inventions, rural artifacts, and African art. The museum is a Juneteenth archive site that maintains material relating to African Americans struggle for freedom. It is a faith-based project of St. Luke Baptist Church. Open 1–5 P.M. Wed.–Fri. and by appointment.

✤ ⊤ ⚘ **River Road African American Museum** (225-474-5553, www.african americanmuseum.org), 406 Charles St., Donaldsonville. This well-planned, small museum is a jewel. Take time to examine the exhibits that focus on the history and heritage of African Americans in this region of the Mississippi River. Learn about contributions of enslaved people, free people of color, doctors, lawyers, folk artists, and inventors. Call ahead for an appointment to tour the museum. Cost is $5 per person. Displays are detailed and heartwarming. Hours are 10 A.M.–5 P.M. Wed.–Sat. and 1–5 P.M. Sun.

✤ ⊤ ⚘ **Southern University Museum of Art** (225-771-4513, www.subr.edu), G. Netterville Dr., Baton Rouge. Situated on the Southern University campus, the museum contains a stunning collection of African and African American Art. Four galleries contain pieces from several regions of Africa. Works are from three major collections: The President Leon R. Tarver II Collection, the Steve and Mary L. Harvey Collection, and the Dr. William Bertrand Collection. Visitors can also view ceremonial masks, clothing, and functional artifacts. The visual arts gallery in

SOUTHERN UNIVERSITY'S LAKE IS A FAVORITE MEETING SPOT FOR STUDENTS AND FACULTY.

Louisiana Office of Tourism

PLANTATIONS
THE GOLDEN AGE OF ANTEBELLUM HOMES

Fortunately, the lower Mississippi River still contains many beautiful antebellum homes built by planters who accumulated great wealth before the Civil War. They furnished their homes with exquisitely beautiful pieces and lavishly entertained their neighbors and friends. According to the customs of the period, people were expected to show off their wealth. While the economy of the time was based on slave labor and many of the customs are contrary to today's mores, the homes that remain are fine examples of outstanding architecture and refined taste. Many that are open for tours are house museums; others are still privately owned. Most tours take about an hour. Remember, the houses were on huge plantations, most with frontage on the Mississippi, which provided transportation to the port of New Orleans. Even today, it takes time to drive from one plantation to another. Usually, you can comfortably visit three plantations in a day, with time out for lunch. The last tours of the day usually begin around 4 P.M. Ask about handicapped accessibility, as many of the homes were built with stairways in a period when there were no elevators. Always call ahead to check on tour times and costs. Admission for most tours ranges from $10–$20 for adults.

♂ ♈ **Bocage** (225-588-8000, www.bocageplantation.com), 3950 LA 942, Darrow. Recently restored by Dr. Marion Rundell with an eye to historic detail, Bocage Plantation House is about 2 miles upriver from Houmas House. In 1801, Marius Pons Bringier built a Creole cottage here as a wedding gift for his daughter Francoise. She was married to Christophe Colomb, a French refugee and a descendant of Christopher Columbus. The current mansion was designed by the architect James Dakin in 1837. View the exceptional collection of antique furniture, including pieces by Charles Lee, John and Joseph Meeks, and John Henry Belter. Bocage also operates as a bed & breakfast. Tours are noon–5 P.M. Wed.–Sun. Cost is $20; free to children under 12.

ROSEMARY LANE, LEFT, AND JUNE SMYTHE VOLUNTEER AS OPEN-HEARTH COOKS AT MAGNO MOUND PLANTATION.

Cynthia V. Ca

✎ ♂ ❀ **BREC's Magnolia Mound** (225-343-4955, www.magnoliamound.org), 2161 Nicholson Dr., Baton Rouge. Just minutes from downtown, Magnolia Mound is one of the oldest houses in the Baton Rouge region. Nothing like the grandiose plantation homes depicted in movies, this simple French Creole house was built in the 1790s. Guides, wearing costumes from the Federal era, discuss the lifestyle and customs of the family who lived here and their connection to the Marquis de Lafayette. Let your imagination take you back to a time without electronics, when the nearest neighbors were miles away. The house contains carefully documented Louisiana-made furnishings. View the open-hearth kitchen, overseer's house, and crop garden. Hours are 10 A.M.–3 P.M. Mon.–Sat. and 1–3 P.M. Sun. Admission for tours and grounds are $10, adults; $8, seniors, teachers, military with IDs; and $3, children ages 4–17. General admission for grounds only is $3.

✎ ❧ ♂ ❀ **Butler Greenwood** (225-635-6312, www.butlergreenwood.com), 8345 US 61, St. Francisville. One of the few plantation homes in the area still owned by descendants of the original family, Butler Greenwood dates from the 1790s. The home is filled with original furniture and a fascinating collection of family heirlooms, including jewelry, clothing, and photographs. Chat with the owner and author Anne Butler to get personal glimpses of this West Feliciana family. The drive to the house is flanked by sunken gardens filled with camellias, azaleas, and sweet olives. Plan a bed & breakfast stay here in separate cottages on the grounds. This is a birder's haven. Daily tours given 9 A.M.–5 P.M. Tour cost is $5.

♂ **Cottage Plantation** (225-635-3674, www.cottageplantation.com), 10528 US 61, St. Francisville. This is the most complete plantation complex in the area. The drive through a dense wooded area leads to the main house, a series of buildings built between 1795 and 1859. The tranquil setting appeals to those who simply want to relax on a rocking chair and be at peace with nature. Out buildings include the old school house, outside kitchen, carriage house, milk house, and slave houses. A bed & breakfast stay includes a full plantation breakfast and tour. Regular tour is $7 per person. Daily tours are held 10 A.M.–4 P.M.

Evergreen Plantation (985-497-3837, www.evergreenplantation.org), 4677 LA 18, Edgard. This privately owned plantation complex has recorded 500 pages of documentation through an archaeological project and ongoing research in oral history and cultural landscape. The tour highlights 250 years of family ownership. Emphasis is placed on the plantation's dependence on slave labor and, later, the labor of freed African Americans that was necessary to

West Feliciana CVB

COTTAGE PLANTATION IS ONE OF THE THE BEAUTIFUL B&BS NEAR ST. FRANCISVILLE

operate such an enterprise. Serious attention is paid to do justice to history. Tours of the house, furnished with beautiful antiques, and the original slave quarters are 9:30–11:30 A.M. and 2 P.M. Mon.–Sat. Gates are open 8:30 A.M.– 2 P.M. Tours cost $20 per person; half price for children age 12 and under.

✒ ⚲ **Greenwood Plantation** (225-655-4475, www.greenwoodplantation.com), 6838 Highland Rd., St. Francisville. Movie buffs will find this is a dream setting. The original house built on a Spanish land grant was struck by lightning and destroyed on August 1, 1960. Walter Barnes and his son Richard purchased the site and 800 acres and rebuilt the plantation home following photographs and detailed research. Designed with massive columns, the Greek Revival mansion was completed in 1984. That year the TV movie *Louisiana* was filled at Greenwood. Since then the house has been the setting for a number of other films, including *Drago, North and South– Book I, North and South–Book II,* and *Sister Sister.* Tours are given 9 A.M.–5 P.M. March 1–Oct. 31, and 10 A.M.–4 P.M. Nov. 1–Feb. 28. Tours are $8, house and gardens, and $3, grounds only.

ORIGINAL SLAVE QUARTERS ARE AN IMPORTANT HISTORICAL FEATURE AT EVERGREEN PLANTATION.

Louisiana Office of Tourism

✒ ⚲ ⚲ ⛨ ⚶ **Houmas House Plantation** (225-473-9380, www .houmashouse.com), 40136 LA 942, Darrow. Glamorous and spectacular, this mansion is a fantasy come true. Restored by the New Orleans

Cynthia V. Campbell

VISITORS STROLL THROUGH
SPECTACULAR GARDENS BEFORE
TOURING HOUMAS HOUSE
PLANTATION.

businessman Kevin Kelly, the antebellum site features 16 acres of legacy oaks, fountains, and landscaped gardens that bloom year-round. Start at the gift shop, filled with tempting goodies, then view the well-prepared video, take a leisurely stroll through the gardens, and arrive at the Big House, created during America's golden era of sugar barons. Guides give lively tours showcasing 14 rooms filled with Louisiana artwork and elegant furnishings. The house was the setting for *Hush, Hush Sweet Charlotte* and other movies. Stop for a mint julep at the Turtle Bar (named for the unique turtle-shaped chandelier), and stay for dinner and wine in Latil's Landing, an exceptional fine-dining restaurant. Other restaurants on the property are Cafe Burnside, Le Petite Houmas Restaurant, and the Wine Cellars of Houmas House. Open 9 A.M.–5 P.M. Mon.–Tues. and 9 A.M.–8 P.M. Wed.–Sun. Tour for house and gardens costs $20, adults, $15 ages 13-18, $10 ages 6-12, and free to children under 6. Garden tour only is $10.

Laura: A Creole Plantation (225-265-7690, www.lauraplantation.com), 2247 LA 18, Vacherie. The 70-minute tour covers more than 200 years of

LAURA PLANTATION, CIRCA 1805, TELLS THE HISTORY OF A FRENCH CREOLE FAMILY.

Laura Plantation

real-life accounts of the Creole plantation owners, women, slaves, and children who lived here. One of the most authentic historic home tours on the Mississippi River, guides here provide a wonderful glimpse of Creole life. The tour concludes in one of the 1840s slave cabins, where West African folktales of Compare Lapin, better known as Br'er Rabbit, were recorded. Tours are 10 A.M.–4 P.M. daily. Tour is $18, adults; to $5, children; younger than 4, free.

Mount Hope (225-761-7000, www.mounthopeplantation.net), 8151 Highland Rd., Baton Rouge. Built in 1817, this landmark one-and-a-half story house is a small antebellum jewel. The traditional central hall is flanked by two large rooms serving as double parlors. There's a gabled roof and wrap-around porches. Beautiful grounds, with ancient oaks, a fountain, and expansive patio, make this a popular spot for private receptions and weddings. The home is not open for individual tours, but people are welcomed to walk the grounds 9 A.M.–dusk.

The Myrtles (800-809-0565, www.myrtlesplantation.com), 7747 US.61, St. Francisville. It doesn't matter whether you believe in ghosts. Most people who visit this home walk away feeling that there's a certain aura about the site. Often called "America's most haunted house," The Myrtles has been featured on A&E, the Travel Channel, the Learning Channel, and *Oprah,* as well as National Geographical Explorer. Ancient oaks laden with Spanish Moss surround the house that boasts a stunning front gallery. The ghost stories are compelling. One tells about a slave named Chloe, who poisoned a birthday cake made for one of the owner's children. Sarah Mathilda Woodruff and two of her children died. Chloe was dragged from the house and hanged on a nearby oak tree. People report they have seen Chloe's ghost about the house and the shades of the two children playing in the garden, usually on a rainy day. There's an elegance to furnishings, which include Baccarat crystal chandeliers and gold-leaf French furniture. The home operates as a bed & breakfast. The Carriage House Restaurant on the grounds serves regional favorites in a romantic setting. Historic tours are 9 A.M.–5 P.M. daily, and mystery tours are 6, 7, and 8 P.M., Fri.–Sat. Historic tours are $8, adults; $4, children 12 and under. Mystery tours are $10 per person. Reservations recommended.

Nottoway Plantation (866-527-6884, www.nottoway.com), 31025 LA 1, White Castle. Cross the I-10 bridge over the Mississippi River to the west bank and head south through Plaquemine on LA 1. In about 18 miles you'll come to Nottoway. Completed in 1859 by John Henry Randolph and his wife, Emily Jane, this is thought to be the largest plantation home in the South. The mansion reopened in 2009 after a multimillion dollar restoration. The tour includes the famous white ballroom, which is popular as a wedding site, and you'll see

ELEGANT CRYSTAL AND CHINA CREATE A
GLAMOROUS FORMAL DINING ROOM AT
NOTTOWAY PLANTATION.

the home's intricate frieze work. Nottoway is operated as a bed & breakfast resort with lavishly decorated guest rooms. Be aware that several bedrooms in the mansion are on the daily tour, and guests staying in these rooms must be out and about by 9 A.M. Ramsay's Mansion Restaurant in the ground-level basement serves breakfast, lunch, and dinner. The menu features contemporary European cuisine with Louisiana touches. Guided tours are 9 A.M.–4 P.M. daily. Guided tours cost $20, adults; $6, children ages 6–12; free to age 5 and under. Ask about senior and military discounts. The mansion is not handicapped accessible.

  **Oak Alley Plantation** (225-265-2151 or 800-44-ALLEY, www.oakalley plantation.com), 3645 LA 18, Vacherie. This grand dame of a plantation is world famous for its spectacular 300-year-old oak alley. The house, built in 1839 with 28 Doric columns around all four sides, still stands majestically facing the Mississippi River. It has been authentically restored and filled with handsome antiques. Facilities include overnight cottages, a restaurant, and gift shop. Daily tours are 9:30 A.M.–5 P.M. March 1–Oct. 31, and 9:30 A.M.– 4:30 P.M., Mon.–Fri., until 5 P.M. Sat.–Sun. Nov. 1–Feb. 8. Admission is $18, adults; $7.50 youths 13–18, and $4.50 children younger than 13.

…VERS AND A FOUNTAIN GRACE THE SIDE GARDEN AT
…OWAY PLANTATION, THE SOUTH'S LARGEST
…EBELLUM PLANTATION.

Oakley Plantation (225-635-3739), 117 LA 965, St. Francisville. The plantation house (circa 1813–1815) and its surroundings have special

Oak Alley Plantation

SPECTACULAR LIVE OAKS FORM A MAGNIFICENT SHADE CANOPY AT THE ENTRANCE TO OAK ALLEY PLANTATION.

appeal. John James Audubon apparently thought so during the summer of 1821 when he lived here. He was hired to teach the owners' daughter, but found time to paint part of his *Birds of America* series. During a tour, be sure to study the architecture, a combination of Anglo and French design, with the jalousied galleries common in the West Indies. The plantation home is part of an Audubon State Historic Site, which includes a kitchen garden, outside kitchen, two slave cabins, an 1870 barn, a nature trail, picnic area, and a museum containing memorabilia from early residents. Open 9 A.M.–5 P.M. daily. Admission is $4, adults; free to children 12 and under and seniors 62 and over. The last tour is at 4 P.M.

Ormand Plantation (985-764-8544, www.plantation.com/home), 13786

THE DINING ROOM IN OAKLEY HOUSE AT AUDUBON STATE HISTORIC HOUSE IN ST. FRANCISVILLE IS SET FOR A FORMAL OCCASION.

Cynthia V. Campbell

River Rd., Destrehan. The main building at Ormond was completed shortly before 1790. Once home to soldiers heading to the Battle of New Orleans, Ormand was bombarded by the Federal Navy in that conflict and captured by the U.S. Navy during the Civil War. Through the centuries, the property has changed owners many times. Currently it's operated as a bed & breakfast and is open for weddings and receptions. Tours take place 10 A.M.–4 P.M. Mon.–Fri. Tours cost $7 a person.

Poche Plantation House (225-562-7728, www.pocheplantation.com), 6554 LA 44, Convent. Civil War buffs will enjoy hearing about Judge Felix Poche in the years during and after the Civil War. The 1867 plantation house features a wide front veranda and a magnificent formal dining room. It's also a bed & breakfast and an RV Park. The property adjoins another registered historic property, the famed St. Michael's Church and Lourdes Grotto, and there are walkways between the two. Open 9 A.M.–7 P.M. Mon.–Sat. and 2–7 P.M. Sun. House tours are $10 per person.

Poplar Grove Plantation (225-344-3913, www.poplargroveplantation), 3142 North River Rd., Port Allen. A unique home, Poplar Grove began life as the Bankers' Pavilion at the 1814 World's Industrial and Cotton Centennial Exposition in New Orleans. In 1886, the building was purchased and moved by barge on the Mississippi River to Poplar Grove and became the home of the sugar planter Horace Wilkinson and his wife, Julia. Five generations of the Wilkinson family have called the place home. The architect Thomas Sully designed ornate Oriental details and a pagoda-styled roofline for the house. The interior features Victorian and Oriental-inspired furnishings A candlelight dinner, lunch, or Plantation brunch can be arranged, as well as weddings receptions. Forty-five-minute tours by appointment only. Call for information.

✎ ♿ ↝ ⏏ 🐾 **Rosedown Plantation** (225-635-3332), 12501 LA 10, St. Francisville. About 25 minutes north of Baton Rouge just off LA 61, this magnificent plantation home dates from 1835. It is now a Louisiana State Historic Site. The original owners, Daniel and Martha Barrow Turnbull, were among the wealthiest families in America in the mid-1800s. The 28-acre garden, planned by Martha Turnbull, has been carefully restored. Walk along the 660-foot oak alley leading to the house and enjoy the camellias, azaleas, and other plants intersected by paths and fountains. The house tour includes furniture original to the house. Programs offered throughout the year include demonstrations of open-hearth cooking, 19th-century crafts, children's games, and parlor entertainment. You can also visit the doctor's office and an excellent gift shop. Admission is $10, adults, $8 seniors 62 and older,

MAGNIFICENT GARDENS SURROUND THE ROSEDOWN PLANTATION HISTORIC SITE AT ST. FRANCISVILLE.

$4 students age 6–7, free to children age 5 and under. Open 9 A.M.–5 P.M. daily. Tours are on the hour with the last tour at 4 P.M.

✐ 🏛 **St. Joseph Plantation** (225-265-4078, www.stjosephplantation.com), 3535 LA 18, Vacherie. One of the few fully intact sugarcane plantations left in the river parishes, St. Joseph is a working plantation with 25,000 acres. The property extends from the Mississippi River as far as the eye can see, and still has its original slave cabins, detached kitchen, blacksmith's shop, and school-house. Many tours are guided by family members themselves, and they relate fascinating stories of past generations who lived here. They also tell how family members and friends volunteered months of their time to restore the home. Cost is $15, adults; $7, youths ages 13–18; $5, children ages 6–12; free, age 6 and under. Ask about group discounts. Open Tuesday, Thursday and Saturday. Tours on the hour 10 A.M.–3 P.M.

Frank Hayden Hall exhibits original paintings, drawings and sculptures by students. Call for hours and admission.

✐ **West Baton Rouge Museum** (225-336-2422), 845 North Jefferson Ave., Port Allen. The museum focuses on the sugar plantation lifestyle of West Baton Rouge Parish. See a 22-foot working model of a sugar mill, the 1850 Allendale Slave Cabin, and the 1830 Aillet House, a French plantation house. Changing exhibits include visual art by regional artists and artisans. Every visitor receives a free sample of locally produced raw sugar. Open 10 A.M.–4:30 P.M. Tues.–Sat. and 2–5 P.M. Sun. Admission is $4 per person and $2, students and seniors.

✐ ✈ ❦ **Bluebonnet Swamp Nature Center** (225-757-8905), 10503 North Oak Hills Parkway, Baton Rouge. The center and swamp feel like a wilderness, yet you are in the middle of an urban area. The 101-acre preserve includes gravel paths and boardwalks through a cypress swamp and a magnolia-beech forest. Birders can view seasonal species during peak migrations. Snakes and turtles can be seen from the trails, and raccoons, rabbits, opossums, squirrels, and foxes are known to inhabit the site. The airy, rustic Nature Center features live animal exhibits. Programs include swamp night hikes. No pets. Open 9 A.M.–5 P.M. Tues.–Sat. and noon–5 P.M. Sun. Admission is $3, ages 18–64; $2.50, 65 and older and full-time college students with IDs; $2, ages 3–17; and free age 2 and younger.

✈ **Cat Island National Wildlife Refuge** (601-442-6696, www.fws.gov), off LA 66 near St. Francisville. Established as the 526th National Wildlife Refuge in 2000, Cat Island is dedicated to preserving, restoring, and managing this native forested habitat for migratory birds, aquatic resources, and endangered plants and animals. Because it is situated along the southernmost, unleveed portion of the lower Mississippi River, the refuge allows natural flooding most years. During the flooding season parts of the refuge are closed. The area is important to migratory birds, including the swallow-tailed kite, black crowned night heron, wood duck, blue-winged teal, woodcock, solitary sandpiper, prothonotary warbler, and pileated woodpecker. Other wildlife in the refuge include river otter, white-tailed deer, wild turkey, mink, and bobcat. Among the numerous trees are bald cypress estimated to be 500 to 1,000 years old. In fact, the National Champion bald cypress, the largest tree of any species east of the Sierra Nevada mountain range, is found in the refuge, 4.8 miles from the entrance gate of the refuge. The refuge is accessible when the Mississippi River gauge in Baton Rouge reaches 18 feet. There is no access to the National Champion bald cypress once the gauge in Baton Rouge reaches 20 feet. The refuge is ideal for birding, photography, and canoeing. However, once the river rises, it can be accessed only by boat from the Mississippi; there are no boat launches on the refuge. To reach by vehicle, take US 61 north of St. Francisville, turn west on LA 66 and then left on Solitude Road, and follow signs to the Cat Island Refuge entrance. More information is available from the West Feliciana Parish Tourist Commission, 800-654-9701 or www.stfrancisville.us.

✐ ✈ ❦ **LSU Hilltop Arboretum** (225-767-6916, www.hilltop.lsu.edu), 118 Highland Rd., Baton Rouge. Tucked between several lovely subdivisions, the Arboretum was given to LSU by Emory Smith and his wife, Annette, as a teaching tool for the School of Landscape Architecture to be shared with the community. Cross a wooden footbridge and enter into a dreamy landscape of towering native trees and flowering shrubs. The 14 acres are a serene place to walk and contemplate the nature's beauty. The Arboretum sponsors plant sales and garden tours during the year, and there's a delightful garden book and nature shop. Open during daylight hours. No admission fee.

✐ ♿ ✈ **Tickfaw State Park** (225-294-5020, www.lastateparks.com), 27225 Patterson Rd., Springfield. East of Baton Rouge via I-12, this is a great spot to experience the sights and sounds of a cypress tupelo swamp, a bottomland hardwood forest, and a mixed pine/hardwood forest. Visitors are welcome to bring their own canoes or rent one here and take a relaxing trip along a section of the Tickfaw River. Bring binoculars, because this is a super birding spot. Skate, bicycle, or

stroll the park's roadways. Ranger programs in the Nature Center delight children and adults. The park facilities include cabins and improved campsites. Visitors also can join nighttime programs or go night hiking. There's a cooling water playground for children. Entrance station is open 8 A.M.–7 P.M. April–September and 8 A.M.– 5 P.M. October–March. Park hours for day visitors are 7 A.M.–9 P.M. Sun.–Thurs. and 7 A.M.–10 P.M. Fri.–Sat. Entrance fee is $1 per person. Free for seniors 62 and over and children age 3 and under.

✳ To Do

♂ ♿ ⇾ 🐾 **BREC's Baton Rouge Zoo** (225-775-3931, www.brzoo.org), 3601 Thomas Rd., Baton Rouge. Baton Rouge's No. 1 year-round family attraction, the zoo is a delight. More than 1,800 animals from around the world live here in well-planned habitats. The newest major attraction, Realm of the Tiger, features Malayan and Sumatran tigers, siamang gibbons, and an Asian aviary. Among the special exhibits are L'Aquarium de Louisiane, featuring fish, reptiles and amphibians from Louisiana, and the otter pond in a Cajun Cabin setting. A fun Safari Playground is next to the Petting Zoo. Plan a mini picnic with items from the Flamingo Café. Take the narrated sidewalk tour in the White Tiger Tram and ride the Cypress Bayou Railroad as it circles the grounds and the animal habits. Open 9:30 A.M.–4 P.M. Mon.–Fri. Admission is $7, adults and teens; $6, seniors; $4, children 2–12; free 1 and younger.

♂ ♿ ⇾ 🐾 **BREC Walks/Jogs** (225-272-9200, www.brec.org). There are some 25 miles of walking and running trails and tracks in parks operated by the East Baton Rouge Parish Recreation and Parks Commission, better known as BREC. Eleven parks have hard-surface walkways and seven boast walking trails. The easiest park to reach from downtown is City Brooks Community Park, where there's ample opportunity to stretch your legs. Local walkers and joggers can be found daily at Milford Warfield Memorial Park, 901 Stanford Ave., and at University Lake. All amenities are compliant with the Americans with Disabilities Act, and there are sidewalks, benches, and a water fountain.

♂ 🐾 ⇾ 🐾 **City-Brooks Community Park** (225-272-9200, www.brec.org), 1650 Eddie Robinson Dr., Baton Rouge. Just minutes from downtown and Louisiana State University campus, this park dates from the 1920s. In 2008 it received a multi-million dollar redesign, and today it is an urban treasure with activities for people of all ages. On any day, visitors can enjoy the nine-hole golf course, basketball courts, Capitol One Tennis Center, and the recreation center. There are bike paths, walking trails, a labyrinth, informal gardens, and a picnic area. View works by local artists in the Baton Rouge Gallery on the grounds or take your dog (on a leash) for a walk in Raising Cane's Dog Park. The park is closed sunset to sunrise. Drugs, alcoholic, beverages, firearms, and cursing are not allowed at any BREC parks in the parish.

♂ 🐾 **Levee Walk,** downtown on River Road between the USS *Kidd* and the Capitol Park Welcome Center, Baton Rouge. Walk or jog along on a paved walk along the top of the levee. The views of the Mississippi River, with barges and ocean-going vessels passing, constantly change. Handsome benches allow visitors to sit and take in the scene, and street lights cast a soft glow over the walkway in the evening. The area is regularly patrolled by city police.

♂ ⇾ **Mike the Tiger Cage** (225-578-0628, www.mikethetiger.com), Stadium Dr., LSU campus, Baton Rouge. Stop by and visit Mike the Tiger, one of America's

Cynthia V. Campbell

MIKE THE TIGER, LSU'S MASCOT, TAKES A LEISURELY STROLL IN HIS 15-MILLION-DOLLAR HABITAT.

most beloved and pampered mascots. Mike VI, born in 2005, is a handsome Bengal/Siberian tiger with beautiful markings. His habitat features semi-tropical plants, large live oak trees, a waterfall, and a stream flowing from a rocky backdrop. The current Mike is friendly and apparently likes visitors. If you catch him early in the day or late in the afternoon, he might be playing with a tough large ball made especially for him.

✔ ✤ **Plaquemine Lock State Historic Site** (225-687-7158, www.lastateparks .com), 57730 Main St., Plaquemine. The lock built in 1909 allowed boats to pass between the Mississippi River and Bayou Plaquemine, opening the Atchafalaya and Acadiana regions to commercial traffic. Boaters, outdoors enthusiasts, and budding engineers find the original lock house and locks fascinating, and the views of the Mississippi are really impressive. Downtown Plaquemine is just blocks away. Open 9 A.M.–5 P.M., Tues.–Sat. Admission $4 per person; free for seniors 62 and older and children age 12 and under. Groups are asked to call in advance.

AMUSEMENT/WATER PARKS ✔ **Blue Bayou Water Park and Dixie Landin'** (225-753-3333, www.bluebayou.com), Highland Rd. and Perkins Rd. East, Baton Rouge. Operating during the hot summer months, this is a cross between the amusement parks of yesteryear and today's snazzy water parks. Dixie Landin' features more than 25 rides, including a looping roller coaster, the Ragin' Cajun. Parents can take toddlers for a ride in a Model T in Gasoline Alley. Get wet and wild in modern, up-to-date water attractions, including the Mad Moccasin slide that twists and turns in darkness. Concession stands offer cotton candy, funnel cake, hot dogs, pizza, and more. Live concerts take place on Saturday. Bring your bathing suit and suntan lotion. Blue Bayou hours are 10 A.M.–6 P.M. Dixie Landin' hours are 2–10 P.M., but vary somewhat at the beginning and end of each season. Admission to both parks is $34.95, 48 inches and taller; $27.99, under 48 inches; $27.99, seniors; and free under 35 inches. Admission prices drop after 6 P.M. Get $5 off your admission when you bring a Coca-Cola can. Open from Memorial Day weekend through Labor Day weekend.

BOWLING ✔ **Circle Bowling Lanes** (225-925-5471), 8878 Florida Blvd., Baton Rouge. Across from Cortana Mall, Circle Bowling offers 25 bowling lanes and an arcade. A section of an alley can be used as a dance floor, and you may find a DJ playing your favorite tunes on the weekend. Pizza and party-style bowling are offered on special nights, with lights and music. Prices vary. Call for hours and bowling times.

✔ **Don Carter Bowling Lanes** (225-925-5471, www.dcbowl.com), 9829 Airline Highway, Baton Rouge. With 64 lanes, Don Carter Bowling is a major indoor attraction with activities for the entire family. In addition to adult leagues, the center arranges short-season leagues for bowlers with limited time. Staff members go out of their way to help visitors. Fees, hours, and times are posted on the website.

⊘ **Metro Bowl** (225-356-1366, www.bowlmetro.com), 4388 Airline Highway, Baton Rouge. Catering to adults and youth groups, Metro Bowl offers opportunities for leagues, tournaments, and the general public. It's a good spot for people who enjoy bowling wherever they go. Christian night is Wednesday, 9:30 P.M.–midnight. The website lists hours and special events. Call for hours and bowling times.

FISHING *⊘ ⇝ ◈* **Parish Fishing** (www.brec.org). Fishing in Baton Rouge's lakes and ponds does not require a special license, just a basic fishing license from the Louisiana Department of Wildlife and Fisheries. The limit is four fish per day. You can catch and release more than four. The lakes include: **City Park Lake**, 2549 Dalrymple Dr.; **Greenwood Park Lake**, 13350 LA 19; **Oak Villa Lake**, 2615 Oak Villa Blvd.; **Doyle's Bayou**, 7801 Pride–Port Hudson Rd.; **North Sherwood Forest Lake**, 3140 North Sherwood Forest Dr.; and Blackwater **Conservation Area**, at the intersection of Blackwater and Hooper roads. The fishing ponds at North Sherwood, Greenwood, and Oak Villa have been stocked with rainbow trout. Your best chances are at North Sherwood and Oak Villa. The Mississippi River here is much too wide and busy with commercial traffic for easy fishing, however, with an hour's drive anglers will find state parks, rivers, and lakes with abundant fishing. For more information contact the Louisiana Department of Wildlife and Fisheries at www.wlf.louisiana.gov. Additional information is available from the Louisiana Office of State Parks, www.crt.state.la.us; the U.S Forest Service, www.fs.fed.us; and the U.S. Fish and Wildlife Service, www.fws.gov.

GOLF *⊘ ⇝ ◈* **BREC's City Park Golf** (225-387-9523, www.brec.org), 1442 City Park Ave., Baton Rouge. Built in 1926 and designed by Tom Bendelow, this is one of 20 courses in the country to be placed on the National Register of Historic Places as the community's first municipal golf course. The short, 34-par, nine-hole course is notable for its natural beauty, mature trees, and lake vistas. Situated off I-10 and Dalrymple Drive, it is convenient to LSU and downtown Baton Rouge. Open 7 A.M.–dark. Fees (twilight–weekend, all ages) range $8–$12.

⊘ ⇝ **BREC's Webb Park Golf Course** (225-383-4919, www.brec.org), 1351 Country Club Dr., Baton Rouge. A favorite with local golfers, this 18-hole course measures 6,656 yards in length. Large oaks line the fairways of this centrally located course off College Drive. It's close to I-10, LSU, and downtown Baton Rouge. Locker room facilities are available for both men and women. Webb Park

GOLF AT ANGOLA PRISON

A game at the **Prison View Golf Course at Louisiana State Prison** (225-655-2978), LA 66, St. Francisville, is a rare experience. Open to the public, the nine-hole course features two tee boxes for an option to play 18 holes. Tee times must be scheduled at least 24 hours in advance by contacting the Pro Shop at the phone number above or by e-mail at www.prisonviewgolf.com. The cost to tee off at the state's only maximum-security prison is $20, which includes cart rental.

has a specially designed fitness area for golfers to work out, with plenty of equip-ment designed specifically to enhance your swing. Tee times may be booked six days in advance.

🏌️ ⇸ **The Island Country Club** (225- 685-0808, www.theislandgolf.com), 23550 Myrtle Grove Rd., Plaquemine. Fourteen miles from downtown Baton Rouge, The Island is in Iberville Parish, west of the Mississippi. It is one of the courses listed on Louisiana's Audubon Golf Trail. Designed by Mike Young, the course has been featured in *Golf Magazine* and on the Golf channel. Water comes into play on nine holes and 17 greens. The distance is 7,010 yards; the course rating, 74.4/135 championship, 71.8/130, standard; the status is semi-private. The clubhouse provides panoramic views of holes 9 and 18. Fees range $16–24, Tues.–Thurs., and $16–$34, Fri.–Sun. and holidays. The restaurant, open to the public, specializes in Cajun cuisine.

🏌️ ⇸ 🏌️ **LSU Golf Club** (225-578-3394, www.golf.lsu.edu), corner of Burbank and Nicholson, Baton Rouge. The course is part of Louisiana State University's huge sports complex. Located just minutes from downtown, this is a public course. The distance is 6,772 yards and course rating 72.3 (blue). There's a pro shop for your convenience. Green fees on weekdays are $18, alumni and public; $15, faculty, staff, and seniors; and $12, students. Weekend fees are $23, alumni and public; $18, seniors; $16, faculty; and $14, students.

🏌️ ⇸ **Santa Maria Golf Course** (225-752-9667, www.brec.org), 18460 Santa Maria Parkway, Baton Rouge. Designed by Robert Trent Jones Sr., Santa Maria has consistently received *Golf Digest's* highest ranking for a municipal course. It is located one mile off Highland Road near I-10, on 150 acres of rolling terrain featuring 15 lakes and two natural waterways. Sand and grass bunkers, exquisite Bermuda grass fairways, and ancient oaks provide the perfect setting for a memorable test of golf. The course distance is 6,826 yards; the rating is 74.1 (gold), 71.8 (blue), 6812 (white), and 70.7 (red). Facilities include a driving range, practice facility, and workout facility. The Champions Grill overlooks the beautiful par-five finishing hole. Open 8 A.M.–dark weekdays and 7 A.M.–dark weekends. Fees (twilight to weekends) range $22–$38.

SKATING 🏌️ **Skate Galaxy** (925-756-2424, www.skategalaxy.com), 12828 Jefferson Highway, Baton Rouge. There's plenty of room here for casual roller skating or an all-out workout. There's rarely a dull moment here. The Galaxy also offers rock climbing and laser tag. There's an exciting arcade, food court, pro shop, and a viewing balcony with TV. Hours are seasonal. Closed Mondays. Skate rentals are $2.

TENNIS 🏌️ **BREC's Tennis Programs** (225-272-9200, www.brec.org), Baton Rouge BREC tennis courts can be found in public parks throughout the city. They are well designed and lighted. We recommend the new courts at **City-Brooks Park** (225-272-9200, 1515 Dalrymple), the **Highland Park Center** (225-766-0247, 140 Highland Rd.), and the **Independence Park Center** (225-923-2792, 7502 Independence). For information and fees at these centers, call 225-272-9200, ext. 549. The **YMCA Lamar Tennis Center** (225-287-2748, 8100 YMCA Plaza Dr.) features 10 hard courts and 10 soft courts. Nonmembers attending with a member pay a $5 fee.

✴ Lodging

✐ ♿ ⊘ ((ɰ)) ♈ **Baton Rouge Marriott** (225-924-5000), 5500 Hilton Ave., Baton Rouge. With 20,000 square feet of banquet and meeting space, the Baton Rouge Marriot is a major, full-service hotel located at I-10, near the I-12 split. A gracious staff welcomes guests in a handsome lobby, and the lobby bar is open for dinner. Some 300 guest rooms feature luxurious bedding with duvets, spacious work desks, high speed wire and wireless Internet access, cable TV, coffee, and dual phones. There are four private floors with concierge service. No pets. Moderate–expensive.

✐ ♿ ⊘ ((ɰ)) **The Cook Hotel** (225-383-2665, www.thecookhotel.com), 3848 West Lakeshore Dr., Baton Rouge. Different and fun, this four-star hotel and conference center is situated on the LSU campus, just off University Lake. Created to accommodate visiting alumni, athletes, and guest lecturers, it's also open to the public. You don't have to be a die-hard LSU fan to enjoy the hotel, but you'll probably leave humming the "Tiger Rag." Throughout the public rooms and guest rooms, the university's colors—purple and gold—appear in subtle shades in carpets, lounge chairs and bedroom décor. Plush Sealy Posturpedic beds, luxurious triple sheeting, and duvets create beautiful guest rooms. Upgrade to a suite or mega-suite complete with fireplace and Jacuzzi tub. Join other guests for a yummy complimentary breakfast. There's high-speed Internet, a 24-hour business center, a fitness center, a great LSU sports museum, and a gift shop. The hotel is usually completely booked months in advance for LSU football games and certain special events. Moderate–expensive.

✐ ♿ ⊘ ♈ **Crowne Plaza** (225-925-2244), 4728 Constitution Ave., Baton Rouge. This is a full-service hotel with spacious conference rooms popular with local organizations. Beautiful guestrooms in a quiet zone have been recently renovated in soft neutral tones and include Sleep Advantage beds, with Euro shams, duvets, and travertine surround bathrooms. Facilities include a restaurant, lounge, gift shop, outdoor pool, and 3,000-square-foot gym. Concierge level available. Nearby restaurants include Ruth's Chris Steak House, Ninfa's, and Chili's. Just off 1-10, the hotel is within minutes of a major shopping area, a medical complex, and downtown. Moderate–expensive.

✐ 🐾 ♿ ⊘ ((ɰ)) **Drury Inn & Suites Baton Rouge** (225-766-2022, www.druryhotels.com), 7930 Essen Park Ave., Baton Rouge. Take time to view historic photographs of Baton Rouge in the gallery just off the lobby and you'll know this hotel cares about this river city. Its location off I-10 puts you with minutes of landmark sites such as the State Capitol and Old State Capitol and the USS *Kidd*. Just across Essen Lane is the LSU Rural Life Museum and Windrush Gardens. Guest rooms are furnished with burgundy and gold bedspreads, drapes, and carpets. For relaxing, there's an indoor-outdoor swimming pool, a Jacuzzi spa, and a fitness facility. Guests receive complimentary popcorn and snacks 3–10 P.M. Complimentary hot breakfast features everything from waffles and cereals to sausage and eggs. Pets are welcomed (the hotel even has its own doggy yard). Moderate.

✐ ♿ ((ɰ)) ♈ **Embassy Suites** (225-924-6566, www.embassysuites.com), 4914 Constitution Ave., Baton Rouge. Not your ordinary suites hotel, the Baton

Rouge Embassy Suites puts Louisiana soul into its service and cuisine. The hotel features complete two-room suites, each with a roomy bedroom and sturdy sleep sofa in the living room. There are two televisions with full cable TV. Guests who want to take it easy and dine in have the convenience of a mini-refrigerator, coffeemaker, and microwave. Guests receive a complete cooked breakfast and a manager's reception with their choice of beverage. There's a small but relaxing indoor swimming pool, sauna, and steam room, and a three-hole putting green. Pets are not accepted. Just off I-10, the hotel is close to numerous restaurants, a Wal-Mart, a shopping area, and medical center. Moderate–expensive.

✆ 🐾 ♿ ✂ ⧫ Y **Hilton Baton Rouge Capitol Center** (877-862-9800, www.hiltoncapitolcenter.com), 201 Lafayette St., Baton Rouge. The Hilton is across the Mississippi River levee in downtown Baton Rouge. Its guest rooms feature contemporary design and furnishings, but this is a historical landmark. Built in 1927 as the Heidelberg Hotel, it was a favorite spot of Governor Huey P. Long. In 1931, the hotel briefly served as the state capitol during a dispute between Long and Lieutenant Governor Paul N. Cyr. Details of the building's façade and lobby reflect the stylish art deco mode of the 1930s. The Kingfish restaurant offers breakfast, lunch, and dinner and features excellent American dishes with a nod to Southern and Cajun cuisine. Executive suite rooms have views of the Mississippi and access to the Executive Lounge, which hosts a continental breakfast and evening reception. There's a $75 non-refundable fee for housing pets. Across the street is the Shaw Center for the Arts. Within close walking distance are the Old State Capitol, the Louisiana Arts and Science Museum, and the USS *Kidd* and Veterans Memorial. One block over on Third Street are more restaurants, wine bars and night spots. Expensive.

✆ 🐾 **Holiday Inn South** (225-924-7021, www.hibatonrougesouth.com), 9940 Airline Highway and I-12, Baton Rouge. The large full-service hotel is centrally located about 6 miles from downtown. Designed with a beautifully landscaped atrium, it offers more than 300 rooms, indoor and outdoor pools, wireless Internet service, an exercise facility, and a full-service restaurant and lounge. Moderate.

BED & BREAKFASTS

✆ ♿ ✂ ↝ ((ᵀ)) **The Stockade Bed and Breakfast** (225-769-7358, www.the stockade.com), 8866 Highland Rd., Baton Rouge. Situated about 3.5 miles south of LSU on historic Highland Road, this inn is on the National Register as a Civil War site. Five guest bedrooms are luxurious and elegant. People enjoy gathering in the great room with fountain, fireplace, piano, and original art work. Enjoy a continental or full Southern breakfast (perhaps garlic cheese grits or vegetable quiche with fruit) in the delightful dining room filled with antiques and fine paintings, prints, and drawings. No pets. The neighborhood community center across the road includes several restaurants and shops. Moderate–expensive.

CAMPGROUNDS *✆ 🐾* BREC'S

Farr Park Horse Activity Center (225-769-7805, www.brec.com), 6402 River Rd., Baton Rouge. This is the home of a fine equestrian facility and RV campground. It offers 180 campsites, many of which are pull-through sites. There are activities for horse lovers, horse boarding, riding lessons, and special events. Inexpensive.

♪ ⇝ ((ᵖ)) ♨ **KOA Campground** (225-664-7281, www.batonrougekoa.com), 7628 Vincent Rd., Denham Springs. East of Baton Rouge just off I-12, this is a large, well-run campground with shady spots, a concrete pull-through, and blacktop streets. There's a 50-foot heated pool, a hot tub, and mini-golf. Campers also are within walking distance of the area's Bass Pro Shops. Inexpensive.

✴ Where to Eat

EATING OUT **Bistro Byronz** (225-218-1433,www.bistrobyronz.com), 5412 Government St., Baton Rouge. Enjoy a delicious meal in a friendly atmosphere. Sandwiches are hearty and filling. Entrees range from a chicken and duck cassoulet to hamburger steak. Hours are 11 A.M.–9 P.M. Mon.–Thurs., 11 A.M.–10 P.M. Fri.–Sat., and 11 A.M.–3 P.M. Sun. Moderate

Y ♨ **Boutin's Cajun Music and Dining** (225-819-9862, www.boutins.com), 8322 Bluebonnet, Baton Rouge. Enjoy the taste and sounds of Cajun Country, without leaving town. The main dining room is centered on a dance floor where you can two-step and waltz before, after, and during a meal of authentic Cajun dishes. Among the specialties are grilled alligator and enchiladas filled with crawfish, a cheese blend, and topped with cumin mornay sauce. Entrées are served with jambalaya, corn maque choux, and hush puppies. Boutin's is perfect for a family outing or to join friends for a festive, informal gathering. Regional Cajun bands play Tuesday through Saturday. Open 11 A.M.–9 P.M. Sun.–Wed. and 11 A.M.–10 P.M. Thurs.–Sat. Moderate.

♪ **Louie's Cafe** (225-346-8221, www.louiescafe.org), 209 West State St., Baton Rouge. This place is a legend among LSU students, alumni, and fans. Never mind the funky diner atmosphere. Louie's has been in business since 1941, and it's still turning out fantastic breakfasts and filling lunches and dinners. Order your eggs any way you like. Omelets are spectacular, as are the hash browns seasoned with Cajun spices. The melt-in-your-mouth biscuits are only served from 6–11 A.M. Hamburgers and gumbo also lunch and dinner staples. Entrees include steak, seafood, and chicken. Open 24 hours daily. Inexpensive–moderate.

♪ Y **Pastime Restaurant and Lounge** (225-343-54-90, www.pastimerestaurant.com), 252 South Blvd., Baton Rouge. A cherished family hangout, the Pastime in Beauregard Town dates from 1945. Because of a 1-mile exclusion law from the LSU campus for any business selling alcohol, it became a college hangout. Alumni return here to relive their student days and mingle with the current generation while munching great pizza, po-boys, and burgers. Customers walk into the kitchen area to write down their orders for the cooks, then pick up their food and gather at tables in a simple, clean dining room. Music drifts in from the bar, which is off limits to anyone younger than 21. The menu includes seafood plates and daily specials such as red beans and rice or meatballs and spaghetti. Older customers belly up to the bar to enjoy their beverage of choice and enjoy the atmosphere, which could easily be a roadhouse scene from a Hollywood movie. You never know who you'll meet in the Pastime. Customers have included Angelina Jolie, Billy Bob Thornton, and Matthew McConaughey. The Pastime has the same menu lunch and dinner. Open 10 A.M.–11 P.M. Mon.–Thurs., 10 A.M.–

midnight Fri., and 10 A.M.–11 P.M. Sat. Inexpensive.

♪ ⅋ **Sammy's Grill** (225-766-7650, www.sammysgrillonline.com), 8635 Highland Rd., Baton Rouge. This cafe has grown from a small neighborhood bar on Highland Road south of the LSU campus into a full-fledged restaurant with great eats. Cars pack the two parking lots during lunch and dinner hours, especially on game days. The salads with lettuce, Roma tomatoes, cucumbers, boiled egg, and Parmesan cheese, are huge. We like the grilled or fried Tiger ($9.95) with fried shrimp, crawfish, and jumbo lump crabmeat with a spicy remoulade. You'll find one of the best half-pound hamburgers in the city here. The chicken-fried steak ($7.95) with mashed potatoes, white gravy, and veggie of the day is as Southern as it gets. Open Mon.–Sat. lunch and dinner; Sun. brunch. Moderate.

♪ ❧ **Voodoo BBQ & Grill** (225-248-6793, www.voodoobbqandgrill), 3347 Nicholson Dr., Baton Rouge. Other locations are 3510 Drusilla Lane and 6409 Bluebonnet Blvd. at the Mall of Louisiana. This is a good place to grab a quick hearty meal of slow-cooked BBQ with a choice of sauces. Specialty meats include brisket, pulled pork, jerk chicken, Cajun sausage, and rack of ribs. Order lunch or dinner at the counter and your meal will be served in record time. If you like Southern cooking, try a side of the well-seasoned gris gris greens, macaroni and cheese, or corn pudding. Kid's meals, such as hamburgers or chicken fingers, come with French fries. Hours are 11 A.M.–10 P.M. Mon.–Thurs., 11 A.M.–11 P.M. Fri.–Sat., and 11 A.M.–9 P.M. Sun. Inexpensive–moderate.

DINING OUT **The Carriage House** (225-635-6278, www.themyrtles

restaurant.com), 7747 US 61, St. Francisville. On the grounds of The Myrtles Plantation, this restaurant presents traditional plantation cooking with flair. We suggest the chicken and dumplings for lunch and the shrimp *etouffee* for dinner. For Sunday brunch, try the eggplant medallions topped with seafood stuffing, a poached egg, and Hollandaise sauce. Open every day except Tuesday. Hours are 11 A.M.–2 P.M. and 5–9 P.M. Sunday brunch is 11 A.M.–2 P.M.

⅋ **The Chimes Restaurant** (225-383-1754, www.thechimes.com), 3357 Highland Rd., Baton Rouge. Other locations are 10870 Coursey Blvd., Baton Rouge, and 19130 West Front St., Covington. At the north gates of LSU, the Chimes has a collegiate ambiance that should not be missed. The menu is varied and anything you choose will be consistently good. Crawfish dishes are delicious and sandwiches are hearty. Try the Louisiana alligator appetizer and the duck and sausage gumbo. The busy bar features more than 100 beers from more than 60 countries. Go anytime and you'll find the Chimes packed with students, alumni, faculty and townspeople. On game days, lines spill out into the sidewalk. Oysters on the half shell are on special 4–7 P.M. daily. Open daily; kitchen closes at midnight Mon.–Sat. The restaurant offers the same menu for lunch and dinner. Moderate.

♿ ♂ ⅋ **Juban's** (225-346-8422, www.jubans.com), 3739 Perkins Rd., Baton Rouge. Located in a drab strip center, Juban's presents Creole-inspired dishes that keep patrons returning time and again. The selection of entrees is varied and includes beef, lamb, veal, and Louisiana fish. Try the signature dish, Hallelujah Crab, a soft-shell crab stuffed with shrimp, crawfish, and crabmeat and topped with a Creole sauce. With one of the area's finest wine cellars, Juban's has been awarded Wine Spectator's Best of Award of Excellence. Many patrons choose to dine in the attractive, well-appointed indoor courtyard bar. This is considered one of the best dining spots in town. Attire is business or dressy casual. Ask about the 25-cent martinis at lunch. Reservations preferred. Open for lunch 11 A.M.–2 P.M. Tues.–Fri, dinner 5:30–10 P.M. Mon.–Sat. and brunch 10:30 A.M.–3 P.M. Sun. Expensive.

Latil's Landing (225-473-9380, www.houmashouse.com), 40136 LA 942, Darrow. Chef Jeremy Langlois at Houmas House Plantation creates exquisite dishes that delight the palate. His signature bisque of curried pumpkin, crawfish, and corn is memorable, as is grilled duck breast with praline pecan sauce. The restaurant is located in the French House, a 250-year old structure with beamed ceilings, and the elegant table setting features French Limoges china. Open 6–10 P.M. Wed.–Sat. and 2–9 P.M. Sun. Expensive.

Mansion Restaurant (866-527-6884, www.nottway.com), 31025 LA 1, White Castle. The glassed-in rotunda at this restaurant has fantastic views of Nottoway Plantation's oaks and expansive lawn. The setting is truly romantic. The menu blends regional south Louisiana dishes with contemporary favorites. Items range from blackened redfish to grilled beef tenderloin filet. The house salad with mixed greens, cucumbers, and tomatoes takes on exciting flavors with blue cheese, crumbled almond brittle, and sugarcane vinaigrette dressing. Open daily. Hours are 7–10 A.M., 11 A.M.–2 P.M., and 5–9 P.M. Sunday brunch is 11 A.M.–2 P.M.

&. Y Mansurs on the Boulevard (225-923-3366, www.mansursonthe boulevard.com), 5720-A Corporate Blvd., Baton Rouge. Start with the brie and crabmeat soup, then move on to one of Mansur's spectacular entrees. The veal Oscar topped with crabmeat and the cedar-roasted redfish are memorable. Attire is business or dressy casual. The restaurant appeals to the crowd with sophisticated tastes in food, décor, and soft lighting. Live piano music and professional service adds to the dining experience. There's an excellent wine list and drinks from the bar. Open 11 A.M.–2 P.M. and 5–9:30 P.M. Mon.–Thurs., dinner until 9:30 P.M. Fri.–Sat., and brunch 11 A.M.–2 and dinner 5–8:30 P.M. Sun. Expensive.

Y Mike Anderson's (225-766-7823, www.mikeandersons.com), 1031 West Lee Dr., Baton Rouge. Established by the former LSU All-American football player, Mike Anderson's continues to draw huge crowds with its great fresh seafood dishes, large crunchy onion rings, and special salads. Regulars like to stop at the bar for a cold beer and charbroiled oysters. Lunch and dinner are served daily. There's indoor and patio seating, but on game nights, this restaurant is packed. Attire is casual and dressy casual. Arrive early or be prepared to wait for that memorable meal. Open 11 A.M.–2 P.M. and 5–9 P.M. Mon.–Thurs., 11 A.M.–10 P.M. Fri.–Sat., and 11 A.M.–9 P.M. Sun. Moderate–expensive.

Y ⌘ Tsunami Sushi (225-346-5100, www.servingsushi.com), 100 Lafayette St., Baton Rouge. One of the most romantic spots in Baton Rouge, Tsunami is on the sixth floor of the Shaw Center for the Performing Arts downtown. Sip on a chilled martini and take in the wonderful view of the Mississippi River, especially as the sun sets on the Western horizon. There's an extensive sushi and sashimi menu. We recommend choosing from the dinner menu. Try the Pacific Rim ribs cooked in sake and pineapple juice. A good choice for dressing up for an evening and going upscale. Open 11 A.M.– 10 P.M. Tues.–Thurs. and 11 A.M.– 11 P.M. Fri.–Sat. Moderate–expensive.

✳ Entertainment

✎ ⛵ **Baton Rouge Little Theater** (225-924-6496, www.brso.brlt.org), 7155 Florida Blvd., Baton Rouge. Founded in 1946, Baton Rouge Little Theatre is one of the longest-running regional theater companies in the United States. In 1951 the actor and director Lee Edwards, who had studied with Lee Strasberg and Max Reinhardt, became the director and brought a new level of professionalism to the organization. Performers include students, amateurs, and professional actors. Through the years, an impressive number of actors, dramatists, and writers have "graduated" from BRLT. Some return from time to time in guest roles. More recent productions have included *Agnes of God, Arsenic and Old Lace,* and *The Elephant Man.* Among the many memorable musicals BRLT has presented are *West Side Story, Annie, Camelot,* and *Evita.* Check the website for a schedule.

✎ & ⛵ **Baton Rouge Rivercenter Theatre for the Performing Arts** (225-389-3030, www.brrivercenter .com), 275 South River Rd., Baton Rouge. The large theater, which seats up to 1,900, is the home of the Baton Rouge Symphony, which presents a Master Works Series as well as the Pennington Great Performance concerts. Guest artists have included Renee Fleming, Chris Botti, Van Cliburn, Joshua Bell, Itzhak Perlman, and Yo-Yo Ma. The Baton Rouge Ballet Theater performances include a Cajun version of *The Nutcracker.* The theater also presents productions by Opera Louisiana and has welcomed touring Broadway shows such as *Rent, Miss Saigon, Les Miserables,* and *Cats.* There is no central aisle at this theater or elevator to the spacious balcony. However, disabled-accessible seating is available, with wheelchair ramps located at side entrances. Check the website for upcoming performances.

& ⛵ ☿ **Belle of Baton Rouge Casino and Hotel** (800-676-4847, www.belle ofbatonrouge.com), 103 France St., Baton Rouge. This three-deck, paddlewheel boat is permanently docked on the Mississippi River at the foot of the

---

MUSIC WITH A "ROUGE" AWAKENING

The Arts Council of Baton Rouge has boosted the city's music landscape by organizing a series of premier music events. FestForAll in May is a celebration of art and music held downtown on North Boulevard. In October and November, the council sponsors Sundays in the Park concerts in Lafayette Park downtown, a casual way to enjoy fine performances with food and drink vendors. Many families with children turn out to enjoy the sunshine, dance, and watch kids play in the Shaw Center's interactive fountain. The Arts Council also is responsible for bringing international artists, such as Wynton Marsalis and the clarinetist Paquito D'Rivera to Baton Rouge in 2010 as part of the River City Jazz Masters series held in the Shaw Center for the Arts.

I-10 bridge. The gaming area is 28,000 square feet of live poker, slots, table games, and video poker. Food is available on board and in the casino's landside facilities. The casino hotel, just across the street, is attached to the Catfish Town Atrium, where concerts, boxing matches, and other entertainment take place.

Y **Boudreaux and Thibodeaux** (225-636-2442, www.myspace.com /boudreauxdowntown), 214 Third St., No. 2D, Baton Rouge. This jiving nightclub features live entertainment three nights a week. The colorful, casual atmosphere in this two-story club is popular with 20somethings and young professionals. The Balcony Bar has a French Quarter atmosphere. Step out on the balcony for one of the best views of downtown Baton Rouge on a Saturday night. Call about nightclub hours, which are subject to change for special events and LSU football games. Hours for balcony bar 4 P.M.–2 A.M. Tues.-Sat.

Y **Funny Bone/Triple A Bar** (225-927-3222, www.tripleabatonrouge .com), 4715 Bennington Ave., Baton Rouge. Don't let the unimposing entrance deter you from having fun. There's double-dip entertainment here. The spacious bar area has room to enjoy your favorite beverage while watching wide-screen televisions, dancing, or playing pool. This area is separated from the comedy area with a double sound-proof wall. Entertainers have included Jeff Foxworthy, Ron "Tater Salad" White, and Phyllis Diller. Open to guests age 18 and over. Those under 21 will not be served alcohol. Funny Bone shows are held at 8 and 9 P.M. on Friday and Saturday and 9 P.M. on Thursday.

& ↑ Y **Hollywood Casino** (800-447-6843, www.hollywoodcasino.com), 1717 River Rd. North, Baton Rouge.

Situated on the Mississippi River just north of the capitol, Hollywood Casino is open around the clock. The casino features more than 1,800 slots and popular table games. Dine in style at the Steakhouse Restaurant or choose the Epic Buffet or Take 2 Deli. Valet parking is convenient. Guests enjoy live weekend entertainment featuring regional bands, such as Geno DelaFose, Gumbeaux Rouge, and Van Broussard, as well as national celebrities.

✍ ↑ **LSU Theater** and **Swine Palace** (225- 578-5128, www.theatre .lsu.edu and www.swinepalace.org), Dalrymple Dr., LSU Campus, Baton Rouge. There's a certain thrill in viewing young budding artists during the period when they are polishing their skills. LSU Theatre dates from 1928, and counts numerous distinguished graduates. Swine Palace was formed in 1992 as a nonprofit professional theater company and gives students an opportunity to work with established professionals. LSU Theatre is one of the few programs in the United States with an affiliated Equity theater. All performances are open to the public. An added perk is seeing a production in the stunning Claude L. Shaver Theatre within the Music and Dramatic Arts Building. To attend a performance, contact the box office at the number listed above.

✍ ↑ **Manship Theatre** (225-334-0334, www.manshiptheatre.com), 100 Lafayette St., Baton Rouge. The Manship is the perfect spot for people who enjoy performances in small, intimate theaters. Situated in the Shaw Center for the Arts, the theater presents a diverse and entertaining mix of dance, music, films, and theater. Among those who have appeared on this stage are the New Orleans music celebrity Dr. John; the singer-songwriter Randy

Newman; and the actor Hal Holbrook. The theatre also features local groups including the Playmakers, who are noted for their innovative productions for children and adults, and Of Moving Colors, a creative contemporary dance group. See the website for a calendar.

⬆ 🍸 **Sullivan's Ringside** (225-237-3055, www.sullivansteakhouse.com), 5252 Corporate Blvd., Baton Rouge. A lively nightspot, just inside Sullivan's Steak House, is popular with young professionals who gather to schmooze and listen to jazz and pop music by local bands. The setting somewhat resembles a boxing ring, with a nod to the restaurant's namesake, the bare-knuckles fighter John L. Sullivan. Hours 9 P.M.–2 A.M. Thurs.–Sat. Music groups also perform in the main bar, open daily 11 A.M.–2 A.M.

⬆ 🍸 🎵 **Teddy's Juke Joint** (225-892-0064, www.teddysjukejoint.com), 17001 Old Scenic Highway, Zachary. If you love blues and jazz, Teddy's is the place for an unforgettable evening. Musicians and people in the know consider Teddy's one of the best places to go to hear authentic American blues. Among the performers who have performed here are Henry Gray, Gregg Wright, Kenny Neal, Larry Garner, and the club's owner, Teddy Johnson. Christmas lights add to the festive atmosphere. Patrons love the soul food cooking from Nancy's Kitchen. Open noon–2 A.M. Mon.–Sat.

🍸 **The Varsity** (225-383-7018, www.varsitytheater.com), 3353 Highland Rd., Baton Rouge. Located next to The Chimes Restaurant at the North Gate of LSU, the Varsity has seen more than 25 Grammy Award-winning artists on stage. Performers have included Robert Earl Keen, the Michael Foster Project, Analog Rebellion, and Barenaked Ladies. With a 300-person capacity, the venue keeps things rocking with everything from modern rock to salsa. The Varsity opens at 8 or 9 P.M. depending on the show. Tickets range from $10 to $90 depending on the show and lead entertainer. Check the website for show schedules.

🎷 ♿ ⬆ **Movie Theaters:** While there are no movie theaters downtown, you'll find first-rate movie houses at shopping centers and malls throughout the city. The theaters show first-run movies, and at times seats sell out early. They include: **United Artist Citiplace 11** (225-216-0056, www.regmovies.com, 2610 CitiPlace); **Rave Mall of Louisiana 15** (225-769-5176, www.ravemotionpictures.com, 6401 Bluebonnet Blvd.); **Rave Baton Rouge 16** (225-753-2710, www.rave motionpictures.com, 16040 Hatteras); **Grand Cinema** (225-755-8888, www.thegrandcinema.com, 15365 George O'Neal Rd.); and **Cinemark Perkins Rowe** (225-761-6905, www.perkins rowe.com, Perkins Rd. and Bluebonnet Boulevard).

✳ Selective Shopping

Backpacker Wilderness Outfitters (225-925-2667, www.backpacker.com), 7656 Jefferson Highway. Established in 1964, the Backpacker has become the premiere wilderness outfitter in Louisiana. Outstanding service is a hallmark of this company, which can provide clothing and gear for any adventure you can dream. The company is an official Boy Scout and Girl Scout supply distributor. It's also home to the C.C. Lockwood Gallery featuring works by Lockwood, an award-winning nature photographer. A travel section organizes outdoor adventure trips and ski trips, including Mardi Gras ski trips to snowy winter destinations. Open 10 A.M.–7 P.M. Mon.–Fri., 9 A.M.–6 P.M. Sat., and noon–5 P.M. Sun.

Brian's Furniture and Appliances
(800-259-0896), 515 Court St., Port
Allen. Just a few blocks from the Mississippi River on the west bank, Brian's is a one-stop place for shopping for rust-free cast aluminum furniture designed for patios and gardens. You'll find iron and fiberglass sugar kettles of various sizes that can be turned into fishponds and or water fountains. The company also specializes in furniture made from reclaimed Louisiana cypress. Open 9 A.M.–6 P.M. Mon.–Fri. and 9 A.M.–4 P.M. Sat.

Caffery Gallery (225-388-9397, www
.cafferygallery), 4016 Government St.,
Baton Rouge. A welcome diversion, Caffery's is packed from ceiling to floor with an eclectic variety of fine art and craft pieces. The pink house in Mid City is jammed with truly innovative paintings, sculpture, jewelry, and more. Open 10 A.M.–5:30 P.M. Tues.–Sat.

Circa 1857 (225-387-8667, www.circa
1857.com), 1857 Government St.,
Baton Rouge. In old Rome, citizens often took stones and sculptures from ancient ruins to enhance new homes or temples. If you love searching for architectural salvage, old doors or windows, then drop by Circa 1857. Shops here also carry antique dishes, candlesticks, retro clothing, and original art. **Rue Cou Cou,** in the same complex, specializes in custom framing and artworks from more than 60 local artists. Open 10 A.M.–5 P.M. Mon.–Sat.

Fireside Antiques (225-752-9565,
www.firesideantiques.com), 14007
Perkins Rd., Baton Rouge. Fireside specializes in fine quality French, Italian, and English antiques and some reproduction pieces. In addition, the store has an extensive collection of mirrors and decorative items as well as garden sculpture and architectural items. Eight large showrooms total more than 18,000 square feet. Nation-wide shipping is available. Open
10 A.M.–5 P.M. Mon.–Sat.

Grandmother's Buttons (225-635-
4107, www.grandmothersbuttons.com),
9814 Royal St., St. Francisville.
Antique and vintage buttons transformed into beautiful jewelry are the focus of this renovated 1905 bank. Step into the old vault to see the Button Museum with buttons dating from the 1760s to the 1940s. Shop owner and jewelry designer Susan Davis has turned this building into a unique shopping haven. Open 10:30 A.M.–5 P.M. Mon.–Sat. and 11 A.M.–5 P.M. Sun.

Louisiana Pottery (225-675-5572,
www.louisianapottery.com), 6470 LA
22, Sorrento. This shop is situated in Cajun Village, a collection of Acadian cottages that make up a small shopping area. Louisiana Pottery is filled with wonderful hand-crafted pots, dishes and art pieces made by Louisiana artisans. As a bonus, you also will find quality souvenirs and cookbooks. Open 10 A.M.–5 P.M. Tues.–Sun.

**Main Street Market/Red Stick
Farmer's Market** (225-267-5060),
501 Main St., Baton Rouge. There are people in Baton Rouge who start their weekend every Saturday at the Farmer's Market, where they pick up locally grown fresh vegetables and fruits from 8 A.M.–noon. While there, have coffee and enjoy some friendly local gossip. The Main Street Market, just inside the ground level of a city parking garage, features courtyard cafes, a coffee shop, retail items, and works by local artists. Hours 7 A.M.–4 P.M. Mon.–Fri. and 8 A.M.–noon Sat.

✑ ♿ ♛ **Mall of Louisiana** (225-761-
0307, www.malloflouisiana.com), 6401
Bluebonnet Blvd., Baton Rouge. This mall spreads out like Spanish moss in oak trees. Anchoring stores include Macy's and Dillard's, and in between you'll find big-brand names and

Cynthia V. Campbell

WORKS BY AWARD-WINNING ARTISTS ARE FEATURED AT THE LOUISIANA POTTERY SHOP IN SORRENTO.

Louisiana goodies. Circling the mall are many of America's best stores, restaurants, and movie theaters. Open 10 A.M.–9 P.M. Mon.–Sat. and noon–6 P.M. Sun. Handicapped parking.

🍴 ♿ **Perkins Rowe** (225-761-6905, www.perkinsrowe.com), Perkins Rd. at Bluebonnet Boulevard, Baton Rouge. Created for people with sophisticated taste in a township setting, Perkins Rowe shops are très chic. Browse for hours in Anthropologie, Francesca's, Orvis, Urban Outfitters, or Barnes and Noble. Then dine at The Grape, Kona Grill, La Madeleine, or Texas de Brazil. If you need a breath of fresh air, stroll about the landscaped square and study the architecture of the apartments built above the stores and cafes. Parking garage and handicapped park-

ing is available. Hours are 10 A.M.–9 P.M. Mon.–Thurs., 10 A.M.–9 P.M. Sat., and noon.–6 P.M. Sun.

Royal Standard (225-344-2311, www.theroyalstandard.com), 2877 Perkins Rd. and 16016 Perkins Rd., Baton Rouge. A delightful shop with myriads of choices, Royal Standard has all types of gifts, including decorative napkins and house and garden wares, antiques, jewelry, and home décor items.

🍴 ♿ **Tanger Outlet Mall** (225-647-9383, www.tangeroutlet.com/gonzales), 2420 Tanger Blvd., Gonzales. This large mall just off I-10 contains numerous popular outlet stores, including Claire's, Guess, Lane Bryant, Nine West, and Gap. Several restaurants and cafes are located in the complex. Open 9 A.M.–9 P.M. Mon.–Sat. and 11 A.M.–6 P.M. Sun.

🍴 **Towne Center at Cedar Lodge** (225-925-2344, www.townecenterat cedarlodge.com), Corporate Boulevard at Jefferson Highway, Baton Rouge. Upscale and snazzy, Towne Center is an outdoor shopping area with everything from Rickey Heroman's Florist to Whole Foods Grocery (organic vegetables and great wines). Among notable shops are Adler's fine jewelry, Mignon Faget custom jewelry, Style Lab for Men, Chico's, and Ann Taylor Loft. Satisfy your taste buds and Zea Rotisserie, Bonefish Grill, Carrabba's Italian Grill, and P.F. Chang's China Bistro. Handicapped parking. Shopping hours are 10 A.M.–9 P.M. Mon.–Sat. and noon–6 P.M. Sun.

✷ Special Events

February–March: **Mardi Gras Season** (800-527-6843, www.visitbatonrouge .com), Baton Rouge. Although not as extensive as Carnival in New Orleans, Mardi Gras here includes private parties, formal balls, and parades with zany costumes and beads. The most unusual parade is the Spanish Town parade, which satirizes national, state and local politics, and local celebrities. Some 70 floats wind through downtown and the historic Spanish Town district. The alcohol-free zone is popular for families with children. Contact the Baton Rouge Convention and Visitors Bureau site above, or visit www.baton-rouge.com/MardiGras.

Audubon Pilgrimage (225-635-6330, www.audubonpilgrimage.info), St. Francisville. Sponsored by the West Feliciana Historical Society, the festive mid-March home and garden tour celebrates the summer in 1820 when the artist and author John James Audubon stayed at Oakley Plantation, teaching the owner's daughter and painting many of his bird paintings. Take in historic demonstrations, cemetery tours, historic churches, homes, shopping, and nighttime events. Volunteer hosts and hostesses dress in colorful replica clothing from the 1820s for the event. Check out the ladies' empire gowns and the men's waistcoats.

St. Patrick's Day Parade (225 -92-8295, www.paradegroup.com), City Park and Perkins Rd., Baton Rouge. Overpass neighborhoods. You don't have to be Irish to have fun at this parade on or near March 17, usually beginning at 10 A.M. Riders in floats, decorated with shamrocks and harps, toss green and white beads to crowds. After the parade, parties continue in cafes and clubs in the Perkins Road area.

April–May: **Baton Rouge Blues Festival** (225-383-0968, www.batonrougebluesfestival.org), downtown, Mid City, and North Baton Rouge. Baton Rouge celebrates its distinctive blues heritage with Sunday in the Park sessions in Lafayette Park and programs at blues venues throughout town. The city is the home of blues

legends Tabby Thomas, Henry Gray, Rudy Richard, Raful Neal, Slim Harpo, and others. Folk-life seminars and locally produced radio shows are part of the festival mix.

Kite Festival (225-344-2920, www.westbatonrouge.net), Port Allen. Children and adults turn their sights and talents skyward for this fun event. Held in the West Baton Rouge Soccer Complex, the festival includes children's competitions, professional kite-flying exhibitions, music and regional cuisine.

International Heritage Celebration (225-930-0901, www.brcwa.com), RiverCenter, River Rd., Baton Rouge. This event salutes the cultures of countries around the world. People turn out for the parade of nations, music, storytelling, dance, international foods, and educational booths.

Louisiana Earth Day Festival (www.laearthday.org) RiverCenter, River Rd., Baton Rouge. Each year, local residents gather downtown by the government complex on the Mississippi River to learn more about the latest developments on green, sustainable living, including stewardship of Louisiana as well as the entire planet's resources. Children and adults participate in hands-on activities from building bird houses out of scrap wood to creating art that celebrates life. Local entertainment features Cajun, zydeco, country, blues, and rock performers.

Red Stick Animation Festival (225-578-0595, www.redstickfestival.org), 100 Lafayette St., Baton Rouge. This contemporary festival headquartered in the Shaw Center for the Arts is growing each year. People are drawn by the cartoon-a-palooza, free screenings of classical films, and workshops by aspiring animation artists.

May: **FestForAll** (225-344-8558, www.artsbr.org), Baton Rouge. Taking place at the city's government complex and along North Boulevard, the two-day festival embraces both visual and performing artists. People stroll along North Boulevard browsing for jewelry, pottery, paintings, and sculpture. Musicians perform in churches and historic buildings.

Jambalaya Festival (225-647-2937, www.jambalayafestival.org), Gonzales Civic Center, Gonzales. There's a good reason the town is called the Jambalaya Capital of the World: You'll never eat better jambalaya anywhere in the world. Come for the two days of cooking workshops, all the jambalaya you can eat, carnival rides, and music that will set you dancing.

Bayou Country Superfest (504-410-4100, www.bayoucountrysuperfest.com), LSU Tiger Stadium, Baton Rouge. Take in a star-studded Memorial Day weekend festival of country music.

June–July: **Feliciana Hummingbird Celebration** (800-488-6502, www.audubonbirdfest.com), 12501 LA 10, St. Francisville. Hummingbirds enjoy flowering shrubbery and long summers in the Baton Rouge region. Attend this celebration and learn how to weigh, measure, and band the tiny but sturdy little hummers. Lots of fun for kids.

Star-Spangled Celebration (225-342-1942, www.usskidd.com), River

Rd., Baton Rouge. Spend the Fourth of July enjoying music by local groups and the Baton Rouge Concert Band, food booths, and a mock air attack on the USS *Kidd*. The day is topped off with spectacular fireworks over the Mississippi River.

Donaldsonville Fireworks and Fais Do-Do (225-323-4970, www.donaldsonvilleddd.org, Crescent Park, Donaldsonville. This historic town observes the Fourth of July on the third day of July. Activities include family fun, music, food, contests and fireworks over the river.

October–November: **Awesome Art in Autumn Gardens Festival** (225-473-7841, www.artgumbo.org), 40136 LA 942, Burnside. Houmas House Plantation welcomes visitors for the two-day festival with artists, musicians, singers ,and dancers sprinkled throughout the spectacular gardens. The festival's Art Show and Sale features some 300 works of art by both youth and adults in competition for blue ribbons. An Arts Fest buffet in the plantation dining room adds up to a splendid day in the country.

Louisiana Book Festival (225-755-3247, www.gbrsf.com), 701 North Fourth St., Baton Rouge. Sponsored by the Louisiana State Library, the late-October event features more than 190 writers, poets, scholars taking part in a day of book talks, readings, and

---

JUST WHAT'S IN JAMBALAYA?

Similar in many ways to Spanish paella, the word *jambalaya* is derived from the Spanish *jamon,* for ham. According to the Jambalaya Festival website, the dish found its way into Creole cooking in the late 1700s, and soon took on the local ingredients. The Cajun/Creole dish is made from a mixture of meats or seafood, rice, onion, garlic, pepper, and other seasonings. It can be made with ham, chicken, sausage, pork, shrimp, oysters all together or in any combination. It's best cooked in a well-seasoned black iron pot, but it also does well in a one-quart pot.

panel discussions in the State Capitol, the State Library, and the State Museum. Children and adults can get their books autographed by a favorite author. Tents are set up for youth, book shopping and signing, book-related arts, food, and beverages. The festival concludes at sunset.

Sugarfest (225-635-6277, www.west batonrougemuseum.com), 845 North Jefferson Ave., Port Allen. The West Baton Rouge Museum celebrates the city's sugarcane growing heritage on the west bank of the Mississippi River. Tour authentic plantation cabins, watch a mule-driven cane grinder in action, and enjoy the cake walk and sugary treats.

December: **Baton Rouge Festival of Lights** (225- 389-5520, www.down townbatonrouge.org), Galvez Plaza and North Boulevard, Baton Rouge. People gather at the plaza in the government complex to enjoy the traditions, art, and music of the holidays. The mayor officially turns on the city's Christmas tree lights and those along North Boulevard. Other activities include a Jingle Bell Jog and ice skating.

Christmas Parade (225-766-2282, www.christmasbr.com). The parade takes place in downtown Baton Rouge in early December. Families with children line the streets to watch holiday floats, marching groups, and horses at the parade that begins at 7 P.M. and ends with the arrival of Santa.

Rural Life Christmas (225-765-2437, www.rurallife.lsu.edu), Essen at I-10, Baton Rouge. Join staff and volunteers at the Rural Life Museum as they present the holiday season as it was enjoyed in Southern communities in the late 1800s. Living history reenactors demonstrate farm crafts and household skills. Enjoy browsing in the gift shop that includes quality hand-crafted items created by Louisiana artisans.

INDEX